∨ B + T
19May81
26.00

D1450791

International Library of the Philosophy of Education

General Editor

R. S. Peters
Professor of Philosophy of Education
Institute of Education
University of London

International
Library of the
Philosophy of
Education

**Philosophers
as educational
reformers**

Philosophers as educational reformers

The influence of idealism on British educational thought and practice

Peter Gordon

and

John White

Routledge & Kegan Paul

London, Boston and Henley

Wingate College Library

First published in 1979
by Routledge & Kegan Paul Ltd
39 Store Street,
London WC1E 7DD,
Broadway House,
Newtown Road,
Henley-on-Thames,
Oxon RG9 1EN and
9 Park Street,
Boston, Mass. 02108, USA
Set in 10 on 11pt Baskerville
and printed in Great Britain by
Weatherby Woolnough, Wellingborough, Northants
© Peter Gordon and John White 1979
No part of this book may be reproduced in
any form without permission from the
publisher, except for the quotation of brief
passages in criticism

British Library Cataloguing in Publication Data

Gordon, Peter, b.1927

Philosophers as educational reformers.
- (International library of the philosophy of education).
1. Education - England - History
2. Idealism, English
3. Education - Philosophy
I. Title II. White, John III. Series
370'.942   LA631.7   79-40223

ISBN 0 7100 0214 9

082551

Contents

Contents

Plates

General editor's note

There is a growing interest in philosophy of education amongst students of philosophy as well as amongst those who are more specifically and practically concerned with educational problems. Philosophers, of course, from the time of Plato onwards, have taken an interest in education and have dealt with education in the context of wider concerns about knowledge and the good life. But it is only quite recently in this country that philosophy of education has come to be conceived of as a specific branch of philosophy like the philosophy of science or political philosophy.

To call philosophy of education a specific branch of philosophy is not, however, to suggest that it is a distinct branch in the sense that it could exist apart from established branches of philosophy such as epistemology, ethics, and philosophy of mind. It would be more appropriate to conceive of it as drawing on established branches of philosophy and bringing them together in ways which are relevant to educational issues. In this respect the analogy with political philosophy would be a good one. Thus use can often be made of work that already exists in philosophy. In tackling, for instance, issues such as the rights of parents and children, punishment in schools, and the authority of the teacher, it is possible to draw on and develop work already done by philosophers on 'rights', 'punishment', and 'authority'. In other cases, however, no systematic work exists in the relevant branches of philosophy – e.g. on concepts such as 'education', 'teaching', 'learning', 'indoctrination'. So philosophers of education have had to break new ground – in these cases in the philosophy of mind. Work on educational issues can also bring to life and throw new light on long-standing problems in philosophy. Concentration, for instance, on the particular predicament of children can throw new light on problems of punishment and responsibility. G. E. Moore's old worries about what sorts of things are good in themselves can be brought to life by urgent questions about the justification of the curriculum in schools.

There is a danger in philosophy of education, as in any other applied field, of polarization to one of two extremes. The work could be practically relevant but philosophically feeble; or it could be philosophically sophisticated but remote from practical problems. The aim of the International Library of the Philosophy of Education is to build up a body of fundamental work in this area which is both practically relevant and philosophically competent. For unless it achieves both types of objective it will fail to satisfy those for whom it is intended and fall short of the conception of philosophy of education which the International Library is meant to embody.

Philosophers as Educational Reformers is an unusual book among the other volumes of the International Library in that it is an inter-disciplinary study, drawing both on the philosophy of education and on the history of education. Its topic is the influence of the British Idealist philosophers of the late nineteenth century on the leading educational reformers of that time and later. It assesses how far the ideas and achievements of these philosophical reformers are still important for us today when we consider fundamental questions about the structure and objectives of our educational system. Part 1 examines those ideas of the Idealists, especially of T. H. Green, which had most bearing on these reforms. Part 2 concentrates on the innovations in the organization and content of education in England and Wales brought about by the administrators and educationalists educated in philosophical idealism. It is not widely known that virtually all the leading figures in educational reform between 1870 and the 1920s belonged to this school of thought: examples are T. H. Green, Arthur Acland, Robert Morant, Michael Sadler, R. B. Haldane, E. G. A. Holmes and R. H. Tawney. These men all helped in different ways, to pioneer a coherent national system of secondary and elementary education, of civic universities and adult education, as well as contributing to the theory of education. After the First World War, enthusiasm for organic reform of this type tended to wane.

Part 3 examines what relevance the philosophical and practical ideas of this interconnected group of reformers have to education today. There are many signs that current educational thought and practice are turning back towards ideas with which Idealists were sympathetic. The belief that educational institutions should be largely autonomous in their curricular arrangements is being increasingly challenged – a challenge which echoes the demand of many of the Idealists that the educational system should be planned as an organic whole. As for the aims of education, there is, similarly, a growing realization that pupil-centred aims need to be supplemented by aims of a community-oriented kind. Light may be shed on this by the thesis of many of the Idealists that a fundamental aim of education is morality or citizenship.

Preface

Prominent among the builders of a national system of education in Britain after 1870 were a group of men who were either influenced by British idealist philosophers or idealist philosophers in their own right. They included T. H. Green, Arthur Acland, R. B. Haldane, Henry Jones, Michael Sadler, Robert Morant – and in a later generation R. H. Tawney, Fred Clarke and A. D. Lindsay. Together, and with the co-operation of others of similar persuasion, they played an indispensable part in laying the foundations of our present system. Much of the impetus towards liberalizing the elementary schools in the 1890s came from them; they were conspicuous in the campaign for state secondary education which culminated in the 1902 Act and in pressing for 'secondary education for all' after the First World War; without them the many universities founded in the first years of this century would not have come into existence, or, at least, not so speedily; they were pioneers of adult education; they helped to shape the 1918 Education Act.

Of course this group, comprising university teachers, statesmen, civil servants and school inspectors, were not responsible for *all* the educational advances in this half-century. Sidney Webb was not a philosophical idealist; neither, though he *was* a philosopher and had crossed swords with the idealists in his writings, was Arthur Balfour. But the idealists' influence was considerable. They had a collective genius for creative administration, throwing themselves with extraordinary energy into the task of building new structures within which their educational ideals could be expressed. These ideals arose directly out of their shared philosophy. It was a philosophy which had given them not only an academic discipline but also a life's work, sending them into the world as missionaries of the spirit.

It may seem strange to some that a philosophy like Hegelian idealism, with its preoccupation with the Absolute, or Eternal Spirit, could come to be connected with the utterly practical, very detailed work of educational administration. But it was not merely connected: it was, in fact, a prime mover. To show how this came to be so is one of the chief aims of this book, especially of Parts 1 and 2. Part 1 is philosophical. It describes in a non-technical way the leading features of nineteenth-century idealism, concentrating mainly on its social and political doctrines, but showing at the same time how these were connected with its metaphysical tenets about the nature of reality, and, above all, how very *obvious* it was to one brought up in this system of ideas that a life devoted to the education of the nation was unsurpassable in its worth. Part 2 is historical. It traces the achievements of these philosophical reformers over the half century from 1870 onwards. It reveals the common threads running through the work of men who, though sometimes separated from each other temporally by one or two generations, or spatially, with Glasgow and Oxford as the twin poles of the movement, were yet interconnected by a set of shared beliefs.

But telling what happened and why is not the only purpose of this book. Philosophical idealism gradually faded away as a movement of thought after the First World War. Its social doctrines – its elevation of the state and its insistence that individuals have their being only as parts of society – became increasingly repellent as the totalitarian dictatorships grew in power. With its decline, its role as the spiritual generator of educational ideas and institutions vanished to nothing. In 1978, the year in which we write, nothing is left, and scarcely anything remembered, of its creative power in this area. But is this power dead beyond recall? Has idealism anything still to teach us? How far are we right to label its social philosophy 'totalitarian' and so dismiss it? Has this association with totalitarianism blinded us to any substantial qualities it may possess, qualities which may be of service to us in our present anxieties about the lack of direction so evident in our educational system? Part 3 will seek to answer these questions.

Acknowledgments

During the writing of this book, we have received assistance from many libraries and record offices, which are listed in the Bibliography. We are particularly grateful to a number of individuals for helping us to locate sources, particularly Miss Trudy Jackson, Temple House, London; Mr E. V. Quinn, the Librarian, Balliol College, Oxford; Mr Alistair Elliot, Assistant Librarian, Special Collections, Newcastle-upon-Tyne University; and Mr F. W. Jessup, formerly Director, University of Oxford Department for External Studies.

For generously allowing us to quote from family papers, we wish to thank Sir Richard and Lady Acland, Killerton, Devon; the Earl Spencer, Althorp, Northamptonshire; The Rt Reverend Stephen Temple, Bishop of Malmesbury; and John Sharwood Smith, University of London Institute of Education.

Permission to quote from the papers of the London Extension Society and to reproduce photographs of Toynbee Hall was given respectively by Mr Brian Groombridge, Director of the Department of Extra-Mural Studies, University of London, and Mr Donald Chesworth, Warden of Toynbee Hall.

Professor R. S. Peters and Pat White, both of the University of London Institute of Education, Professor W. H. G. Armytage, Sheffield University, and Dr J. H. Higginson, were good enough to comment on the manuscript, although of course the final responsibility for the work is our own.

We would like to thank Gabriella King and Lynn Cairns for all their help in preparing the typescript, and Tessa and David Gordon for their bibliographical and other help at various stages of the writing.

We are indebted, finally, to Mr W. S. Fowler, whose article 'The Influence of Idealism upon State Provision of Education', in *Victorian Studies,* June 1961, first prompted us to write this book.

The authors and publishers would like to thank the following for permission to use illustrations: Plate 2: The Bodleian Library, Oxford (MS. Top. Oxon, d.242); Plate 3: John Constable, from M. Sadleir, *Michael Ernest Sadler* (1949); Plate 6: Hodder & Stoughton Ltd, from *Richard Burdon Haldane: An Autobiography* (1929); Plate 7:

Acknowledgments

Greater London Record Office. Further, Plate 1 is taken from R. L. Nettleship (ed.), *The Works of T. H. Green*, vol. 3, *Miscellaneous and Memoirs*, Longmans (1891); Plates 4 and 5 from A. Mansbridge, *An Adventure in Working-Class Education, Being the Story of the Workers' Educational Association 1903-1915*, Longmans Green (1920); Plate 8 from A. L. Illingworth (ed.), *The Life and Work of John Richardson Illingworth*, John Murray, 1917.

Philosophical idealism and education

part 1

Introduction

British philosophical idealism of the late nineteenth century was founded on the philosophy of Hegel and drew its inspiration also from the thought of Kant and Fichte, and, more anciently, from Plato and Aristotle, all four of which writers had contributed much to Hegel's thought. Between Hegel and the British idealist whose work will figure prominently in this volume, T. H. Green, there are, of course, considerable differences, both in conclusions and in arguments. But they both hold certain beliefs in common. For both of them reality is not to be identified with the physical world or even with a dualist combination of a physical with a mental world: reality is essentially mental or spiritual. What we call the realms of matter and mind – the everyday world of physical objects on the one hand and the everyday world of our thoughts and feelings on the other – are not the ultimate, irreducible constituents of reality. To understand the physical world, we have to look behind it to the foundation on which it rests, that in virtue of which it is what it is. This foundation is thought, not the thought of individual human beings, but an eternal consciousness (or God, or Absolute, or Spirit), existing outside time and space. Man, as well as the world he lives in, is also linked to the eternal. *His* link is more intimate. For man, unique among animals, is capable of reason. *Qua* thinker he becomes a part of or a reproduction of the eternal thought which underlines all things. But man is essentially a social creature. His being is inseparable from that of the state, the political community within which he lives and which includes smaller-scale social groups, such as the family, to which he belongs also. Man is, therefore, connected to reality as a whole not as an independent individual, but as a participant in a shared social and political life, that is, as a citizen of a state. His education, which is the means whereby he becomes a citizen, is thus one of the state's foremost concerns. For at least the spiritual and political leaders of the state – and, as we shall see, in Green's case, for others too – it is at the same time an intellectual education, developing their powers of thought so that they come to partake of eternal thought: in this way the state will be able to realize its proper fuction, of mediating between the human and the divine.

This conception of the links between nature, man, the state, and

God will have to be filled out, with reference to the British idealists in particular, in later sections. But even this sparse account of the connexions is enough to show us how very different from the prevailing metaphysical and social ideas of mid-nineteenth-century Britain the new idealism was. The dominant thought of the time, deriving from the Enlightenment of the eighteenth century, was empiricist, individualistic, utilitarian. While the idealist saw reality as an organic, interconnected whole, no part of which was independent of the rest, the empiricist saw it as an aggregation of atomic entities, the physical atoms of Newton and Locke and/or the sensations, or ideas which were the atoms of the mind. Each atom could be understood, and could only be understood, in isolation from the rest. Science, physical or mental, was to begin from these irreducibly simple entities and show how they are associated together to form more complex phenomena. Man was one example of such complexity. While the idealists saw him as essentially a part of a community, the empiricists held him to be essentially an independent, a-social individual, complex in relation to the physical and mental atoms of which he was constituted and in terms of which he was to be understood, but atomic in relation to the other individuals with whom he was associated in a society. On this view the state was not a community of citizens sharing a common good, but a kind of machinery of government instituted to preserve the liberty of the individual. The ethical principle of utilitarianism – that man should aim at bringing about his own and others' happiness – was not derived from reflection on man's social and spiritual nature, but from his innate tendency, in common with other animals, to seek pleasure and shun pain. In educating children, consequently, one's master-aim was the promotion of the general happiness. There was no theoretical reason why the state should do anything to promote this education.

Nothing could be further from this prevailing orthodoxy of the mid-nineteenth century than the idealism which was to challenge it and for a time upstage it between 1870 and 1920. But idealism did not burst upon the old order quite unheralded with the publication of the first British neo-Hegelian philosophy around 1870. The previous half century had already witnessed a growing dissatisfaction, both among literary men and among theologians, with the old Enlightenment order. Carlyle's was the most powerful voice, declaiming in tones which tend to jar on our modern ears, but which deeply affected his contemporaries, against the absence of spiritual values in the new industrial society. Though too unsystematic a thinker to be called a philosopher, Carlyle's leading ideas were philosophical none the less, being inspired directly by

German idealism, especially that of Fichte. This metaphysics – Kant's and Schelling's, perhaps, more than Fichte's – was also the source of Coleridge's religious and political thought.˙ It is via Coleridge that Wordsworth came to incorporate in his poems the idealist conception of the spirituality of nature and hence its educative influence. Coleridge's *Church and State* (1830) took over from the idealists the thesis that the state is a spiritual entity, mediating between man and God. Just as Fichte argued for a class of scholars to devote themselves to raising the spiritual level of the state, not least by their educative influence on the rest of the population, so Coleridge, for similar reasons, advocated a 'Clerisy', that is, a large body of clergymen, scholars and teachers who were to form part of a 'National Church', engaging in scholarship, advanced teaching and more general parochial work of an educative kind, thus leaving no corner of the country 'without a resident guide, guardian and instructor' (Willey, 1949, p. 46, quoting from Coleridge, op. cit.). State funds were to be provided to support the work of this National Church.

Coleridge's belief that the Anglican church, though imperfect, could, through its network of parochial influences, as well as through its dominance in educational, especially university circles, provide a foundation for a Clerisy, was taken up by two leading religious thinkers of the early nineteenth century, Thomas Arnold and F. D. Maurice. Arnold is known to us today as the prig lampooned by Lytton Strachey in *Eminent Victorians.* But Strachey's perception was cruel and one-sided, doing less than justice to Arnold's creative role in nineteenth-century social reform. Like Coleridge before him and like the Rugbeian R. H. Tawney in our own times, he deplored the separation of secular affairs ˙from spiritual, opposing the divorce which evangelicals and puritans made between them and advocating a 'Broad Church', that is a liberal Anglicanism which could embrace other forms of Protestantism within it. Church and state were an indissoluble unity. Like Coleridge, and again like Tawney, Arnold wanted part of the national wealth 'saved out of the scramble of individual selfishness and set apart for ever for public purposes' (Willey, p. 57, quoting from Arnold's *Principles of Church Reform*). In Tawney's age such funds would be used for what would then be considered the purely secular activities of a welfare state. To many of us today Arnold's view that more public money should be spent on the Establishment, in the shape of the Anglican church, may seem reactionary. But his end – the spiritual enlightenment of the nation – was the same as Tawney's. Like Coleridge, he saw the educational possibilities of having a Christian scholar in every parish. In his work as headmaster of Rugby, imbuing his pupils with the gospel of hard work, not for purely intellectual but for the higher moral and spiritual ends to which these were subordinate, he helped to give the idea of 'Clerisy' a practical embodiment.

F. D. Maurice was another disciple of Coleridge, important as the co-founder, with Kingsley, of 'Christian Socialism' in 1848. Maurice shared many of Arnold's ideas: latitudinarianism, a belief in the spirituality of the state as expressed through a national church, a passion for education. His 'socialism', inspired by the revolutionary fervour of 1848, led him to advocate co-operative rather than private ownership of capital and to work with co-operative associations and trades unions. It also led to his founding of a working men's college in London in 1854.

Carlyle, Thomas Arnold and Maurice were still influential figures, either in their own person or via their disciples, in the intellectual world of the 1870s with which our story begins. This is perhaps especially so for Oxford. Carlyle's most famous follower was John Ruskin, who was Slade Professor of Fine Art at Oxford (1870-9) and who united Carlyle's denunciations of *laissez-faire* and Fichtean belief in a new class of spiritual leaders with a passion for the history of art. Matthew Arnold, the son of Thomas, had been appointed Professor of Poetry at Oxford in 1857, a post which he held concurrently with the school inspectorship which remained his main career. Matthew Arnold's *Culture and Anarchy* appeared in 1869. The influence of his father, and through him of Coleridge and the Germans, is evident in his criticism of the narrow 'Hebraism' of the dissenters, or Philistines, and in his reliance on the state to educate men of 'culture', that is 'Hellenists' committed to the values of spirituality and rationality, whether expressed in literary, religious or political activity. We shall see later and in more detail how Arnold's general social theory led him to press for a national system of secondary education, on Continental lines, to raise the 'intelligence', as he put it, of the largely dissenting middle classes. For the moment it is enough to note that there was nothing of exclusive élitism in this call for middle-class education. Arnold, like Coleridge and Thomas Arnold, wanted educated values to permeate the whole nation. 'The men of culture', he claimed, 'are the true apostles of equality.' By its attachment to critical reason, its opposition to stock notions and narrow prejudices, culture 'seeks to do away with classes' altogether (Arnold, 1869, p. 44).

In his attachment to the state as a spiritual organism, Arnold, according to his biographer, Lionel Trilling, generally passed for a disciple of Hegel 'probably without ever having read him' (Trilling, 1939, p. 90 fn.). The genealogy of his ideas which we have sketched in part (the Greeks and Wordsworth were among other major influences) may help to explain why this was so. German idealism came to England first not as a worked-out philosophical system but embedded in the literary, religious and socio-political works of writers like those whom we have mentioned. In the 1870s and later it became systematized. The ease with which this occurred, and the rapidity with which its ideas, in their systematized form, were able to permeate the intellectual world, were due not a little to the already widespread influence of idealist ways of thinking which we owe to these men.

It was at Balliol College, Oxford, in the 1860s and 1870s that this systematization took place. A leading figure here was T. H. Green (1836-82), who was a Fellow of Balliol from 1860 until his death. It was he, pre-eminently, who wove together the various idealist strands of thought of an unsystematic nature and reconnected them with the Greek and German philosophy which inspired them. But the creation of a British school of idealism was not all due to Green. More must be said about the role which Balliol College had in this process, and more particularly, about the influence of Green's tutor, Benjamin Jowett.

Jowett (1817-93) is important in several ways. First, it was he who introduced Hegel's philosophical system into England. In 1844, some ten years before Green went up to Oxford, Jowett, then a young tutor at Balliol, visited Germany to make a study of current philosophical writings; he quickly became absorbed in Hegel, whose influence in his own country was then beginning to decline. According to his official biographers, Jowett remained for several years after this an ardent, though an independent, student of Hegel. It added a new dimension to his thinking, which was manifested through his teaching and informal associations with students, rather than in his writings. Jowett had no interest in constructing philosophical systems; and when Green came to develop his own system out of Hegel and other idealist influences Jowett was less than lukewarm. For all his later distrust of Hegelian systems, however, he acknowledged as late as the 1880s that he had received a greater stimulus from Hegel than from anyone else.[1]

Jowett's interest in Hegel was only one aspect of his idealist cast of mind, which permits us to classify him with Coleridge, Carlyle, Maurice and the two Arnolds as one of the pre-systematic progenitors of British idealism. Plato was an abiding influence. Jowett's translations of the dialogues, especially of the *Republic,* are now classics. He saw his Balliol undergraduates rather as Plato saw his Guardians, urging them to work hard not only in the pursuit of academic excellence alone, but also in order to devote themselves,

7

having left Oxford, to public service of one sort or·another. How far he was influenced here by Hegel in particular is unclear. Certainly Hegel's insistence in his *Philosophy of Right* on a rigorously educated 'universal class' of civil servants and teachers who were to maintain the spiritual unity of the state against individualistic pressures from below has affinities with both Jowett's thought and practice. But then, as we have seen, this kind of Platonic solution to the problem of social disintegration was a commonplace among the other idealist-inclined thinkers we have mentioned, from Fichte, through Coleridge and Carlyle, to both Thomas and Matthew Arnold.

Between Jowett and the Arnolds there were also more particular connexions. It was under Jowett's regime at Balliol, first as tutor, then, after 1870, as Master, that the famous link between the college and Rugby School became firmly welded. Jowett's gospel of hard work and public service was little different from Thomas Arnold's. Another link with Matthew Arnold is that he was an undergraduate at Balliol in the early years of Jowett's fellowship.

Jowett's Platonic conception of the links between the university and public life made him an enthusiastic supporter of the campaign for university reform. He helped to turn Oxford away from medievalism and bring it into closer touch with the leading social, intellectual and political movements of the day. One of his 'pet crotchets', which, as we shall see, was shared by T. H. Green, was to raise the value of scholarships, so as to 'provide the means for many more persons of the middling class to find their way through the University into professions' (Faber, 1957, p. 197).

T. H. Green's idealism owed not a little to the work of his teacher and colleague Jowett and the other pre-systematic idealists we have been describing. In broad outline Hegelian, with a strong Kantian emphasis, it also, especially in its ethical and political doctrines, brought to bear these other, native, lines of thought, fusing them with German-inspired philosophy in a new synthesis.

Green, the son of an evangelical clergyman, was a pupil of Rugby and Balliol. Melvin Richter mentions the 'faith he constructed, like so many others in his age, out of Wordsworth, Coleridge, Dr Arnold, Carlyle, F. D. Maurice and Kingsley' (1964, p. 47). Of these, Maurice's influence on him is of particular interest, since one of Maurice's best-known disciples, D. J. Vaughan (1825-1905), vicar of St Martin's, Leicester, and the founder of what became the Vaughan Working Men's College in the same city, was Green's uncle. Green never lost hold of his uncle's Christian Socialist principles. He used to visit him regularly throughout his life (op. cit., p. 42).

Through his critiques of empiricism in his posthumous *Prolegomena to Ethics* (1883), in which he outlined his positive metaphysical views and the ethics he built on them, and his *Lectures on the Principles of Political Obligation* (1895), Green built up a wide-ranging and eclectic idealist philosophy, Hegelian in its broadest outlines, as we have said, but argued through without the head-breaking abstractions of Hegelian logic. It rapidly became enormously influential, both in the development of British philosophy and, more generally, as an inspiration for social reformers.

Speaking of the new idealist philosophy as a whole, Anthony Quinton stated in a recent lecture: 'In less than ten years (from 1865) a series of works came out, bearing a strong Hegelian imprint, from those who were to be the leaders and inspirers of a whole generation of British philosophers. For the next thirty years absolute idealism maintained an unchallenged primacy, both in volume of publications and in its hold over the loyalties of university students' (1971, p. 14). Among Green's disciples and fellow idealists in the 1870s were A. C. Bradley at Balliol, his brother F. H. Bradley at Merton, Bernard Bosanquet at University College and William Wallace at Merton. The best known of these in philosophical circles today is F. H. Bradley (1846-1924), whose *Appearance and Reality* (1893) reargued Hegelian metaphysics on a new logical foundation. Bradley led a retired academic life in Merton College, Oxford, and lacked the concern for public affairs typical of the idealists. His *Ethical Studies* (1876), however, reinforced the Greek-Hegelian insistence that an individual is essentially a member of a society and stressed, in a somewhat un-Hegelian way, as we shall see, that it is that society which lays down one's ethical code for one in the shape of 'my station and its duties'.[2]

Green's influence was not restricted to professional philosophers. Collingwood recorded in his *Autobiography:* 'The school of Green sent out into public life a stream of ex-pupils who carried with them the conviction that philosophy, and in particular the philosophy they had learnt at Oxford, was an important thing, and that their vocation was to put it into practice. . . . Through this effect on the minds of its pupils, the philosophy of Green's school might be found, from about 1880 to about 1910, penetrating and fertilizing every part of the national life' (1944 edn., p. 17). Green's philosophy, as will become more evident later, achieved this remarkable effect because it met so exactly the spiritual needs of young men brought up in some orthodox Christian faith who, like Green himself in his youth, could no longer accept without qualification both that faith and also the religious vocation which, for university students, so often went with it. Green taught his readers that the saintly ideal of a parish priesthood was not the only, and perhaps not always the most effective, way of helping to realize God's purposes. Not only his readers: his hearers, too. As the first layman to fill the office of tutor at Balliol (1860), Green continued the clerical tradition, later emulated by his friend Edward Caird, by delivering sermons to the undergraduates. Published posthumously, two of them, 'The Witness of God' and 'Faith', subtitled 'Two Lay Sermons', contained passages which, ascribed by Mrs Humphrey Ward in her novel *Robert Elsmere* to the 'Professor Grey' whom she modelled on Green, inspired Elsmere to seek for 'great ideas' and 'great causes'. Towards the end of his second sermon, delivered in 1878, Green told his audience:

> Those of us to whom University life is merely an avenue to the great world, would do well betimes to seek opportunities of co-operation with those simple Christians whose creed, though we may not be able exactly to adopt it, is to them the natural expression of a spirit which at the bottom of our heart we recognize as higher than our own. In the everyday life of Christian citizenship, in its struggle against ignorance and vice, such opportunities are readily forthcoming (pp. 102-3).

The 'struggle against ignorance', we should note, is uppermost in Green's mind. We shall see later, and in more detail, the tangible results of this exhortation: in the educational work of his friend and colleague Arthur Acland, for instance, and that of Acland's follower, Michael Sadler. Robert Morant, Britain's most famous educational civil servant, was inspired by Green's lay sermons as an undergraduate at New College; and Edmond Holmes, the author of that bible of early progressivism *What Is and What Might Be,* also fell under his spell at St John's. The story of these men's achievements must wait until Part 2 of this book, since in this part we are more concerned with presenting the philosophy of Green and other idealists than with the details of the reform movement which they initiated.

But the philosophy and the educational history cannot be kept tidily in different boxes. If Green were the only source of inspiration, this might be possible: one could first give an account of Green's ideas and then describe his own and his followers' achievements. But Green, though pre-eminent, was not alone.

In his early days as an undergraduate at Balliol, Green belonged to a small radical and intellectually very powerful essay and discussion club called the Old Mortality Society. Apart from John Nichol, its chairman, Algernon Swinburne, A. V. Dicey, and James Bryce (later to lend his name to the Bryce Commission on Secondary Education in 1895), its membership included T. H. Green (who 'preached Hegel with the accent of a Puritan' (Knight, 1896, p. 159)) and Edward Caird. Caird (1835-1908) was a Scot from Glasgow University, a lifelong admirer of Carlyle, who studied philosophy at Balliol from 1860 until 1866 and, like Green, was one of the earliest of the British disciples of Hegel and a radical in politics. His biographer describes Green and Caird as 'Knights of the Spirit', riding into battle with the same weapons (Jones and Muirhead, 1921, pp. 32-3). Caird returned to Glasgow from Balliol in 1866, as Professor of Philosophy, coming back to the college in 1893 as its Master, following Jowett's death. Caird is important in this study in several ways. He attracted about himself in Glasgow much the same kind of socially-committed disciples as Green did in Oxford. Some of these were later to become, in their turn, not merely professors of idealist philosophy but, like J. S. Mackenzie, John MacCunn, Henry Jones and J. H. Muirhead, professors of idealist philosophy of a peculiarly practical turn of mind, many of whom became prominent in educational reform as well as in other fields. The educational work of Henry Jones and John MacCunn, in particular, the first mainly in the practical field and the second in educational theory, will receive our detailed attention in Part 2. There we shall see also how Caird himself was involved in practical educational reform, not least as regards the higher education of women. When he returned to Balliol in 1893, he had far from lost his inspirational powers. He is a link, indeed, between an earlier generation of idealist reformers and a later. R. H. Tawney fell under his influence while an undergraduate at Balliol, so did William Temple and William Beveridge. Philosophically he was much more avowedly Hegelian than Green. Perhaps for this reason his strength lay in exposition rather than, as with Green, in the forging of a semi-independent system.

Graduates of Oxford and of Glasgow constitute all but one of the main educational reformers we shall be discussing in detail in Part 2. The exception is R. B. Haldane (1856-1927). A leading figure in Liberal politics from the 1890s to the First World War, he is perhaps best known to us today for his army reforms before that war. But his dominant and persisting passion was for education, his influence, especially in the area of post-school education, being as we shall see enormous. Haldane was an idealist philosopher in his own right. His *The Pathway to Reality* (1902-3, 1903-4) exhibits the same explicit debt to Hegel as does Edward Caird's philosophy. This and others of his writings are, like Caird's, mostly now of historical interest only. But in his heyday Haldane was a leading member of the group of young idealist philosophers influenced by

T. H. Green. With Caird, Henry Jones and others he contributed to the *Essays in Philosophical Criticism* (1883) dedicated to Green and edited by Seth and Haldane. Unlike virtually all the other disciples of Green and Caird who appear in this book, however, Haldane was not a student of either of them in the institutional sense. He was a graduate of Edinburgh, having first been drawn towards idealism by his reading of Fichte and Hegel, during a term spent at Göttingen in 1874 under the philosopher R. H. Lotze (Haldane, 1929, pp. 6-19).[3]

There is one other idealist philosopher, of greater eminence than Haldane and whose impact on educational reform was even more powerful, who like Haldane, was deeply affected by Green's philosophy without having been one of his students. His philosophical and educational achievements will, however, gain him little more than a paragraph or two in Part 2. This is because he was an American and his educational work was within the American, not the British system. We are referring to John Dewey (1859-1952). Some may find it strange to find this torch-bearer of progressivism placed in a common bracket with all these Hegelians. But a Hegelian Dewey most certainly was in his early days; and it was the shattering effect upon him of reading Green that turned him into one.

T. H. Green's central place in this network of philosophical influences on education should now be fairly plain and will become even plainer as we go on. Partly for this reason, and partly because of the scope, accessibility and interconnectedness of his ideas, the ensuing philosophical sketch of idealist metaphysics, ethics, political and educational thought will draw heavily on his works, especially on the *Prolegomena to Ethics* and the *Lectures on the Principles of Political Obligation*. But, as we have seen, other philosophers, Kant, Fichte and Hegel in particular, were influential in their own right on the educational reformers, not only via whatever mediate influence they had on Green. Their contribution will be shown in what follows in two ways: by indicating, where appropriate, Green's dependence on them: and by sketching out those others of their educationally-relevant ideas which were important in their own right. In Chapter 2 we will begin with a sketch of idealist views about the ultimate nature of reality, proceeding to ethics in Chapter 3 and political philosophy in Chapter 4. Chapter 5 will conclude Part 1 with a discussion of idealist educational theory.

Nature, man and God

Reality for the idealist is an organic whole. It is not basically a mass of discrete, unconnected atoms as empiricists believe. Neither is it divided, as many of the latter also believe, into two sharply distinguished realms of being, the material and the mental. Reality is of one kind only – spiritual. The world of nature and the world of our mental life are interconnected embodiments of this spiritual reality. This is not to say that this reality constitutes a single substance, within which all the distinguishing features of natural phenomena and human consciousness are engulfed. Hegelian idealism is no featureless monism. Reality – the Absolute or Eternal Spirit – lives in and through the variegated concrete phenomena which constitute it. For the whole to flourish, the parts, too, must flourish, in all their manifold variety.

To understand this metaphysics we have to go back briefly to Kant's revolutionary critique of eighteenth-century empiricism. David Hume had shown that experience can teach us less about the physical world and about our minds than earlier empiricists like Locke and Berkeley believed. Experience alone cannot inform us of the existence of material substances, only of certain perceptual impressions: in more modern terminology, in looking at an apple, for instance, we can have experience only of certain red, shiny and round sense-data, not of an apple-substance. We cannot experience, either, a substantial self, or mind: all we can know of by introspection is feelings, ideas, images, which succeed each other in time. Causal relations, whether between items in the physical world or between mind and matter, are just as unknowable as material or mental substances. Our common – and scientific – view of reality as a network of phenomena in causal interaction comes, Hume claimed, not from experience alone, as empiricism strictly demanded, but from psychological habits we have acquired of imputing a *necessary* connexion between spatially contiguous events which can be known by experience merely to have regularly succeeded each other in time. If we leave common sense for philosophy, we end up in scepticism over whether anything can exist except the disconnected sense-data and data of introspection which we experience.

13

Wingate College Library

Kant's philosophical revolution consisted in examining the empiricists' central concept, that of experience, and showing that it was far from the simple idea which they had assumed it was. For experience to be possible, Kant argued in his *Critique of Pure Reason*, it had to be the experience of a unitary self, operating within a spatio-temporal world of physical substances in causal interaction with each other. The argument for this remarkable conclusion – the deduction of a world of selves and objects from the mere fact that experience exists – is long and intricate. It does not concern us here. What *is* important for our purposes, however, is that this world which Kant so deduced was only the world as experienced by creatures with our (human) kind of sensibility and powers of understanding – a world, that is, of 'phenomena', not of 'noumena'. The noumenal world is a world of 'things-in-themselves', real objects (including selves) lying behind the 'phenomena' of which they are the causes, but objects inaccessible to our understanding.

There is, therefore, in Kant's philosophy a fundamental dualism, a gulf between the world as it appears to us and the world as it really is. *Theoretical* understanding can provide no knowledge of the latter. Our only insight into it, according to Kant, can come from reflection on the presuppositions of our *moral* experience. As moral beings we have free will. We cannot, therefore, belong to the phenomenal world, since that world is governed only by causal relations between phenomena and such a total determinism leaves no room for free action. As moral selves we must belong, then, to the noumenal world. But morality would not exist – we would not have room for talk of moral 'duties' and 'obligations' – unless there were also a non-moral part of our nature which required to be kept under control for the sake of moral ends. We have such a nature: we desire happiness in different forms and seek to avoid pain. But this part of us does not belong to the noumenal, but to the phenomenal world. The fundamental dualism divides our self in two as well. It sets up an unbridgeable gulf between our real or moral self and the world of nature.

Kant is an important influence on the British idealist reformers whom we are studying, in three ways: via his disciple Fichte (1762-1814); via Hegel; and in his own right.

One of the central difficulties in Kant's metaphysics is his postulation of a realm of noumena, or things-in-themselves lying behind and causally responsible for the phenomena of nature. The difficulty is this. If all one's knowledge of nature is restricted to phenomena, then how can one know that there are noumena lying behind them? Fichte sweeps away the difficulty by refusing to postulate the existence of these noumena. Nature comes to be confined to phenomena alone. In so confining it, Fichte transforms the Kantian system into idealism. The duality between the world of consciousness and the physical world disappears. There is now nothing but consciousness. But *which* consciousness? The existence of the phenomenal natural world still poses a problem. How and why has that world come about?

Before answering that question, let us turn back from Fichte's account of nature to his account of man. Here, far from rejecting Kant's perception of man as a moral being *par excellence,* Fichte sharpened and enlarged it. Where Kant's main preoccupation was to reconcile, if possible, the claims of physical science on the one hand and morality on the other, Fichte, brought up as a theological student, had little interest in science: ethico-religious questions about the destiny of man were all-important to him. Not only are individual men, according to Fichte, to be seen under moral categories; so, too, is reality as a whole. Nothing exists which is not related to a single underlying moral purpose. This is as true of nature as it is of man. Man, clearly, has not created nature, even in its phenomenal form. Nature owes its being to what Fichte calls the Ego, or the Absolute Ego. It is this absolute that has brought the natural world into existence via its productive imagination. Nature is thus the creation of an ultimate spiritual reality. As to why this Ego has taken the trouble of creating nature, the answer is clear. The underlying purpose of all things is ethical. The only intrinsic good, not only of individual men but of the universe as a whole, is the free exercise of the good will, the autonomous acceptance of a self-imposed moral law. But morality, as Kant himself pointed out, implies a conflict between duty and contrary inclinations. These inclinations derive from the fact that we are embodied, that is, a part of the order of nature. The cosmic significance of nature, in Fichte's eyes, is that it has been created for a moral purpose, to allow the Absolute Ego and the individual egos which are its vehicles a field in which their moral strivings can take place.

One would be correct in judging that to a thinker like Fichte, with his intense ethical interests, education, especially an education directed towards moral ends, would be of great, indeed cosmic, importance. This, as we shall see below, is indeed the case. Via Fichte and via Fichte's influence on British educational thinkers like Carlyle, Green and Haldane, Kant's ethical and metaphysical doctrines came to have an indirect influence on the idealist reform movement in education, quite apart from the direct influence which Kant had himself.[1]

But the most influential of the German philosophers was almost certainly G. F. Hegel (1770-1831). In this necessarily brief sketch of a notoriously difficult philosophical system, we shall highlight those features most relevant to an understanding of the idealist educational reformers, beginning with Hegel's picture of the individual human being and then showing something of the wider metaphysics in which this picture is set.

All Hegel's philosophical work was dominated by a desire to combine the lessons learnt from the Enlightenment, culminating in Kant's philosophy, with the neglected Greek conception of reality as an organic whole. Neither tradition was satisfactory on its own. The Enlightenment had championed the individual's liberation from the old bonds which restricted him: arbitrary laws, dogmas and superstitions, ancient customs, religious rituals and obligations. This ideal of individual autonomy reached its highest expression in Kant's ethics: the moral agent is he who, by the light of his reason alone, decides where his duties lie. This stress on the moral autonomy of the individual was clearly an advance, in Hegel's eyes, on the less rational, non-individualistic forms of social control which preceded it. But was it enough to call, as Kant and Fichte had done, for the freedom of the individual moral conscience? As individuals shook off the social bonds which had earlier restricted them, they would each become a separate centre of moral striving, isolated from others. The demotion of customs, traditions, rituals cut both ways: it liberated the individual, but at the same time turned him into a moral island. Man's social nature counted for nothing. In so far as the Enlightenment programme succeeded, society would increasingly be deprived of the interpersonal linkages which were essential to its being. It would become a mere aggregate of autonomous atoms, or, as Hegel put it in a chillingly apt image, nothing but a 'heap' (Hegel, 1821, paras 302-3). The fruits of the Enlightenment programme were evident to Hegel in the French Revolution and its aftermath. In destroying the old order, the Revolution had created a citizenry of free individuals, no longer hampered by oppressive laws and customs. In doing so, it destroyed the intermediate institutions which used to stand between the individual and the state: political society now consisted of a mass of autonomous individuals on one side, the state on the other. The situation was ideal for the imposition of a new tyranny: it was 'absolute freedom', as Hegel saw all too clearly in his *Phenomenology of Mind* (1807), that led directly to the Terror (pp. 599-610).[2]

To check these disintegrative tendencies of the Enlightenment, Hegel, following Rousseau, revivified the Greek idea that society should be seen as an organic whole. Individuals, on this view, are not conceivable as isolated, independent atoms: they are by their nature social creatures, necessarily linked to others within a common life. Yet while attaching the highest value to the well-being of the state as a whole, the Greeks placed too little emphasis on individual autonomy and creativeness. What was lacking from the Greek conception was precisely what the Enlightenment thinkers had seen as so important: that only if individuals are liberated from their intellectual and social shackles can they acquire that independence of thought which is essential not only for autonomous moral agency but also for creative advances in art, science and philosophy.

Hegel's philosophy is, in part, an attempt at reconciling the twin ideals of community and freedom. It proceeds by locating this polarity against a larger metaphysical background.

Hegel's metaphysics is one step further away from Kant's than Fichte's. By dropping Kant's postulation of noumena behind the phenomena of nature, Fichte converted Kantianism into idealism. Reality now is wholly spiritual. But, at the same time, Kant's division between the moral world and the world of nature still persists, though not in the same form. In Kant, nature, owing to the noumena which underlie it, has a certain independence from the moral world. This independence vanishes in Fichte: nature exists only as a field for moral activity, as an antipathetic power which it is man's duty to combat. But is this the correct interpretation of nature? Or are man and nature more closely interlinked, as Wordsworth, for instance, would have us believe? Wordsworth held that nature, like man, is an embodiment of divine spirit: hence the affinities which we, as men, feel with it, and hence its educative power over us. This line of thought was partly formed by Wordsworth's vicarious experience, via Coleridge, of German idealism, especially that of F. W. Schelling (1775-1854). Schelling's belief in the spirituality of nature was taken up by Hegel and woven into his own idealist system.

Absolute Reality for Hegel is Thought or Spirit. This Absolute – and here Hegel seeks to incorporate the insights of the Enlightenment – is not a featureless unity, but is by its nature differentiated into particulars. It exists, that is, expresses itself, only through the individual parts which constitute it: remove variety, particularity, and you remove the whole. Nature has now a more positive role in the universal order than Fichte could have contemplated. It is one form in which Spirit comes to express itself. To understand Hegel, we have to share his vision of Reality as purposive, as working towards its intrinsic goal of self-realization. What is it for Spirit to realize itself? The end of Thought, on this view, must be to become fully conscious of itself. The *telos* of Reality is self-knowledge, thought about thought. The world of nature is one expression of this cosmic urge towards self-consciousness. If man were not part of nature, if, that is, man did not exist, spirit would not exist either, since its self-awareness would have no vehicle. Only man, alone among natural things, has a capacity not only for consciousness, but also for self-consciousness. In this reflexive activity – his thought about himself as a thinking being – the cosmic process finds its final expression, its ultimate end. Individual men find their own self-realization in their own thinking about themselves; and as they themselves are vehicles of Spirit, so Spirit, too, realizes itself in their self-realization.

But what is it for man to think about himself? He is, as we have seen, no atomic entity, but necessarily a part of a larger social whole. This social whole is itself a part of a wider, metaphysical reality, that is, Spirit. It thus mediates between man on the one side and Spirit on the other. So in thinking about himself, man is necessarily thinking about these larger, social and metaphysical wholes. Philosophy, as the most fully developed form of such thinking, makes an essential contribution, therefore, to the progressive expansion of the Spirit's self-consciousness. So, in a less explicit way, can art and religion. This is why the Greek idea of the individual as a part of a political community is insufficient on its own: it is only when individuals are free to realize their power of creative thought – in art, religion, philosophy – that they can fully participate in this eternal process of self-awareness. The period, indeed, between the Greeks and Hegel's own time has been, in the latter's view, a notable stage in this process, owing to the heightened awareness of reality as a whole which the intellectual liberation of the individual since the seventeenth century has brought into being.

But an individual's progress towards an awareness of reality as a whole is bound to be slow and arduous. He has to pass through many intermediate phases of partial understanding, each one of which is seen to have contradictions within itself which can only be resolved when one's thinking reaches a higher level. This is not the place to go through the detailed progression – from lower forms of consciousness, to the individual's awareness of himself as an individual, to his realization of his social nature and to his awareness of himself as a part of the Absolute – that Hegel elaborates in his *Phenomenology of Mind* and elsewhere. The most significant point for us to remember is the cosmic significance of intellectual education from a Hegelian viewpoint. Initiating students into art, religion, the history of thought, philosophy is not justified, as it has been for others, because these forms of thought are intrinsically worthwhile: it is important because it is only when men have fought through to these higher levels of consciousness that they can become adequate vehicles of Spirit in its eternal quest.

In this brief discussion of Hegel's thought we have concentrated on those features which will prove of especial significance in the educational reform movement under consideration. There is much, of course, that we have left out, not merely details but also something quite central to Hegel's philosophy, the new logical apparatus which he introduced to make clear the structure of the Absolute and its connexions with the particularities of nature and of human life. We have left this out, because it was not Hegel's logical apparatus but his broader theses about reality, society and the individual, which most deeply affected T. H. Green, Haldane and the other idealists in our story.

T. H. Green's metaphysics, as we have already seen, was enormously influential. But it does not rest on the complex battery of concepts found in Hegel's *Logic*. While the framework of Green's thought is distinctively Hegelian – Green would accept virtually all the Hegelian theory we have briefly sketched – the name of Hegel is not mentioned even once in the metaphysical Book I of the *Prolegomena to Ethics* (henceforth *PE*). We stated earlier that Kant influenced the British idealists in his own right as well as via his influence on Fichte and Hegel. Nowhere are Kantian conceptions more prominent among the idealists than in the writings of Green, not least his metaphysics. His basic argument for the spiritual nature of reality is, compared with the tortuous triads of Hegel, simplicity itself – and it springs directly from Kant. Green begins by distinguishing between our knowledge of nature and nature itself. Nature itself, following Kant, can only be conceived as a single and unalterable system of relations – the spatio-temporal world of substances in causal interaction which we mentioned earlier. Our consciousness of nature is not itself a part of nature and its origin cannot therefore be discovered by natural science. Neither can the origin of nature itself: science can teach us much about the relations of which nature consists – it can provide us with causal laws which explain how events and substances are interconnected – but it cannot explain how the whole system of relations, nature itself, came into being. Now nature, as a system of relations, is necessarily mind-dependent. Natural phenomena only exist as objects for some consciousness or consciousnesses. They can only be said to be 'related' within a single, all-inclusive system if there is something to do this relating. Human intelligence provides us with one example of a relating agency. But if these relations are

19

real and do not merely exist *for us,* they must be the product not of human intelligence, but of something analogous to human intelligence. This Green calls the eternal consciousness. It is a consciousness outside space and time, for these belong to the world of nature in which it is embodied.

How does man fit into this picture? His consciousness of nature is not, as has been said, a part of nature, even though it is dependent on a part of nature, a human body, for its existence. Its origin cannot, therefore, be found in nature: one must look for it elsewhere. The answer is not hard to find. Human consciousness, at least those higher forms of it which are not part of our animal nature, is a 'reproduction' or 'self-realization' in us of an eternal consciousness. Green's first brief account of this relationship in the *Prolegomena* is worth quoting in full:

> The true account of [the growth of knowledge on our part] is held to be that the concrete whole, which may be described indifferently as an eternal intelligence realized in the related facts of the world, or as a system of related facts rendered possible by such an intelligence, partially and gradually reproduces itself in us, communicating piece-meal, but in inseparable correlation, understanding and the facts understood, experience and the experienced world
> (*PE,* para. 36).

A Hegelian framework is very evident here. Nature, man and God are inseparable. The eternal intelligence is not a transcendent being apart from nature and responsible for its creation. It is 'realized' in that nature, embodied within it. It gradually reproduces itself in us as we grow in knowledge. This is because this is a growth in our *self*-knowledge (which includes a knowledge of nature since our self is inseparable from reality as a whole). The eternal intelligence 'realizes itself' (para. 74) in the growth of our consciousness, since as we become more self-conscious the eternal intelligence elsewhere described as a 'self-distinguishing consciousness' (para. 52) or a 'self-consciousness which is not in time' (ibid.) does also.

The thought here is Hegelian. It embodies, as elsewhere in Green, a teleological conception of reality, the same, in fact, that we noted in Hegel himself. The eternal intelligence is an active, goal-oriented power, realizing its end as it embodies itself in nature and reproduces itself in our growing consciousness. In Green, as in Hegel, human history is a part of this cosmic process: it is the story not only of man, but of the eternal intelligence in its timeless realization of its end.

There are a number of points about Green's metaphysics which we will need to keep in mind when discussing his influence on educational reform. The first is akin to one we have already made about Hegel (above, p. 18). Green could have had no doubts, holding the metaphysical views that he held, about the supreme importance of intellectual education. In educating a man, one is raising his consciousness above the purely animal level, gradually imparting to him knowledge about man, nature and reality as a whole. As one does so, one is participating in an eternal process, enabling the eternal intelligence to reproduce itself in him, and enabling the pupil thereby to participate in the spaceless, timeless activity of that intelligence. Failure to educate a man is a missed opportunity of cosmic significance. Green would have been the first to echo Carlyle when he said: 'That there should one Man die ignorant who had the capacity for Knowledge, this I call a tragedy, were it to happen more than twenty times in the minute, as by some computations it does' (Carlyle, 1831, p. 207). He would also, as we shall see, have echoed the universal sentiment expressed in this passage. Education is for all who have the capacity for knowledge, that is, for the many, not the few. In this egalitarianism, Green differs radically from Hegel. Hegel, like Plato, had stressed above all the arduousness of intellectual education: the path upward from the Cave and the journey through the stages picked out by Hegel's system are both long and difficult. They are not intended for the ordinary man but for the rulers, Plato's Guardians and Hegel's 'universal class'. This is not to say that Green thinks that acquiring knowledge will be effortless, only that there is nothing in his thought which suggests that it is out of the intellectual reach of the ordinary citizen. He does not, as Plato did, seek to justify educational élitism by a doctrine of difference in innate intelligence. There is no evidence that Green himself believed in such differences. On the contrary, his metaphysical outlook made him see all men as alike: in so far as they were capable of thought at all, they were capable of having that thought developed so that they could become vehicles of the eternal consciousness. Hence Green's deeply felt enthusiasm, about which we will be saying more later, for universal education.

A second point to bear in mind about Green's metaphysics is the impact it had on the young men who came in contact with it, as his pupils or through his writings. The second half of the nineteenth century was a time of religious doubt. Enlightenment philosophy, not least that of Hume and Kant, challenged traditional arguments for the existence of God. Nineteenth-century science, especially by its geological discoveries about the age of the earth and by its biological theory of evolution by natural selection, had undermined the biblical accounts of the origin of man: Darwin's *Descent of Man* was published in 1871. At the same time, biblical scholarship was casting further doubt on the literal truth of the Christian story. Christianity, it seemed, was no longer reconcilable with reason. It was increasingly difficult for the religiously-minded young men who came up to the universities from the middle of the century onwards, many of whom intended to become either clergymen (including university dons) or Christian schoolmasters, to preserve their faith intact, without denying the claims of rationality altogether. For the most reflective of them it seemed impossible.

One of the latter was George Sylvester Morris (1840-89). Morris plays no part in our story, except as the teacher of John Dewey at Johns Hopkins University in 1882-4. We take *him* as an example of someone who fell under Green's influence, rather than, say, one of the Oxford students who studied under Green or was fired by his lay sermons, because although Morris lived three thousand miles away from Oxford and never met Green, only coming across him in about 1878-82 through his writings, the effect on him of Green's metaphysics was cataclysmic. It restored to him, as it restored to young John Dewey in a similarly dramatic way, the confidence in a religious interpretation of reality which had long forsaken him. Originally a divinity student intent on the ministry, Morris went through a painful crisis of faith on reading Hume and other empiricists in the mid-1860s. He gave up thoughts of a religious career and turned to philosophy, attempting, but failing, to find a secure theological underpinning to his thought by studying under F. A. Trendelenburg in Berlin. For a dozen or more years, including the first eight years of his university teaching at Michigan (1870-8), he remained in a spiritual desert. Then he discovered Green. As Neil Coughlan, whose *Young John Dewey* is our source for Morris's career, writes:

> Morris can hardly have begun reading Green much before 1880, yet within a year or two he had adopted Green's philosophy almost whole. Between 1882 and 1889, when he died, Morris, who had not written a book in the twelve or thirteen years since his return from Europe, wrote four of them (p. 25).

Green spoke to Morris's spiritually empty condition in the same way as to Dewey's. For both men faith was threatened by science and the empiricist philosophy which championed it. Green, in his *Introductions to Hume's Treatise of Human Nature* (1874) and his critique of Herbert Spencer and G. H. Lewes (Green, T. H., 1885-8, vol. 1), had tried to show, in young Dewey's words, that empiricism 'was no more compatible with science than it was with religion; that a consistent interpretation of Empiricism sapped the roots of knowledge as well as of faith' (Dewey, 1969, p. 18). Hume's scepticism was the outcome of Locke's empiricism: if nature cannot be known by experience to possess causal relations, then science is immediately in jeopardy. It is a condition of our having any experience of nature at all, and of our scientific knowledge of it in particular, that an eternal consciousness is seen to underlie it in the way we have already sketched. In Dewey's words:

> It was the main work of Green's speculative philosophy to show that there is a spiritual principle at the root of ordinary experience and science, as well as at the basis of ethics and religion; to show, negatively, that whatever weakens the supremacy and primacy of the spiritual principle makes science impossible, and, positively, to show that any fair analysis of the conditions of science will show certain ideas, principles or categories - call them what you will - that are not physical and sensible, but intellectual and metaphysical (op. cit., p. 17).

The central thread of Green's metaphysical arguments seemed to lead, economically and unambiguously, to a conclusion which was not only intellectually acceptable to such men as Morris and Dewey and their counterparts in contemporary Oxford, but was also able to restore to them a purpose in living, to revive that spiritual fervour which they had inherited from earlier generations but against which the doubts of the new age had anaesthetized them. Green had shown, or had appeared to show, that Christianity was not only compatible with reason: it was rational through and through. For he sought, in Thomas Arnold's Broad Church tradition, to shift the focal point of Christian doctrine away from the fundamentalist attachment to literal biblical truth so prominent among evangelicals and puritans, away even from the figure of Christ himself, to the more general conception of the necessary spirituality of the world which he derived from idealism. In doing so, he seemed to prove that the central truths of religion could be seen to be so by rational reflection alone. Whatever new revelations about the Bible or the nature of the universe or of man's evolution which science or history might yield between them could not undermine the basic argument. Religion could not be proved false by empirical means: its truth was vindicated *a priori.*

The very simplicity of Green's central argument contributed greatly to its impact. In the light of this simplicity, it is remarkable that it was not questioned by his disciples more than it was. But when a plank is thrown over the abyss one doesn't stop to inspect it for woodworm.

Morality and community 3

Kant's ethics stresses, as no ethical theory did before, the autonomy of the moral agent. Moral action demands that one does what one does not because something outside oneself (e.g., law, custom, public opinion) tells one to do it, but because it is dictated by one's own reason. The 'external' influences on one's will include one's own desires and aversions: it will be remembered from Chapter 2 that in Kant's view these are not part of one's moral self, since they are a part of nature. But how can reason alone tell one what one ought to do? Kant's answer lies in his theory of the categorical imperative: those maxims should be followed which can be willed without contradiction to hold universally. Making lying promises, for instance, can be ruled out by this criterion, in Kant's opinion: for one could not will it to be a universal law that everyone should make lying promises when so inclined, since in that circumstance the whole institution of promise-making would collapse (Kant, 1785, ch. 2). A central failing of Kant's criterion, as many later commentators have pointed out, is its emptiness. All sorts of maxims seem to pass the test even though they could scarcely be said to be moral duties. One could will without contradiction, for instance, that every child born on a Tuesday should wear blue clothes. Something less formal, more substantive, is needed as a criterion if it is to be a practical guide to action.

Hegel believed he could provide this. The trouble with Kant's ethics, he held, was that it was too subjective: in putting all the weight on the autonomy of the individual, Kant had overlooked the fact that individuals are necessarily members of society and that society brings with it its own moral code, enshrined in its laws, customs and institutional practices. Ideally this social morality – which Hegel termed *'Sittlichkeit'* in opposition to subjective morality which he called *'Moralität'* – should determine the whole moral life of the individual, as Aristotle had argued and the Athenians tried to put into practice.[1] The empty formalism of Kant's system was replaced in this conception by the concrete obligations of what Bradley came to call 'my station and its duties'. This is not to say that in Hegel, at any rate, morality was simply a matter of obedience to the laws and customs of one's society

25

whatever these were like. The morality of *Sittlichkeit* was an ideal. In actual empirical societies one might sometimes have to go against received morality: Socrates and Jesus, whom Hegel much admired, did just this. But a reflective morality, where the individual has consciously to forge his own criterion of what is right in opposition to the criteria he finds in his community, could not be the ideal form of morality which we all should aim at possessing.

Hegel's ethics is closely tied to his metaphysics. Individuals are parts of the Absolute, but are linked thereto by the mediate link they have with the state. This link itself is also mediated. Hegel, as we saw in Chapter 2, was horrified by the effect of the French Revolution in helping to destroy the intermediate links between man and the state. Between the two comes a man's family and his social class, in Hegel's view: each of these, as well as the state as a whole, brings with it its own customs and rules to guide his conduct (1821, pt 3)[2]. By this graded series of attachments, the individual feels himself united with the state-community and thereby, since the Absolute realizes itself through the historical development of the state, with reality itself. Morality is no longer, as for Kant, a matter of a strong-willed endeavour to fulfil one's obligations in the face of a hostile nature: one is at home in the world, no longer a divided self. The sphere of *what ought to be* is not now separated by an unbridgeable gulf from the sphere of *what is*, for it is from reality, the Absolute, via the state and its subordinate communities, that one's moral duties come.

All this is not to say that Hegel wrote off Kant's moral theory completely. Far from it. As pointed out earlier, he was not advocating a full-scale return to the Greek *polis*. The individual, even though ideally he is to be guided by the *Sittlichkeit* of his community, is not to accept this blindly. He should ideally understand the reason why this social morality is to be accepted; that is, he should see its connexion with the Absolute in the way described. In following *Sittlichkeit*, he is still guided by reason: although the social maxims which he follows are not his own in the sense that he has originated them, he is still acting autonomously because he can freely accept them as rationally demanded.

Hegel's ethical ideas influenced the idealist educationists both directly and via T. H. Green. Green's own ethics is an amalgam of Hegel and Kant. The framework is Hegelian. Individuals are not atomic entities. It is wrong to believe

> that the individuals could be what they are, could have their moral and spiritual qualities, independently of their existence as a nation. The notion is conveyed that they bring those

qualities with them ready-made into the national existence, which thereupon results from their combination; while the truth is that, whatever moral capacity must be presupposed, it is only actualized through the habits, institutions and laws, in virtue of which the individuals form a nation (*PE*, para. 184).

Hegel's metaphysical backing for this *Sittlichkeit*, together with his incorporation of Kant's insistence on autonomy, is also echoed in Green:

It is the very essence of moral duty to be imposed by a man on himself. The moral duty to obey a positive law, whether a law of the State or of the Church, is imposed not by the author or enforcer of the positive law, but by that spirit of man – not less divine because the spirit of man – which sets before him the ideal of a perfect life, and pronounces obedience to the positive law to be necessary to its realization (*PE*, para. 324).

But within this Hegelian framework, Green outlines an ethic which is in many ways reminiscent of Kant. Both Green and Kant put themselves in the position of an autonomous individual looking for a guide to conduct, a criterion of right and wrong. Both find their criterion in a single principle. Both are adamant that the supreme principle is resolutely adhered to against likely counter-inclinations.

Where Kant and Green differ is over the supreme principle. For Kant, this is the categorical imperative; for Green, the injunction to promote the common good. Even here, the difference between the two should not be overemphasized. Kant's second formulation of his categorical imperative is that one should treat all men as ends in themselves, never merely as means. This principle, regardless of whether it is equivalent, as Kant thought, to the first formulation, already cited, whereby maxims must be universalizable, is implicit, as we shall see, in Green's ethics.[3] Kant's first formulation, moreover, although pronounced vacuous by Hegel and others, does give *some* practical guidance. What it stresses is impartiality or fairness. If my maxim is to be a universal law, I must follow it consistently, not ignoring it, for instance, when it seems more in my interests to do so; in particular, I must apply it to myself as I do to other people, and vice versa. This implicit egalitarianism in Kant is powerfully echoed, as we shall also see, in Green's theory. Both writers, therefore, lay great stress on respect for persons as ends in themselves; both are egalitarian in their opposition to unjust privilege. Where Green goes further than

Kant, however, is in his demand that it is the community which provides the locus for the individual's moral strivings: he incorporates Hegel's revival of this ancient Greek belief.

Another way of putting Green's fundamental principle is that our highest duty is our own self-realization. At first glance this might appear to be a selfish ethic, implying that we ought only to bother about our own fulfilment and to ignore other people. But enough has been said about Hegelianism and Green's version of it in particular to make it quite obvious that this interpretation is false.

> The self of which a man thus forecasts the fulfilment, is not an abstract or empty self. It is a self already affected in the most primitive forms of human life by manifold interests, among which are interests in other persons. These are not merely interests dependent on other persons for means to their gratification, but interests in the good of those other persons. . . . The man cannot contemplate himself as in a better state, or on the way to be best, without contemplating others, not merely as a means to that better state, but as sharing it with him (*PE*, para. 99).

A Kantian respect for persons is combined in this passage with the Hegelian insistence that an individual's good cannot be treated as something apart from the good of others within his community.

But what is this 'good' and what is this 'community'? Unless we can give these terms a more determinate sense, Green's fundamental principle, that one should promote the common good, will face the same charge of vacuousness that has been levied against Kant's. Let us look first at the 'good'.

We cannot know for certain what this is, according to Green. 'For the moral good is the realization of the moral capability, and we cannot fully know what any capability is till we know its ultimate realization' (*PE*, para. 172). This ultimate realization is the self-realization of the eternal consciousness. How then can an individual man, who is only a fraction of the whole, understand what this might be? Green's answer is that since the divine spirit is at work through human history, we can gain a partial grasp of the ultimate ideal from the moral progress which human societies have already exhibited. From past improvements we can extrapolate to the final end.

> The practical struggle after the Better, of which the idea of there being a Best has been the spring, has taken such effect in the world of man's affairs as makes the way by which the Best

is to be more nearly approached plain enough to him that will
see (*PE*, para. 172).

But even though we cannot know the good directly and in detail,
we do, Green implies, have some understanding of the kind of
thing it is. Self-realization is the development of those spiritual
capacities within us which we possess as vehicles of the divine
consciousness. The good, therefore, cannot be identified with
pleasure, as the utilitarians believe: it is nothing less than the
spiritual perfection of man. As moral beings, we are enjoined to
develop in ourselves and others those capacities whose actualization
is only possible in a non-temporal, eternal world: our powers of
thought in different forms, not the transient capacities we share, for
instance, with the animals.

There is more to be said in a moment about the kind of life
Green believes we should lead in order to realize this good. But let
us first look at what he understands by the 'community' whose
good we are to consider. In the first passage quoted from him above
(pp. 26-7), he writes of the individual forming a part of the *nation*.
This, again, is a legacy of Hegel: when both Hegel and Green speak
of the state as the locus of individuals' endeavours, they have in
mind not the Greek *polis* but the modern nation-state. But it would
be very wrong to read Green with hindsight as arguing for 'nationalism' as this is often understood today. He is not saying that
our supreme duty is to promote the interests of our own nation
even at the expense of others. Neither is he reifying the nation (or
state), making it an entity in its own right over and above the
persons who compose it.

The truth of these points should be evident from his discussion
of these matters in *Prolegomena to Ethics* and the *Lectures on the
Principles of Political Obligation* (henceforth *PO*). In *PE* he affirms the
view that individuals are necessarily parts of society. But 'there can
be nothing in a nation however exalted its mission, or in a society
however perfectly organized, which is not in the persons composing
the nation or the society. Our ultimate standard of worth is an
ideal of *personal* worth' (para. 184; Green's italics). Societies,
including nations or states, are nothing but individuals in certain
relationships. In working for the good of society, one is working for
persons' well-being, therefore, not for the good of some mythical
suprapersonal entity called society, the nation or the state. In
taking this line, Green is again following Hegel: because Hegel
translations have been wont to render capitalized German nouns
like 'der Staat' as capitalized English nouns like 'the State', many
have wrongly assumed Hegelianism to imply a monistic view of

29

the state, as an entity within which individuals become unimportant and the whole all-important. As we saw in the previous section, for Hegel wholes only exist as embodied in their parts. Just as the Absolute is not a transcendent entity but exists only in its natural and human embodiments, the same, *mutatis mutandis*, is true of the state.

Green goes on to argue in *PE* that one index of the moral progress made by humanity is 'the gradual extension ... of the range of persons to whom the common good is conceived as common' (para. 206). In the remote past this conception was limited to those who were outside the community, like the Greek slaves excluded from the citizen-community, or the members of an alien tribe, who were not thought to be the subjects or objects of mutual obligations. But by Green's day 'it is almost an axiom of popular Ethics that there is at least a potential duty of every man to every man' (ibid.). We now speak of 'a human family, of a fraternity of all men ... or we suppose a universal Christian citizenship' (ibid.). Our widest community is now humanity itself.

How does Green's predilection for the nation square with this? Again, with Hegel, he is very alive to the importance of mediating communities between the individual and the largest social wholes. He mentions in particular the family (*PE*, para. 229) and the town one lives in (*PE*, para. 237; *PO*, para. 119) and the nation-state. This is for him

> an organization of a people to whom the individual feels
> himself bound by ties analogous to those which bind him to
> his family, ties derived from a common dwelling-place with its
> associations, from common memories, traditions and customs,
> and from the common ways of feeling and thinking which a
> common language and still more a common literature
> embodies. Such an organization of a homogeneous people the
> modern state in most cases is (*PO*, para. 123).

In Hegel's term, the nation has, for all the reasons which Green mentions, a special *Sittlichkeit* of its own.

At the same time – and it is crucially important to grasp this – the nation is not to be seen as an exclusive community, as one whose special claims can be allowed to override those of other nations or groups. Love of one's nation is a step towards an embodiment of one's wider attachment to the community of all mankind.

> The love of mankind, no doubt, needs to be particularized in
> order to have any power over life and action. Just as there can

be no true friendship except towards this or that individual, so there can be no true public spirit which is not localized in some way. The man whose desire is to serve his kind is not centred primarily in some home, radiating from it to a commune, a municipality, and a nation, presumably has no effectual desire to serve his kind at all. But there is no reason why this localized or nationalized philanthropy should take the form of jealousy of other nations or a desire to fight them, personally or by proxy. Those in whom it is strongest are every day expressing it in good works which benefit their fellow-citizens without interfering with the men of other nations (*PO*, para. 171).

So much, in brief, for Green's views on the extent of the community whose good we should foster. Putting these together with his views on 'the good', we can see that his injunction that one should work for the common good is not empty but does indicate to his readers the kind of moral road they should follow. The ultimate objective is to develop the spiritual capacities of all the members of one's community – which is, at the limit of its extension, humanity as a whole.

What particular road to this destination, though, should one follow? How best can one promote the growth of spirit? Many young men of Green's time would have agreed with this central objective (though not usually with Green's Hegelian backing for it) and looked to a career in the church as a way of realizing it. Many others would have agreed with the objective but had doubts about the church. Green's ethics spoke to the uncertain situation of the latter. It pointed out to them that there was not one route to the common goal, but several.

In particular, one could seek to enlarge the domain of spirit directly, as a clergyman, for instance, would, or indirectly, by helping to remove obstacles to that enlargement. The man who devotes himself to improving the sanitation of a town is working for the common good (*PE*, para. 237) just as much as the parson. He is indirectly helping the growth of spiritual consciousness by bringing about one of its necessary conditions, i.e. freedom from disease. Green's own particular interests as a social reformer neatly illustrate this distinction between the direct and indirect routes. Apart from education, his chief work was for the temperance movement: drink, like disease, was an impediment to the spirit.

Many of Green's followers who were more drawn to the direct route, at least as far as their own vocation was concerned, must have agreed with him that they could do more to develop the

31

spiritual capacities of the people as lay educators, working within and expanding a national system of education, than as parsons. We shall have to see in Part 2 how far this is true of the educational reformers we are considering. For some, as we shall see, a clerical career and the vocation of educational reformer did not present themselves as an exclusive either-or.

How else could one realize one's moral end? Was one bound to throw oneself into some kind of social work, using that term very broadly to cover any spiritually-oriented work for the community as a whole, whether direct or indirect, including under direct work both its pastoral and lay educational varieties? What if one felt that one's vocation lay along a more solitary path than in social work? Suppose one felt drawn towards an artistic career, for instance, or towards a life of religious contemplation: could one still be said to be working for the common good if one adopted it?

Green discusses both these options in the course of *PE*, comparing them in each case with the vocation of social reformer. He asks, for instance, whether the latter's work is of higher value than that of the 'saint', the man who is dedicated to living a perfect human life in 'self-abasement before an ideal of holiness' (para. 302). Does not the social reformer do more to promote the well-being of the community? Green's reply is:

> If the end by reference to which moral values are to be judged were anything but the perfect life itself, as resting on a devoted will, it would be right to depreciate the obscure saint by the side of the man to whose work we can point in the redress of wrongs and the purging of social vices. But if the supreme value for man is what we take it to be – man himself in his perfection – then it is idle to contrast the more observably practical type of goodness with the more self-questioning or consciously God-seeking type. The value of each is intrinsic and identical (*PE*, para. 303).

Even if all social wrongs were righted, all vices eradicated, there would still be a need for saintliness of character, if no longer for reforming zeal. Saintliness cannot, then, be inferior. But this is looking at the matter in a very long time-perspective. It may be all right to be a saint in the well-ordered society say of a millennium hence; but could it be one's duty in nineteenth-century England? Here Green is unspecific. He says that 'under certain conditions of society, of individual temperament and ability, it [the same spiritual principle of action] takes the one form, under other conditions the other' (ibid.). But many of his young readers and listeners, inclined by their previous upbringing to put saintliness above all else, must have read in Green the message, intended or not, that in a society where so much practical good work cries out to be done, absorption only in one's own progress to perfection is really a form of self-indulgence.

On the choice of an artistic way of life, Green is more specific. Right at the end of *PE* he discusses the hypothetical case of a man who wishes to devote a large part of his life to gratifying his taste for music, for which he has an excellent talent. Should he do so? Again, this depends partly on his own abilities but also on the social conditions around him. A long passage from Green on this point is worth quoting in full:

> In some Italian principality of the last century, for instance, with its civil life crushed out and its moral energies debased, excellence in music could hardly be accounted of actual and present value at all. Its value would be potential, in so far as the artist's work might survive to become an element in a nobler life elsewhere or at a later time. Under such conditions much occupation with music might imply indifference to claims of the human soul which must be satisfied in order to the attainment [*sic*] of a life in which the value of music could be actualized. And under better social conditions there may be claims, arising from the particular position of an individual, which render the pursuit of excellence in music, though it would be the right pursuit for others qualified as he is, a wrong one for him. In the absence of such claims the main question will be of his particular talent. Has he talent to serve mankind – to contribute to the perfection of the human soul – more as a musician than in any other way? Only if he has will he be justified in making music his main pursuit. If he is not to make it his main pursuit, the question will remain, to what extent he may be justified in indulging his taste for it, either as a refreshment of faculties which are to be mainly used in other pursuits – to be so used, because in them he may best serve mankind in the sense explained – or as enabling him to share in that intrinsically valuable lifting up of the soul which music may afford (*PE*, para. 381).

Few of Green's readers who were torn between an artistic career and one concerned more directly with social service could have doubted, after reading such a passage, which path they should follow. Unless they felt themselves to be most unusually talented – and there were objective grounds to support this feeling – they had better give up all thoughts of a musical career. Even if they were musically gifted, it still would not be clear that they should devote themselves to music, owing to the massive imperfections of contemporary British society.

It is on the basis of passages such as this that Green has been accused, for instance, by Melvin Richter, of puritanism or 'Hebraism', as Matthew Arnold called the doctrine that strict moral values are all-important, as contrasted with the 'Hellenism' which holds that these values are subordinate to the superior claims of intellectual and aesthetic culture (Richter, 1964, p. 219). But this is not a fair judgment on Green. We must leave aside a detailed exegesis of what Arnold meant by the slippery terms 'Hebraism' and 'Hellenism', stating only that the main object of Arnold's critique seems to have been not so much those who put morality above the contemplative life – for the Hellenist is one whose whole life, and not merely a hived-off portion of it, is guided by critical reason – as those who favoured the pre-eminence of a particular form of narrowly conceived morality, that is, the sectarian morality of the dissenters. On this issue, Green and Arnold would have been on the same side. But even if we did interpret Arnold's contrast to be between morality as such, that is, *any* form of morality, and the contemplative life, it still would not be certain that Green was a Hebraist. We see from the end of the passage just quoted that music may provide an 'intrinsically valuable lifting up of the soul'. It can assist directly, that is, in the perfection of man, raising his consciousness so that it becomes one with the eternal spirit. Not only art, but the pursuit of knowledge, too, can have this effect. R. L. Nettleship, a pupil and co-fellow of Green at Balliol, wrote of him in his Memoir:

> Recognizing as he did in the effort to assimilate truth or to appreciate beauty a liberation of the human spirit from its own littleness, a self-development through self-renunciation, not different in kind from that which takes place in moral discipline, he could not but see in the men who have lived to find what is true or to express what is beautiful, fellow workers with prophets and statesmen in the furtherance of human freedom (Green, 1885-8, vol. 3, p. cxlviii, hereafter cited as *Works*).

Green is no Hebraist, even in a wide sense. It is true that he leaves the issue of the ultimate relation between theoretical and artistic values on the one hand, and moral values on the other, unsettled in *PE*. He is uncertain whether values of all these kinds fall under a unitary concept of the good or whether the two kinds of value split apart into separate goods (para. 289). At the most, however, this suggests that moral values are equivalent in worthwhileness to intellectual or aesthetic ones, that the good will involves just such a heightening of spiritual consciousness as intellectual/aesthetic activity. While there is nothing to suggest he held the kind of view held later by G. E. Moore, which subordinated moral to cultural values, there is equally nothing to suggest he believed the reverse of this.

Green puts more emphasis on the vocation of social reformer than on the vocation of scholar or artist only because of the age in which he lived:

> It is no time to enjoy the pleasures of eye and ear, of search
> for knowledge, of friendly intercourse, of applauded speech or
> writing, while the mass of men whom we call our brethren,
> and whom we declare to be meant with us for eternal
> destinies, are left without the chance, which only the help of
> others can gain for them, of making themselves in act what in
> possibility we believe them to be (*PE*, para. 270).

The ancient Greeks, whose civilization was based on slavery, could enjoy these aesthetic and other pleasures without self-sacrifice, but

> where the Greek saw a supply of possibly serviceable labour,
> having no end or function but to be made really serviceable to
> the privileged few, the Christian citizen sees a multitude of
> persons, who in their actual present condition may have no
> advantage over the slaves of an ancient state, but who
> in undeveloped possibility, and in the claims which arise out
> of that possibility, are all that he himself is (ibid.).

Another telling comparison which Green makes between his own age and that of the Greeks concerns attitudes to *temperance*, not in the anti-alcoholic sense, but as one of the cardinal virtues in Greek thought. To Plato it involved the renunciation of desires arising from one's embodied nature such as greed and lust. One indication of mankind's moral progress since the Greeks, so Green believes, is that our concept of temperance has now altered. It is not now that we should deny ourselves the pleasures of food, drink and sex in order that we may devote ourselves to intellectual activity: it is these very aesthetic and scientific pursuits we must now forgo for the sake of a more widespread human perfection (*PE*, paras 261ff).

4   Society and the state

For all the idealists *the state* is the central political concept. The state provides a mediating link between the individual and the eternal spirit. It is conceived as a spiritual community, inspired by the ancient Greek *polis*, but going beyond the *polis* in two important ways. It is, first of all, a territorial or national, not a city-state. And, second, it is one in which individuals are ideally autonomous moral agents, living within the *Sittlichkeit* of the community not simply because it is there to be obeyed, but because they find these laws and customs rationally justified.

Hegel has often been accused of holding a totalitarian political theory, whereby individuals' interests and liberties are wholly subjugated to the superior interests of the state. Karl Popper, for instance, has for this reason put Hegel in the same category as Plato, as an enemy of the 'open society' and an intellectual forebear of the twentieth-century totalitarian state (Popper, 1945, ch. 12). But this accusation is wholly unjust.[1] Hegel criticizes Plato's *Republic* precisely on the grounds of its lack of pluralism:

> It might seem that universal ends would be more readily attainable if the universal absorbed the strength of the particulars in the way described, for instance, in Plato's *Republic*. But this, too, is only an illusion, since both universal and particular turn into one another and exist only for and by means of one another (*Philosophy of Right*, para. 184, addition).

The state is nothing but a community of individuals; its well-being, the common good, is merely the well-being of its constituent members. Part of that well-being is individual autonomy, the freedom to determine one's own actions and way of life.

> In Plato's state, subjective freedom does not count, because people have their occupations assigned to them by the Guardians. In many oriental states, this assignment is determined by birth. But subjective freedom, which must be respected, demands that individuals should have free choice in this matter (ibid., para. 262, addition).

Hegel, unlike Plato, stresses the importance of social mobility (see also his *Philosophy of Right* (henceforth *PR*), para. 206).[2]

Hegel's state is not, therefore, a monolithic structure. It contains mediating institutions, or forms of life, between itself and the individual, all of which possess a certain autonomy. This comes out in more than one way. It is seen, most noticeably, in Hegel's trichotomy between the family, civil society, and the state. The family provides, according to Hegel, the individual's first experience of community life. It is a community where the distinction between one's own and others' private interests is unknown: all equally contribute to and share in the well-being of the family as a whole. The individual is thus far very much in the position of a citizen of the Greek *polis*, his own well-being unreflectingly identified with that of the whole. When he leaves the family circle he enters what Hegel calls 'civil society'. Civil society is the society of the classical economists, a society whose prime motive is not the well-being of the whole, but self-interest. Men live as individuals, each bent on his own end. They live, of course, within a framework of laws and institutions, but these are seen as necessary only so that private purposes can be the more effectively pursued. In civil society, subjective freedom counts for everything, community for nothing.

The state is the reconciliation of these opposite ideals. It restores to men that sense of belonging to a community of which civil society has deprived them. No longer are they alienated individuals, opposing themselves to society and its institutions, which comes to seem something over and against themselves, a soulless machine; which at best hedges round their independence but promotes, rather than diminishes, their sense of isolation from their fellows; and at worst – and here Hegel saw acutely how the *laissez-faire* economic system of civil society tends to create large-scale poverty and excessive division of labour – crushes them into a new serfdom. The state is organized in such a way that all its members work together for a common well-being. Controls are necessary on the economic and other institutions of civil society, so as to ensure that they now serve this common end and not simply private ends. A new class is created, the 'universal class' of state officials, including teachers, doctors, lawyers, as well as civil servants. These are, like Plato's Guardians, motivated predominantly by considerations of what is in the interests of the state as a whole: they help to direct the work of the agricultural and commercial classes below them so that they promote this end. But civil society still preserves its independence to a very great extent: subjective freedom is important as well as fraternity. Economic life, although finally *controlled* by the state, in the form, for instance, of a guaranteed minimum standard of living, price controls, and taxes designed for a redistribution of income, is not *undertaken* by the state, in the form of state industries or state farms. Hegel envisaged a free economy in the latter sense. Not only that: he accepted that civil society is still largely motivated by self-centred desires, such as the maximization of one's profits or wages. Its members may still be working for the common good even though they do so unconsciously; but this depends on the power of the universal class to ensure that private interests and public do converge.[3]

Green's theory of society and the state, as presented in his *Lectures on the Principles of Political Obligation* (*PO*), owes much, as one would expect, to Hegel. But one difference between them should be noted immediately, as it may lead to confusion. Hegel attributes the widespread poverty of industrial society, the creation of a 'rabble' of propertyless individuals, to the operation of a capitalist economy: the multiplication of material needs, real or fabricated, leads to the overproduction of goods which the poor cannot buy, at the same time subjecting them to a dehumanizing division of labour.[4] While Green is as sensible as Hegel to the horrors of urban poverty – indeed he spent much of life, directly or indirectly, in helping to remove them – he believes that poverty is due not to capitalism but to landlordism: it is partly produced by the growth of large estates, forcing smallholders and labourers away from the countryside and into the cities, and partly by the servile habits of the urban poor, inherited from their agricultural ancestors (*PO,* para. 229). Capitalism is not necessarily connected with poverty, Green argues. If industrial workers were less servile, less prone to drink, better educated and more thrifty, they could well prosper under a capitalist system: there is, in fact, 'nothing . . . to prevent them from being on a small scale capitalists themselves' (*PO,* para. 227).

This contrast between Green and Hegel is noteworthy because, while Green is now often thought of as a prime mover of the modern welfare state and politically a radical, Hegel is usually placed firmly on the right wing: yet their views on poverty seem to reverse these positions. What one should remember, however, is that Hegel's 'anti-capitalist' insights were worked out in his early *Jenaer Realphilosophie* which remained unpublished until the 1930s. The same themes are found here and there in his better known *Philosophy of Right,* but, as Avineri points out, there they were 'nothing more than a marginal phenomenon. When writing the *Philosophy of Right* Hegel thought that he had already found an answer to his problem [of industrial society], and hence the criticism appeared as secondary, while the proposed solution came to occupy the centre of the argument' (Avineri, 1972, p. 98). Whether

Green and other idealists would have come out more vehemently against capitalism if they had read the *Realphilosophie* we cannot say. As it was, Green and other leading figures in this book like Acland and Haldane were too closely associated with the Liberal Party not to believe that it was land rather than capital which stood most in the way of social reform. A later generation of idealist thinkers, that of Tawney and Lindsay, would find them-selves closer to Hegel than Green, although unwittingly so. Green himself, had he lived longer, may have come to switch from the Liberal to the Labour Party (as did Haldane in his old age). There was certainly room for him to do so within his political theory. To Green, as to many of his radical contemporaries living at the highpoint of Victorian prosperity, the material benefits which capitalism was providing for the poor were more evident than its evils: it was not until after the social surveys of Booth and Rowntree after Green's death that the extent and depth of urban poverty they revealed prompted non-revolutionary radicals to reflect more fully on its causes. But Green had no time for the claim that property rights were absolute. The possession of property, he argues, following Hegel, is only justifiable if it is a necessary condition of the self-determination one requires as a citizen, i.e. as a contributor to the common good (*PO,* para. 216). He has as little enthusiasm for 'functionless' property as Tawney. Had he the economic turn of mind and empirical evidence which were to lead Tawney towards his passionate critique of *laissez-faire* capitalism, he may well have joined him as one of the leading theorists of democratic socialism. Even despite his reluctance to pin the blame for social distress on capitalism rather than on landed interests, there is evidence that Green was seen by those who knew him intimately as a 'socialist'. His brother-in-law, J. A. Symonds, wrote to Green's widow as follows:

> Green's practical grasp on political conditions and his
> sympathy with the vast masses of a nation, the producers and
> breadmakers, the taxpayers and inadequately represented,
> strike all alive. Personally I may say that he inducted me into
> the philosophy of democracy and socialism ... [He had] the
> faculty of feeling by a kind of penetrative instinct that
> modern society had ripened to a point at which the principles
> of democracy and socialism had to be accepted as actualities.[5]

We mentioned just now that Green is usually seen as a radical and Hegel as a conservative. One historical reason for this may be traced to Green himself. This was certainly his own assessment of the difference between them. In one of the few places where Green

explicitly mentions Hegel, his essay *On the different senses of 'freedom'
as applied to will and to the moral progress of man* (*PO*), he acknowledges
his debt to Hegel for his notion of a 'system of social relations, with
laws, customs, and institutions corresponding' [i.e. *Sittlichkeit*],
which supplies interests to a man 'of a more concrete kind than the
interest in fulfilment of universally binding law because universally
binding [i.e. Kantian *Moralität*], but which are yet the product of
reason' (para. 5; our brackets). He agrees, too, with Hegel, that 'the
modern state does contribute to the realization of freedom, if by
freedom we understand the autonomy of the will or its deter-
mination by rational objects' (ibid.). Where Green disagrees,
however, is in his claim, *contra* Hegel, that the realization of this
freedom is 'most imperfect' even in the best society that has ever
been:

> To an Athenian slave, who might be used to gratify a master's
> lust, it would have been a mockery to speak of the state as a
> realization of freedom; and perhaps it would not be much less
> so to speak of it as such to an untaught and underfed denizen
> of a London yard with gin-shops on the right hand and on
> the left. What Hegel says of the state in this respect seems . . .
> hard to square with facts (ibid., para. 6).

Green's implication here is that for Hegel the state as it is is the
state as it ought to be. This is an early expression of the view which
was later to become orthodox among British thinkers, that Hegel
was a state-worshipper, believing that state laws should always
be obeyed. But Hegel's early radicalism, as shown in his
Realphilosophie, should make us hesitate to accept this too readily.
So should his enthusiasm for such social critics as Socrates and
Jesus Christ. Although he put *Sittlichkeit* ultimately above *Moralität*,
it was not *any Sittlichkeit,* but that of an ideal state whose laws and
institutions would be fit vehicles of its members' self-realization.
Hegel's view of the relation between actual empirical states and the
ideal state was not, in fact, very different from Green's. Both were
reluctant to identify the two; and while Hegel, admittedly, believed
that actual states were a partial embodiment of the ideal, as the
latest stage so far in the manifestation of *Geist,* this was no different
from Green's own belief in moral progress, a belief which led him
to claim that we should normally obey the laws of the state (*PO,*
para. 144), and that philosophy can show us how the impulse after
the moral ideal has expressed itself in authorities and institutions
of all kinds, which we learn to obey for this reason (*PE,* paras
321-6). Just the same forces pulled Green towards conservatism as
pulled Hegel; other, humanitarian, forces pulled both towards a

very similar radicalism. The differences between them are less striking than what they share in common. Green was more of a Hegelian than he knew.

This is not to say, however, that the fact that Green *thought* that Hegel was more of a worshipper of the *status quo* than he was in fact is not important for our purposes. We shall have to see later how far it is. But let us now turn, in any case, from Green's general political attitudes to more particular themes in his political thought. The point made above about property rights gives us an entrée. Green stands foursquare against the view, prominent in earlier British political philosophy, that there exist certain 'natural' rights, whether to liberty, property or whatever, which belong to individuals *qua* individuals. Individuals may well have rights to such things, but this is not because these in some sense 'naturally' belong to them, but because without them they could not live as members of a community. Liberty is important for the Hegelian reason, already mentioned, that individuals need it to be able to act as autonomous self-determining citizens. The right to property follows from the right to liberty: one needs 'a certain permanent apparatus beyond the bodily organs, for the maintenance and expression of that [free] life' (*PO*, para. 215).

Green's opposition to the individualist tradition centres around its conception of political authority. If men are conceived not primarily as social creatures but primarily as individuals wanting to pursue their own ends without hindrance, the state comes to be seen as something external to them, instituted by them with either absolute power, as Hobbes thought, or limited powers, as Locke thought, to create a framework of security and law-abidingness in which individuals can better pursue their own ends. But suppose a man finds it not in his interest to do what the law enjoins him to do: why should he obey the state? He has no reason except fear of the state's penalty. Coercion proves to be the ultimate basis of political obedience.

Green objects in a well-known chapter that 'will, not force, is the basis of the state' (*PO*, section G). Green sees the state as something superimposed on and growing out of communities already in existence. Men are not related to it as atomic individuals to a machine which serves their purposes. An atomic, a-social individual is inconceivable. Individuals are necessarily parts of society, members of communities. So before states come into being, men are bound together by customs and duties in the common life of families and tribes. The political institutions of the state-codified laws (a state bureaucracy, etc.) evolve out of these primitive institutions, are systematizations of them. There is no clear cut-off point which determines how far this process of systematization must have gone before we can really talk of a 'state'. Individuals conform to the basic morality of their pre-political society not out of fear, but out of the recognition of a common well-being which is at the same time their own well-being. Their obedience to the state springs from the same motive:

> To ask why I am to submit to the power of the state, is to ask why I am to allow my life to be regulated by that complex of institutions without which I literally could not have a life to call my own, nor should be able to ask for a justification of what I am called on to do. For that I may have a life which I can call my own, I must not only be conscious of myself and of ends which I present to myself as mine; I must be able to reckon on a certain freedom of action and acquisition for the attainment of those ends, and this can only be secured through common recognition of this freedom on the part of each other by members of a society, as being for a common good (*PO*, para. 114).

State institutions are seen as necessary conditions of individual liberty not in the individualist way, which makes that liberty an absolute value, but in the Hegelian way, whereby the liberty is important because without it individuals could not participate autonomously in the life of the state-community, thus helping to realize the divine purpose for which it has come into being.

The state is nothing alien to the individual, therefore, but grows out of a more primitive community life in which the individual also felt at home. In describing the emergence of the state in this way, Green diverges in an important way from Hegel. Hegel sees its origin in terms of contradictions and reconciliations. Civil society is the antithesis of family life: universal self-interest supersedes the primitive sense of community. The state is the higher synthesis of both the family and civil society, incorporating the communitarianism of the former and the subjective freedom of the latter. For Green, on the other hand, the state grows *directly* out of a primitive community, differing from it only in degree of systematization. The interpolation of civil society, with its anti-communitarian ideology, is thus absent from Green's account. This bears out our claim that while Green's philosophy in general retains the framework, the leading conclusions, of Hegel's thought, it is no slave to his logic. It is thus not committed to any of the particular dialectical triads, like that of family–civil society–state, which arise from that logic.

42

The state is, in Green, a more inclusive community than the family and tribal communities it supersedes. We have already shown in Chapter 3 how closely Green associates state with nation. We do not need to labour what we said there about possible misconceptions of his theory. Nationalism is not incompatible for Green with internationalism. He sees man's attachment to his nation-state as helping to realize a wider brotherhood of all men. Just as state institutions are superimposed on those of a more primitive community, he foresees the possibility of inter-state institutions being superimposed on those of the state. While he believes there is no reason why governments should not privately arrive at a 'passionless impartiality' in dealing with each other, bias in one's own favour may sometimes be hard to avoid. But in such circumstances 'the dream of an international court with authority resting on the consent of independent states may come to be realized' – a result, incidentally, which is in Green's opinion 'very remote' (*PO,* para. 175).

How far does membership of a state imply, in Green's opinion, that one should work consciously for the common good? We have seen that this is not implied in Hegel, except for the 'universal class'. Members of other classes can be left free to devote themselves to their own private interests as long as these do not impair the common weal. Green does not make such a sharp distinction as Hegel between the motivations of the leaders of the state and its other members. His egalitarianism, arising partly from Kant and partly from the Christian Socialist belief in the brotherhood of man, tends to make him see all men in their spiritual aspects as the same, or at least as potentially the same. Nowhere in his writings does he suggest that an individual is justified in leading a purely self-centred life on the grounds that the work he does *in fact* promotes the common good, even though he does not intend it to do so. Napoleon is no counter-example. Even though his leading motive was self-glory, he could only achieve this by personifying the greatness of France as a deliverer of oppressed peoples. In this way the national spirit worked upon his egotism: 'his motives ... were made for him by influences with which his selfishness had nothing to do' (*PO,* para. 129). The motives, then, were not purely self-centred.

> The pure desire for social good does not indeed operate in
> human affairs unalloyed by egotistic motives, but on the other
> hand what we call egotistic motives do not act without
> direction from an involuntary reference to social good, –
> 'involuntary' in the sense that it is so much a matter of course

that the individual does not distinguish it from his ordinary state of mind (*PO*, para. 128).

Although Green does make a distinction between the 'ordinary citizen' and the patriotic citizen who devotes himself to the service of the state, the dividing line is intentionally blurred and there is no implication that not all ordinary citizens could turn into patriotic ones. If we take seriously Green's belief in the progressive expansion of the human spirit, this belief could only imply that the more patriots there are in the community the more spiritual progress it has made. Both ordinary citizen and patriot are governed by a conception of a common good served by the state. The former's understanding of it is more limited in content:

> Very likely he does not think of it at all in connexion with anything that the term 'state' represents to him. But he has a clear understanding of certain interests and rights common to himself with his neighbours, if only such as consist in getting his wages paid at the end of the week, in getting his money's worth at the shop, in the inviolability of his own person and that of his wife (*PO*, para. 121).

The ordinary citizen's morality is still the *Sittlichkeit,* the unreflective social morality originating in the pre-political community. Once the state comes into existence a 'higher' morality, 'the morality of the character governed by "disinterested motives", i.e. by interest in some form of human perfection, comes to differentiate itself from this primitive morality consisting in the observance of rules established for a common good' (*PO*, para. 117), although 'this outward morality is the presupposition of the higher morality' (ibid.). In Hegel's language, *Moralität* comes to be built on the foundation of *Sittlichkeit.* It is this 'higher', autonomous morality which differentiates the 'intelligent patriot' from the 'loyal subject', blurred though this distinction is. The former 'so appreciates the good which in common with others he derives from the state – from the nation organized in the form of a self-governing community to which he belongs – as to have a passion for serving it, whether in the way of defending it from external attack or developing it from within' (*PO*, para. 122). This distinction, between two forms of state service, is explored in more detail in *Prolegomena to Ethics.* Just as our moral progress since the Greeks is evident in our broader conception of temperance (as implying the renunciation of our 'higher' enjoyments, not merely our animal ones), so there has been a similar extension of the virtue of fortitude. Whereas the Greeks conceived of this only as the physical

bravery of the soldier, we have come also to include under it
another form of self-renunciation, the moral heroism found in
service to suffering humanity:

> Every day and all about us pain is being endured and fear
> resisted in rendering such service. The hopelessly sick are being
> tended; the foolish and ignorant are being treated as rational
> persons (*PE*, para. 259).

As part of his service to the state, the patriot 'must have a share
direct or indirect [in its work], by himself acting as a member or by
voting for the members of supreme or provincial assemblies, in
making the laws which he obeys' (*PO*, para. 122). He must come to
feel passionately bound to the state by the same kind of ties which
bind him to his family, 'ties derived from a common dwelling-place
with its associations, from common memories, traditions and
customs, and from common ways of feeling and thinking which a
common language and still more a common literature embodies'
(*PO,* para. 123). In short, Green's patriot is someone whose life
pivots about the well-being of the state, promoting it not only by
some kind of internal or external social service but also by participating in democratic government at different levels. Few could
have better exemplified his ideal than Green himself, with his work
in education and temperance reform on the one hand and his
activities as Oxford City councillor and Liberal Party propagandist
on the other.

One of the specific ways in which Green helped to shape, or,
rather, reshape Liberal Party policy was in the very broad conception he had for his time of the functions of the state. He had no
sympathy with the extreme individualism which would keep the
area of state activity to a minimum, largely the internal and
external security necessary to allow individuals the freedom to lead
the lives they wanted. The state's function is to promote the
common good. But to say that the 'state' is to do this is to say that
those individuals should do it who make up the state community.
But suppose many of these cannot work for the common good
because they are debarred by, for instance, ignorance or ill-health?
The state as a whole will suffer. It is to prevent this that Green
insists that the individual has a claim 'to be enabled positively to
realize his capacity for contributing to a social good which is the
foundation of his right to free life' (*PO*, para. 207). To put it
another way: the state has the right (and duty) to promote
morality. But this must not be misunderstood. The state cannot
make men act for the common good. Moral action must be
autonomous, the product of the agent's free will: the notion of

enforced morality, brought about by laws and penalties, is unintelligible. If one tries to enforce morality, one merely stunts men's
moral capacities. So

> the effectual action of the state, i.e. the community as acting
> through law, for the promotion of habits of true citizenship,
> seems necessarily to be confined to the removal of obstacles
> (*PO*, para. 209).

Green's first example of this is directly relevant to our central
theme in this book. He argues that the state should require parents
to

> have their children taught the elementary arts. To educate
> one's children is no doubt a moral duty, and it is not one of
> those duties, like that of paying debts, of which the neglect
> directly interferes with the rights of someone else. It might
> seem, therefore, to be a duty with which positive law should
> have nothing to do, any more than with the striving after a
> noble life. On the other hand, the neglect of it does tend to
> prevent the growth of the capacity for beneficially exercising
> rights on the part of those whose education is neglected, and it
> is on this account, not as a purely moral duty on the part of
> the parent, but as the prevention of a hindrance to the
> capacity for rights on the part of children, that education
> should be enforced by the state (*PO*, para. 209).

The state has similar reasons for interfering with other freedoms.

> The freedom to do as they like on the part of one set of men
> may involve the ultimate disqualification of many others, or of
> a succeeding generation, for the exercise of rights. This applies
> most obviously to such kinds of contract or traffic as affect the
> health and housing of the people, the growth of population
> relatively to the means of subsistence, and the accumulation or
> distribution of landed property (*PO*, para. 210).

Green argues that governments of his time have been too ready to
remove constraints on individual liberty, largely for reason of
class-interest:

> We have been apt to take too narrow a view of the range of
> persons whose freedom ought to be taken into account. . . .
> Hence the massing of population without regard to conditions
> of health; unrestrained traffic in deleterious commodities;
> unlimited upgrowth of the class of hired labourers in
> particular industries which circumstances have suddenly

stimulated, without any provision against the danger of an impoverished proletariate in following generations (ibid.).

There is work enough for the state to do in remedying these evils. Not that all the initiative should come from it. Voluntary action of individuals could also contribute. Green mentions this distinction but considers it out of place in this philosophical work to discuss what the division of labour should be between state activity and voluntary work in particular cases.

A word, finally, on the relationship of state and church. For Green these were necessarily closely connected. The state was not a mere machine of government, but a spiritual entity, mediating between God and man. Green's religious attachments, following his Arnoldian inheritance, were to a Broad Church, the opposite of narrow or sectarian: not only were there no frontiers between its clerical work as such and wider commitments to social and public improvement, but its only doctrine was that which reason demanded – that same reason, in fact, of which the state was an embodiment. This belief, that religion was basically rational, coloured the whole outlook on life of the educational reformers whom we shall shortly be studying in Part 2. We will find it useful to bear this in mind in tracing through their history. Otherwise it will be difficult to understand how the national system of schools, universities and adult education institutions which the idealists had such a large hand in creating, and which they have bequeathed to us, could have been *both* the practical embodiment of a widespread religious zeal *and* the organized, rational structure, for many of us quite divorced from any religious connexions, which it has come to be seen as today.

5 Education

With one exception – Fichte – none of the leading idealist philosophers wrote extensively about educational theory. Green, for instance, wrote very little directly on this topic, even though he produced several lengthy essays and speeches on practical suggestions for specific educational reforms. Yet Green's general philosophy, like that of Hegel and other idealists, is full of educational implications, some of which we have already seen in previous chapters. Philosophical idealism does not need a *separate* philosophy of education to go alongside its metaphysics, ethics and political philosophy. Its whole *raison d'être* is educational. It is concerned with teaching the individual what it is to realize himself and how that self-realization is to come about. We shall try to make explicit in this chapter the views largely implicit in idealism about such matters as the aims of education, its distribution (are all to be educated, or only some?), the role of the schools and other formal educational institutions in the educational process, and the educational functions of the state. To a large extent this will be a drawing together of points already made in previous chapters.

But before we do this, we must say something more specific about the views of Fichte, the one idealist thinker who *did* write more than incidentally about general educational matters, since, as we shall see, his influence on the British educational reform movement, direct and indirect, was considerable. Fichte, as we saw in Chapter 2, deepened Kant's gulf between the world of moral agents – the only real world – and the world of nature, which was merely a world of appearances. He applied the doctrine of the priority of morality to the problem of German recovery after the disasters of Napoleon's early campaigns. His *Addresses to the German Nation,* delivered in 1807-8 after Prussia's crushing defeat at Jena in 1806, is a passionate appeal to the Germans to work together to build a new nation on the ashes left by Napoleon. This can only be done in one way: by education. What Germany needs is a national educational system, based on the German language and literature, not on the French culture which has dominated German academic life for many years. It will have to be universal, for every citizen without distinction. Its aim is the development of moral agents, of citizens who bend all their efforts to promoting the good of the whole community. Intellectual learning is important, but never for its own sake, only as a necessary condition of moral agency. On top of this system of universal education Fichte superimposes another system. Those who, when they have passed through the first system, give evidence of high intellectual ability, now undergo a scholarly education. Like Plato's Guardians in the *Republic,* they devote themselves to advanced intellectual studies, which are still, however, subordinate to a central moral purpose. Fichte's scholars will be the leaders of the new state, not only its teachers but also its rulers. While the mass of the people will have been equipped through their education to maintain the society at its present level of spiritual development, the scholars' job will be to move society forward beyond this point. The expansion of education is not something which can be left to private persons, helpful though these may be. It is essentially the function of the state to introduce and enforce such a two-tier national system.

This is not the place to go into other aspects of Fichte's educational theory: his insistence that children should be brought up apart from their parents, or his enthusiasm for Pestalozzi. But his theory in general is important in our story in a number of ways. First, Fichte's call for a national education system in Germany affected the Prussian minister Humboldt who, two years after Fichte's *Addresses,* that is, in 1809-10, initiated a wholesale reconstruction of the education system, a task continued and perfected by Süvern and Altenstein between 1810 and 1818. It was to this system that British educational reformers looked for models from the mid-nineteenth century onwards. Matthew Arnold, as we shall see again later, visited Germany in 1859 in connexion with the Newcastle Commission as well as in 1865 for the Taunton Commission. His recommendations proposed reforms on German lines, including the division of the country into a number of educational provinces. T. H. Green was impressed, via Arnold's Taunton Report, by the distinction between *Gymnasien* and *Real-Schule;* Haldane, independently of Arnold, by the higher technological education to be found in Germany. All this was the fruit of that German educational revolution on which Fichte's thought was so influential.[1]

Second, Fichte is important to us for his profound influence on Carlyle, in whom one sees the same passion for national education, together with the same tension between an egalitarian and an élitist conception of it, about which we shall be saying more later. Third, Fichte's most famous pupil at Jena was J. F. Herbart (1776-1841), whose lifelong interest in educational theory was derived from Fichte. Although he came to reject Fichte's idealism, the central notion in Herbart's *The Science of Education* (1806) – that the aim of education is morality and that while the content of that education is highly intellectual, knowledge is never important for its own sake but only as demanded by morality – is pure Fichte. Herbart is interesting to us since the period of educational reform in Britain with which we are concerned, roughly from 1870 until the First World War, was also the time when Herbart's educational ideas first became widely known in this country and came to occupy a dominant position in teacher-training institutions. (In America Herbartianism was equally in vogue during this period: John Dewey, indeed, was at one time on the executive council of the National Herbart Society in that country (Dunkel, 1970, p. 6).) At a time when educational thought and practice were becoming permeated with idealist notions, Herbart's theory, with its insistence on high intellectual standards in the service of a moral aim, found a ready audience. (Herbart in one very important way went beyond Fichte and later idealists: unlike them, he addressed himself to psychological and pedagogical questions about how pupils assimilate and store the knowledge they receive and how, on the basis of such understanding, instruction should be carried out.) Like idealism, Herbartianism declined dramatically in popularity after the First World War.[2]

But Fichte's importance for us lies not so much in his influence on subsidiary figures like Carlyle, Herbart and the Prussian reformers of the 1800s. Central characters, Green and Haldane especially, were influenced by his writings; and while neither of the latter shares his extremer nationalist or élitist tendencies, it is remarkable how Fichtean many of their ideas were. In both we find the same enthusiasm for a national and universal educational system, morally oriented and state-directed. In Haldane we find a Fichtean insistence on advanced scholarship as a means of forwarding the spiritual progress of the state-community: Fichte's advocacy of university expansion, both in his *Addresses* and in the work he did in the creation of the University of Berlin, is mirrored, as we shall see, in Haldane's remarkable achievements in founding universities, not least the University of London. In Green we find a Fichtean interest in problems of personal vocation, which is too pronounced to be purely coincidental. We have already seen evidence of this above in Chapter 3: ethics is not for Green a purely analytical branch of philosophy but helps to point out the kind of path one ought to be following in life. He was, of course, particularly concerned with the vocational problems of his Balliol undergraduates. Both in his ethics and especially in his lay sermons, he led these young men, doubtful as they were that they could conscientiously follow a clerical career, to see that they could find God as much in a life of social service as in the Church. Fichte had a similar interest in vocational guidance. His *Vocation of Man* and *Vocation of the Scholar,* which we know from Nettleship's *Memoir* of Green were probably among the most important intellectual influences on him while still an undergraduate, were, like Green's work, designed to help his own students in their problem of choosing a way of life (Green, *Works,* 3, p. xxv). Not only this; Fichte's message was, at bottom, identical with Green's. Although Fichte urged his students towards scholarship and Green towards social reform, both men held the same Kantian belief that the highest life is that of the autonomous moral agent, of the man whose master-motive is the pursuit of moral perfection: scholarship and social reform were for each respectively worthwhile only under this aegis.[3]

The aims of education

Let us turn from the educational views of Fichte in particular to those embedded in idealism as a whole, beginning with views on educational aims. Each of our idealist philosophers would have endorsed Hegel's contention that:

> Education is the art of making men ethical. It begins with pupils whose life is at the instinctive level and shows them the way to a second birth, the way to change their instinctive nature into a second, intellectual nature, and makes this intellectual level habitual to them (*Philosophy of Right,* para. 151 (addition)).

We see in this passage the same unwillingness to separate ethical and intellectual values which we found in Fichte (and in Herbart). But Hegel and his British followers have a different understanding of this connexion. Whereas Fichte and Herbart made the moral life supreme and intellectual activity a means thereto, the Hegelians' position is less clear-cut. Morality had been for Fichte the highest expression of reason, so, clearly, moral values could not be subordinate to intellectual. But for the Hegelians the moral bonds which bind individuals to their communities are only mediating links between the individual and reality as a whole. Reason is found in nature as well as in morality because reality as a whole is rational. In developing one's intellectual powers as far as possible, one becomes increasingly a vehicle of, or reproduction of, the eternal spirit. So isn't the *fundamental* aim of education for the Hegelian

idealist the development of intellect, or, more broadly, of consciousness, rather than moral character? And isn't there, then, a
more direct theoretical and/or aesthetic course of study? It would
seem that the more one knows about science, history, philosophy,
art and so on, the closer one's consciousness comes to the divine;
so why bother with mere morality? In Chapter 3 we saw T. H.
Green wrestling with this fundamental problem about the relations
between moral values on the one hand and intellectual/aesthetic
values on the other (see p. 34). He failed to reach a solution in his
unfinished *Prolegomena,* as we indicated. For all that, however,
neither he nor any of the other idealists could have agreed that
education could by-pass moral development altogether. On the
contrary, even though morality is subordinate to eternal reason,
individual men cannot have a purely intellectual education; i.e.,
one sufficient in itself and hived off from all non-intellectual
concerns, because they are not atomic entities but necessarily
participate with other individuals in a common life. They must,
therefore, as Hegel says, be 'made ethical'. Even those who are
most intellectually capable are still inseparable parts of a community. Although their consciousness *seems* to be raisable to a
divine level by an education from which moral development is
absent, it is not really so. One cannot realize one's full powers as an
alienated, a-social individual: realizing oneself is realizing the
superordinate whole – the family, the work-community, the
town-community, the state – of which one forms a part.

It is not easy to pigeonhole the British idealists' views, implicit or
explicit, on the aims of education under categories familiar today.
Shall we say that Green and others thought the individual pupil's
good all-important, given their emphasis on self-realization? Or did
they think, rather, that education should promote the good of the
community, given what they said about the 'common good'? To
the idealist this familiar dichotomy would have appeared misconceived: as has just been mentioned, to aim at self-realization is
nothing other than to aim at the common good. Did they hold that
the aims of education were 'intrinsic' in the light of their claim that
pupils' consciousness should be raised to higher and higher levels,
not because of any application this might have to social or other
problems, but for its own sake? Or should we rather say that they
held an 'extrinsic' conception of educational aim, since, after all,
consciousness-raising was not strictly important in itself but only
for an ultimately metaphysical or religious purpose, that is, to
bring men closer to Spirit? If they did advocate knowledge for its
own sake, this was not in the hived-off sense, detached from a
metaphysical rationale, in which we tend to think of this today.

Again, this 'intrinsic' aim, of the pursuit of knowledge for its own sake, is today sharply contrasted with citizenship as an aim: people take sides on the relative importance of these two, often partly on political grounds, conservatives inclining rather towards the intrinsic aim and socialists towards citizenship. But, once again, for Green and his followers, citizenship and knowledge for its own sake were much more closely connected, since the good citizen will wish his own and others' consciousness to be raised as far as possible. Equally the British idealists would not have objected to the proposition that the function of education is to serve the state. They would have objected to this no more than to the view that the aim of education is the worship of God, despite the mutually antithetical nature of these two orientations as many would see it today. The state or national community is a mediator between the individual and the divine: to serve the interests of the state is not to submit oneself to a leviathan which has no purposes beyond itself, since to realize the good of the state is to further a divine purpose.

Dewey, as is well known, inveighed against the tyranny of dichotomous thinking on educational matters, dissolving away duality after duality: individual good *v.* social good, liberal education *v.* vocational education, development according to nature *v.* social efficiency, etc. This holistic cast of thought was something he shared with the British idealists and derived from his own early attachment to their philosophy. For them the aim of education could indifferently be expressed as: realizing the good of the pupil, realizing the good of the state, developing moral character, realizing God's purposes, promoting understanding for its own sake. In the context of their philosophy as a whole, the apparent differences between these emphases were, it was claimed, unreal. But the identification of each with the other depended entirely on a commitment to this whole philosophy. As we shall see, there were those among the 'idealist' reformers in the later phase of the movement who accepted idealism only in part. Depending on what part they accepted, certain of these aims became more salient, being progressively detached from others with which they had been previously identified. As idealism thus paled, the differences between the aims became more and more marked, culminating in the very sharp distinctions between them which we make today. When we come, in Part 3, to assess the legacy of the idealists we shall be better placed to see whether these contemporary views on the aims of education are adequate, or whether we have still something to learn by returning to the idealist source from which they originate.

The distribution of education

Let us turn from the aims of education to its distribution. Who, in the eyes of the idealists, are to receive the kind of education just described? Is it for the whole population? Or only for a few? On this issue one finds a division, or tension, between two wings of idealist thinking, an élitist and an egalitarian wing. Sometimes, as with Hegel's élitism, it is easy enough to put a thinker in one or other of those camps. At other times, as with Fichte, Carlyle and Arnold, this is more difficult.

Fichte is an élitist in that he draws a distinction between the education of the scholar and the universal national education. But there is no unbridgeable gulf between the two. For one thing, future scholars must pass through the universal national system: they acquire their basic education there, but instead of then devoting themselves to manual work, they apply themselves to higher learning in the interests of the moral progress of the community. Second, universal education is, like the scholars', intellectually oriented, although at less abstract a level of thought. This comes out clearly in Fichte's attitude to manual skills. He distinguishes among these between those with little intellectual content, like knitting and spinning, and those, like agriculture, gardening and cattle rearing, which have a scientific basis. He disagrees with Pestalozzi for including activities of the first type in the curriculum along with more intellectual subjects: 'In my opinion, instruction must be represented as so sacred and honourable that it requires the whole attention and concentration, and cannot be received along with something else (Fichte, 1807-8, vii, pp. 424-5). But with manual activities of the second type, 'the chief consideration is that, so far as possible, the pupils must understand the principles of what they do, and that they have already received the information necessary for their occupations concerning the growing of plants, the characteristics and needs of the animal body, and the laws of mechanics. . . . Further, their mechanical work is even at this stage ennobled and made intellectual. . . . Even though associated with the animal and with the clod, they do not sink to the level of these, but remain within the sphere of the spiritual world' (ibid.). Fichte's two-tier system of education is far from Plato's division in the *Republic,* between the elementary education which is apparently intended for all citizens, and the higher education of the Guardians which comes after this. Plato constantly emphasizes what *divides* the Guardians from the people, Fichte what *binds* his scholars to them. The mass of the people are to be raised as far as possible to the higher spiritual levels at which the scholars live. The scholars, as rulers of the state, must compel them to be educated to the limits of their capacity. All who show an aptitude for scholarly learning must be permitted to engage in it: 'every talent of that kind is a precious talent of the nation, and may not be taken away from it' (ibid., vii, pp. 426-7). With the passage of time, as the scholar-rulers advance the spiritual achievements of the nation, the intellectual and moral standards expected of mass education may be expected gradually to be raised.

Fichte's vision is, therefore, no doubt owing to Kant's influence, as egalitarian as it is élitist: the more people the scholars succeed in hauling up behind them into the realms of the spirit, the better; the best possible society is one where everyone without exception lives at that level. We shall see in a moment further examples of this Fichtean conception of education and society among the British idealists. But before turning to this, let us first look at the very different conception of this relationship that we find in Hegel's *Philosophy of Right.*

Hegel, like Fichte, draws a distinction between two types of education: that of the 'universal class' of civil servants, teachers, etc., on the one hand, and that of the rest of the population on the other. Here the gulf between the two is much deeper. Most often, when Hegel speaks of education (*Bildung*), he is referring only to the former, the education of the 'universal' class, sometimes also called the 'middle' class, because it mediates between sovereign and people, whose combined pressure from above and below prevents it from 'acquiring the isolated position of an aristocracy and using its education and skill as a means to an arbitrary tyranny' (*PR,* para. 297). The role of the educational system, Hegel argued in his address as Rector of Nürnberg gymnasium in 1815, is to prepare civil servants for the state. It is of this élite which he is thinking when he says that 'the final purpose of education ... is liberation and the struggle for a higher liberation still; education is the absolute transition from an ethical substantiality which is immediate and natural to the one which is intellectual and so both infinitely subjective and lofty enough to have attained universality of form' (*PR,* para. 187). Becoming educated is an arduous process through the complexities of dialectical thought necessary to see the logical structure of reality and the place of the state within it. 'It is part of education ... that the ego comes to be apprehended as a universal person in which all are identical' (*PR,* para. 209). It is a 'hard struggle against pure subjectivity of demeanour, against the immediacy of desire, against the empty subjectivity of feeling and the caprice of imagination' (*PR,* para. 187).

While the intellectual agonies of high learning are more

pronounced for Hegel's civil servants than for Fichte's scholars, Hegel makes the upbringing of the ordinary citizen correspondingly less arduous. It is not even clear that Hegel thought, as Fichte did, that there should be a national *system* of education for those not intended for the 'universal' class.

> When a father inquired about the best method of educating his son in ethical conduct, a Pythagorean replied: 'Make him a citizen of a state with good laws' (*PR*, para. 153).

For men in general, education is not so much a matter of formal instruction as of becoming sensitized to the *Sittlichkeit* – the laws, customs, institutions – of the community. It does not have to be so theory-laden, since ordinary citizens, rich and poor, do not have their eye always on the well-being of the state as a whole; as we have seen, in their economic life they can be left to a large extent to pursue their own selfish interests, as long as these are so regulated by the civil service that their satisfaction in fact subserves the common good, even though it was never intended to do this. In wishing to submit men to the easy yoke of *Sittlichkeit*, Hegel sought to free them, as G. A. Kelly has pointed out, from the academic coercions of Fichte's scholar-state (Kelly, 1969, pp. 346-7). While Fichte would have children taken away from the possible corrupting influence of their parents and neighbours and instructed in state boarding schools, Hegel believed that it is only by continuing to remain in the community and imperceptibly conforming to its mores, that the individual can be transformed into an ethical being.

While Hegel was not an élitist in the sense that he wanted to make the 'universal' class a closed class – he was as firm a believer as Fichte in unrestricted social mobility for the talented of any class to become civil servants – he shows none of the egalitarianism which led Fichte to blur the distinction between the education of the scholars and the education of the people at the same time as he seemed to sharpen it.

Both Fichte and Hegel influenced the thinking of the British idealists. In their own educational work and in that of those influenced by them, both élitist and egalitarian tendencies are visible, as we shall see. The predominating attitude, however, inclines towards egalitarianism. In this respect, British idealism, especially as represented by the thinkers considered in this book, is Fichtean (and Kantian) more than it is Hegelian.

Fichte's first and most prominent English disciple was Carlyle. His writings share the tension which we noticed in Fichte between élitism and egalitarianism. He is remembered today as a fiery critic of democracy, ready, like Fichte, to exalt the leader over the mass and forming, like him, an early link in the chain that led to National Socialism. But *his* élitism, too, hides a more fundamental egalitarianism. The masses of the 1830s cannot be entrusted with political power because they are intellectually and spiritually unequipped to use it. Will they necessarily always be so? Must society be eternally divided into Fichtean-inspired spiritual heroes on the one side and ordinary, limited individuals on the other? Not so. In perhaps the best-known passage from his influential *Sartor Resartus,* which we reproduce in full, Carlyle expresses quite the opposite opinion:

Two men I honour, and no third. First, the toilworn
Craftsman that with earth-made Implement laboriously
conquers the Earth, and makes her man's. Venerable to me is
the hard Hand; crooked, coarse; wherein notwithstanding lies a
cunning virtue, indefeasibly royal, as of the Sceptre of this
Planet. Venerable too is the rugged face, all weather-tanned,
besoiled, with its rude intelligence; for it is the face of a Man
living manlike. O, but the more venerable for thy rudeness,
and even because we must pity as well as love thee!
Hardly-entreated Brother! For us was thy back so bent, for us
were thy straight limbs and fingers so deformed: thou wert our
Conscript, on whom the lot fell, and fighting our battles wert
so marred. For in thee too lay a god-created Form, but it was
not to be unfolded; encrusted must it stand with the thick
adhesions and defacements of Labour: and thy body, like thy
soul, was not to know freedom. Yet toil on, toil on: *thou* art
in thy duty, be out of it who may; thou toilest for the
altogether indispensable, for daily bread.
  A second man I honour, and still more highly: Him who is
seen toiling for the spiritually indispensable; not daily bread,
but the bread of Life. Is not he too in his duty; endeavouring
towards inward Harmony; revealing this, by act or by word,
through all his outward endeavours, be they high or low?
Highest of all, when his outward and his inward endeavour are
one: when we can name him Artist; not earthy Craftsman
only, but inspired Thinker, who with heaven-made Implement
conquers Heaven for us! If the poor and humble toil that we
have food, must not the high and glorious toil for him in
return, that he have Light, have Guidance, Freedom,
Immortality? – These two, in all their degrees, I honour: all
else is chaff and dust, which the wind blow whither it listeth
(op. cit., pp. 171-2).

Doubtless Carlyle dichotomizes here, making a clean cut between the manual and the spiritual worker. But at a deeper level than occupation there is a common humanity, a fraternity. Both these men are essentially creatures of spirit: in both there is a 'god-created form', even if in the manual worker this fails, society being what it is, to be unfolded. The job of the spiritual worker is to liberate the manual worker, to toil so that he have light and freedom. Carlyle's ideal is not permanent class-division, but the union of spirit and matter. He goes on:

> Unspeakably touching is it, however, when I find both
> dignities united; and he that must toil outwardly for the lowest
> of man's wants, is also toiling inwardly for the highest.
> Sublimer in this world know I nothing than a Peasant Saint,
> could such now anywhere be met with. Such a one will take
> thee back to Nazareth itself; thou wilt see the splendour of
> Heaven spring forth from the humblest depths of Earth, like a
> light shining in great darkness (op. cit., p. 172).

As we shall see in detail later in this volume, virtually all the idealist reformers were deeply committed to workers' education, especially through adult classes. Many of them, and perhaps especially Green, Caird and Henry Jones, looked back to Carlyle as an inspiring force. As well they might, for the sentiment he expresses is identical with that which created Toynbee Hall and the WEA.

> What I do mourn over [continues Carlyle, returning to the
> condition of the manual worker] is that the lamp of his soul
> should go out; that no ray of heavenly, or even of earthly
> knowledge, should visit him. . . . Alas, while the Body stands so
> broad and brawny, must the Soul lie blinded, dwarfed,
> stupefied, almost annihilated! Alas, was this too a Breath of
> God; bestowed in Heaven, but on earth never to be unfolded!
> – That there should one man die ignorant who had capacity
> for knowledge, this I call a tragedy, were it to happen more
> than twenty times in the minute, as by some computation it
> does. The miserable fraction of Science which our united
> Mankind, in a wide Universe of Nescience, has acquired, why
> is not this, with all diligence, imparted to all? (ibid.).

R. H. Tawney was a century later to protest against the belief that

> there is a class of masters whose right it is to enter at
> manhood on the knowledge which is the inheritance of the
> race, and a class of servants whose hands should be taught to
> labour but whose eyes should be on the furrow which is

watered with their sweat, whose virtue is contentment,
and whose ignorance is the safety of the gay powers by whom
their iron world is ruled (Tawney, 1964 (1966 edn), p. 76).

Tawney's dichotomy is between masters and servants rather than
between spiritual and manual workers, and his language lacks
Carlyle's extravagances; but the underlying thought is identical, as
is the high indignation with which it is expressed. This similarity
owes nothing to coincidence. Carlyle's radicalism deeply affected
his fellow-Scotsman, Edward Caird; and it was Caird who, as
master of Balliol when Tawney was an undergraduate, explicitly
challenged his students to find out why England had poverty
alongside riches, and do something about it – a challenge to which
Tawney's decision to devote himself to social work owed most.

Carlyle influenced Green no less than he did Caird. Among the
letters of condolence which Green's widow received after his death,
correspondent after correspondent mentions the link between the
two. Henry Sidgwick remembers that it was Green, perhaps while
they were both schoolboys at Rugby, who 'made me feel the depth
and reality of Carlyle's sympathy with the Puritans as compared
with Milton's'. He mentions, too, Green's Carlylean 'religious
earnestness in politics', their common 'aloofness' and 'unlikeness'
from other men, their 'deep, grave, humour'.[4] A. V. Dicey writes of
his student days with Green at Oxford:

> The more I think this matter over, the more I am struck with
> the fact of his having when so young thought so much more
> than most of us about the state of the poorer classes and the
> necessity of making their material and moral welfare a main
> object of politics. This I fancy was in part the result of his
> great admiration which when first I knew your husband, he
> felt for Carlyle.[5]

J. A. Symonds adds that 'Carlyle influenced him in many ways,
especially in the German direction of his mind'. Bryce in his essay
on Green in *Studies in Contemporary Biography* echoes this last point:
it was Carlyle, he says, who had led Green to the German
philosophers.

We have already said enough in previous chapters to show that
Matthew Arnold and T. H. Green were educational egalitarians.
Arnold's 'élite' of men of culture was not an end in itself: they
were, he said, the 'true apostles of equality'. Green's radicalism has
also been made abundantly clear. Wordsworth, Carlyle, Maurice,
Kant and Fichte had all urged him towards the same conclusion:
we should see all men, not just a few, as potential vehicles of

eternal spirit; as such, we have a duty to raise all men's consciousness as far as possible.

As far as Green is concerned, we have already seen, too, that his failure to see the social efforts of *laissez-faire* capitalism should not be allowed to count against his egalitarianism. In Part 2, when we look at Green's practical involvement in educational reform, we shall see that, like Matthew Arnold, one of his chief objectives was the improvement of 'middle-class education'. Today a fighter for this cause would be seen as a right winger, as someone who wanted to shore up class divisions, not remove them. But the support which Green and his circle lent to the cause of the same name was inspired by quite opposite motives. Their belief in the divine potentialities in every individual could never have led them to lower the portcullis at the boundaries of the middle class or at any other point. It was the education of the whole community that mattered finally. Middle-class education was important at that time because, so they believed, only when that class was educated could the mass of the people become similarly enlightened: the masses would need educators – not only teachers, but also writers, artists, journalists, politicians, administrators – and these the middle class would initially, at least, for the most part provide. Some of us may scoff at the naïveté of this point of view in the light of the long and still-continuing battle which many from the middle class have fought this century for the preservation of their educational privileges. But the intention, if not always the outcome, was far from élitist.

Similar problems of interpretation arise when we turn more specifically to the idealists' views on social mobility. We shall return later to Arthur Acland's claim that 'the object of education is not to make us rise above our surroundings', and that we should not 'get above our friends and neighbours'.[6] One way of taking this would be as the expression of the belief, familiar both to Acland's age and our own, that working-class pupils must be kept in their place as members of a lower order. But it is very doubtful whether Acland *did* hold this belief. He certainly did not think that working-class education should be a form of indoctrination into passivity and obedience, since in his adult education work and elsewhere he kept to the mainstream idealist policy of making working people as enlightened about society and its operations as was possible within the practical constraints. His point in the passage quoted was about fraternity, not repression. He was assuming, in fact, that some individuals from the working class *would* become more highly educated than most: just because they were so, he was saying, they should not think themselves above their fellows.

There is nothing about this that a socialist would find unacceptable today.

Green's (and others') support for the 'ladder of ability' is another case in point. Today those who believe, like Green, that bright children from primary schools should be selected for high-level secondary education, are again found on the right wing. Contemporary radicals favour a common school. But the 'ladder' concept was egalitarian enough in Green's day: those who climbed the ladder were not, after all, or so the theory ran, doing so to enjoy the privileges of an élite: they were in the vanguard of a national movement of enlightenment.

We have been at pains to emphasize the egalitarian tendencies of the idealist reformers. But we should at the same time make it clear that theirs was an *educational* egalitarianism, not invariably an egalitarianism of any other sort. That is, their fundamental belief was that everyone, of whatever class or occupation, had the moral right to a high level of education. This did not always entail a change in the class structure. The ideal, for some, was to bring the upper and lower classes closer together, to allow them ultimately, through their common education, to recognize their common humanity and the need to co-operate for a common good. But this aim was quite compatible with the continued existence of the two classes. Many of the reformers were Liberals in politics and shared that party's unwillingness to go along the socialist road towards a classless society. Henry Jones, another of Caird's disciples, is a good example. Although no one could have been more enthusiastic in pressing for an expansion of educational provision for the working class, we find him, for instance, delivering an anti-socialist speech to a union meeting of North Wales quarrymen in 1911. In it he warns that socialism threatens the old Liberal regard for 'tolerance and consensus which was the basis of democracy'.[7] Some of the reformers, especially those of the later generation like Tawney and Lindsay, did become egalitarians of a more thoroughgoing sort, impelled, perhaps, by a keener perception of economic realities. But it was a belief in the common educational needs of men as men which bound them to the earlier idealists, and through them to Carlyle and Fichte, a belief implicit in their common underlying philosophy.

The predominating attitude among the reformers, we have said, was egalitarian in the sense just described. But idealism, as we saw with Hegel, could also lead to educational élitism, especially if the Platonist elements in it were allowed to outweigh considerations of human fraternity. Plato was certainly an influential figure in British idealism. Jowett's translation of the *Republic* soon became famous; and both Nettleship and Bosanquet wrote commentaries on the text. F. H. Bradley's influential essay 'My Station and its Duties' reinforced the Platonic message, though not without serious qualifications, that we can best do what is morally right by carrying out the obligations attached to our allotted social station. But of the educational reformers it is only of Robert Morant, who was, in any case, only marginally an idealist, that one can argue, as Eric Eaglesham has done, that he was an élitist, rather than an egalitarian, although even with him the verdict is not clear-cut. The case rests on Morant's sharpening of the line between secondary and elementary education by removing the higher-grade schools which were allowing elementary schools to grow in a secondary direction and adjusting school curricula to make the secondary more broadly humanistic and the elementary more practical and oriented to the demands of manual work. But the verdict is not clear-cut because it is possible to see Morant less as an ideological Platonizer than as a civil servant conscious of the muddle created by the uncontrolled growth of post-elementary education and anxious to remove it. Certainly his interest in working-class adult education and his association with such unconservative reformers as Sidney Webb and Haldane should at least give rise to doubt as to whether he should definitely be classified as an élitist.

The organization of education

We have discussed the idealists' thoughts on the aims of education and on its distribution. It would be surprising if, given the supreme value they placed on universal education, they did not also have thoughts about how this might best be brought about, that is, about means as well as ends. They were, indeed, particularly attentive to questions of organization. Part 2 will show us how fertile their thinking was in this area, as well as how energetic they were, without exception, in translating their schemes into practice. In this section, where we are concerned not with historical detail but with the influence of idealism on educational thinking, there is naturally less to say about the means than about ends; but, even so, there are still two important points that must be made.

As we shall see in Part 2, one of the hallmarks of the idealist reform movement was its vision of the educational system as an organic whole. Its achievements – in adult education, universities, elementary and secondary education – were not the product of isolated enthusiasms, as educational innovations, especially in England, often tend to be. The parts were to fit together to make an articulated whole. Of course, one does not have to be influenced by idealist philosophy to be a global planner. Sidney Webb, for instance, was not. Neither should one underestimate the economic and social pressures which were pushing late-nineteenth-century Britain, like so many other countries, towards increasingly systematic state involvement in education. Systematic organization was not the preserve of idealists alone. On the other hand, the holistic cast of mind which philosophical idealism engendered was not something easily confined to pure philosophy. Hegelian idealism did not, in any case, erect fences between itself and practical affairs. On the contrary: the attempt to realize the divine idea entailed scrupulous attention to detail, since the universal only existed in its concrete embodiment in particularity. Hegel himself, notoriously, logically deduced the existence of the police force from the Absolute. His British followers were less swayed by the power of pure logic to generate such practical results; but they were at one with him in working towards organizational details from the first principles, rather than adopting the piecemeal empiricism more characteristic of their nation. Haldane, after his appointment to the War Office, was asked by the Army Council what notion he had of the British army: he replied, he tells us, 'A hegelian army' (Haldane, 1929, p. 185). In his educational reforms, as in his military, Haldane, as we shall see later, worked in a similar direction, from a comprehensive scheme towards its detailed institutional embodiment. He was not alone.

Idealism was also distinctive among philosophical movements in the importance it attached to the national state. It was essentially a national system of education which the idealists were intent on creating; and a system in which the role of the state was of the first importance. Both T. H. Green, as we have already seen, and J. S. Mill believed that the state had a duty to insist on compulsory education for all children. But whereas it was difficult for Mill to establish this conclusion on utilitarian premises – after all, it was not even clear that education itself conduced more to pleasure than to pain – for Green there was no problem. If education was desirable, on metaphysical grounds, for all members of the national community, then the state, as the political organization of that community, had a duty to insist on it, given that it would never come about if things were left to chance. For all the idealists, the state was more than an efficient governmental machine which could be used (as the Webbs, for instance, sought to use it) to remedy social evils. It was a spiritual power, whose essence was to bring man closer to God. As such, it was not clearly distinguishable from an ideal church, or indeed, from any other social institution which had the same spiritual porpose: all had their being in the state.

This brings us to the second, and connected, point about means to ends. Following Hegel's stress on *Sittlichkeit,* or the educative influence of social institutions, the British idealists did not see formal instruction as the sole, or even in some cases as the chief, way of educating the nation. Schools, universities and adult classes were all, of course, indispensable; and most of the reformers' effort went into their improvement and extension. But society educates, or mis-educates, also. Churches, factories, families, political and legal systems are also potential educators. In bringing organized religion closer to society, in industrial and economic reform, in extending political democracy, in temperance work and in the creation of systems of social welfare, one could be furthering educational ends as much as if one were a teacher or educational administrator. The idealists sought in their different ways to alter the overall 'tone' or ethos of society. Many of those who did so, Beveridge, for instance, will receive scant mention in this book, since we shall concentrate on those whose work had more directly to do with the education system. But the significance of these wider reforms for the progress of education should not be forgotten. As we shall see, both of the idealists who wrote most explicitly about educational theory – MacCunn and Fred Clarke – put, if anything, more stress on social influences than on direct instruction. And in the work of R. H. Tawney we see the impossibility of divorcing the extension of educational opportunity from fundamental changes in the structure of industry, changes designed, above all, to bring about a new ethos, a shift from status, arbitrary power, and social divisiveness towards function and fellowship.

The work of the educational reformers

part 2

The Oxford influence 6

The educational background

In the first part of this book, Green's views on education were explored. As we shall see in the course of what follows, Green also attempted to devise a plan for a national system which accorded with his philosophical principles. His range of educational interests extended over all stages: elementary, secondary, university and adult. To place Green's thinking on education in an appropriate context, it will be first necessary to sketch in the situation prevailing in schools and universities in England in the 1860s.[1]

So-called 'popular' education, which had become fairly widely available following a Parliamentary grant towards school buildings in 1833, was for the most part equatable with denominational education. The main providers were the National School Society of the Church of England and the British and Foreign School Society; the grant was extended to Catholics in 1847. This state provision contradicted the main principles of the prevailing doctrine of *laissez-faire* which looked to an improvement in society by allowing individuals to improve their condition of life by their own efforts. But at least, if state involvement in education was unavoidable it was important, many advocates of *laissez-faire* held, to prevent it from becoming too great a burden on the taxpayer. This view was reflected in the policy of Robert Lowe, Vice-President of the Committee of Council on Education (Sylvester, 1974, ch. 2). Expenditure on elementary education during the 1850s had risen forty-fold since the grant was first made. As a result, a commission under the chairmanship of Lord Newcastle was appointed in 1858: 'to consider and report what measures, if any, are required for the extension of sound and cheap elementary instruction to all classes of people'. The Report in fact was centrally concerned with the cost of education of the poor alone and Lowe adopted one of its main recommendations, the system of payment by results which came into effect with the Revised Code of 1862. As he told the House of Commons during the debate on the Code, 'If it (elementary education) is not cheap it shall be efficient; if it is not efficient it shall be cheap' (*Hansard Parliamentary Debates*, 3, clxv, col. 229).

Henceforth a school's income would depend on its pupils' ability to pass annual examinations in the 3Rs, with the addition of plain needlework for girls.

But the provision of elementary education was intended to serve wider purposes than simply achieving standards of attainment. Basic schooling was urged as a means of combatting crime and social and political unrest. The social order could also be reinforced through schools by including a religious content in the curriculum which would be conducive to inculcating moral principles. Since church schools provided the larger part of elementary education, such provision was an intrinsic part of their instruction. After the Liberals came into power in 1868, the agitations of the National Education League, representing largely nonconformist and radical interests and adopting for its slogan 'universal compulsory, free and unsectarian' elementary education, led to a breach in church monopoly. Under the 1870 Elementary Education Act, steered through the Commons by W. E. Forster, local school boards, elected by eligible householders, were able to build schools where existing denominational provision was inadequate. Moreover, it was left to the boards to decide whether or not to include religious instruction; if it was included, it was to be of an undenominational character. A 'conscience clause' was inserted in the Act, which guarded the right of withdrawal from religious instruction even in church schools.

Green's interest in elementary education had first been aroused some fourteen years earlier. He had read an essay on National Education in the *Oxford Essays* (1860) (see Part 2, Chapter 9) contributed by Frederick Temple, himself a Balliol man. For Green, the essay materially embodied the aspirations of the National Education League, but the Forster Act did not match up to them: a dual system of board and voluntary schools had been created which coexisted uneasily, and although the administration of schooling after 1870 was different, the views as to its purpose expressed by Lowe still largely prevailed.

When we turn to examine the provision for secondary education it would be true to say that there was much less of a national debate before the 1860s. The great public schools had sunk to a low ebb until the 1830s, when the reforming zeal of such headmasters as Thomas Arnold at Rugby and Hawtrey at Eton helped to reassert the position of their schools as suitable places for the education of the upper classes, though the content of the curriculum remained narrowly classical. In 1861 the nine leading public schools were investigated by the Clarendon Commission; its reports, whilst advocating reform along the lines of the German

Gymnasium or classical school, nevertheless justified the leading place occupied by them in the education system.

The use of the word 'system' in this context is somewhat misleading. Besides these nine endowed grammar schools, there were another three thousand or so, ranging from those of public school status to others which offered an education below the level of an average elementary school. The common denominator was that, at some time in the past, an endowment had been earmarked by a donor for the education of the poor in specified localities. Many of the endowments had decayed and widespread abuses of them were public knowledge. Following the investigation of the Newcastle and Clarendon Commissions, the Government appointed, in 1864, a third commission headed by Lord Taunton, 'to enquire into the education given in schools not comprised within Her Majesty's two former Commissions'. During the following three years, assistant commissioners were appointed to visit and report on the 782 endowed schools offering an education of a post-elementary standard. It was on the advice of Frederick Temple, now one of the Taunton Commissioners, that Green was appointed to an assistant commissionership in the following year.

By this time the growing population justified the creation of new centres of higher education.[2] The fact that Oxford and Cambridge Universities excluded Dissenters and others by religious tests brought about the founding in London of University College (1828), the first non-sectarian institution of its kind in England. The church countered this move with the establishing of King's College, London, two years later and Durham in 1832. Perhaps of even more importance was the granting of a charter to London University to act as an examining body in 1836, not only for the two colleges but in addition for anywhere in Britain or the Empire approved by the Government (Berdahl, 1959, pp. 24-5). In Manchester a scheme to open an anti-test college where the fine arts, arts and manufactures and medicine could be studied, bore fruit in the form of Owens College in 1851. This combination of new curricula in new colleges without religious restrictions highlighted the need for reform at the two ancient universities. Both were scrutinized by royal commissions between 1850 and 1852; the outcome was the beginning of central government concern with the universities. By 1871 religous tests had been abolished in respect of fellowships and other teaching posts.[3]

Green's educational thought and practice

From the time when Green entered Rugby in 1850, where he

gained a reputation as a 'dreadful radical' and hero-worshipped Cromwell,[4] he began to form decided views on educational matters, especially those relating to universities. Writing of Oxford in 1854 shortly before he became a student at Balliol, Green remarked that:

> The inside of the colleges are strangely incongruous with the outside. The finest colleges are the most corrupt, the functionaries from the heads to the servants being wholly given to quiet dishonesty, and the undergraduates to sensual idleness (Green, *Works,* 3, p. xvi).

Politically, he was a follower of Bright and Cobden. In his first undergraduate year (1858) he had brought forward a motion, at the Oxford Union, eulogistic of Bright though independent in his views on nationalism, being especially critical of it where it was an expression of political vanity. On the other hand he attached the highest importance to national life and the necessity of peace in order to introduce social reforms for ameliorating the plight of the poor. Although the son of a Church of England clergyman, Green looked for his own answers in religion. He did not wish to share what the Established Church enjoyed to the exclusion of Dissenters, and attended meetings on the abolition of university tests.

Green gained a lectureship at Balliol in ancient and modern history in April 1860, and in November of that year became a Fellow of the College. The next four years were an unsettled period for Green, during which he contemplated entering the church, began a number of literary works, including an edition of Aristotle's *Ethics* with Edward Caird, which was never completed, and paid visits to Germany and Switzerland. After unsuccessfully applying for the Chair of Moral Philosophy at St Andrews in July 1864, he accepted the offer in March 1865 to investigate and report on the state of schools in the Midlands on behalf of the Taunton Commission.

His Balliol colleague and biographer, R. L. Nettleship,[5] tells us that some of the commissioners were dismayed at Green's appointment as he was considered to be an extreme man, an ultra-radical in politics, an ultra-liberal in religious opinion (Green, *Works*, 3, p. xiv). Green denied this charge, stating that he could be considered radical only in so far as he believed that participation in a common rational nature conferred on every man the duty of furthering that development in himself as in others.[6] Green, who had shortly before contemplated applying for a school inspectorship, saw this as an opportunity to become practically involved in educational affairs. As he wrote later, he was looking forward, in common with many of those with whom I was associated at Oxford to a reconstitution, at no very distant time, of the middle and higher education of England, and, if not to a reconstitution of society through that of education, yet at least to a considerable change in its tone and to the removal of many of its barriers (Green, *Works*, 3, pp. xlvi-xlvii).

Before we look in detail at Green's work for the Taunton Commission, it will be useful to examine the kind of educational reconstruction he favoured in common with other Oxford thinkers. Of the latter the most articulate, and one whose ideas were very close to Green's,[7] was Matthew Arnold. Arnold, also a product of Rugby and Balliol, held that nothing less than a total reformation of national life was necessary, especially via a system of national education. This was the theme of his three books published in the 1860s: *The Popular Education of France, with Notices of that of Holland and Switzerland* (1861), *A French Eton, or Middle-Class Education and the State* (1864), and *Schools and Universities on the Continent* (1868). *A French Eton*, which appeared shortly before Green embarked on his work as assistant commissioner, set out many of the major issues which concerned

> that large class which wants the improvement of secondary instruction in this country – secondary instruction, the first great stage of a liberal education, coming between elementary instruction, the instruction in the mother tongue and in the simplest and indispensable branches of knowledge on the one hand, and superior instruction, the instruction given by universities, the second and finishing stage of a liberal education, on the other (Arnold, 1864, pp. 4-5).[8]

He called the middle classes, which were growing daily in power and wealth 'nearly the worst educated in the world': they thus became increasingly alienated from the upper classes. Arnold warned that the time had come for England to organize its secondary instruction.

Arnold pointed to the systems prevailing in France and Germany, which he had visited in 1859 in connexion with the enquiry into popular education. He advocated a minister of education directly representing all the interests of learning and intelligence in the country, and who would be aided by a High Council for Education, made up of leading men from a wide spectrum of interests. Taking the German pattern, Arnold favoured dividing the country into a number of provincial boards which would be units of educational administration. He did not argue for a uniform society in which one education should be suitable for all its members. 'We have to regard the condition of classes, in dealing with education; but it is right to take into account not their immediate condition only, but their wants, their destination' (ibid., p. 137).

Looking to higher education Arnold, like Green, saw that the diffusion of knowledge did not lie exclusively within the province of Oxford and Cambridge. Arnold wrote in 1867:

> We must get out of our heads all notion of making the mass of students come and reside ... at Oxford or Cambridge, which neither suit their circumstances nor offer them the instruction they want. We must plant faculties in eight or ten principal seats of population and let the students follow lectures there from their own homes with whatever arrangements for their living they and their parents choose. It would be everything for the great seats of population to be thus intellectual centres as well as mere places of business (Berdahl, 1959, p. 41).

The chief cultural organ of the state which Arnold desired to see in England was based on the model of the French Academy. It was, however, to be especially concerned with education: it was to set standards, create educated opinion and rebuke those who fell below these standards. Arnold believed that such an agency would unify society and act as an inspiration towards perfection (Connell, 1950, p. 81). His concept of a state which was above all classes and sects was not in conflict with that of democracy. In an article on 'Democracy', he suggested that it was no longer progressive and revolutionary to demand freedom from the state. In Arnold's view, democracy could be achieved within the nation by a State Church comprising the various sects, making for unity instead of separatism. This would also incidentally diminish the grounds for exclusiveness in admitting pupils to church foundations.

Secondary Education

When we examine Green's own views, it is clear that he shared Arnold's belief that the first necessary step toward a national system of education was adequate provision for the middle classes. But Green was concerned with middle-class education not only for those who could afford it but as a commodity which should be more widely available. The so-called 'public schools' which were heavily endowed had been beyond the means of all but the 'squires, capitalists and richer professional men'. Green's commitment to social equality, like Arnold's, looked to the middle classes to give a lead. He was disappointed to find, on his visits to schools, the absence of any middle-class tradition of a liberal education.

There is lacking in this class the public sentiment in favour of the sort of learning which requires many years for its attainment. It is not from the successful men of the class, as a rule, that any germination of this sentiment can yet be looked for. Only by a special grace, can any one bred amid the keen interests, the obvious profits, the 'quick returns' of prosperous commerce, be drawn into the devious and difficult paths which lead to the knowledge that is its own reward. Among men, however, not made to get on, men whose heart is with their few books, or in the Lord's house, while they are behind the counter or at the clerk's desk; among those, again, who, having the instinct for letters, yet spend their life in teaching arts not 'ingenuous' to the children of commerce, and among them preachers who deal with the intellect of men of business at the intervals when it is open to other interests than those of the immediate present: here the lacking sentiment already exists, and only needs an open path for its development and realization (Schools Inquiry Commission, 1868 (hereafter *SIC*), vol. 8, pp. 236-7).

The main solution as Green saw it was to recast the whole educational system so that these sentiments could be released. He recognized that educational reform in England was bedevilled by subtle class distinctions, 'between those who claim to be gentlemen and whose claim is conceded, those who claim to be so but whose claim is not yet conceded, and those who do not claim to be gentlemen at all' (Green, *Works,* 3, p. 403).

J. H. Muirhead, who had known Green, recalled that he had an old-fashioned affection for the phrase 'the education of a gentleman'. A gentleman was, in Green's eyes, one who possessed definite capacities of knowledge and emotion, access to which, instead of being the privilege of a few, ought to be the acknowledged right of all (Muirhead, 1908, p. 82). Both he and Arnold recognized that the public schools which were essentially Church of England foundations provided for a comparatively small number of children. There was no good reason why they should lay claim to the prerogative of being the sole providers of a liberal education.

After this brief survey of Green's general position in regard to some educational problems, we can now look at his activities on behalf of the Taunton Commission. He was actively engaged in visiting the schools allocated to him first in Warwickshire and Staffordshire and then Northamptonshire and Oxfordshire during the period September 1865 to June 1866. His reports, subsequently published with the evidence taken before the Taunton Commission, appeared in 1868. They voice clearly his concern with the lack of religious and social justice and include trenchant comments on a number of issues which drew criticisms from Robert Lowe and others. Green was aware that he had had no experience of practical life, as he called it, and in Birmingham he was at first embarrassed on having to 'poke into back-shops and small manufactories (such as abound here) and explain to parents and old pupils of the school what one was about. Now I don't mind it much' (Green, *Works*, 3, p. xlvi). His remarkable seriousness of expression and intellectual disposition, and the apparent remoteness which had given rise to a sense of alarm when Bryce first met him, probably made a striking impact on his visits. Green's subsequent judgments on the reforms needed in education were firmly based on the knowledge gained during his day-to-day visits to schools. At Brackley, Northamptonshire, for example, he heard a lesson from the first book of the *Aeneid*, listened to pupils reading Caesar and Smith's *Principia* and set an essay on Caesar's invasion of Britain. He also examined one group on the outline of English history down to the end of the Wars of the Roses and another in geography, as well as testing younger boys in arithmetic (*SIC*, vol. 12, pp. 319-20). At Daventry Free Grammar School, which was little more than elementary in standard, Green gave the upper class 'a rather hard piece from a *Times* article', which he admitted did not yield good results (ibid., p. 336).

He condemned inefficiency in straightforward language. 'The grammar school at Towcester is, to speak plainly, in an utterly bad and useless state', opened one report. Green was appalled at the misuse of endowments: in some instances, children could hardly read, absent headmasters delegated their work, and the number of pupils attending was low. He remarked on the separation of classes in the schools. 'It appeared that the farmers of the place [Burton Latimer] seldom sent sons to the school. The poor people of the place are mostly shoemakers, and the farmers probably object the more on this account to the mixture of their sons with the poor boys' (ibid., p. 325).

Green reserved his weightiest criticisms, however, for the obstructive attitude of the church towards reforming the endowed schools. In one case, at Clipstone, Northamptonshire, where trustees were anxious to raise the character of a school so that it could act as an upper department to the surrounding elementary schools, the local clergyman who was one of the trustees, Green reported, 'was unwilling that a new scheme should be applied for, lest it should introduce a "conscience clause", as the place being full of Baptists, it probably might'. And at Wellingborough, where there was nothing in the scheme to exclude them, Dissenters had scarcely ever been admitted. The situation was more complex at Birmingham. Here Green was asked by the Commissioners to direct his attention to the conditions, both internal and external, affecting the conduct of the King Edward VI Free School. This was a consequence of the activities of an association, which consisted of a wide range of interests within the city, for the reform of the Grammar Schools. Green voiced one of the association's main concerns, the constitution of the Board of Governors:

> So far as I could ascertain, the Board has fairly represented the upper or more select section of society in Birmingham, so far as this section is politically conservative and attached to the Established Church. . . . Thus, a Board composed of conservative churchmen, of good social position, had necessarily been antagonistic to the town council, and careless or contemptuous of local politics. Social and municipal distinctions have not coincided, and hence the Board has been an object of public animosity, irrespectively of the manner in which it has exercised its function (*SIC,* vol. 8, pp. 91-2).

One evil resulting from this was that 'as dissenters or radicals, the Board has excluded most of those who would be disposed to move, and likely to move with discretion'. Green complained that the Dissenting congregations in Birmingham were not only as numerous as those of the Establishment, but included as many persons of intellect and intelligence. A second evil was that so long as the right of nominating scholars was exercised by individual trustees, preference was likely to continue to be shown to the children of churchmen as against those of Dissenters.

It was fortunate for Green that the Commissioners had selected the King Edward School, because of its size and importance, as one of the endowments to be especially studied as a possible model for other schools to follow. A close scrutiny of the curriculum offered to the different social classes attending the foundation led Green to formulate a blueprint for such schools. We have already seen that Green had been disappointed at the lack of enthusiasm by the middle classes for a liberal education. At Birmingham, Green had remarked that the existence of two departments at the grammar school – the classical and the English departments – was based on social, not educational, grounds, The classical department, consisting mainly of boys from 'genteel' homes and therefore higher in social estimation, taught Latin, Greek and mathematics. The

English department drew its pupils from sons of shopkeepers and small manufacturers and offered a basic education sufficient to equip them as clerks or superior artisans. Green considered both schemes showed a lack of 'general cultivation, an absence of intellectual interest and an obtuseness for distinctions of thought'. (It was also on these grounds that Green denounced private schools, which had an even narrower view of education.)

Lacking in intellectual aspirations, the grammar schools were not passing their more able pupils on to the universities. Green's scheme to reform the structure of the schools was set out in full in his Report (*SIC,* vol. 8, p. 191A). First, grammar schools should insist on a larger amount of knowledge at entrance; and second, the learning of Greek should be postponed in order to secure for the average boy a good standard in the basic subjects. There should also be established a number of 'high' schools in geographically convenient areas, to which the poorer grammar schools could pass on their best boys with exhibitions. The high schools would have two departments, one for potential university candidates, the other for those studying a combination of subjects such as modern languages, mathematics and physical science. Such a system would eliminate the 'mischievous separation' of smaller grammar schools into classical and English (or commerical) departments and provide a common curriculum and incentives for their pupils.

This experiment was subsequently tried out with great success in the Potteries, which Green had visited as an Assistant Commissioner. He had noted then that 'an oppressive atmosphere of well-to-do ignorance hangs over the district', with no intellectual pursuits available, such as evening classes and popular lectures. By 1876 a first-grade high school at Newcastle-under-Lyme was sending boys to universities; there were middle schools at Newcastle, Burslem and Tunstall, girls' schools at Burslem and Stoke, with increasing numbers matriculating for London University; night classes, science classes and crowded popular lectures. The headmaster of Newcastle-under-Lyme High School, F. E. Kitchener, who had been at Rugby and later an Assistant Commissioner with Green, mentioned his companion's great interest in the reorganized schools in an address delivered shortly after Green's death (Kitchener, 1882, p. 11).

Although the Taunton Commission's recommendations followed much along the lines of Green's suggestions, many of the attempts to implement them met with difficulties from the various interested parties. The notion of a central agency with a number of provincial authorities proceeded no further than a Parliamentary Bill. Local opposition to the regrading of schools was often successful, mobility between grades of schools was officially discouraged, and inspection was not enforced. The opportunity for a fundamental reform of secondary education was not taken.

Elementary Education

Green was equally active in promoting elementary school reform. As already noted, he supported the programme of the National Education League. The 1870 Forster Act did not seem to Green to go far enough. He looked forward to a time when school boards would be universal and the influence of the church, especially in rural districts, weakened. A large part of his two lectures on 'The Elementary School System of England' (1878) was concerned with expounding the need to regard the provision of elementary education as a matter of public duty and not as an object of sectarian zeal. Under the existing system, the ordinary citizen was taught to regard the schooling of his own and other people's children as a matter which could be left, for the most part, to the endeavours of the religious elements of the community. Green argued that casual action by charitable persons was no substitute for the collective action of society:

> The whole body of citizens ought to be called upon to do that as a body which under the conditions of modern life cannot be done if everyone is left to himself (Green, *Works,* 3, p. 432).

Green's views were coloured by the situation prevailing in Oxford. There the School Board, formed in 1871, had no schools directly under its control, as sufficient accommodation had been supplied by denominational effort during the time allowed after the 1870 Act came into force. The Board remained under church domination for the rest of its existence.[9]

We know from Nettleship that the question of popular education was the social subject which interested Green most. He had no false sentiment about the proletariat: as MacCunn said, 'a proletariat could be nothing in his eyes but an index of the failure of civilization' (MacCunn, 1910 edn, p. 250). During the 1860s, especially after Gladstone had been elected to office, Green held a high opinion of the working classes. After visiting the elementary department of the Birmingham Free School, Green stated that:

> A school which was supplied regularly with boys of 12 years old, knowing as much as these boys knew, though it might not turn out just the type of scholar now sent forth from the foundations of Eton and Winchester, would not fail to produce

plenty of men of the sort who now get first classes at Oxford, and became wranglers at Cambridge (*SIC,* vol. 8, pp. 105-6).

His views changed as a result of growing acquaintance with the weaknesses and poor qualities of the working classes, according to an Oxford friend, C. A. Fyffe. After the return of a Conservative government in 1874, Green told him, 'We held our heads too high during Gladstone's ministry. We thought the working classes had made more moral progress than they really had.'[10] What Green had especially in mind in talking about the working classes' moral weaknesses was drunkenness. Their élite had rallied to the doctrine of prohibition; if this minority could, in time, as Green believed, become the majority, this would be a great achievement. The way Green saw this end being realized was worked out fully in one of his late lectures, 'Liberal Legislation and Freedom of Contract', where he argued that there must be legal prohibition on the purchase and sale of any commodity – including drink – if the general result of allowing such freedom 'is to detract from freedom in the higher sense, from the general power of men to make the best of themselves' (Green, *Works,* 3, p. 383).

Clearly, by the time he wrote this lecture, Green had long given up the belief that the working classes could reform themselves entirely by their own efforts. The principle of self-help was supplemented now by the principle of state intervention. Education could play a major part in combatting drink. He told Sir William Harcourt, then one of the MPs for Oxford, in 1872:

> The education of the families of the sober has no effect on the families of the drunken. Unless the vice is first checked by a dead lift of the national conscience, education and comfortable habits are impossible in those very families which are to be saved from drunkenness by them (ibid., p. cxvii).

There is a close connexion in Green's thinking between temperance and education: in both instances, the working class could be elevated in character to good citizenship only by state intervention. He played an active part in promoting temperance. Nationally, Green was Vice-President of the United Kingdom Alliance. Locally, he was President of the Oxford Band of Hope Temperance Union; in 1875 he started a coffee house and evening school in the St Clement's district of Oxford with the help of some of his undergraduates.

In order to ensure that children of working-class families benefited from the provision of universal elementary education, Green saw the necessity for compulsory attendance. Ideally, the education of families could be safely left to the parents; but in a situation where large masses of the labouring poor existed, the collective action of society was required. Green suggested that compulsory attendance should be attained as quickly and with as little annoyance to the poor as possible, by training the public conscience into harmony with it. He fortunately lived long enough to witness the introduction of universal compulsory attendance by the Liberal government in 1880. After his election to the Oxford School Board in 1874, Green had been active in promoting this. At a meeting of the Board in 1881, he persuaded members to address a letter to the Education Department on the new regulations, pointing out that 'the Code was not necessarily known to the Parents and in practice was not known or acted upon so generally and so accurately as could be wished *even by the teachers'*. The Education Department were requested to provide a fuller explanation of the meaning of the Code for all parties concerned.[11]

Green lamented the low standard of work achieved in the elementary schools, laying much of the blame on the large classes and the piecemeal nature of educational provision. He postulated the need for larger authorities based on existing school boards, with extensive powers over secular teaching within their areas. This would enable several schools within a radius of about a mile, in conjunction with the inspector for the district, to assign advanced pupils to one, those of Standard IV to another, and so on. In this way, each group would have the undivided attention of one or more masters (Green, *Works*, 3, p. 451).

A scheme for national education

Towards the end of his life, Green sketched out a scheme of national education (in three public addresses), starting from the principle that it was the business of the school system in the interest of the common good to modify or remove pre-existing social class differences. True citizenship could not be attained whilst superficial standards relating to social worth bedevilled the discussion of educational questions. The lines of education then existing, Green noted, did not intersect social strata but ran parallel to them. A properly organized system of schools, he argued, would level up without levelling down.

> It would not make the gentleman any less of a gentleman in
> the higher sense of the term, but it would cure him of his
> unconscious social insolence just as it would cure others of
> social jealousy. It would heal the division between those who

look complacently down on others as vulgar, and those who
angrily look up to others as having the social reputation which
they themselves have not, uniting both classes by the
freemasonry of a common education (Green, *Works,* 3, p. 460).

Green anticipated the possible rejoinder to his belief that the school
system of England fostered the spirit of social exclusiveness only
because the system is an effect, not a cause, reflecting existing lines
of social stratification. Green pointed out that it did not by any
means simply follow the natural divisions in society. For one thing,
the exclusion of Dissenters from universities and grammar schools
was not based on social class differences; for another, the
unreformed state of endowed schools and colleges, the only avenues
to higher learning, made for wide differences in the opportunities
available to those who could benefit from a sound education. Green
looked to a grading of schools which allowed for flexibility of entry
and at the same time provided opportunities based on intellectual
development rather than on accidents of birth or wealth.

Speaking roughly, we want three orders of schools
distinguished according to the age to which education is
continued in each. There are boys, and those the great
majority, including all of the labouring class, whose parents
cannot reasonably be expected to keep them at school after the
age of thirteen. There are others who may be induced to stay
till fifteen or sixteen, when they will be put into some business.
A few again may stay at school till eighteen, when they will
pass on to the universities. ... We thus want three grades of
schools, each aiming at a different standard of learning
according to the ages to which the pupils continue in them
(ibid., pp. 461-2).

Fees would normally be charged 'on the simple principle that
people should not have a present made of what they can well
afford to pay for' (ibid., p. 412). These fees, together with surpluses
from endowments, could be applied to the establishment of more
university classes to accommodate the products of the remodelled
system. There were three important conditions to be fulfilled before
such a scheme could be successfully carried out. First, he envisaged
a time when a common education at elementary schools would be
possible. Green nevertheless recognized that social prejudice would
have to be overcome before the 'parents of refinement' of the boy
whose schooling was likely to continue until eighteen years of age
would be willing to use the elementary schools. In time, Green
hoped that differences in habits and language would be overcome
and that common schools at this level would flourish.

Second, there was no reason why pupils should not successively pass through schools of all three grades according to their stages of development. Third and most important was, to use Huxley's phrase which Green acknowledged, a 'ladder of learning' which could take promising boys through the schools to the universities. Thirteen years previously, he had suggested that such funds were to come from a strong central initiative which had so far been lacking. If there were no class impediments, Green had no doubt what the logical gradation of schools would be. He took as his model the German and New England systems, which had common elementary schools. Their élite would transfer at the age of ten to a middle school where they would meet boys who had reached the same standard of education at more select schools. A broad education would be followed at the age of fourteen with a choice between a classical or a 'modern' or 'real' school, the latter catering for commerce or for higher civil servants, the former for potential university students. Free education should be liberally granted as a reward for merit in the entrance examinations: educational endowments which were associated with charitable foundations for the relief of the poor would be used for this purpose 'to efface demarcations of class (and) to give a freedom of self-elevation in the social scale other than that given by money' (*SIC*, vol. 8, p. 232).

Green recognized that such opportunities would be limited in number. Progress from one grade of school to the next, in Green's scheme, was dependent on high attainment in competitive tests. He saw this *corps d'élite* as educational missionaries to the class from which they had sprung and envisaged it as a palliative for 'workmen of keen intellectual interests' who became embittered by the feelings that their full powers were not being employed.

> Perhaps not one in a hundred of the soldiers in the French
> revolutionary armies ever really obtained promotion to the
> rank of an officer, but the knowledge that the promotion was
> open to every one gave a spirit unknown before, and a unity
> higher than mere discipline can produce, to the body of citizen
> soldiers (Green, *Works,* 3, p. 475).

The different grades of school within a town, representing different standards, should be connected to each other either by the headmaster of the highest or a small board of supervision.

> For every group of schools, affording instruction according to
> each of the grades, there ought to be one pair of eyes which
> can traverse the whole and see that the élite from the lower

grade are carried on, through the middle to the higher, according to a system which makes the most of their time at each stage (ibid., p. 401).

Green doubted the wisdom of leaving the direction of a school's fortunes solely in the hands of a board of governors, and advocated the setting up of county boards throughout the country. This would bring the grammar schools nationally into more systematic relationship with the elementary schools and facilitate the establishment of appropriate schools where they might be needed. A more rational distribution of resources and overall planning would ensue. Green did not address himself to the problems of social justice which such a system would pose, merely pointing to the improvement that would accrue to the working classes.

As a practical token of his enthusiasm for a coherent secondary system, Green assisted in the creation of a new Oxford High School for Boys in 1877. There was already adequate provision in Oxford for a third-grade school which met the needs of small shopkeepers and farmers. Accordingly, Green proposed that it should be an amalgam of a first-grade school, catering for pupils preparing for university, and a second-grade, for those entering business or the civil service. Two sets of scholarships were provided: one for promising boys from the elementary schools and the second for boys under fifteen, enabling them to stay on for a further three years. At that age, it would be necessary to decide whether they should leave for business or aim at the university. Those who decided on the latter would be able to enter for a second order of scholarship which Green hoped to establish. Exhibitions would cover the cost of tuition at university. Green contributed both to the cost of the buildings and the endowment of one of the yearly scholarships for boys from Oxford elementary schools.

He was also instrumental, together with his friend R. W. Dale, the Birmingham Congregational leader, in remodelling the schools of the King Edward VI Foundation, Birmingham. Green, as a teachers' representative on the governing body, took a great personal interest in putting some of his ideas into action. In the years 1880-1 the Lower Middle and Middle Schools were fused into the 'Grammar School' of the foundation, and A. R. Vardy, the headmaster, gratefully acknowledged Green's part in this operation. [12] In spite of persistent bad health, Green rarely missed travelling to Birmingham for the governors' meetings.[13]

As we have seen, the extension of the benefits of university education to a larger section of the population was a logical corollary of Green's conception of a school system which allowed for wider access by different classes and groups within society. It was not likely that the impulse towards a liberal education which Green detected among the middle classes in large towns would be sustained without teachers of vision and commitment. These, he believed, could be supplied only by men from the universities who were willing to devote themselves to this cause. It was essential 'that if people were to be made scholars, the scholar must go to the people and not wait for them to come to him'. Green told a teachers' meeting in 1877:

> He must sink his pride so far as to offer them his wares in the universally accessible day school, instead of expecting them to seek him out at the boarding school. Perhaps it is one of the first-fruits of university reform that men are now forthcoming from Oxford and Cambridge who will enter, without any of the caste-spirit of the conventional university man, but with unabated zeal for the knowledge which 'does not pay', into the educational life of cities. The influence which such men may have in eliciting the latent capacity for learning in the less wealthy middle class, is what we are only just beginning to appreciate. I can myself bear witness that, so far as we are drawing to Oxford young men of promise from classes outside those which we are used to, it is through the action of day education under such men as I have spoken of. It is the day scholars of Birmingham, Manchester and the City of London school, the day students of the Scotch universities, sent us by professors whom we have sent there, that are bringing hopeful new grist to our mill (Green, *Works*, 3, pp. 409-10).

At Oxford University, an unofficial Extension Committee of the Delegacy came into existence in 1865 with the aims of, amongst other things, assisting poor students to prepare for the ministry or medical profession and providing a new college in Oxford where expenses would be low. Green had shown in his Report to the Schools Inquiry Commission how the cost of Oxford and Cambridge colleges deterred boys of high intellect from entering.

> Their parents are either unable to bear the expense of a university course, or if they are prosperous men who have risen from the ranks, generally unwilling. The college system, maintained at Oxford and Cambridge, by putting a certain mystery about the University career and raising its expense, increases the difficulty (*SIC*, vol. 8, p. 172).

Jowett and Green outlined a scheme to make more places available to deserving scholars. In order to attract this 'new class', the subjects of examination were not confined to Latin and Greek but included physical science and mathematics. As Jowett noted, the great difficulty 'in working it out was the present state of the grammar school'. In 1867, Balliol Hall, consisting of a lodging house in St Giles' Street, was founded for men students; no college fees were payable. Green moved into residence at the Hall and in the following year helped to promote exhibitions at Balliol itself.

The movement to promote the higher education of women also received his strong support: together with Henry Nettleship, R. L. Nettleship's brother, Green set on foot the Association for the Higher Education of Women in Oxford.[14] One of the movement's early successes was the establishment of a University College at Bristol in 1876, the first one to be open equally to men and women. Green was a member of the Council. Balliol and New College initially provided funds and scholarships for women until this was found to be illegal. It was later discovered that an anonymous donor who contributed for some time to sustain these funds was Green (Temple, 1921, pp. 263-4). He was also prominent in the initial stages of the university extension movement, which will be discussed later.

Another group of university students with whom Green was concerned were those from Dissenting families. There was a danger that, as undergraduates, they might become attached to the Church of England or lose their faith altogether. This, as Richter has pointed out, would have had long-term implications for the Liberal Party (Richter, 1964, p. 361). Green told R. W. Dale, 'You are bound, as soon as you have secured the opening of the universities for your sons, to follow them when you send them here, in order to defend and maintain their religious faith and life' (Dale, 1902, p. 496). The notion of setting up a college for the training of congregational ministers in Oxford was Green's. Six years after his death, Spring Hill College was transferred from Birmingham to Oxford, taking the name of Mansfield College (Marriott, 1946, p. 181).

Green deplored the isolation of the university and its members from the community in which it was situated. Democratic citizenship for Green involved active participation in local affairs. From the time of the Second Reform Act (1867) he became involved in the political and educational life of Oxford. As a member of the School Board from 1874, he made a detailed study of problems affecting the poor families of the city. In the following year Green stood for election to the City Council as a lay rather than a university candidate. In his election address, he proposed greater expenditure of rates on health and education and reiterated the need to raise boys from elementary schools to higher ones, in this case, the proposed grammar school. R. L. Nettleship mentions that Green's example – the first college tutor to become a town councillor – laid the foundation for a bridge between the city and the university (Green, *Works,* 3, p. cxix). His political interests were connected with education and temperance as means of the moralization of the people. Green advocated cheaper Parliamentary elections so that M.P.s concerned with the interests of the suffering classes of society could be better represented. He also pressed for the purifying of elections. Green's energetic involvement in the Oxford elections of 1880 and the by-election of 1881 brought about a successful petition to unseat the Conservative victor on the grounds of corrupt practice.[15]

No account of Green's work in connexion with education would be complete without some reference to his own teaching activities within the University. Passmore has remarked that Green, like other idealists, was predominantly a teacher (1957, p. 55). He had been active in introducing philosophy as a separate academic discipline at Oxford. Before Green's election to the Whyte's Professorship of Moral Philosophy in 1878, there had been no systematic lecturing on philosophic subjects except in ethics and the works of Plato and Aristotle. Jowett for his part was reluctant that philosophy be taught as Green wished it, independently of classical authors (Richter, op. cit., p. 153). As a philosophy tutor, Green impressed his hearers with the substance of his lectures. One of his most able students wrote of him, 'To other real or imagined great people in Oxford I took off my *hat,* but before Green I felt as if I could take off not the hat only but also the *head*' (Muirhead, 1908, p. 2). Although Green did not always express himself clearly, he worked out his ideas with a conviction which attracted and inspired many students, both in his own time and later. Herbert Asquith, the future Liberal Prime Minister, contributed an anonymous tribute to his teacher in *The Spectator:*

> Even those, and there were many, students who never
> penetrated into the inner shrines of the Hegelian temple found
> that under his teaching the narrow nature of the schools was
> gradually enlarged and vivified and their own philosophic
> reading converted from a dry analysis of books and a laborious
> accumulation of 'tips' into a living interest in the historical
> development of human thought.[16]

More significantly, as R. G. Collingwood wrote:

> The school of Green sent out into public life a stream of
> ex-pupils who carried with them the conviction that

philosophy, and in particular the philosophy they had learnt at Oxford, was an important thing, and that their vocation was to put it into practice (Collingwood, 1944 edn., p. 17).

One field in which many of Green's pupils came to apply his ideas was education. Balliol had already a long tradition of involvement in this area. This stemmed initially from Jowett, who desired to secure reforms in government and the civil service. Through his efforts, an impressive number of links had been formed with the Committee of the Privy Council on Education from its inception in 1839. 'Patronage,' as Richard Johnson has remarked, 'was now being exercised through the educational institutions of the mid-Victorian intelligentsia, initially through a college well-emancipated from aristocratic and ecclesiastical ties' (Johnson, 1972, p. 121). A few examples will suffice: R. R. W. Lingen,[17] who became a Fellow of Balliol in the same year that P. Cumin[18] (a close friend of Matthew Arnold at Balliol) and F. R. Sandford[19] entered the college (1841), were successive secretaries to the Education Department from 1850 to 1890. G. W. Kekewich, the last Secretary of the Department (and the first of the Board of Education 1890-1903) was also a Balliol man. Matthew Arnold was appointed secretary to the Lord President in 1847 before becoming a school inspector. Frederick Temple, later a Taunton Commissioner, became the first principal of Kneller Hall, a training college for workhouse schoolmasters, in 1848 (see p. 167 for subsequent career). F. T. Palgrave, Temple's first vice-principal, and Arthur Hugh Clough later both took up posts in the Education Department.

It would be tedious to list the growing number of Balliol men who entered the education service as the century progressed. Many were directly influenced by Jowett's and Green's ideas, though to different degrees. They included W. N. Bruce, Principal Assistant Secretary to the Secondary School Branch of the Board of Education 1903-20, J. W. Mackail, Assistant Secretary, 1903-19; H. L. Withers, Professor of Education, University of Manchester, 1899-1902; and T. G. Rooper, one of Her Majesty's Inspectors, 1878-1903. Balliol continued to be strongly represented in the higher branches of educational administration during the present century. Its graduates include the first Parliamentary Secretary to the Board of Education, and a former Vice-Chancellor of Oxford, Sir William Anson, 1902-5; E. H. Pelham 1931-7 and M. G. Holmes 1937-45, both Permanent Secretaries; and influential individuals such as H. M. Lindsell, first head of the Legal Branch of the Board of Education and D. R. Fearon, who carried out notable work as an inspector, an assistant commissioner for the Taunton Commission, and later as secretary to the Charity Commission, 1886-1900. Central and local inspectorships were often held by Balliol men, who were also strongly represented on Royal Commissions and Consultative Committees of the Board: members of the latter included R. H. Tawney, Arthur Acland and T. H. Warren. The First Viscount Burnham, who looked after the interests of Whitechapel on the London County Council from 1897 to 1904 and was a prime mover in securing votes for women in 1918, is best remembered as chairman of the standing joint committee of teachers and local education authorities whose deliberations form the basis of national pay scales in the teaching profession (Compact Edition of the *Dictionary of National Biography* (hereafter *DNB*), 1975, vol. 2, p. 2745). Not all of these men were as closely connected with Green's school of thought as those whom we are considering in detail in this book, although as products of Balliol few were likely to have been wholly uninfluenced by it.[20]

It was unfortunate that Green did not live long enough – he was forty-six when he died in 1882 – fully to work out his educational ideas. We are left only with his early reports as a Schools Inquiry Assistant Commissioner, a handful of speeches and a number of scattered references in his colleagues' and disciples' writings. As an active Liberal with radical tendencies, Green saw education as of first importance in promoting the self-realization of the individual in a society oriented towards the common good. It was left to those who followed him to search for various ways of achieving this aim. Even those of his disciples who did not enter the education service as such often took up careers in which they could work for the same broad educational ends.

Some (notably Henry Scott Holland, Charles Gore and William Temple) accepted Green's view of religion as Christian citizenship and entered the church. At a further remove from formal education institutions, concern with the community through social work (Plant, 1974, pp. 6-7) occupied the attention of individuals such as C. S. Loch, Bernard and Helen Bosanquet and Arnold Toynbee. Their work for the relief of the poor took shape, for instance, in the operations of the Charity Organisation Society, in the encouragement of self-help, and in temperance reform. These activities were closely connected with the study of the economics of welfare, which challenged the orthodox view of economic man. One forum for its expression in the 1880s was the Oxford Economic Society, which included D. G. Ritchie, Sidney Ball, W. J. Ashley, Michael Sadler, H. Llewellyn Smith and W. A. S. Hewins. Journalism was another field in which the work of national enlightenment could proceed. Here we have in mind not only influential newspaper editors such as J. A. Spender[21] and E. T. Cook, but also the impressive number of individuals who could be called upon to propagate their views in the press when vital issues arose. Politics, finally, provided a congenial outlet for educational ambitions. Liberal intellectuals, notably James Bryce, Arthur Acland, Thomas Ellis and R. B. Haldane, made outstanding contributions to educational reform through their political offices (Harvie, 1976, ch. 9). Some, such as Alfred Milner and his 'Kindergarten' of Oxford men in South Africa at the beginning of the century, were attracted to Liberal Imperialism, which was concerned with the spiritual as well as the constitutional aspects of Empire.[22] This theme was also explored by lawyers, notably A. B. Keith and L. G. Curtis, who helped to create the Institute of International Affairs.

Many of Green's contemporaries, as well as others attracted to idealist philosophy, remained within universities, propagating their views through lecturing and writing. As a body scattered over the country, they were active in promoting reform within their own institutions, helping to forge new links between the university and the local community. One of the commonest means by which many of them sought to realize this aim was involvement in adult education. In the next chapter we shall examine in more detail the idealists' contribution to this movement.

Adult education

Co-operation

An important feature of the idealist movement was that most of its activities were carried out within the framework of existing institutions which could be transformed in the course of time. The case of adult education provides a good illustration.

In 1816 Robert Owen had advocated the setting up of co-operative communities – associations of middle- and working-class farmers, mechanics and tradesmen – to remedy unemployment. The education of its members, both children and adults, formed a major part of the Owenite programme. Halls of Science were opened from 1839, where lectures were given on scientific, economic and political subjects. At the same time, the Chartist movement, which demanded electoral rights for the working classes, established reading rooms, libraries and lecture halls and a range of publications aimed at educating and informing fellow Chartists (Simon, 1960, pp. 193-276).

After the failure of the Chartist movement in 1848, a group of Broad Churchmen who looked towards ecumenicalism, expounded the view, taken from Coleridge, that the Church should play a leading part in initiating and participating in social action and defending workers against exploitation. The leading members were J. M. Ludlow, F. D. Maurice and Charles Kingsley, and the movement gained a number of supporters including Ruskin and Tom Hughes. Deeply affected by the prevailing widespread poverty, their main theme was that in an industrial society Christian co-operation should supersede competition. Efforts to found Working Men's Associations, self-governing productive organizations, failed from the members' lack of education. Maurice was instrumental in establishing a Working Men's College in London in 1854.[1] One of Maurice's aims in founding the College was to bring together through education social classes which had been alienated from one another (Maurice, 1884, vol. 2, p. 220). His important work in the fields of education and social reform sprang directly from his theological beliefs that the Kingdom of God was in the present, not the future. Maurice cared little for religion unless it was put into practice (Saunders, 1942, p. 239). The failure of the movement has been attributed to the attempt to transpose Thomas Arnold's ideal of 'Muscular Christianity' into a proletarian key. 'Team athletics and the spirit of "manliness", it was thought, would combine to produce Christian gentlemen in working clothes' (Altick, 1973, p. 143).

Edward Denison, a friend of Ruskin and son of the Bishop of Salisbury, was moved to investigate the causes of distress in the East End of London, settling there in 1867. His views on the treatment of poverty were largely governed by the principle of self-help rather than charity. Denison advocated settlement in poorer areas by educated men, based on Maurice's principle that 'the remedial influence of the mere presence of a gentleman known to be on the alert is inestimable' (Pimlott, 1935, p. 13). Education was an important instrument in Denison's plan to ameliorate the plight of the poor. In August of that year, he organized weekly classes in Bible teaching and began an evening class for working men, using quotations from Wordsworth, Tennyson and even Plato (Leighton, 1872, pp. 40-1). Many of Denison's ideas for social reform appealed to Oxford men in the following decade.[2] A number of them took part in Ruskin's scheme of road-making at Hinksey in 1874. One of the most influential of these was Arnold Toynbee. Under Toynbee's influence, undergraduates extended their activities to include visits to workhouses, instruction of pupil-teachers, and charity organization work. Of more important significance, they laid down the guide-lines for a working class adult aducation movement.

Toynbee had arrived at Oxford in 1873, absorbed in thoughts of religion. He was later taken up by Jowett and established a close friendship with Green and Nettleship.[3] His circle of admirers included Alfred Milner, T. H. Warren, later to be Vice-Chancellor of the University, and A. C. Bradley. Toynbee was appointed tutor to those Balliol students who intended to qualify for the Indian Civil Service. Like Green, he was convinced that idealism could justify its existence only by energetic devotion to the good of mankind. After studying the philosophy of history, Toynbee devoted his time to investigating the science of economics, in order to improve the condition of the working classes. His unfinished *Industrial Revolution*, based on a course of lectures delivered at Balliol and published posthumously in 1884, was a study of the laws governing the production and distribution of wealth: studying the work of earlier economists, Toynbee hoped to show how the forces of competition and self-interest could be utilized by corporate action for the common good.[4] This approach had two outcomes: first, it encouraged other like-minded individuals to pursue the study of economics and economic history to good effect; second, as Alfred Milner, a contemporary of Toynbee, has testified:

> The years which I spent at Oxford, and those immediately succeeding them, were marked by a very striking change in the social and political philosophy of the place, a change which has subsequently reproduced itself on the larger stage of the world. When I went up to the *Laisser-faire* [*sic*] theory still held the field. All the recognized authorities were 'orthodox' economists of the old school. But within ten years the few men who still held the old doctrines in their extreme rigidity had come to be regarded as curiosities (Toynbee, 1884, p. xxv).

Toynbee looked forward to a democratic state which controlled excessive competition but also allowed for the exercise of free play on the part of the individual, a view which was neither socialist nor utilitarian.

If true citizenship were to be achieved, Toynbee argued, a start could be made with existing voluntary associations of free men which pointed towards the higher life. Toynbee saw in the co-operative movement rather than the trade unions a closer outward resemblance of a united life possessing high ideals (ibid., p. 241). In the spirit of the medieval guilds, the co-operative movement aimed at ending competition which divided men into capitalists and labourers. But Toynbee was also aware that though they differed from other societies in possessing an ideal aim, co-operative societies did not claim to cover the whole range of human life. In the light of this, what particular contribution. Toynbee asks in a lecture on *Education for Co-operators*, could the co-operative movement make to the cause of education? Many bodies were involved in providing different aspects of education. Elementary education was the responsibility of the state; secondary schools were in the process of being reformed; university colleges belonged to the civic communities. Technical education, at first sight a likely candidate for co-operators was, in Toynbee's estimation, best left to employers and the state. What then remained for co-operators? Toynbee wrote:

> The answer I would give is, the *education of the citizen*. By this I mean the education of each member of the community, as regards the relation in which he stands to other individual citizens, and to the community as a whole. But why should co-operators, more than anyone else, take up this part of education? Because co-operators, if they would carry out their avowed aims, are more absolutely in need of such an education

than any other persons, and because if we look at the origin of the co-operative movement we shall see that this is the work in education most thoroughly in harmony with its ideal purpose (ibid., p. 243).

The break-up of the medieval pattern of work with the coming of the Industrial Revolution resulted in the dissolution of brotherhood and citizenship. Robert Owen, in founding self-contained communities based on the principle of equal association and the pursuit of a moral life, had helped to restore the balance. But new factors had now to be taken into account: workers were being given more share in the government of the country at a time when the conditions of industrial life were exhausting their energies and dulling their intelligence. Industrial development had degraded the individual from a man into a machine. For these reasons, a scheme of education of the citizen in his duties was indispensable.

Toynbee outlined only a few headings rather than an elaborate scheme. They related to:

(a) Political education. A description and history of local and central political institutions in England and the history of political ideas.

(b) Industrial education. A history and description of the industrial system and institutions of England, a history of the material conditions of the working classes and a history of social ideas and schemes of reform.

(c) Sanitary education. The duties of citizens in relation to the prevention of the spread of disease (ibid., p. 245).

Several objections to such a scheme could be anticipated. There was a danger that political education might be taught in a partisan way. This, said Toynbee, was a challenge to co-operators to prove that men's deepest interests are not the peculiar possessions of factions and parties, but the rightful inheritance of every citizen. Possibly the greatest obstacle to the success of the plan was the apathy of co-operators in acquiring such knowledge. Workmen were less interested in political and social questions because of their prosperity: material comfort can diminish spiritual energy. But if political progress was to be maintained, the effort must be made to devise a programme which would capture the workman's imagination. A third objection was that, even if co-operators were willing to adopt such subjects as part of their education, there was a shortage of teachers with a broad yet impartial knowledge of social and political questions. Toynbee hoped that they could be recruited from the ranks of co-operators themselves, but to a greater extent he was convinced that in the universities, there were many suitable persons

> who have studied political and social questions with all the keenness of partisans, but without their prejudice. The fact that these men will often, of course, have reached definite practical conclusions will not destroy their influence as scientific teachers (ibid., p. 246).

It was to Oxford that Toynbee looked for assistance in this work. Whilst he was tutor and Senior Bursar at Balliol, he drew together an informal society, consisting of the most studious of his younger contemporaries, each of whom selected a special study in some aspect of politics; from the society's inception at Oxford in June 1879, meetings were held termly for discussion and exchange of information (Montague, 1889, p. 36). Toynbee was sure that the masses were eager for knowledge on economic matters and would be delighted to follow intelligent men who were sincere and frank. In January 1880 Toynbee delivered the first of his series of popular addresses at Bradford (on Free Trade, the Law of Wages and England's Industrial Supremacy) and during the following years lectured on political economy to a class of working men, meeting at the Oxford Co-operative Stores. He also gained the confidence and devotion of large audiences of workmen in many parts of England. Towards the end of his last meeting in London, in January 1883, which was concerned with Henry George's *Poverty and Progress.* Toynbee said:

> We – the middle classes, I mean, not merely the very rich – we have neglected you; instead of justice we have offered you charity, and instead of sympathy. we have offered you hard and unreal advice; but I think we are changing. If you would only believe it and trust us, I think that many of us would spend our lives in your service (Toynbee, 1883, p. 53).

Toynbee's early death at the age of thirty in 1883 at a time when he was actively engaged in charity organization work, church reform and co-operation inspired others to respond to the call for continuing his work.

Arthur Acland

One of Toynbee's greatest admirers, who played a leading part in the co-operative education movement, was Arthur Acland, third son of Sir Thomas Dyke Acland, head of one of the largest landowning families in England. During Sir Thomas's undergraduate years at Christ Church, he made two lifelong friends, William Gladstone and F. D. Maurice. Maurice's writings had a profound influence on him as did those of Coleridge: 'The spiritual Philosophy of Coleridge', he wrote in 1892, 'was as the breath of life to young men half a century ago.' (Acland, 1902, p. 51). Arthur Acland's interest in educational reform was not surprising in view of the devotion of his father to the same cause. Sir Thomas had become a leading figure in the establishment of the Oxford school examinations ('Locals') from 1857 and in the reform of middle-class education in his home county of Devon. He set out the path for his son on entering Christ Church:

> The main object of your Oxford education is . . . to fit you to be a political animal in the wide sense. I mean a man whose special responsibility is to be morally and socially useful to his fellow men, rather than to have a speculative insight into the laws of converting matter, or a practical power of advancing the material comforts of this world at large.[5]

From the first, Arthur was destined for the church and a family living, having been brought up in a near-Tractarian household. It is clear from a study of his personal diary that his friendship with T. H. Green was one of the main factors which led Acland to consider himself 'Broad Church' from about 1874 and eventually to resign his orders in 1879.[6] The surviving correspondence between Green and Acland is somewhat fragmentary, but the closeness of the two men emerges from it. During a long holiday in Italy in the spring of 1876, Acland and his wife joined the Greens at Florence. The men spent their time there learning about the social state of the people and the conditions of education, and investigated the normal schools (Green, *Works,* 3, p. cxxvi). During the fifteen years 1870-85, Acland, between graduating and entering politics, apart from a short spell as curate in a Northumberland parish,[7] lived in or near Oxford: up to 1875 as tutor at Keble College, and for the next two years as Principal of the Military School at Cowley. After his break with the church, Acland returned to Christ Church as Steward, a post which allowed him ample time for his other interests. He was responsible in 1884 for convening a number of fellows and undergraduates, forming a small club called the Inner Ring, to discuss political, economic and social issues;[8] the club continued to meet after Acland left Oxford (Sadleir, 1949, p. 68 fn.). Most of the leading members were from Balliol, including Cosmo Lang, A. Hope Hawkins, J. A. Spender, as well as Michael Sadler of Trinity and H. Llewellyn Smith of Corpus Christi.

As we shall see later (p. 102), Green employed Acland as secretary in 1878 for his early scheme of university extension. In 1880, in a letter concerned with the General Election then taking place, Green suggested that Acland might consider standing for the new post of provincial lecture secretary, combining it with the responsibility for local examinations. Green told him 'You would no doubt have strong support for the place, if you would try. I think you would find it more interesting work than housekeeping at Ch: Ch: [Christ Church]'.[9]

When in April 1883 Acland was offered the Senior Bursarship of Balliol by the Master and Fellows, a post previously occupied by Toynbee, he explained the attractions of the post to his father:

> The real reason why I should be extremely sorry not to accept the offer, and to miss the opportunity which may never recur, is that it would give me a permanent link with a college where there are more men to whom I believe I can be of use than anywhere else. The things that I really care most about are the things that working men are doing for themselves or the work of Charity organizations and other matters of that kind and it is just on these matters more than at any time previously in my knowledge of Oxford there are many young men (chiefly at Balliol and New College) genuinely anxious to be interested – genuinely anxious to make themselves useful in work for the poor and others – men some of whom are going to be clergymen some of whom may find conscientious difficulties but who none the less wish to be doing real good and self denying work. I know that I can be of some little use to such men and at Ch. Ch. there are very few such. With a room at Balliol and the power to dine in Hall and go to the Common Room etc I should get a footing in the place which would make my life here much more to me than it is now. At Ch. Ch. except Holland[10] who is one of my best and oldest friends and who is liberal-minded enough to forget that I thought it right to give up orders or rather not to let it influence him, I find very little sympathy among the Dons with the things I care most about.[11]

Acland's historical interests had already resulted in *A Handbook of the Political History of England,* written with Cyril Ransome in 1881, and a handbook of English politics the following year for co-operative readers. He helped to organize the Co-operative Congress held at Oxford in 1882 at which Toynbee spoke (Bellamy and Saville, 1972, p. 6). This event made an everlasting impression on him. Nine years later, recalling Toynbee's address on the duties of citizens, Acland told a co-operative audience that the occasion lingered with a certain special flavour in the memory . . . the fresh life, and hearty, vigorous interest in our affairs, which suddenly you brought into the University town for a few days were sources of the greatest pleasure (Acland, 1891, p, 4).

He saw the co-operative movement as a way of elevating the artisan through education (Armytage, 1947, p. 548), expressing the belief that

you can gradually educate even very ignorant people by making them feel their responsibility and that only by the steady improvement of public opinion (which *is* going on) can you shame local bodies out of jobbery and extravagance such as it often perpetrated in our towns.[12]

For this reason Acland encouraged co-operators to participate in school board and town council work on a wider scale than hitherto, but he warned members that one of their most important tasks was to combat 'one of the gravest of the social questions of our day': to set an example on the question of temperance (Acland, 1891, p. 20).

Like Green and Toynbee, Acland saw that voluntary associations of working-class men, aided by interested members of the middle classes, would be a first step to reconciling the claims of employers and workers. In Richter's words, 'by a spontaneous recognition of their mutual obligations to the whole community . . . their members accepted obligations imposed by their collective purposes and so transcended mere individualism' (1964, p. 324).

Acland and Benjamin Jones (the latter a leading figure in the co-operative movement) open their book *Working Men Co-operators* (1884) with the words

The power of association to lift the masses of the people in every country to a fuller and higher citizenship – to give them a steadily increasing influence not only on the conditions of their own lives, but on national affairs and on national life – is the most obvious as well as the most important phenomenon of this last half of the nineteenth century in which we are living (p. 10).

The book, the authors say, is aimed to stimulate young co-operators to a fuller sense both of their responsibility and power . . . A further purpose will be served if this book leads some who have not much acquaintance with working men's co-operation to study the matter more fully in books or in 'real life', and themselves to assist the work in one or other of the many ways which may be open to them (ibid.).

During December 1882 and January 1883, Acland delivered a series of lectures to Co-operative Society audiences in Lancashire;[13] these were reprinted under the title *The Education of Citizens* in 1883 with an apt quotation from Toynbee on the title page. The lectures dealt with three topics: the nature of education, methods of teaching, and the content of a proposed syllabus.

The nature of education

Acland envisaged lifelong education: 'I speak to those who feel more and more assured every day they live, that while the period of *instruction* may cease before we are twenty years of age, the work of *education* is the work of our lives, and that education in the true sense ends when our lives end.' In considering the subjects to be chosen, individuals should be concerned with their own daily lives as part of the great body of working people, as English citizens, and as neighbours of the suffering and the poor. Education should lead to self-restraint and self-reliance, and to individuals' becoming more tolerant of other people's opinions (p. 8).

Methods of teaching

As the sole object of the teaching would be to encourage thinking, it must be continuous and systematic. Discussion would be a vital element. Acland stressed that 'the object of education of this kind is not to make us rise out of our surroundings. We may and ought to rise above our worst selves; but if we get above our friends and our neighbours . . . it does not at all follow that we thereby move in the right direction. All I can say is that if young men come to us and go back in any sense ashamed of that from which they came, we in the universities ought to be ashamed of ourselves' (pp. 16-17). Education, therefore, does not necessarily elevate the individual or bring material benefit but brings increased strength, power and wisdom 'which must add force to individual men'.

Acland too looked to the universities to provide lecturers who had investigated and would be capable of answering questions on social, economic, industrial and historical problems. They should be men of real capacity, able to arrange facts well and clearly, indicate how to form a right judgment about men. 'Individual reform must be the groundwork of social progress.' The practical and systematic education of co-operators as English citizens should be open equally to men and women if future generations were to become reasonably and rationally educated.

The content of education

In enumerating areas to be studied, Acland excluded scientific subjects as having less effect on social aspects of citizenship. He suggested *social and economical* subjects such as co-operation, the citizen in his locality, education and health of the citizen and the state. The second, *literature,* was directed to books which bore more on life, less on the facts of science, economy or politics. Acland acknowledged that the first class of subjects may prove to be 'too hard and dry' for students, whilst literature could inspire and stimulate and give an insight into the meaning and moral purpose of many of the characters. Like Green, Acland warned against worthless books called 'light literature' and recommended authors such as Dickens, Eliot and Kingsley. Biographies of noble and heroic people were also of great value. The life of Thomas Carlyle was selected by Acland as an illustration of the latter point: the detailed examination of his work occupies a substantial proportion of the whole pamphlet.

The third heading, *history,* is briefly treated, consisting of a suggested study of decisive movements which have helped to shape our society and institutions. Again the study of great lives is recommended.

Such programmes of study by co-operative societies, Acland wrote in his preface, would help to raise, through education, the general level of intelligence among the working classes and so increase both their happiness and their efficiency.

One of Acland's younger supporters in his work was Michael Sadler, who had entered Trinity College, Oxford, in 1880 and was a great-great-nephew of M. T. Sadler, the factory reformer. Sadler and Acland had much in common. They had spent their school days at Rugby, where the basis for their later views and beliefs was formed. Sadler, looking back half a century to Rugby in the 1870s, wrote:

> My masters were enthusiastic upholders of Oliver Cromwell and of the Puritan Revolution. Without knowing it, some of them were ardent propagandists of Liberal ideas . . . Soon I found myself in critical revolt against the Cavalier and Anglican tradition, though I appreciated its beauty and the loveliness of its personal example (1926a, p. 342).

Sadler in his undergraduate years was tending towards political and economic radicalism, a tendency which was strengthened after hearing Arnold Toynbee read a paper at Oxford in 1882 on the factory movement (Sadleir, 1949, p. 30). As with Acland, his inclination for public service took the form of involvement in educational work. 'The things in national education which act most powerfully for good,' he wrote, 'are the spiritual and moral forces which are at work in the social life of the nation.' Sadler later publicly acknowledged his personal obligation to Acland, Toynbee and Green, who 'did much to touch existing forms of adult education in England with a new spirit of citizenship' (Sadler, 1907a, p. 263). He had met Mr and Mrs Green in June 1881 at Trinity and the meeting left a vivid impression on his mind. Even before this encounter, Sadler had fallen under Green's spell. Recalling his undergraduate days some years later, he told an audience:

> You can imagine, therefore, what was the state of mind of a
> youth of nineteen who, with such a preparation as this
> [reference to his memories of Winchester and Rugby], came up
> to Oxford in 1880 and found T. H. Green stemming the now
> slack tide of Herbert Spencerism with the gnarled and sturdy
> convictions of the *Prolegomena to Ethics*. My optimistic
> Liberalism was challenged. Here was a man, a Liberal of
> Liberals, who showed by every deep furrow in his face what a
> fight he had passed through in order to win for himself firm
> foothold in a spiritual view of the universe. If such a man as
> Green had passed through such torture of thought in order to
> gain by honest conviction a belief in the spiritual guidance of
> human affairs, how cheap ought to seem to such a tyro as
> myself any easily held and clearly gained opinions on these
> vital things. Green's very figure, the tones of his voice, the
> piercing glance of his deep-set eyes, all meant that the
> apparently dominant forces of modern thought were running
> against the plain acceptance of the Christian faith. He had
> won a foothold at a cost greater than any young man could
> measure. How sleepy and out-of-date the Rugby state of mind
> began to look! (Sadler, 1913).

There were other influences. He was also an admirer of Ruskin, whom he had heard address a meeting of the Palmerston Club at Oxford in 1882.[14] Sadler acknowledged that English education owed a great deal to the philosophers Fichte and Hegel.[15]

For the next twenty years, the careers of the two men overlapped. Sadler had already known Acland as a member of the Inner Ring, and as an undergraduate had visited the Aclands'

Oxford house to discuss political and social questions.[16] Sadler's son records that his father developed for the elder man 'a sort of hero worship' (Sadleir, op. cit. p. 68). Immediately after graduating in July 1884, he wrote to Samuel Barnett (see below), 'I have told Mr Acland that I will begin Political Economy (i.e. the lectures to co-operators) about the end of August' (ibid., p. 52). We can gain an insight into Sadler's thinking at this time from a paper he wrote entitled 'Christian Philanthropy and Rationalistic Philanthropy', in which he analysed both of these schools of thought. The first group had taken the economic system of their time for granted and were assured that wrongs would be righted in a life beyond the grave. The second group, worshipping Progress, were assured that the lot of man would improve in time, and distributed tracts on economics even to the very poor. The main cause of change in both groups of philanthropists later was a gradual realization of the significance of social economics and a perception of the justice of the claim for greater economic equality.[17] Sadler and Acland worked together effectively in the north of England (Sadler himself came from the West Riding of Yorkshire) and over the years their friendship deepened.[18]

By the following year, Sadler had delivered a series of lectures in Lancashire, saving for the Rochdale Equitable Pioneers, the home of the movement, a lecture entitled 'The History and the Achievements of the Working Classes in Union and Co-operation'. He shared with Acland a passion for social justice: during his Lancashire tour, he spent several weeks attempting to understand the truth concerning a strike of cotton operatives at Oldham. Sadler did not, like Acland, seek to enter politics, but he provided enthusiastic help when Acland stood for Rotherham as a Liberal candidate and was elected M.P. in December 1885.[19]

The two men were also linked together with Toynbee through the activities of the Toynbee Memorial Fund. At the first meeting of the Committee in March 1884, it was resolved to appoint some competent person 'to give a course of systematic instruction in Political Economy, arranged primarily for the working classes in some important centre of industry'.[20] Whoever was appointed would make a special study of the economic conditions of the town and should be resident there for four months, undertaking no other work during that time. Another stipulation was that the lectures should be repeated at Oxford. Following Toynbee's route, the first course of lectures was to take place in Newcastle-upon-Tyne and the next at Bradford.

Acland, who was Secretary,[21] and William Markby, a Fellow of Balliol,[22] were appointed to superintend the investment of the

Trust. The Committee of seven comprised (besides Markby and Acland) Henry Sidgwick, Professor Foxwell, Alfred Milner, R. Spence Watson and the Chairman, the 13th Earl of Dalhousie. The last mentioned, a contemporary of Toynbee at Balliol,[23] was succeeded as Chairman on his early death in 1887 by Acland. Sadler was at first an assessor to the Committee, though the records show that he also played an active part in the proceedings. H. Llewellyn Smith investigated 'The movement of industrial population from Trade to Trade and Place to Place' in 1889; and the Committee published the findings of L. L. Price of Oriel College in a pamphlet entitled 'Industrial Peace' the year before. An offer was made to Charles Booth of an 'inquirer' in connexion with his social research, but this was not accepted.[24] In 1889, towards the end of the Committee's existence, a protracted discussion took place 'as to lecturers, places for lectures, economic investigations and persons fitted to conduct them'. Prophetically, in view of later developments in the area, it was decided that 'Mr Acland should communicate with Mr Sadler with the view of finding a centre where lectures might be given, and more particularly, to inquire with regard to the Potteries as a possible scene of operations.'[25] By now Sadler, in his capacity as Secretary to the Oxford University Extension movement (see below), was also employing the Fund's lecturers;[26] the Committee's work virtually came to an end with Acland's resignation in 1890.[27]

University Extension

The co-operative movement with its aim of adult education was only one channel into which some of the followers of Green and Toynbee expended their energies. Another, which had wider implications, was the field of 'university extension'. The term had become current in Oxford from 1850 when William Sewell, a former Professor of Philosophy, had advocated in a pamphlet, *Suggestions for the Extension of the University,* at a time when a Royal Commission was investigating the university, that Oxford should expand its services throughout England: 'Though it may be impossible to bring the masses requiring education to the University, may it not be possible to carry the University to them?' Sewell's plan was to establish endowed professorships and lectureships in towns such as Birmingham and Manchester and to provide examinations locally. In this way, both the ancient universities 'would become the great centres and springs of education throughout the country, and would command the sympathy and affection of the nation at large'.[28] The only immediate result was the beginning of the Oxford and Cambridge Local Examinations in 1857, a move encouraged by Jowett and Temple as extending the university influence into schools (Roach, 1971, pp. 68ff.). At Oxford in 1865, a University Extension Committee was set up with the aim of providing a new college at Oxford for poor students and allowing undergraduates to live in lodgings without a college connexion. As we saw earlier, Green was closely associated with this venture.

The initial impetus for the movement came from James Stuart at Cambridge, who first established a system of local lectures in 1873 (Stuart, 1911, p. 172). The idea of a peripatetic university for working classes in large towns grew from a series of lectures by Stuart in and after October 1867 to the North of England Council for the Higher Education of Women (Ashby, 1955, p. 5; Welch, 1973, pp. 25-44). A Syndicate, with Stuart as Secretary, sent out university lecturers to large towns. Stuart's work, aimed at establishing local colleges, led to the foundation of University Colleges at Sheffield (1879), Liverpool (1879), and Nottingham (1880).

At Oxford, Jowett had taken up the cause in 1877. Giving evidence before the Royal Commission on the University of Oxford, he stated that there was considerable demand for adult education in the large towns and recommended that the University should be involved in it. He suggested that there should be a university extension office with a secretary paid by the University, and the creation of non-resident fellowships for those who undertook the work.

The time was ripe in 1878 for the formation of a Standing Committee of the Oxford Delegacy for Local Examinations, responsible for lectures in both England and Wales, but excluding London. Green was its active first Chairman and Acland the Secretary. Acland's first report to Committee stated that 'on the 25th of September [1878] Mr Johnson began at Birmingham his courses of twelve lectures and classes in Modern History. Professor Green was present on behalf of the University.'[29] The scheme conformed closely to Green's views of education: that the dissemination of knowledge would act both as a unifying force to all grades of society and as a means to the moralization of the people.

Oxford had entered the field during the worst part of the great economic depression, and the movement at first lost impetus: but from the mid-1880s onwards it played a leading part in the movement. Michael Sadler took over the Secretaryship from

Acland in 1885[30] after a reconstitution of the Delegacy by Dr
Percival and Jowett. Sadler's methods were direct. John Marriott,
a lecturer in Politics at New College who later succeeded Sadler as
Secretary, recalled that Sadler burst into his rooms at college and
opened with 'I want you to go and give a course of lectures at Bath'
(Marriott, 1946, p. 91).[31] During the next fifty-three years,
Marriott was to give no fewer than 10,000 lectures for the
movement. The cause attracted a great number of Green's and
Toynbee's followers, including W. J. Ashley, who had studied
economics with Toynbee, and W. A. S. Hewins, who became first
Director of the London School of Economics. Ashley, prevented by
family circumstances from pursuing his chief interest, philosophy,
graduated in history from Balliol in 1881 (Ashley, 1932, p. 23).
Impressed by the standard of historical scholarship on visiting
Göttingen the previous year, Ashley followed Toynbee in applying
the historical method to a study of economics.

Both Hewins and Ashley became important in assisting the
formulation of ideas about economic and social change in high
places (Shannon, 1976, p. 299). Ashley conducted some of the
earlier extension courses before becoming head of the school of
commerce at Birmingham University, the first of its kind, in 1901.
Whilst at Oxford, Hewins had been responsible, along with Sidney
Ball, tutor at St John's, and H. Llewellyn Smith, for establishing
a Social Science Club. Its main object was to question the
philosophy underlying orthodox economics, using modern historical and scientific methods to collect facts and disseminate
members' views.[32] Hewins developed systematic economic teaching
throughout the country. He found inspiration in the writings not
of economists, but of Kingsley, Ruskin and Carlyle. 'I wished,' he
explained in his autobiography, 'to make life worth living for all
these people – troubled with great anxieties owing to the break-
down of the industrial machine' (vol 1, 1929, p. 15). Others
prominent in the extension movement were H. J. Mackinder the
geographer, R. G. Collingwood, Cosmo Lang and Acland.

The rekindling of the movement was assisted by a number of
events relating to the social conditions of the time. In October
1883, the publication of *The Bitter Cry of Outcast London: An Inquiry
into the Condition of the Abject Poor* highlighted the depressed conditions under which a large section of London's population existed.
It quickened an interest initiated by the Christian Socialists and
demonstrated by Toynbee in aiding and educating the poor.
Besides the revival of the political ideas formulated by Hyndman
in the Social Democratic Federation and the birth of the Fabian
Society within two years (1882 and 1884), there was agitation for

a widening of the franchise after 1884. These events confirmed the belief of those taking part in university extension of the need for adult education, especially in the field of citizenship.

Toynbee had frequently stayed in the East End of London with Samuel Barnett, the vicar of St Jude's, Whitechapel (Barnett, 1918, vol. 1, p. 306). Both had been involved in the work of the Charity Organisation Society which had its offices in Commercial Road. Barnett, who had been a friend of Green's wife – then Charlotte Symonds – since childhood, was invited to Oxford to give a 'Toynbee lecture' in Autumn 1883. The aim of the lecture, which was to be part of a series, was to promote zeal for the study of social questions and to unite different classes in the work of social reform. The lecture was given in the rooms of his friend Sidney Ball at St John's on 17 November 1883, and was entitled 'Settlements of University Men in Great Towns'. Among those present were Sadler, Acland, J. A. Spender, E. T. Cook, A. Hope Hawkins and Cosmo Lang.[33] Barnett suggested a settlement of university men in the midst of some great industrial centre. A director who was also a teacher would be appointed to supervise the work of the settlement. Full and part-time members would be welcomed to help in a range of activities: as visitors for the Charity Organisation Society, managers of elementary schools, and members of committees concerned with such matters as sanitation. For those who could spare evenings only, there were clubs to be organized and teaching to be done. An important feature of the establishment from its beginning would be the accommodation made available for the extension classes. In Greenian language, Barnett stated that the settlement would afford 'an outlet for every form of earnestness. No man need be excluded from the service of the poor on account of his views.'

The excitement which the idea generated, especially among Balliol men, led to a meeting early in 1884 at that college,[34] which adopted resolutions by Acland and Ball for a university settlement in East London: Barnett was appointed as warden, with Sadler and Lang as the first two undergraduate secretaries. In January 1885 the appropriately named Toynbee Hall opened in Whitechapel as an experiment in social living. As one of its wardens expressed it: 'An educated and politically conscious working class and a socially conscious upper class were indispensable prerequisites of the democratic state. Toynbee Hall was established for the education of both' (Pimlott, 1953, p. 43).

Most of the Hall's residents and visitors[35] were attracted by the evangelical opportunities presented by the settlement to educate the working classes. Amongst those were Cyril Jackson, Robert

Morant, Acland, Sadler, Sir John Gorst, H. Llewellyn Smith and J. A. Spender.

Milner, until his death in 1925, took an active interest as Chairman of the Council.[36] A second generation included Haldane, Clement Attlee, R. H. Tawney and his brother-in-law William Beveridge. Beveridge, inspired by Caird's advice to investigate the causes of and cure for poverty, left Balliol to be sub-warden at Toynbee Hall in 1903. He shared courses of lectures with Tawney on industrial and political questions and campaigned widely for university settlements (Beveridge, 1953, pp. 24-31). Beveridge also ran election courses, served as a school manager in East End schools, supervised the students resident at Toynbee Hall (their accommodation was named after Balliol and Wadham Hall), and taught Greek to a small group of them.[37]

Barnett saw the settlement primarily as a Working Man's University and placed high priority on this work.[38] A proportion of the students attending the lectures were pupil-teachers, some of whom were awarded scholarships enabling them to proceed to universities. This was part of the policy of the Education Reform League, which originated from Toynbee Hall and which had amongst its objects the better training of teachers, the provision of evening classes in board schools, the bridging of the gap between elementary and secondary education, and the election of residents of the Hall to the School Board for London in order to implement these policies. Barnett appreciated that voluntary effort alone was not enough. He told his brother in 1895, 'As I get older I feel that every thing a Government can do is second to what it can do for education.'[39]

During the existence of the London Society for the Extension of University Teaching (1876-1902) a voluntary body eventually taken over by London University, Toynbee Hall became its most important centre with a wide range of courses being offered (Burrows, 1976, p. 8).[40] Thanks to Barnett's close links with the colleges, Oxford men, particularly those from Balliol, came to London to deliver lectures.

Sadler argued that services to learning and the community were complementary rather than incompatible. In a speech to the American National Conference, he confirmed the mutual benefits arising from extension. The movement had been accompanied by a concentration and development within the University itself. 'The movements for University Extension and University Intension are concurrent elements in the history of the University. And by itself superintending the diffusion of knowledge the University familiarizes the public with the idea of, and so protects the higher interests of, research' (Grier, 1952, p. 7).

Sadler envisaged four types of student to whom extension would appeal: those with the ability to pursue a university education but who for a variety of reasons were unable to do so; second, those who desired a liberal education; third, women who had few opportunities for higher education; and fourth, 'the great mass of the people each year more directly charged with the ultimate settlement of great problems, each year feeling a greater need for judgment and the judgment which comes from knowledge'. Sadler believed that a generous public provision of adult education was essential; meanwhile more immediate difficulties had to be solved. He wrote to F. S. Marvin, then an assistant inspector, a former Toynbee Hall resident and a friend of Sidney Ball, about an extension lecture to be given at Hebden Bridge, Yorkshire, the home of one of the few successful examples of a producers' cooperative (Harrison, 1961, p. 237):

> As for working men's audiences, we can only expect them
> when working men get up the lectures for themselves. This
> they can't do except when they have friends. Friends they only
> have in the Education Department and Co-operative Societies.
> These Departments are not always intelligently or energetically
> managed. When they are so managed, e.g. Oldham, Hebden
> Bridge, etc., our lectures succeed, in the hands of the right
> men, excellently. But it is no good being impatient. Things are
> moving slowly in the right direction.[41]

A good example of the success of this movement was to be found among the Durham miners during the years 1879 to 1887, where Mansbridge reported that the results were more comparable with a religious revival than with an educational undertaking (Mansbridge, 1940, p. 53).

Among the more optimistic developments from the 1887 Oxford Conference on Extension were the summer meetings, based on the American pattern, which consisted of month-long conferences: the first, at Oxford in the following year, attracted some 900 members (Draper, 1923, p. 121).[42] Unlike the meetings which were started at Cambridge two years later, Oxford welcomed all who cared to come, without reference to educational qualifications and whether extension students or not (Roberts, 1891, p. 88). There were other changes in the methods used in the courses given in the 1880s (Welch, 1976, pp. 41-2). To allow the audience a chance to discuss the points at leisure, planned courses extending over six terms often took the place of individual lectures, and women members especially were active in requesting syllabuses for use with difficult lectures (Grier, op. cit., p. 8). The substitution of the tutorial class for the lecture course was to become a feature of the Workers' Educational Association.

The Workers' Educational Association movement

Barnett, amongst others, remarked that fewer working people were attending extension lectures as wider provision was made. By the beginning of the present century the lectures had become more suited to the needs of the middle classes, as was reflected in the composition of the committees (Barnett, 1918, vol. 2, p. 108); they were condemned as condescending and patronizing by militant workers (Rowbotham, 1969-70, p. 71).

The main hope of the Oxford Delegacy – that audiences in industrial towns would be eager for instruction in economics – was not realized, although Acland had arranged local courses under the joint auspices of the Co-operative Union and the Delegacy in 1891.

Albert Mansbridge, whose own formal education had ended at fourteen, had gained much by attending extension lectures in London. His own background of co-operative and trade union activities (he was an employee of the Co-operative Wholesale Society) enabled him to analyse the failings of the extension movement and to suggest a solution. Working people, as Sadler had stated in the letter quoted above, proved in the main unresponsive to facilities devised for them by other people. Mansbridge considered that universities should be enlisted to inspire, not to create, the demand for education, but that this should not be confined merely to intellectual subjects. In other words, adult education should be concerned with every legitimate activity or expression of man. But this could not be achieved by working people alone. Mansbridge sought help from Oxford and Cambridge for the success of the new movement, to create the right development of mental and spiritual power (Mansbridge, 1940, pp. 54-5).[43]

As we have seen, the links between Oxford and the co-operative movement had been earlier established: the third element necessary to forward the plan, the trade union movement, had no direct educational tradition. Mansbridge had in 1899 given an extension address at Oxford on the relation of the co-operative movement to the education of citizens, analysing the reasons why the movement had not reached working men. Four years later in the last of three articles contributed to the *University Extension Journal*, Mansbridge suggested an alliance of the four extension authorities with co-operators and trade unionists.[44] The encouragement of Barnett,

Sadler, Marriott and Ball led to the formation of an Association for the Higher Education of Working Men, since 1906 known as the Workers' Educational Association (WEA), with Mansbridge as Secretary. A platform for its launching was provided by the summer school at Oxford in August 1903. A preliminary meeting of the Association in. May had established that its membership should consist of co-operators, trades union and university men in equal proportions.[45]

One of its primary aims was to develop extension teaching in a wider range of subjects which were not 'particularly co-operative', so as ultimately to constitute an alliance between the university and working-class movements (Price, 1924, p. 14). At the same time, in order to develop the intellectual capacity of workmen and enable them to reach the level required by extension, educational effort should be provided through co-operative classes, trades union meetings and reading circles.

The subsequent history of the WEA does not concern us here,[46] but the existence of the Association provided a ready appeal to those following the Green-Toynbee tradition. Some, like Sidney Ball, a Fabian and the recognized head of Socialism in the University, regarded the WEA as a logical outcome of this tradition (Ball, 1923, p. 242). At Balliol in April 1899 he had, together with Caird, shared a platform at a meeting in favour of Labour co-partnership. He also later conceived the idea of a university settlement at Oxford, Barnett House, which became a lively centre for the WEA. Another important figure in the movement was A. L. Smith, Master of Balliol (1916-24), who had been befriended by Green and Nettleship as an undergraduate and had absorbed their high ideals. His devotion to the college extended over fifty years. He taught history to generations of students, holding that the significance of the past lay in great moral truths. He offered his gardens for the first WEA Summer Conference in 1910, before Balliol and other colleges acted as hosts (Smith, 1920, p. 283). Smith was also Chairman of the important Adult Education Committee of the Ministry of Reconstruction, whose report was issued in 1919. It contained a survey of the history of the movement and discussed philosophical aspects of it. In a covering letter to the report addressed to Lloyd George, then Prime Minister, Smith wrote:

It is a truth brought out by the war that there is latent talent in the mass of our people, a capacity far ·beyond what was recognized, a capacity to rise to the conception of great issues and to face the difficulties of fundamental problems when

these are visualized in familiar form. They only require
teachers whom they can trust (quoted in Adam, 1956, p. 4).

R. H. Tawney, who played a leading role in the development of
the Association, rejected at this stage both traditional Fabianism
and Guild Socialism. He distrusted political or industrial
philosophies which were concerned with details of structure and
administration. As a Christian who had been influenced by idealist
thought, Tawney looked rather to human associations which
brought about alterations in morals and standards of conduct
which affected people's daily lives (Winter and Joslin, 1972, p. xix).
'Modern society,' he wrote in 1912, 'is sick through the absence of
a moral ideal.' If the external arrangements of society appeared to
contradict what men felt to be morally right, this could only be
changed by 'a deepening of our individual sense of sin, and by
objectifying our morality' (ibid., p. 9). It was Tawney who suggested to his Balliol friend, William Temple, that the latter should
attend the first national conference of the Association. Temple
subsequently became its first President (1908-24). Both he and
Tawney had been influenced by Caird's teaching: their work at
Toynbee Hall convinced them of the need for an educational
system which was relevant to citizens and the moral well-being of
the state. Temple saw the WEA as a 'brotherhood' in pursuit of
knowledge, a national starting point for the realization of the better
life. He argued in later years that the real root of social problems
as seen by the leading minds in the Labour movement was spiritual. 'What Labour is resenting is not so much poverty, short of
destitution, but rather the insult to the personality of the poor man
.... Until education has done far more work than it has yet had
an opportunity of doing, you cannot have society organized on the
basis of justice' (Iremonger, 1948, p. 78).

The legacy of Christian Socialism can be seen during the early
days of the WEA. A private conference was held at Balliol in
November 1905 to examine 'the possibility of putting the work
done for working men at Oxford in touch with the Delegacy'
(Lowe, 1972, p. 54). Tawney, Percival (then Bishop of Hereford).
Barnett, Ball and Mansbridge were at the meeting. A suitable
platform for the expression of reforming views was provided by a
Conference on Working Class and Educational Organizations at
the extension Summer Meeting at Oxford on 10 August 1907.
Bishop Charles Gore (see Part 2, Chapter 9), Tawney's tutor and
a follower of Green, took the chair.

The subject for discussion was 'What Oxford Can Do for
Working People'. Ball introduced the subject for the University,

quoting Green and Toynbee in his preamble. He quoted from Toynbee's address at his last Co-operative Congress in 1882 on the education of co-operators: 'Enthusiasm can only be kindled by two things – an ideal which takes the imagination by storm, and a definite intelligible plan for carrying out that ideal into practice'. Ball also quoted Green's lecture on the work to be done by the New Oxford High School for Boys that 'common education is the true social leveller' and looked forward to the time when the education of gentlemen became a phrase that would have lost its meaning 'because the sort of education which alone makes the gentlemen in any true sense will be within the reach of all' (Ball, op. cit., pp. 253-4). It is interesting to observe that Ball, in preparing his talk, wrote to Barnett in March 1907 for 'any statement of the experience of Toynbee Hall in connexion with the "higher teaching" of working men': in fact it was Tawney who eventually supplied the background information for both Ball and the presenter of the other paper, Walter Neild.[47]

At the conference it was agreed that seven members of the University and 'seven representatives of labour' nominated by the WEA should meet to discuss the problem of the wider dissemination of education. Ball, Marriott, A. L. Smith and Zimmern, the latter joint secretary of the Committee with Mansbridge, were among the representatives. Their first meeting was held at Balliol on 27 December 1907. The report *Oxford and Working-class Education*, published in 1908, recommended an extension of educational opportunities, to unite learning broadly based on the facts of experience with theories developed by scholars.[48] Because of the contacts which had by now been built up between universities and working-class movements through university extension, co-operatives and settlements, it was possible to stimulate the demand for higher education among the working classes. The report, which excited much attention at the time, was largely written by Tawney (Terrill, 1974, p. 38), although the hands of other members of the Committee, notably A. L. Smith, can be discerned (Davis, 1963, p. 38). Its main recommendation – the setting up of a joint committee in Oxford with equal numbers of WEA and Delegacy members to organize tutorial classes – was adopted by Congregation at Oxford in October 1908. The Oxford model, whereby working men were for the first time associated with the actual administration of and part of a university's work (Mansbridge, 1913, p. 35) was followed by other universities.

Before the Conference took place, Mansbridge had approached the Oxford Delegacy with a view to establishing two experimental university tutorial classes, one organized by the Rochdale branch of the WEA and the other at Longton, Staffordshire, to be set up by a group of mainly industrial workers who had been attending extension lectures there. Such classes required regular attendance by their members, and tutorials rather than lectures were the basis of the course. Membership was largely made up of working men and women, many of whom were trades union leaders and representatives of other working class organizations. The responsibility for admitting students and managing local details rested with the Association. In nearly all cases, the general management of the work and the appointment of lecturers were in the hands of a joint committee, consisting of an equal number of university and Association representatives. Courses were mainly in the field of economic history and theory or industrial history, but some offered English literature and natural science.[49]

R. H. Tawney, then a lecturer in economics at Glasgow University, was chosen as the first tutor, and in January 1908 started tutorial classes at Longton and Rochdale. Tawney's religious and educational view that education was a spiritual emanicipation of the individual harmonized with Mansbridge's. His selfless dedication to the work was impressive. L. V. Gill, the local secretary at Longton, reported to Mansbridge on one of the earliest ventures:

> About the class and Tawney, it is a case of love at first sight on both sides. His lectures are brilliant, illuminating, simple, lucid, eloquent – just the very thing, something between a lesson and a lecture. He obviously has a big grasp of his subject and yet a penetrating knowledge of his audience. He lectures each time for an hour, then an hour or more sustained, unflagging question and discussion. He is perfectly happy – in every sense – here.[50]

These classes were an immediate success. Within four years there were 117 of them throughout England. In two respects Tawney's influence was significant. First, he became not only an educational but also a political figure in the areas in which he taught. The secretary of the Rochdale class remarked in his report for 1909-10, 'he [Tawney] has established for himself a position in the town, especially among the Labour men, and his withdrawal from Rochdale would be looked upon as a calamity' (quoted in Terrill, op. cit., p. 42) Second, his educational philosophy was manifested throughout his teaching and influenced other extension bodies, such as London, who were involved in tutorial work.[51] As a contributor to the Association's magazine remarked in 1911, 'Birkenhead, Birmingham and Swindon, Belfast, London and

111

Longton, are at the moment grappling with R. H. Tawney upon the need for a unifying centre for ethical precept' (quoted in Winter and Joslin, op. cit., p. 12).

The university tutorial class movement continued to attract a line of scholars who were directly influenced by Green, Toynbee and Caird. A. D. Lindsay, Master of Balliol 1924-49, who studied under Henry Jones and Edward Caird, serves as a typical example. He had, under his tutor A. L. Smith, been introduced to working-class education and knew Temple and Tawney as fellow Balliol undergraduates. From the first decade of the century until his absorption in plans for setting up a new university at Keele some forty years later, Lindsay was involved in both tutorial class and WEA work in Staffordshire.[52] He became a joint secretary of the Association in 1911 and influenced a generation of tutors by his example. He educated, in a wide sense, the classes with which he was associated. In turn, as Lindsay's biographer mentions, his students' needs became part of his thinking about education and this led him to reformulate his philosophy. He saw his task as trying to help class members understand and answer their fundamental questions. He once told them:

> I am sure that the real beginning of philosophy is when one really does feel some urgent problem has got to be solved. It is not the business of philosophy to play about with jolly little puzzles .... The real thing in philosophy is to try and understand the kinds of things in men's outlook with which the modern world is faced (Scott, 1971, p. 70).

The summer schools, which were an important feature of tutorial classes and which brought students into the universities, afforded the opportunity of an exchange of views with college tutors. The first school was held at Balliol in July and August 1910, and Lindsay lectured at almost every summer school until he left Oxford.

The dedication of a large band of men, particularly those of Balliol and New College, to the aims of the Association had far-reaching effects. To quote one writer on the subject:

> By the leaders of the nation, watching the trend of working class opinion and policy, it was recognized that many official calculations and assumptions had been upset: it could, for instance, no longer be maintained that there was no demand for higher education among workers (Iremonger, 1948, p. 86).

Not all academics were satisfied with what had been achieved. A. E. Zimmern, an early New College recruit, and an honorary treasurer to the Association, writing at the end of the First World War on 'The Evolution of the Citizen', considered that more adult education of itself was not a sufficient answer:

The two spheres, that of education and that of religion, not only overlap, but interpenetrate one another. The tendency to divide them, to classify our moral and intellectual life into separate and watertight compartments, is precisely one of the curses of our present dissatisfaction and *malaise*. The life of the spirit is a seamless garment, not a miscellaneous patchwork composed of Sunday services and week-night Committees, of sermons and lectures and evening classes, spiced with a dash of modern 'advanced' sociology and fiction. This incoherence, this indiscriminating and irregular appetite, this insensitiveness of the intellectual palate, constitutes a substantial aggravation of our condition (Zimmern, 1923, pp. 33-4).

But against this could be set more positive achievements. A. L. Smith declared in a much-quoted statement that twenty-five per cent of the essays written by WEA students were as good as those done by men who obtained first-class honours in the final school of modern history at Oxford (Mansbridge, 1920, p. 40). The Association's work was recognized and financially encouraged by the Board of Education. H. A. L. Fisher, President of the Board, whose views will be discussed below, wrote to Temple shortly after his appointment, 'All power to your elbow with the WEA. I shall want to help you in any way possible' (Iremonger, op. cit., p. 86). It is interesting to note also that the two sympathetic H.M. Inspectors who were appointed to inspect the work were J. Dover Wilson,[53] later Professor of Education at King's College, London, and A. E. Zimmern, who was an inspector at the Board of Education 1912-15. When the latter resigned, his place was taken by Joseph Owen, the only working-man student who had proceeded to Oxford in connexion with the extension movement. A special report on the classes was prepared for the Board of Education in 1911 by J. W. Headlam, H.M. Inspector, and Professor L. T. Hobhouse, the latter one of the original members of the Inner Ring. Fourteen classes, including those at Longton and Rochdale, were inspected. The report concluded that: 'The treatment both of History and Economics is scientific and detached in character. As regards the standard reached, there are students whose essays compare favourably with the best academic work.'[54]

The Association fitted well into the framework of idealist thought. It provided exceptional opportunities for breaking down barriers between universities and the cities in which they were located. It also enabled many Oxford men in the Balliol-Toynbee Hall tradition, such as Tawney, to combine effectively political and scholarly interests with their moral commitments (Winter and Joslin, op. cit., p.xv). It was a justification of their faith, as expressed by R. B. Haldane, a member of the Council of the WEA, that it was neither capital nor labour which created wealth, but mind (Ashby and Anderson, 1974, p. 11).

The London Ethical Society

Alongside the many idealists who were involved in practical and educational activities, there were other followers of Green and Caird who regretted the relative neglect in these schemes of the philosophical view of the nature and ends of human life. It was the promotion and dissemination of ethics to a wider audience which drew together the Glasgow and Balliol philosophers in London in the mid-1880s.

Samuel Barnett and his wife at Toynbee Hall showed little direct interest in this aspect of the work, but a group of young residents and visitors, notably J. H. Muirhead, James Bonar, and J. Murray Macdonald, took up the cause. An Ethical Culture movement had been started in the USA a decade previously by Felix Adler. One of its leading members, Dr Stanton Coit, came to live briefly at Toynbee Hall in January 1886, and discussed with the group – now enlarged to include Bernard Bosanquet and J. S. Mackenzie – the formation of a similar society in London.

By July, Bonar and Muirhead had drafted a leaflet stating the aims of an Ethical Society. Members would subscribe to the view 'that the moral and religious life of Man is capable of a rational justification and explanation apart from authority and tradition. They believe that there is at present great need for the teaching of a reasoned-out doctrine on this subject, especially where old sanctions and principles have lost their hold' (quoted in Spiller, 1934, p. 2). The challenging tone of this statement was later modified. There was a need for an exposition of the actual principles of social morality, generally acknowledged but imperfectly analysed in current language, and the presentation of the ideal of human progress. Therefore it was a further duty of the Society 'to use every endeavour to arouse the community at large to the importance of testing every Social, Political, and Educational question by moral and religious principles'.

The first meeting to consider ways and means took place on 20 November 1866 in University Hall, Gordon Square. Muirhead read a paper entitled 'The Ethical Point of View'.[55] On the following evening, the first course of twelve Sunday lectures on 'Morality and Modern Life' began at Toynbee Hall. Speakers included Mackenzie, Muirhead, C. S. Loch, Bosanquet, Henry Jones, and Barnett himself. Muirhead (who became the Secretary) mentions in his autobiography that the Society's Scriptures were summed up in Bradley's *Ethical Studies:*

> In morality what we know we feel or see and cannot doubt. There is nothing to believe against appearances. But in religion, despite of appearances, we have to believe that some thing is real. We must have an inward assurance that the reality is above the facts, and that we must carry this out against the facts, in which we cannot see the inward reality, and seem to see what is contrary thereto (Muirhead, 1942, p. 75).

In the light of such a statement the Society hoped to be, and was, successful in attracting people from a wide range of interests. Besides academics, the Society's committee consisted of economists, businessmen, schoolteachers, Government officials, members of the Fabian Society and the Charity Organisation Society. Some of the eminent Presidents included William Wallace, Sidgwick, Leslie Stephen and Haldane. The work of the Society was directed towards organizing systematic ethical instruction in connexion with working men's colleges, clubs and co-operative societies. It was also concerned with university extension and the education of the young.

For the first year of the Society's existence, the key posts were filled by idealists. Caird was President, Muirhead the Secretary, Bonar the Treasurer and Bosanquet served as a committee member. Caird's interest in the Society was not surprising. Like his friend Green, he was a radical in politics, religion and philosophy. As Professor of Moral Philosophy at Glasgow since 1866, he had preached to large and enthusiastic audiences of students his view that morality was not a hopeless struggle against the overwhelming odds of a nature innately and irretrievably corrupt but might be seen as a series of hard-won triumphs and a sure advance. This view was based on a history of philosophy which was obviously Hegelian in origin; namely, that modern civilization had learnt the lessons from atomistic and individualistic criticisms of Greek monism and was now characterized by a more mature form of monism (Davie, 1964, p. 330).

Caird brought from Scotland a more ardently Hegelian philosophy than that of his contemporaries, Green and Nettleship, and actively promoted it through various channels. At Glasgow it had already found one expression in the founding of a society, the Witenagemote, in the winter of 1879, which resembled in many ways the Old Mortality mentioned earlier (see Part 1). Meetings were held in Caird's lodgings at Glasgow University, where students discussed a range of philosophical issues. This was an outcome of Caird's stated endeavour in teaching, namely to plant a few 'germinative' ideas in his pupils' minds (*DNB*, p. 2548). These students, whom Caird called 'his young lions' (Jones and Muirhead, 1921, p. 90) regarded the master with reverence and affection and propagated Caird's views to a considerable extent after leaving university. Amongst the members were Muirhead, later Professor of Philosophy at Birmingham; J. S. Mackenzie, Professor at Cardiff; W. P. Ker, Professor of Poetry at Oxford; Henry Jones, Professor at Glasgow; and Pringle-Pattison, Professor at Edinburgh; many of these later contributed to the activities of the Ethical Society.

Caird saw the Society as an opportunity not only for encouraging his old pupils and those of Green, but also for venturing into a field in which he had little previous experience, that of practical politics.[56] He had for some years been engaged in writing a second volume on *A Critical Account of the Philosophy of Kant*, eventually published in 1889, in which he now developed some of these ideas. Caird agreed with Kant that the full development of the capacities of a human being was only possible in a society where an individual was able to transcend and transform his natural ties, as individual morality transforms and transcends the rational instincts: 'The very anticipation of a higher moral unity, however vague, leads to a kind of emancipation of the individual from the State' (vol. 2, p. 376).

These ideas were developed in two addresses to the Ethical Society, on 'The Moral Aspects of the Economic Problem' (1888) and 'Individualism and Socialism' (1897). In the latter Caird envisaged the aim of social development as when man is put in possession of his true freedom as a spiritual being. This could be found by emancipating individuals from direct social pressure and by limiting the worst forms of competition and the exploitation of the weak by the strong. To achieve this, it would be necessary to seek a form of competition 'which is only the natural process whereby the individual is pressed up or down, till he finds his proper place – the place in which he can best serve the community'. How this could best be accomplished by the Ethical Society was questioned by Bosanquet. He saw its object not as moral suasion but as enabling audiences to be put in a position to help themselves. The Society, he believed, should aim at organizing the material of a noble life so as to bring it within the reach of all. But since there was a danger of the Society's emulating the semi-religious American model, Bosanquet warned members in an open letter: 'Teach moral philosophy (among other things) by all means; but for Heaven's sake do not mix up your teaching with your preaching' (Muirhead, 1935, p. 49). Lecturers had the difficult task of keeping a balance between teaching and sermonizing at Sunday meetings.

One of the contributors to the work of the Society was William Wallace, a reserved and retiring man, who had succeeded Green as Whyte Professor of Moral Philosophy in 1882. Much to the surprise of the committee members, Wallace accepted an invitation to speak at a Sunday evening meeting and continued to do so over a period of ten years. He summed up the purpose of the Society in the course of a Gifford lecture on 'The Ethical Movement in Religion' (1895) as follows:

A few human beings linked in action for the purpose of bettering the general standard of ethical feeling, may seem rather a subject of jest. But they are one indication of a widely prevailing want of satisfaction with the results both of religious and scientific teaching; and the initiation of an effort after something better, which the historian of the future will not count unworthy of regard (Wallace, 1898. p. 61).

Some members saw the Society as a continuation of the practical direction of social effort advocated by Green. One of the most active of the Society's supporters was the philosopher Bernard Bosanquet. Green had said that he was 'the best equipped man in the College', paying the compliment in 1872 of asking Bosanquet to take over his course of lectures on Aristotle's *Ethics* (Bradley, 1924, p. 2). Bosanquet remained a lifelong admirer of Green. Apart from spending five years as Professor of Moral Philosophy at St Andrews, a post for which he was recommended by Haldane, Bosanquet's activities were centred in and around London (Muirhead, 1942, p. 102).

A contemporary has pointed out that although F. H. Bradley was undoubtedly the pioneer in the new development of idealistic philosophy, Bosanquet more than any other was prepared to seize on its implications and carry them out in every field of thought and practice with relentless logic.[57] He had been drawn to the work of the Charity Organization Society by his elder brother, Charles, a founder and its first secretary, and C. S. Loch, the second secretary and a Balliol contemporary.[58] Bosanquet lectured on behalf of

117

various movements of a philosophical nature and, as we have noted, was a founder member of the Ethical Society; but he did not consider that the concept of the settlement (e.g., Toynbee Hall) provided any solution to those wishing to advance citizenship. In an essay on 'The Duty of Citizenship' (1891), Bosanquet wrote that he was not against settlements, but

> against the glorification of the settlement life as one specially
> set apart for the service of men. Here, as throughout, we must
> demand that the specialization which is an indispensable
> feature of modern life shall not isolate us from the citizen
> spirit, the pulse-beat of the social heart (1895, p. 26).

For Bosanquet, the higher life lay in the opposite direction: in the home, the family and the commonplace neighbourhood. Similarly, the strain of practicality is found in Bosanquet's philosophical writings, notably *The Philosophical Theory of the State.* Recognizing that social psychology had advanced since Green's times, he set out to apply conceptions of recent psychological theory of state coercion and of the General Will, and to explain the relation between social philosophy and social psychology. In the Preface to the work, Bosanquet wrote, 'It is my conviction, indeed, that a better understanding of fundamental principles would very greatly contribute to the more rational handling of practical problems' (1899, p. vii).

Some of Bosanquet's lectures to the Ethical Society have survived, fortunately reprinted in his *Essays and Addresses* (1889). They deal with topics such as 'Some Socialistic Features of Ancient Society'. 'How to Read the New Testament', and 'Individual and Social Reforms'. This last throws some light on his attitude towards educational reform; in particular, Bosanquet examines the question in a larger context. The operation of law consists in ratifying by the sanction of public power certain expressions and resolutions of the public mind in so far as the individuals who constitute it co-operate for social judgment or for social action. The question of educational reform cannot be seen in isolation from other issues. The cry for such reform then prevailing, Bosanquet forecast, would probably lead to local self-government, throwing upon citizens in each locality responsibility and powers for the education of their children. He hoped that 'a circle of men and women of the wage-earning class who have had something of a humanizing and formative training' would come forward as managers of their schools (1899, p. 28).

But educational reform consisted of more than organizational details. Schools should become concerned with aesthetic awareness in art and handicraft. This would lead to a citizenship that meant a common life worth living and would help break down 'the brutal exclusiveness of classes'. Ultimately, these educational influences would affect industry itself in two ways: the public would see that the products of handicraft were an expression of the life of crafts-men, and that production cannot be divorced from a sense of duty towards the producer. It would also place the craftsmen in higher public esteem.

> Thus our two examples coalesce in a practical and practicable ideal: we look forward to a society organized in convenient districts, in which men and women pursuing their different callings will live together with care for one another, and with all the essentials, the same education, the same enjoyments, the same capacities. These men and women will work together in councils and on committees: and while fearlessly employing stringent legal powers in the public interest, yet will be aware, by sympathy and experience, of the extreme flexibility and complication of modern life which responds so unexpectedly to the most simple interference: they will have pride in their schools and their libraries, in their streets and their dwellings, in their workshops and their warehouses. In such a society it appears to me to be a mere question of practical efficiency how far the organizations of labour should be the salient servants of the State or as they are now its moral trustees (ibid., p. 45).

Bosanquet's stress on aesthetics sprang from his own interests in the topic. He had met William Morris whilst at Oxford, and later translated Hegel's *Aesthetik* (1882-8). His own *A History of Aesthetics* was praised by A. C. Bradley as being the work of the only British philosopher of the first rank who had dealt fully with this part of philosophy (Bradley, 1924, p. 8). Bosanquet himself was aware of his presumptuousness in enunciating definite views on certain social problems without practical experience (Bosanquet, 1889, p. v.), but his contribution to the Ethical Society was considerable. Besides lecturing, Bosanquet, together with other idealists such as D. G. Ritchie, Mackenzie and Muirhead, reached a wider audience through contributing to various volumes of the Ethical Library, on themes such as political and social ethics, humanism and the civilization of Christendom.[59]

For a number of reasons, the London Ethical Society decided in October 1897 to carry on its work by forming a new body called the London School of Ethics and Social Philosophy.[60] Growing disquiet had been voiced by Bosanquet and his colleagues about the way in which the ethical movement was drifting towards positivism. From the winter of 1889-90, weekly evening lectures were begun at Essex Hall, off the Strand. The Society was responsible for providing lecturers, but the lectures were given under the auspices of the University Extension Scheme, which had already formed a centre at Essex Hall. As this arrangement restricted the scope of the Society's activities, in 1891 the lecture courses were taken over and run entirely by the Society.

One of the most notable Hegelian members of the Society, D. G. Ritchie, was converted to Fabianism, a step which Bosanquet could not contemplate (Muirhead, 1935, p. 74). To save the Society from further fragmentation, Bosanquet and Muirhead called a conference in March 1897, as a result of which an independent School of Ethics and Social Philosophy was established under its director, E. J. Urwick. It was to cater for the large number of people in London who required philosophical lectures but who were unable to attend university. The Society's acitivities were not confined to lecturing. Among the Bosanquet papers, there survives a letter from A. C. Bradley, Professor of English Language and Literature at Glasgow, assessing the examination papers of a ladies' class following a study of Aristotle's *Poetics*.[61]

When in 1899 the London University Commission was receiving new applications for admission to the University, Bosanquet advanced the claims of the School for recognition, primarily on the grounds that there was inadequate provision in London for the teaching of philosophy and kindred subjects. When this application was refused, Bosanquet replied in a spirited public memorandum, pointing out that:

> It did not occur to the Committee that a fear of undue competition would be aroused by an offer to take part in such a work. If teaching were needed, for example, dealing with the Ethics, or the Republic, or with the ethical or social philosophy of Kant and his successors, or with others of a large number of subjects which a teaching University would naturally attempt to deal with, the School might very probably be able to furnish one or more of the courses needed, which otherwise, perhaps, it might be impossible to furnish at all.[62]

Finally, on the reconstitution of London University, the School of Ethics and Social Philosophy was taken over by the London School of Economics, Urwick becoming its first Professor of Social Philosophy.[63]

Unlike the other educational movements in which the idealists participated, the Ethical Society was much more explicit in its evangelistic role. It hoped not only to educate its audiences and classes in universal principles of well-doing and well-being, but also to provide a blueprint, if not at all times apparently clear, for change. As its first Report of July 1886 stated:

It holds that truer views of the nature of human life must issue in juster laws and political institutions. It holds, moreover, that the improvement of the present surroundings of man is an indispensable condition of the moral welfare of all. In this sense the Society may be said to aim at political and social reforms (quoted in Spiller, 1934, p. 6).

University reform

We have already noted that Green and a number of his contemporaries stressed the importance of forging links between the university and its local community. The growing demand for higher education in the 1860s and 1870s provided an opportunity for re-examining the role which Oxford and Cambridge could play in fostering new institutions. A change in attitude towards the provinces was in the first instance necessary (Armytage, 1955, p. 216).

The lead was given in the first place by Jowett, who early in 1872 raised a committee at Balliol to consider how the benefits of university education could be extended to other places (Ward, 1965, p. 285). In September of that year, Dr Percival, then head of Clifton School, published an open letter to the Oxford colleges entitled 'The Connexion of the Universities and the Great Towns'. Percival was anxious to involve the colleges in founding new universities in order to avoid local influences, which would tend towards providing the practical wants of the neighbourhood but which would 'produce little or nothing in the way of liberal culture' (Temple, 1921, p. 261).[64] One of the main features of Percival's plan was that the wealthier colleges should convert some of their non-resident Fellowships into Professorships, to be held in towns such as Birmingham, Bristol and Leeds; each appointment would be for a term of ten or twelve years. Suitable buildings would be provided by the towns and all students who attended courses of instruction and passed the appropriate university examinations should be entitled to a degree.

Such a scheme appealed to Jowett and Green especially. A Royal Commission was at that time investigating Oxford and Cambridge colleges, and a far-reaching programme of university reform seemed possible. Balliol went further than Percival's scheme, putting forward a plan for the foundation of ten colleges in addition to those at Manchester, Durham and Newcastle. There was, however, much criticism and jealousy amongst the Oxford colleges at the prospect of giving away college funds, and the scheme had only a limited success. Perhaps the most notable achievement was the foundation of the University College at Bristol in 1876, which was initially financed by Balliol and New Collegei. Advice, experience and encouragement were provided for the new institutions. When Firth College, Sheffield (which was later to be a university in its own right and which promoted technological studies) advertised for a Principal in 1881, Green and Jowett used their influence to secure the post for a promising Balliol student, Viriamu Jones (Morgan, 1908, p. 306).[65] Green served as one of the academic members of the Council and was succeeded first by Toynbee and then by Percival (Jones, 1921, p. 57).

Two distinguishing features of the idealist movement in relation to the greater provision of university places were the reform of existing institutions and the championing of women's education. Looking at Germany in 1885, James Bryce, then a Professor of Law at Oxford, pointed out that that country, with a population of 45 million, had 24,187 students, whereas England, with a population of 26 million, had only 5,500. 'Nothing,' he wrote, 'could more clearly illustrate the failure of the English system to reach and secure all classes' (quoted in Armytage, 1955, p. 233). Giving evidence before the Royal Commission on Oxford University in October 1877, Jowett had advanced views which if implemented would have anticipated some of Bryce's later criticisms. His sympathy for the poorer student was seen in the proposal to provide a hall, library and system of tutoring for non-collegiate men. New studies and the extension of teaching to other towns and other institutions were also recommended:

> Oxford may be justly charged with having failed to encourage
> new subjects hitherto. It is not here, but at the British
> Museum, or at the Royal Institution in London, that some
> new study is begun (Abbott and Campbell, 1897, vol. 2,
> p. 127).

The professions could be brought nearer to the University by establishing scholarships in the studies preparatory to them. Green also appeared before the Commission, stating the need to democratize the election of Fellows and to appoint a number of

Readers to promote the attainment of a higher standard of learning; the study of new subjects would thus be facilitated without adding to the existing professoriate.[66]

Other idealists were later prominent in pursuing internal reforms. Sidney Ball, for instance, played a leading part at Oxford in two conferences of members of Congregation held in 1903 and 1904 where problems connected with the better co-ordination of teaching resources were discussed in detail. He was also a leading figure in the formation of a University Reform Association in 1907 which examined the power of the Board of Faculties and looked to the encouragement of research (Ball, 1923, pp. 196-7).

The admission of women on an equal footing with men was another of the reforms which was sought. F. D. Maurice and Charles Kingsley, within the Christian Socialist movement, had provided an opportunity for the higher education of women with the establishment of Queen's College, Harley Street, London, in 1848. We have already noted the founding of Bristol University, where men and women were equally admitted. Bryce had played an active part in the founding of Girton College, Cambridge (1873), which was originally opened at Hitchin in 1869; he also lectured in Greek History at both colleges (Fisher, 1927, p. 115). Percival was one of the prime movers in establishing of Somerville College, Oxford (Temple, 1921, p. 76). The main campaign, however, was fought in Scotland. Single courses of lectures in botany had been given to women at Glasgow University as early as 1845, but without making much impact. Edward Caird, shortly after his appointment to the Chair of Moral Philosophy, campaigned in 1868 for the full admission of women to degree courses. As a constant advocate of a fuller life for all, Caird also actively worked for better conditions for women in factories and in the professions (Jones and Muirhead, 1921, pp. 118-25).

Together with other young professors – Nichol, Veitch and Young – Caird and his brother John offered lecture courses for women, at the same time attempting to persuade Senate to admit them to the University. In 1877, Caird presented Senate with a petition from the recently-formed Association for the Higher Education of Women, asking for the institution of examinations. By the following year, certificates were being issued and permission to use classrooms had been granted (Green, 1969, pp. 115ff.). When the Association for the Higher Education of Women was finally incorporated into the Queen Margaret College in 1883, Caird was appointed to its governing body and delivered lectures there (Jones and Muirhead, op. cit., p. 99). In February 1892, a year before Caird left Glasgow for Oxford, women were admitted as matriculated students to the University for the first time. His campaign had lasted twenty-five years in all.

New universities

The spread of extension teaching was an important force in establishing new colleges in the 1870s (Mackie, 1954, p. 300). At Exeter, Colchester, Reading, Leicester and Southampton, local colleges flourished. On a more ambitious scale, a university college was set up at Sheffield in 1879, where the Firth College was the natural outcome of the Cambridge Extension Classes. A similar development took place at Nottingham two years later (Bryce Report, 1895, I, p. 253). Other university institutions, such as the federal Victoria University in Manchester and Liverpool (1880), continued to fulfil their community role, offering, for example, lectures for teachers both in their own teaching subjects and for those wishing to continue with their studies.

One stumbling block to the realization of 'local' universities springing from the extension movement was the attitude of the Treasury towards providing annual grants. Arthur Acland convened a meeting of local organizers of extension teaching in June 1890 with the object of obtaining financial support for two colleges, then known as the University Extension College, Reading, and the Exeter Technical and University Extension College. A deputation met Lord Cranbook, the Lord President of the Council, in December, 1891; it stressed the novel nature of these institutions, which catered for small centres of population, stating that they 'should be placed in a position to offer a well-balanced curriculum, for as they grow they will almost certainly become models for similar institutions in other parts of the country'.[67]

By the following August, Acland himself, by the turn of political fortunes, was Vice-President of the Committee of Council on Education, and the Reading College was officially recognized (Exeter was established in 1893). Its first Principal, H. J. Mackinder, had entered Christ Church, Oxford, in 1880, the same year as Michael Sadler, and they became close friends. Mackinder was an enthusiastic Oxford extension lecturer from 1885, speaking up and down the country on the 'new geography' of which he was the leading exponent (*DNB*, vol. 2, p. 2772). He regretted that the intelligent working people in extension audiences were more interested in scientific analysis than the spirit of historical method. If the historian could 'throw off the academical gown ... he would have little to fear from scientific competition'. Mackinder blamed this timidity and lack of initiative on the fact that lecturers were copying the procedure of the old universities and 'because we have not selected an idea on which to frame our methods of exposition and our curricula. In a democratic age, what nobler idea on which to build a system of historical and economic teaching than the training of citizens?' (1893, pp. 247-8).

He collaborated with Sadler in writing *University Extension: Has It A Future?* in 1890. It was their recommendation in the book, that state grants should be given to extension authorities, which led to the meeting called by Acland and others on this topic.[68] Mackinder's energy was boundless, for in 1895 he was, in his own words, 'a pluralist', holding simultaneously posts at Oxford, the London School of Economics (of which he eventually became Director) and Reading. He left no autobiography, but in his major work *Democratic Ideals and Reality* (1919), he endeavoured to consider, in the light of historical events, how to adjust ideals of freedom to the realities of the world. His view of geography was influenced by his friendship with Milner; together with other young Imperialists, they formed a club in 1902 called the Coefficients, in order to explore how each department of national life could be raised to its highest possible efficiency (Mackenzie, 1977, p. 190).[69] Mackinder saw geography as a unity, as men living in a world that cannot be broken into regions. He applied the subject to the problems of society and state, putting forward the need for planning long before this term became generally recognized. Mackinder was also a trained historian and regarded geography, history and religious knowledge as the three subjects where we learn where we are in space, in time and before God. To him, geography was the prime element in the 'new humanism', and in schools the teaching of it should be brought to bear on the training of citizens. At a higher level, he envisaged that departments of geography at universities should be schools of concrete philosophy (Gilbert, 1977, pp. 174-5).

The success of Reading College in particular was largely due to Mackinder's far-sightedness in establishing an institution which stimulated public interest in higher education.[70] The University was to be, in Mackinder's words, 'the focus of local patriotism'. It provided facilities for adult students as well as for pupils fresh from secondary schools, and a training college was established for pupil-teachers. The university extension system which had flourished in the town for five years was combined with science and art classes. This co-ordination of educational agencies within a town was especially praised by the Bryce Commission on Secondary Education which reported in 1895 (Report, III, pp. 253-4). Captain W. de W. Abney, the Director for the Science and Art

Department, held it out to be a model for others to follow. The
project had only been made possible because Sadler, as Steward of
Christ Church, obtained financial support for Mackinder from the
College. It was a piquant moment when Sadler as a member of the
Bryce Commission asked Abney 'One of the Oxford Colleges took
the initiative, did it not?' to receive the answer 'Yes, Christ Church'
(Evidence, II, Q. 1337-8).

Such enterprise was not generally emulated by others of the new
university colleges. Many followed as Mackinder had indicated the
Oxford or Cambridge traditions, offering humanities courses and
with no clear idea of their purpose. The federal principle, which
was favoured in the north of England, pointed the way towards a
more unified system, but fell into disfavour after internal dissen-
sions between the various parties (Armytage, 1955, pp. 245-6). By
the turn of the present century, the autonomous civic college was
firmly established. To idealists, however, the universities were still
out of the reach of the majority of people. As Tawney later wrote
about this period:

> It was necessary that the whole subject of University education
> should be discussed from a new angle, and that the relation of
> the Universities to the State, to the new classes knocking at
> their door, and to the educational system as a whole, should
> be revised (Green, 1969, pp. 122-3).

Many thought that it was Oxford which should give the lead.

There were a number of different and sometimes overlapping
groups which called for reform within the Oxford colleges. After
1903 the WEA movement had sharpened up some of the issues
which confronted universities. William Temple, then a Fellow at
Queen's and deeply involved in the Association's affairs, was,
according to his biographer, largely responsible for the 'Six Tutors
Campaign' (Iremonger, 1948, p. 89). Besides the influence of the
Fabian Society which was growing at Oxford, a small but
influential Catiline Club, consisting of younger dons with a 'leftish
slant', was formed. The group consisted of W. H. Fyfe, Richard
Livingstone,[71] J. L. Myers,[72] A. E. Zimmern and Temple. They
met weekly at an 'Unholy Lunch' and hatched the plot which
culminated on 24 July 1907 when Bishop Gore of Birmingham
called in the House of Lords for a Royal Commission on the two
ancient universities. Temple persuaded Gore to raise the subject
and also drafted the resolution and recommendations of the group
(ibid., p. 89). Tawney, though not himself a member, kept in close
touch, writing under a *nom-de-plume* a series of articles in the

Westminster Gazette in the early part of 1906 on the élitism of Oxford and Cambridge (Terrill, 1974, p. 32).

It was Tawney who, towards the end of his first stay at Toynbee Hall (1903-6), encouraged Canon Barnett to work towards securing a Royal Commission on university reform. Amongst those from whom Barnett gained support were Acland (now Chairman of the Consultative Committee of the Board of Education), Sir William Markby (Senior Bursar at Balliol), Gore, and J. A. Spender. Spender, who had at one time been resident at Toynbee Hall, and was then the editor of the *Westminster Gazette,* proved an able ally, being able to call on a number of writers such as Tawney with first-hand knowledge of social questions (Spender, 1937, p. 62).[73]

One of the leading figures in the group, and whose part has not been adequately acknowledged, was A. E. Zimmern of New College, who described himself to Beveridge in 1906 as 'an independent and discontented classical don, with grievances and no solutions'.[74] Briefly, he favoured the apprenticeship approach to 'business' in the widest sense of the word:

> that it is at 22-25 that men's minds are most receptive to synoptic study – men must go straight from school to the desk or warehouse – and then *back* to University. I believe that is the only system which would ever induce the English manufacturer to believe in University study.[75]

An Oxford Reform Committee, to widen the entry basis to Oxford and to endow Ruskin College with funds from other colleges, had been meeting regularly at Toynbee Hall since 1903, and Zimmern acted as Secretary.[76] He, like Tawney, propagated the case for university reform through his journalistic writings.[77] A series of articles written by Oxford dons in *The Times* in 1907 was collected together, reprinted and reviewed in newspapers largely on Zimmern's initiative. Zimmern favoured internal reform 'or in the event of the reformed constitution not producing any better results, to have an overwhelming case for a Commission',[78] even approaching Lord Curzon, the Chancellor of the University, on the matter.[79] After the failure to secure a Commission, Zimmern directed his energies towards ensuring the success of the University Joint Committee and later in the activities of the WEA itself.[80]

Barnett's house became the centre where proposals were brought and plans for action decided. Although a Commission on the University was delayed until 1921, the campaign had sparked off the need for change. Curzon conducted inquiries into some aspects of university and college organization and the results were published in *University Reform* in 1909.[81] Many of the recommendations fell far short of what Barnett and Temple had hoped for, but the campaign had served one immediate purpose. A few weeks after Gore's speech, the Conference on Oxford and Working-Class Education (see, pp. 109-10) took place. The work of Temple, Barnett, Tawney, Zimmern and others paved the way to a closer liaison between universities and outside bodies as seen, for example, in the establishment of university tutorial classes.

R. B. Haldane

A much more thorough-going and philosophical approach to the question of university reform was advocated and successfully implemented by Richard Burdon Haldane. Haldane's Scottish parents would have liked their son to go to Balliol, but holding evangelistic views dreaded the Anglican atmosphere of Oxford. Instead, he studied at Göttingen University with Lotze in 1874,[82] completing his education at Edinburgh and becoming an intimate friend of Andrew Seth, afterwards Seth Pringle-Pattison. Haldane came to know Hutchinson Stirling, the author of *The Secret of Hegel,* and the writings of Green and Caird impelled him in the direction of idealism (Haldane, 1929, p. 7). He edited and contributed, with Pringle-Pattison, to *Essays in Philosophical Criticism* (1882), and dedicated the volume to the memory of T. H. Green. The second essay, 'Philosophy and Science', written in collaboration with his brother J. H. Haldane, put forward

> the idea of a 'sort of scale of modes of existence', and
> corresponding series of categories which may be arranged in an
> ascending scale according to the degree of adequacy with
> which they interpret the complex whole. In such a scale we
> rise from the categories of mechanism to those of organic life,
> and from the categories of life to those of Consciousness in all
> its varieties (Pringle-Pattison, 1928, p. 433).

The idea of a stairway of categories was taken up some twenty years later in the Gifford Lectures entitled *The Pathway to Reality* (1903). Here, Haldane states that the problem of philosophy is simply to account for the actual world of the plain man:

> We ought to be prepared to believe in the different aspects of
> the world as it seems – life for example as much as
> mechanism; morality as much as life; religion as much as
> morality – for these belong to different aspects of the world as
> it seems, aspects which emerge at different standpoints, and are
> the results of different purposes and different categories in the

organization of knowledge. And if philosophy gives us back what Science threatens to take away, and restores to plain people their faith in the reality of each of these phases of the world as it seems, then Philosophy will have gone a long way to justify her existence (p. 119).

The second volume of Gifford Lectures also contains Haldane's exposition of Hegel's doctrine of God and man. Aristotle and Hegel are mentioned throughout as the two supreme thinkers of the world; Hegel, Haldane claimed, 'first taught the world how to read Aristotelian philosophy'.[83]

Haldane's main interest lay in the field of higher education. Towards the end of his life in 1923, he looked forward to the establishment of universities in every centre of population, which would be recognized as great national institutions and potent instruments for social advancement:

> We wish this both for the sake of the people and for that of the Universities themselves. A nation's stature is closely bound up with its enlightenment, and without work from the Universities the fullest enlightenment cannot come. What we rely on is the passion which the working classes, like other classes, have for what is of high quality. That passion manifests itself only in a comparatively small class of individuals. But their numbers tend to grow, and leadership naturally passes to these men. They influence not only those around them in their own homes, but others with whom they come in daily contact. The general standard tends to rise appreciably, and is likely to rise still higher the more the opportunities of grasping it become more diffused (Haldane, 1923, pp. 12-13).

Haldane took Germany as the model on which educational reform should be based. In 1901 he contrasted education in Germany and Great Britain: in England only the elementary stage of education was compulsory, whilst in Germany not only were elementary, secondary and technical schools and the universities controlled, organized and brought into close relation to each other by the state, but they were in a large measure compulsory (Haldane, 1902, pp. 10-11). At the top of the system, the universities, Haldane believed, ought to be permeating our education system in *Geist,* 'I mean the larger intelligence and culture without which education not only cannot be interesting but cannot be sufficiently comprehensive to take on practical business' (Ashby and Anderson, 1974, p. 163). This meant that there were two great aims to an

129

educational system: culture for culture's sake and, equally important, the application of knowledge to industry.

From the early years of this century, Haldane's educational
interests were threefold: to provide a network of regional universities; to set up educational provinces for improved primary and
secondary education; and to establish continuation and adult
education classes, with the universities playing a major part (Haldane, 1902, p. 163). The second point will be dealt with more fully
in the next chapter. Adult education, in the form of the WEA,
particularly absorbed his attention and he played an active part in
its proceedings. Haldane was also the driving force behind the
setting up of the British Institute of Adult Education: he did not
envisage this body taking part in direct local administration, but
rather in working out standards and forms of organization 'on
something like a general staff principle' (Mansbridge, 1940, p. 151).
Haldane believed that educational reform would break down class
barriers and create a new class structure founded on achievement.
As he somewhat naïvely told an audience of Scottish teachers,
'Educate your people, and you have reduced to comparatively
insignificant dimensions the problems of temperance, of housing,
and of raising the condition of your masses' (Haldane, 1902, p. 39).

There were two ways in which it was possible to influence events:
by entering politics and by becoming known to the Establishment.
Haldane as a man of action chose both methods. He successfully
stood as a Liberal candidate for Parliament in 1885, arranging a
neighbouring constituency for his fellow barrister and friend,
Herbert Asquith, in the following year (Haldane, 1929, p. 84). A
small group of young radical Liberals gathered around Asquith:
Edward Grey, a former Balliol man, but lacking in academic
distinction (Trevelyan, 1940, p. 20), Arthur Acland, Thomas Ellis,
Sydney Buxton and Haldane. The group worked closely together in
opposition (1886-92) with Haldane occupying the *via media* (Oxford
and Asquith, 1928, vol. I, p. 157), and Acland keeping the group
in touch with the 'labour people and their mind' (Morley, 1917,
vol. I, p. 234). Acland was to write later: 'powerful minds are not
the order of the day in politics. We want about fifty men like
Haldane scattered through the different Progressive Groups in the
House of Commons and the Lords.'[84]

The breakaway faction of Liberal Imperialists under Rosebery's
leadership, which included Asquith, Haldane and Grey amongst its
members, had as a cornerstone of its policy national efficiency. The
group saw that of all the factors impairing such efficiency the lack
of an effective system of education was most important, especially
in the face of German economic expansion and the threat which

this posed (Matthew, 1973, p. 228). The 'Lib Imps' provided Haldane with a platform from which to air his views on higher education.

Haldane was much sought after by London society – he was a successful Queen's Counsel as well as a Member of Parliament – but he did not stay with any one social group. Although basically not in agreement with their views, Haldane was intimate with members of the Fabian Society and studied their stimulating ideas (Haldane, 1929, p. 93). With the Webbs, he was responsible for setting up the London School of Economics in 1895 (E. S. Haldane, 1937, p. 200). He cultivated not only the Webbs but also civil servants such as Robert Morant, the Permanent Secretary of the Board of Education.[85] for his most ambitious scheme: to launch a higher technological institute in London, a 'British Charlottenburg'. This culminated in the establishment of the Imperial College of Science and Technology.[86] Haldane was also prepared to support Morant and the Webbs against his Liberal colleagues in a campaign to replace school boards by a more efficient education system managed by experts (Mackenzie, 1977, pp. 197-9). Earlier, in 1898, he had played a leading part, again with Sidney Webb, in the negotiations which led to the University of London Act: this gave the University teaching as well as examining functions. Haldane's advocacy before the Privy Council of the granting of separate charters for the Liverpool and Manchester Colleges in 1903 opened the way for further university expansion. The following year he headed a small group whose deliberations eventually led to the creation of the University Grants Committee, a national body which recommends the allocation of money to universities. He also brought his full influence to bear as Chairman of two Royal Commissions on university education, in London (1909-13) and in Wales (1916-18).[87]

Haldane's achievements in university reform were, overall, impressive. He followed Green's precept of entering wholeheartedly in serving society in order to attain self-realization. Perhaps his view of society was an over-simplified one: his vision of the world as objectified reason and of knowledge as the remedy for societal ills proved to be over-optimistic (Haldane, 1903, vol. 1, pp. 81-2). The Hegelian strain of idealism is seen in Haldane in a purer form than in many of his English contemporaries.

The final phase

A late outcrop of university reform in the idealist tradition was associated with A. D. Lindsay and the founding of Keele University. He had studied philosophy first under Henry Jones at Glasgow and then at Oxford. Although an undergraduate at University College, Lindsay wrote essays for Edward Caird, then Master of Balliol, who was a close family friend. Lindsay was elected Fellow of Balliol in 1906 and five years later was appointed Jowett lecturer in philosophy at the college at the age of thirty-one. In his inaugural lecture at Glasgow in 1922 entitled 'Idealism', he dissociated himself from the brand of idealism which asserted that all reality is spiritual: rather, he held the view that moral experience gave knowledge of reality and was responsive to a Good in the 'nature of things' (Scott, 1971, p. 390). Lindsay's belief in democracy was rooted in his strong Christian convictions. Politically, as he asserted in *The Essentials of Democracy* (Lindsay, 1929), democracy was only meaningful as a form of government if it was the object of sincere belief and if citizens would be willing to make sacrifices on its behalf.[88]

Relating this political philosophy to university education, Lindsay saw such education in terms of service to the community. Universities, in his view, should equip the most intellectually able people to serve the community in any way which proved best. The nature of the university course should enable the student to experience scientific and historical matters at first hand and to participate in the discussion of moral, intellectual and aesthetic questions (Gallie, 1960, p. 43).

In 1922 Lindsay had taken the lead in establishing a Modern Greats School – philosophy, politics and economics – at Oxford, but failed to get approval for a Science Greats which would have combined philosophy with natural science (*DNB*, vol. 2, p. 2753). Later, an embryo 'Foundation Year' in which college tutors gave general lectures to all their undergraduate students was attempted. The chance to carry out the experiment of a university as a self-understanding society came with the establishment of the new University of North Staffordshire (now the University of Keele) in 1949; Tawney had first stimulated the local authorities of the area four years previously to investigate the possibilities of a college. At the age of seventy, Lindsay was appointed its first Principal. It was a return to an area where he had conducted classes for the WEA many years before (see p. 112, above).

Keele broke with the traditional university course structure. The four-year undergraduate course included a foundation year in which science and art students became acquainted with each others' disciplines. In the next three years, now fewer than four subjects were covered, thus avoiding narrow specialization. Such a scheme reflected Lindsay's view that social awareness was the essence of a successful university education (Mountford, 1972, p. 129). He believed that the intellectually gifted should understand that there are many university subjects which are 'about' society, not only history, social sciences and literature, but also, perhaps less obviously to some, the physical and biological sciences. Lindsay attempted to translate Haldane's concept of the functions of a university in a practical way which accorded with his idealist beliefs. These owed much to Green's and Bosanquet's view that the development and direction of intellectual interests should be at the service of church and state in a modern society (Gallie, op.cit., pp. 75, 79).

8 Towards a national system of education

Green's hopes for establishing a co-ordinated educational system were, by the end of his life in 1882, far from becoming a reality. Some of the important recommendations of the Schools Inquiry Commission, especially the need for provincial authorities responsible for secondary schools, as advocated by Green, were not adopted. The provision of schools for the middle classes remained divided, much of it outside the purview of the state. Elementary schools, apart from the granting on a small scale of scholarships which enabled poor boys to continue their education, remained isolated. Frequently, too, there were no efficient schools at which such scholarships could be held, and often the curricula offered by secondary schools were unsuitable.

We know that by 1886 Acland had mapped out a radical programme of social reforms which could be translated into Liberal legislation, and he divided the proposals amongst his associates for study.[1] He personally concentrated on educational policies, especially in relation to rural communities. Other political colleagues interested in education at this time were Thomas Ellis (see following pages), Haldane, Sydney Buxton (M.P. for Poplar) and Asquith (Jenkins, 1964, p. 48).

Writing in 1892, shortly before becoming Vice-President of the Committee of Council on Education, Acland was certain that the most urgent need of the time was

> to provide facilities for the secondary education of workmen's children, and in the interests of all classes, it is highly desirable that this education should be given as far as possible in the same schools as those attended by the middle class (Acland and Llewellyn Smith, 1892, p. 307).[2]

The grading of schools, the settling of relationships to one another, the assistance of local university colleges and the appeal to patriotism might be effected through Provincial Boards based perhaps on the new County Councils. But Acland, following Arnold, saw that there would be much work remaining for a 'High Council of Education'. It would link together the various kinds of education under public control and it would give valuable advice in subjects of instruction and methods of study. One of its tasks would be to effect the registration of teachers, ensure easy interchange between 'the best elementary and secondary teachers', and in the future look to a common system of training for them (ibid., pp. 315, 318).

Welsh educational reform

That such a scheme was possible had been demonstrated a few years before in Wales, and it was from this that Acland took his model. Together with other like-minded colleagues, Acland had seen the rise of Welsh national feeling as an opportunity for providing a unified educational system on the lines of his stated principles. The Aberdare Committee was set up by the newly elected Liberal Government in 1880 to examine the condition of intermediate and higher education in Wales. Within a year it had completed its findings: the Report revealed a startling shortage of secondary provision. There were twenty-seven endowed schools in the whole country and a correspondingly small number of university students. It recommended a system of 'intermediate education', that is, that between elementary schools and the university, the establishment of two more colleges and the creation of a University of Wales; and it suggested methods of funding. The Report of the Aberdare Committee set out the aims of this restructuring:

> That system of education is most desirable for Wales which while preserving the national type, improves and elevates it, and at the same time gives opportunity for the development of any literary or intellectual attitudes which may be characteristic of the nation (Aberdare Report, 1881, pp. xlvi-xlvii).

Changes in government during the period following the Report delayed the implementation of the Committee's proposals. The establishment of County Councils in 1888, however, was a step towards their realization and in the following year a Welsh Intermediate Education Act provided rate-aided intermediate and technical education for both sexes.[3] The passing of this Act was for many Welsh patriots a notable step forward. The cause had attracted such people as Viriamu Jones, who had left Sheffield in 1883 to become Principal of the newly created University College, Cardiff. He was, as mentioned earlier, a Balliol man who both knew and had been influenced by Green (K. V. Jones, 1921, p. 276). Jones's belief in the wider diffusion of higher education led him to campaign vigorously for intermediate aducation (ibid., pp.

202-18). To advance the cause more directly, Acland gathered together at his summer house in Clynnog, Caernarvonshire, a small party of enthusiasts, all but himself Welshmen, who were interested in the subject and keen to exploit the possibilities of the Act.

One of the leading members of the group, Thomas Ellis, a political nationalist and regarded by many as the potential Parnell of Wales, based his philosophy on a mixture of Celtic culture and Green's organic state (K. O. Morgan, 1963, p. 70). Ellis had been at New College, Oxford, and shared Acland's interest in education. He believed that education should last from 'baptism to burial' with a broad curriculum embracing technical and artistic subjects, and night schools for adults based on those existing in Norway and Sweden (Griffith, 1959, pp. 25-6).[4]

Both Ellis and Acland had been elected Liberal M.P.s in the 1885 Election. They had struck up a friendship in the early 1880s, at the Oxford University Palmerston Club, and gained common political experience as members of the Inner Ring. Acland became an ardent admirer of Welsh nationalism as expressed by Ellis; both were actively involved in promoting the Liberal cause during the Welsh County Council elections (Spender, 1930, p. 22). Their campaign for leasehold enfranchisement was spurred on by their knowledge of the hardships endured by the quarrymen living in North Wales, and they also led the movement for free education there in 1890.[5]

Another member of the group was Henry Jones, who held the distinction unique among the idealist philosophers of having been the headmaster of an Ironworks School. He went on to study at Glasgow University, where he came under the influence of Caird, Nichol and A. C. Bradley, and this was followed by a brief spell at Balliol. Jones's deep study of Hegel led to an unsuccessful attempt to translate into Welsh the *Philosophy of Religion*; but some philosophical classics and a number of his own lectures were issued in that language (Hetherington, 1924, p. 33). He had also been privately commissioned in 1883 to assist in drafting a constitution for a new college in North Wales at Bangor, where, in the following year, he was elected to the first Chair in Philosophy. Moving to St Andrews in 1891, he finally succeeded Caird in the Chair of Philosophy at Glasgow in 1894.

The group's main self-appointed task was to decide on the most appropriate disposition of the new intermediate schools: whether to build a small number of well-equipped schools, one per county, or whether to disperse a much larger number of more modest ones in every centre of rural life. All agreed upon the desirability of the latter alternative. In old age, Henry Jones recalled:

We indicated the places in which we believed the schools in
the Northern Counties of Wales should be placed by sticking
pins into a map: and before we had done the map was
bristling with them. We were well aware that we were
indulging ourselves in constructing a scheme that was ideal. I
do not think that any one of us believed it to be attainable
(1924, p. 184).

In fact the subsequent campaign by the group exceeded their
expectations. Schools were built at all the places which had been
chosen and many others in addition. Different strategies were
adopted by the group's members for advancing the cause. Jones
wrote long articles and letters in North Wales newspapers and held
weekly meetings in that region to promote the movement. It was
also decided to gather their deliberations into a book aimed at
informing public opinion.[6] Provision for a National Council of
Education for Wales had been deleted during the passage of the
Intermediate Education Act. Instead, a Joint Education Committee of five members was constituted in each county, consisting of
three members nominated by the County Council and two by the
Lord President of the Council, preferences being given to residents
in the county. This gave an opportunity for political manoeuvring.[7]
Ellis became the first leader of Caernarvonshire County Council
and Acland the Chairman of its Joint Education Committee. The
work of instituting public inquiries into existing educational endowments and claims of localities for new schools was vigorously
pursued. At nearly all these meetings W. N. Bruce, the Assistant
Charity Commissioner, and a friend of Toynbee, was present.

At its first meeting after the passing of the Act, the Caernarvonshire Joint Committee passed a resolution suggesting a
conference of the six joint committees of North Wales. Six
conferences were held between 1890 and 1892, at one of which
Acland strongly urged a Central Education Board (L. W. Evans,
1974, p. 185).[8] However, some of the inspiration and driving power
of the movement was lost when Acland relinquished his Welsh
connexions in August 1892 to take up the post of Vice-President of
the Committee of Council in Gladstone's last Ministry, and Ellis
became first Junior and then Chief Whip. Within three years,
Acland had retired from political life on account of poor health,
and Ellis died before the end of the century at the age of forty.

None of the three men saw intermediate education in isolation
from the other stages. Acland had envisaged a University of Wales
based on the federal principle, a concept endorsed at a conference
in 1891. As Minister for Education, Acland granted a Royal

Charter of Incorporation two years later, from which time the three university colleges became constituent colleges of the University of Wales. As late as 1916, Henry Jones, who continued to be involved in Welsh education and politics,[9] became a member of the Royal Commission on University Education in Wales, chaired by Haldane. Fellow-members from Balliol on the Commission included W. N. Bruce[10] and Sir Owen M. Edwards (Lloyd, 1964, pp. 91-9), former Chief Inspector for Wales, who had played an important part in shaping educational policy from 1896 onwards.

Acland in office 1892-5

In England, Acland also looked to a reconstruction of the education system. Whilst the 1892 Government was being formed, some of the Liberal progressives pressed for a separate Ministry of Labour and Technical Education under Acland; Gladstone rejected this radical proposal (Davison, 1972, p. 236). One of Acland's keenest supporters, Haldane, wrote to Sir Algernon West, the unofficial head of Gladstone's secretariat at this time:

> I am convinced that the man in our ranks who possesses, beyond anyone else of his standing, the confidence of the Labour party, using the term in its widest sense, is Arthur Acland. He has, as none of the younger men has, the personal respect of not only prominent leaders like Tom Mann and Burns, but the great body of artisans of the northern and midland counties. He is looked on by them, and I think rightly, as having done more really good work in the House of Commons in the last five sessions than any other member of his standing. . . . I believe that I am expressing the sentiments of the bulk of the rank and file in the House when I say that it will be a deep disappointment if he is not placed in a position under Mr Gladstone where he may exercise real influence and attract to us still more of that confidence of the industrial classes on which we greatly depend today for our future (quoted in Sommer, 1960, p. 88).[11]

Acland then set about persuading senior members of the Party of his fitness for the post of Vice-President of the Committee of Council on Education.[12] Unusually for a Minister of Education, Acland was made a member of the Cabinet. He had been actively involved in a number of movements which looked to reform such as the National Association for the Promotion of Technical and Commercial Education, started in 1887, and the National Education Association with its unsectarian aims in 1889. In Parliament, he had successfully campaigned in the following year for County Councils to be allowed to use revenue from liquor duties (known as 'whisky money') for the benefit of technical education.

A stream of reforms flowed from the Education Office during the next three years. The school-leaving age was raised to eleven and payment by results came to an end, thus releasing the teacher, in theory at least, from a tightly controlled curriculum. The Education Code of 1895 encouraged, for instance, outside visits to museums and galleries and in schools, constructive infants' play; categories of pupils previously ignored, the blind, deaf and dumb, were provided for from 1893. In that same year, he put before the Cabinet a scheme to reorganize educational authorities in rural districts.[13] He was anxious to ensure that inefficient schools were refused grants and that inadequately provided and insanitary buildings were reported to the Department by Inspectors. (See Sutherland, 1973, pp. 319ff. for fuller details.)

Acland was also concerned about the problems facing the teaching profession. He told Sadler in October, 1892:

In your first letter giving your experience as to teachers at
Oxford, their separation into layers, their need for greater
unity, their aspirations for a more human method of teaching,
I seem to hear an echo of much that goes coursing through my
own head as I meditate abroad on the difficulties which I have
to encounter.[14]

Acland took a personal interest in the implementation of the Free Education Act which had been passed by his Conservative opponents shortly before their leaving office, seeking speedy returns from the authorities who provided elementary education. Protests by parents concerning the operation of the Act were investigated, and Acland ordered local enquiries by H. M. Inspectors sometimes in the face of internal opposition from the Department.[15] For the benefit of pupils who wished to continue their education after leaving school, the Evening Continuation School Code of 1893 was promulgated.

Acland, together with Sadler, saw that the inadequate provision of secondary education rendered adult education ineffective. An Act, corresponding to the Welsh one, was needed to create an efficient and comprehensive system of such schools. Acland had attempted to present a Secondary Education (England) Bill in April 1892 (Holmes, 1964, p. 133), but upon assuming office was persuaded by Sadler not to introduce immediate legislation. Instead, he asked Acland to receive a deputation from the Oxford Delegacy for the Extension of University Teaching, publishing a

139

letter signed also by Mackinder and T. H. Warren. The letter called for a National Council of Education 'containing representatives of the Government and of the great educational institutions of the country'. If the organization of secondary education was to be entrusted to County Councils, they stated, the latter should be required to appoint an Educational Board consisting partly of councillors and partly of teachers and other educational experts, with advisory representatives of the state and the universities.[16] These views accorded closely with Acland's. He had urged Sadler a few months previously to

> note down some of the things which you think I could usefully
> do to link together and stimulate our various educational
> activities. I have in view ... some informal conference between
> Headmasters, Conference Teachers, Guild College of
> Preceptors, County Council Assn. and Univ. Ext. Auths. etc.,
> one or two from each – at the Education Office on Secondary
> Education Organ. and Registration and Training of Teachers
> etc.[17]

Acland also wished to link together the different government agencies concerned with education: the Education Department, Science and Art Department and the Charity Commission.[18]

Sadler wrote personally to a large number of resident members of the University asking them to petition the Hebdomadal Council to invite a conference to meet at Oxford to discuss secondary education. The Conference was held in October 1893 and was attended by nearly two hundred men and women representing organizations concerned with secondary education. At the Conference Gladstone requested that before any legislation was enacted, a Commission should be appointed to 'inquire into the present state of secondary education within the Kingdom, the further needs of Her Majesty's subjects in this respect and the best means whereby those needs may be met'. Acland pressed Gladstone to set up a strong Commission at once and began canvassing Cabinet colleagues on the matter.[19] Eventually the key post of chairman was given to Acland's Scottish Cabinet colleague, James Bryce.[20] The appointment was a shrewd one. Bryce had been involved in educational reform some thirty years previously when along with Green he had been working as an Assistant Commissioner to the Taunton Commission. In his published report for Lancashire (1868) Bryce called for a national organization of education.

> The whole thing is a chaos and the first step to educational
> reform is to recognize the necessity of having all places of

instruction organized upon some general and definite principles
so as to form parts of one ordered and comprehensive whole.
. . . In every one of our great towns, in Manchester,
Birmingham, Leeds, Liverpool, Bristol, Newcastle, Sheffield,
there ought to be besides the schools an institution like a
Scotch or German University . . . giving instruction of a high
order in the most important branches of literature and
science.[21]

Bryce's views had been influenced by his contemporaries, such as
Nichol at Glasgow University and then at Oxford, where both
became members of the Old Mortality Club. He was a lifelong
friend of A. V. Dicey, three years his senior and for a short time his
tutor. Bryce's admiration for Green, dating from the time when
they were fellow undergraduates, is clearly displayed in a sketch of
his friend in *Studies in Contemporary Biography* (1903, pp. 85-99).
Green's widow told Bryce, 'You knew and understood him in many
ways better than any one else', and during Green's last illness,
Bryce had been a constant visitor.[22] Discussing the obstacle to good
citizenship some years later (Bryce, 1909), he assigned it to three
causes – indolence, selfish personal interest and party spirit – an
analysis which would have met with Green's approval.

Bryce's diaries from his undergraduate days show that the two
men had much in common. His views were not always popular
with his fellow-students. 'I have to sustain constant arguments on
the subject of Oliver Cromwell,' he wrote in 1858, 'whom I of
course entirely admire and love.'[23] The subject of the Old Mortality was an 'unfailing source of chaff' from fellow undergraduates, but this did not deter him from holding meetings in
his rooms. Complaining of the absence of 'motion' and 'progress' at
Oxford in the 1860s, Bryce looked to Germany for intellectual
refreshment. In 1863 he took a party to Heidelberg to study law,
and fell in with two other Oxford reading parties led by Dicey and
Green (Fisher, 1927, vol. 1, p. 58). In April 1892 he had written a
lengthy introduction to Acland and Llewellyn Smith's *Studies in
Secondary Education*, calling for a Ministry of Education which would
'draw to a centre the still unconnected threads of our educational
system', the creation of local education authorities, and the need to
establish harmonious and mutually helpful relations between the
universities and the secondary schools, and between the secondary
schools and the elementary (op. cit., pp. xxiv-xxvi). Many of these
features were incorporated in the recommendations of the Bryce
Report.

Bryce saw the organization of secondary education in terms not only of material prosperity and intellectual activity 'but no less in that of its happiness and moral strength'. Sadler was, at the age of thirty-three, one of the most active members of the Commission and perhaps the chief architect of the Report (Grier, 1952, p. 32) but later insisted that Bryce had drafted most of the recommendations.[24] The Report, whilst looking to more central direction in education, encouraged local and individual initiative. The recommendations went far beyond the original terms of reference:[25] a central department responsible for elementary and secondary education under a Minister responsible in Parliament was proposed. This would be conducted by a national council called an 'Educational Council' consisting of experts from various fields who had direct knowledge of educational work and who could advise the Minister: the latter's function would be to supervise and not override local initiative. As a counter-balance, local authorities were to be established to administer secondary education, able to levy a rate, and with membership based on the pattern existing in Wales since 1889. Secondary teachers were to be trained by universities and a register of teachers was called for; the independent Education Council would supervise and organize the register on lines similar to those of other leading professions. An important feature of the Commission's recommendations was the provision of scholarships for able elementary school pupils to enable them to benefit from the reformed system of secondary education (Bryce Report, 1895, I, pp. 256-328).

The principles expounded in the Report accorded closely with those enunciated by Green. By the time the Commission had completed its work in August 1895, the Liberals were out of office and an attempt to implement some parts of the recommendations was defeated in the following year. One result of the Report was the rationalization of central administration with the creation of the Board of Education following the 1899 Act. Another was the establishment of local education authorities who were to be responsible for co-ordinating all forms of education. As Lynda Grier noted, it was half a century before most of the important ones were carried out (Grier, op. cit., p. 46).

Whilst the Bryce Commission was still deliberating, Acland became in his own words 'the sole inventor and patentee'[26] of a new office which, he hoped, would help the Education Department to 'appear and not only appear but be more conscious of setting a high example and of giving help to educational workers' (Grier, op. cit., p. 49).

The Office of Special Inquiries and Reports was established early in 1895 charged with the duty of keeping a systematic record of educational work and experiments both in Britain and abroad. Acland had already, in connexion with the campaign for Welsh intermediate education, contributed to a manual on the workings of the 1889 Act in which he had described other educational systems (Ellis and Griffith, 1889, pp. 71-83). The idea of a Special Office had been mooted by Sadler during a holiday spent with Acland and Ellis in Switzerland in summer 1894.[27] In October of that year, whilst Sadler was serving on the Bryce Commission and was still Secretary of the Oxford University Extension, he was offered the Directorship of the new office by Acland. 'It is a great opportunity', wrote Acland, 'for us to combine in laying the foundations quietly for a great modification of the State to National Education.'[28] Until the Office came into being some five months later, Sadler spent much time rescuing and reading dusty foreign reports from the Department's cellars and discussing with Acland some of the tasks which the Office would carry out. The Permanent Secretary of the Department, G. W. Kekewich, a Balliol man, to whom Sadler was responsible, welcomed the appointment as a means of enlivening the work of the Department.[29]

Sadler began with nothing but a chair, table and writing materials.[30] By the time he had resigned his post in 1903 a great deal had been accomplished. Information was available on the standard of specified examinations and certificates in Britain, the colonies and foreign countries; an assessment of training colleges in France, Germany, Switzerland and the USA had been carried out; and an analysis and composition made of central and local authorities for education in all West European countries, the British colonies and the USA. The Office prepared the first return of boys and girls attending secondary schools in England and had made an inquiry into curricula and staff at public, secondary and higher-grade schools in selected towns. It also provided research and information for politicians, civil servants and inspectors of the Board.

However, the Office's most permanent legacy was the issue of several volumes of Special Reports on Educational Subjects containing vast quantities of information on the curriculum organization of institutions in various countries.[31] Sadler himself had written fourteen articles in the eleven volumes issued during his time at the Office. They included studies of the *Realschulen* in Berlin; the *Oberrealschule* at Charlottenburg (1896-7), which was read by and influenced Haldane; problems in Prussian secondary education for boys with special reference to similar questions in England (1898); and the place of the preparatory school for boys in English secondary education (1900). The total permanent staff consisted of Sadler, an Assistant Director, a librarian, a clerk, a translator and a messenger boy.

It would be interesting to speculate how far Acland and Sadler would have been able to influence the existing pattern of education and public attitudes towards it if Acland had remained in office.[32] Sadler later wrote to his mother:

> What is really at stake is the intention with which the colossal power of the State shall be brought to bear in the spiritual side of education. It is a new form of a very old controversy. All that is most difficult in political philosophy and much that is most impressive in history, is involved in it.[33]

As it was, the Liberals were defeated in June 1895. Although the work of the Office of Special Inquiries as a research unit continued, Sadler became involved through the new Vice-President, Gorst, in the political controversy arising out of the abortive 1896 Education Bill[34] and his efforts to press for an independent Education Council and a Teachers' Registration Council came to nothing. Shortly after Sadler had resigned from the Directorship in 1903 as a result of the well-known conflict with Robert Morant, the new Permanent Secretary of the Board, Morant admitted some of the difficulties under which Sadler had laboured: the lack of a strong central Board of Education dealing with all aspects of schooling, and the absence of an independent body by means of which the Office's findings could be sifted and if necessary acted upon.[35]

By the time Acland had left office, he could boast to his father that he was one of the six most influential members of the Cabinet. Much uncompleted business remained to be done. Writing to his ex-cabinet colleague and friend Herbert Asquith in 1899, Acland encouraged him to achieve 'practical results' on three subjects – franchise reform, the House of Lords, and education – 'by sitting down to them and giving more time to them than we could give in the scraps of time between 1892 and 1895.'[36] With a none-too-robust constitution aggravated by severe overwork,[37] Acland never returned to office, although he had entertained hopes of becoming Leader of the House of Lords with a seat in the Cabinet in the 1906 Liberal Administration.[38] Whilst remaining active in politics – he was Chairman of the National Liberal Federation from 1906-8 – Acland devoted much of the remainder of his public life to educational work. This was where his true interests lay: even in his early days as a young cabinet minister he had advised Gladstone to pursue a course of action on one matter, stating, 'I do not urge it *politically* but educationally.'[39] The breadth of his later activities would have taxed a normally fit person. Living in Scarborough, he was one of the most prominent members of the West Riding Education Committee, keenly interested in the establishment of new secondary schools following the passing of the 1902 Education Act. Acland was involved in the Yorkshire College at Leeds and took part in the proceedings leading to its receiving its charter as a University in 1904. He was also the first Chairman of the abortive Teachers' Registration Council.[40]

The opportunity to become involved again at national level in the educational sphere arose through the Board of Education Act in 1899. The Act established a Board of Education, replacing the separate Education and Science and Art Departments and the Charity Commission by a single body, and charged with the superintendence of education in England and Wales. The Act attempted to implement some of the recommendations of the Bryce Commission, notably to harmonize the different branches of the Board, though without extending its authority to detailed administration of secondary education (see Gosden, 1962, pp. 44-60). The notion of an Educational Council was re-examined but a body with more limited powers was set up. The Consultative Committee became the official body, which was to advise the Board on any matter referred to it; more specifically it was responsible for framing regulations for the registration of teachers. Membership consisted of not less than two-thirds of persons qualified to represent the views of universities and other bodies interested in education.

Acland told an ex-cabinet colleague, Earl Spencer, that he hoped he (Acland) would be appointed to the Committee.[41] Salisbury, the Conservative Prime Minister, was not enthusiastic. The Lord President, the Duke of Devonshire, wrote to Salisbury whilst the membership of the Committee was being chosen:

> I am sorry to have to trouble you again on the distasteful
> subject of Education. This time it is again the question of the
> Consultative Committee. You warned me against Acland as a
> 'Hardworking Beaver' and no doubt his nominations will
> provoke an outcry.[42]

In fact Acland's subsequent appointment as Chairman gave the new Committee the leadership and experience which was needed. Much was accomplished during his lengthy term of office (1900-16), thanks to the support he received from such members as Sadler, Mansbridge, H. R. Reichel, the first Vice-Chancellor of the University of Wales, and another Balliol man, T. H. Warren.

One of the most notable reports which bears Acland's name is that on Examinations in Secondary Schools (1911). The Committee's terms of reference was 'to consider when and in what circumstances examinations are desirable in secondary schools for boys and for girls'. The Committee supported a single system of public examinations for school-leavers at sixteen to take the place of the many which were offered by a variety of bodies; this led to the Secondary School Certificate Examination a few years later in 1917. Acland also chaired the proceedings on devolution by county education authorities and on school attendance of children below the age of five, both in 1908; on attendance at continuation schools the following year; on practical work in secondary schools in 1913; and, of particular interest to Acland, on scholarships for higher education in 1916.[43] His achievements as Chairman of the Consultative Committee have not received their full recognition. The opportunities presented by means of the Committee's investigations were perhaps the nearest to those which would have been available to a fully representative Educational Council.

Morant and a central authority for education

It might be considered surprising that we should include Robert Morant as a person influenced by idealist thought. Morant, as Permanent Secretary of the Board of Education from 1903, is best remembered for his part in shaping and implementing the 1902 Education Act; for engineering the Cockerton Judgment in 1900 which brought about the end of higher-grade schools; and for the firm separation of elementary and secondary schools into different compartments with different sets of codes and regulations. Morant's overbearing personality also colours much that has been written about him: his bullying of officials, including Ministers of Education, and the manner in which he engineered the overthrow of his friend and then chief, Michael Sadler.[44] What follows is not a defence of Morant but rather an assessment of some of the elements in his thinking and actions which indicate his leanings towards an idealist view of education.

Morant went up to New College, Oxford, in 1881 with the intention of entering the church, and gained a first in Theology. He formed a 'Brotherhood' at college at which theological matters were discussed. B. M. Allen, his biographer, mentions that the publication of Green's *Lay Sermons* is linked with a change in Morant's attitude towards religion (Allen, 1934, pp. 26-7). He discussed his religious doubts at this time with Canon Gore, and he was later attracted to Buddhism.[45] He also acquired a sense of social mission in his undergraduate days, which manifested itself more immediately in his conducting services in poor lodging houses

6 Richard Burdon Haldane, c. 1896

THE PIONEER UNIVERSITY TUTORIAL CLASS AT ROCHDALE, 1907.

Tutor: R. H. Tawney, Balliol College, Oxford.
Subject: Industrial History.

5 The pioneer University Tutorial Class at Rochdale, 1907. Seated, first row of chairs, sixth from left, is R. H. Tawney

4 The Joint Committee on Oxford and Working-Class Education, Oxford, December 1907. Members (both academics and workers' representatives) include—standing: fourth from left, Sidney Ball; third from right, J. A. R. Marriott; seated: second from left, A. E. Zimmern; middle, T. H. Warren; second from right, Albert Mansbridge; extreme right, A. L. Smith

3 The 'Inner Ring', 1883. Members include—standing: first on left, Cosmo Lang; extreme right, Anthony Hope Hawkins; middle row: centre, A. H. D. Acland; second from right, M. E. Sadler; extreme right, J. A. Spender; front row: first on left, L. T. Hobhouse

2 The Old Mortality Society, c. 1858. Standing: middle, T. H. Green; second from right, James Bryce. Seated: second from left, Algernon Swinburne; middle, John Nichol; second from right, A. V. Dicey

1 Thomas Hill Green

7 Residents of Balliol House Students' Residence, Toynbee Hall, November 1895. R. L. Morant, then Censor, is the tallest figure, third row from the front, eighth from the left. Canon Barnett, seated, is in the second row from the front, fifth from the left

8 The Lux Mundi Party at Longworth Rectory, Oxon, 1902. Members include—standing: left, J. R. Illingworth; seated: left, H. Scott Holland; second from left, R. C. Moberly; third from left, Charles Gore

at Hinksey.[46] In 1886 he applied for the post in Siam as tutor to the King's nephews and subsequently to the Crown Prince. Morant wrote at the time that his object was above all 'to develop the highest side of their character in the effort to serve others and to reach the ideal of life in its varying forms' (Allen, op. cit., p. 46).

Siam was at that time undergoing a transformation brought about by the exploitation of resources by Western countries. Modernization of many aspects of life, including education, was carried out, though it was not to be at the cost of losing a sense of national identity. Prince Damrong, a keen reformer, toured Europe to study educational systems and in 1892 inaugurated a Ministry of Public Instruction with Morant as his chief adviser. The Ministry developed innovatory functions, urging schools to achieve higher standards, inspecting schools and devising means by which educational policy could be implemented.[47] Before Morant arrived in Siam, the Prince had introduced public examinations into schools and a standardized curriculum. The cornerstone of the system was a Textbook Bureau, which produced materials in all subjects; the examinations were based on the contents of the books.

Morant, as Examiner to the Government Schools, was involved in constructing a unitary system of education ranging from primary to university preparatory schools (Wyatt, 1969, pp. 149-50). Morant's last important task was to implement a scheme for teacher training and two schools for the royal children in 1892; that same year, the Prince and Morant, for internal reasons, were transferred from their offices, and Morant left Siam in 1894. During his time in Siam, Morant had written textbooks in a *Ladder of Knowledge* series on reading and translating into English, and it is noteworthy that he prepared a new edition of at least one of these books as late as 1901.[48]

Returning to England, Morant went in April 1895 to Toynbee Hall,[49] where Acland and Sadler had been active. He there became Censor of Wadham and Balliol Houses, where young men wishing to study and experience common living resided, compiling a competent report for Barnett on suggested reforms of the course (Barnett, 1918, vol. 2, pp. 16-17). Within a few weeks, Sadler had appointed him as his Assistant at the Office of Special Inquiries, but he continued to reside at Toynbee 'as being a good place to keep in touch with educational matters'.[50] This was certainly true. Gorst, the Vice-President in Salisbury's new Government, came to Toynbee Hall in November to discuss the proposed Education Bill then before the Cabinet which, in Barnett's words, would 'cut a path through the jungle of laws and customs of competing authorities'.[51] Sadler later wrote:

> When I first met Morant, he had about him a dim halo of
> Buddhist austerity, and felt the power of Oriental mysticism.
> ... At that time he was as near a saint as might be a sadhu or
> a Buddhist Monk.[52]

Another aspect of Morant's personality which emerges from
Sadler's papers and which both his biographers omitted to mention
is summed up in a note written by Sadler in 1934, 'T. H. Green
taught me to think about Moral Obligation. R. L. M. started me
on the Philosophy of History.'[53]

Morant's well-known article on Swiss education, written in 1898,
set out his opinions on the deficiencies in the English education
system at that time: in it, he asked for a balanced system of
democratic education in which each type of school would be fitted
into its proper place and receive appropriate support from a strong
central government (Morant, 1898).

Although there were differences of emphasis between the views
of Sadler and Morant, there was fundamentally common
agreement.[54] In an unpublished document which Sadler wrote in
1896 on 'The Relation of the Charity Commission to the Central
Authority for Secondary Education' he supports a 'strong and
comprehensive' central authority for a number of reasons: first,
local authorities would become too powerful; universities and
teachers did not believe that local authorities knew enough about
secondary education to be trusted with such powers; and third,
greater co-ordination between the different stages of education was
essential.[55]

Sadler would have included representatives of the universities
and the teaching profession as an integral part of a central
authority through an Educational Council. Morant, however, in
one of his few recorded comments on the nature of authority in a
democracy, looked rather to

> the willing establishment and maintenance *by* the democracy,
> of special expert governors or guides or leaders, deliberately
> appointed by itself for the purpose, and to the subordination
> of the individual (and therefore limited) notions to the wider
> and deeper knowledge of specialized experts in the science of
> national life and growth.

Morant showed that nothing had been done to provide a
directive centre for education and put forward the view that there
was 'a necessity for having a really expert Central Authority for the
whole of our National Education, a localized "guidance of brains",
which will watch, consider and advise upon *all* our national

educational arrangements of all grades, of every type, *as one whole*' (Allen, op. cit., pp. 125-6).

After the passing of the 1902 Act, with which he had been heavily involved, Morant attempted now to put these ideas into practice. Each stage of education was carefully examined and its aims enunciated. Eaglesham (1967, pp. 53-4) has pointed out that Morant's plan for elementary education – what has been called education for followership – had more vision than subsequent interpretations have given it credit for. Morant's view, in the context of his time, was a practical and reasonably enlightened one. The school, according to Morant, was to form and strengthen the character and to develop the intelligence of children, to assist boys and girls according to their needs to fit themselves practically and intellectually for the work of life. Exceptional children were to be selected for secondary education.

The Introduction to the Code of 1904 for Elementary Schools was widely praised by contemporaries, including *The Times,* which stated that:

> It means that an English Board of Education has definitely abandoned the old crude idea that its functions were merely financial and administrative, viz., to devise means by which the country might get tangible value for an expenditure more or less grudgingly bestowed. ... For the first time the child, rather than the official or the taxpayer, is recognized as the most important consideration (quoted in Allen, op. cit., pp. 213-14).

Morant's main interest was in providing a system of national secondary schools, and for the first time an Act enjoined local authorities to consider the total educational needs of their areas. Morant looked to the classical and literary traditions of secondary education with a curriculum which ensured a good general education free from vocational overtones. By the 1904 Secondary Regulations,[56] a stipulated curriculum was laid down, with fairly precise guidelines on what could be taught. His achievement was to establish a coherent pattern of secondary schooling with recognizable boundaries, as Green, Acland and others had looked for. Morant disliked the old pupil-teacher system and he abolished it, substituting for it proper teacher training in colleges. Potential teachers were to be given a good general education in the new secondary schools.

Any assessment of Morant's contribution towards a national system must be controversial, as the writings of educational historians testify. Certainly, as we have seen, Haldane greatly admired

149

him, not only by asking Morant to serve on Royal Commissions, but by adopting for his own use some of Morant's administrative principles (Heath, 1928, p. 19).[57] Similarly, Morant had congratulated Haldane on the appearance of his collection of educational addresses, *Education and Empire* (1902), sympathizing

> with your impatience at the smallness of vision which seems always to limit our education rulers and education speeches. Our marvellous old office in Whitehall seems never to get a glimpse of the *width* of the problem which it *ought* to be solving, and of which it is really touching the mere surface or edges. The dry old office gropes along, busy with minute details of doles of state money, only wearisomely giving in now and then to persistent pressure from outside and then and only then letting a few isolated new ideas and ways have a chance. I hope you may imbue many in authority with the realization of what England needs: and I for one thank you for the encouragement that your volume contains.[58]

He was also a willing conspirator with Haldane in the founding of the Imperial College of Science (see p. 131). Haldane's plan for bringing university finances totally under the Board's jurisdiction, and thus achieving a more unified system, was eagerly supported by Morant.[59]

After the return of the Liberal Government in 1905, Morant's views broadened.[60] His dislike of technical and vocational education abated, and in 1907 the possibilities of teaching commercial subjects in England were investigated both here and on the Continent. A Report on Commercial Education in 1909 was accepted by Morant. The following year, he set about the replanning of technical and further education: with two sympathetic colleagues, F. Pullinger, the new Chief Inspector of 'T' Branch, and an assistant secretary, E. K. Chambers, Morant outlined schemes of education for 'Industrial Citizenship', which aimed at bringing about a marriage of culture and vocation (Eaglesham, op. cit., p. 69). Morant's departure from the Board shortly after delayed these plans.

Another remarkable achievement was the founding of the School Medical Service in 1907. In that year, Morant attended a private meeting of the Independent Labour Party, with Keir Hardie in the chair, and pledged support for the work of Margaret MacMillan for the physical well-being as well as the teaching of children (Leese, 1950, p. 249). Morant's Circular No. 576 (November 1907) begins: 'The broad requirements of a healthy life are comparatively few and elementary, but they are essential, and should not be regarded as applicable only to the case of the rich' (see also Eaglesham, op. cit., pp. 12-13).

Morant has often been depicted as hostile to the notion of the working-class pupil rising above his station. This picture is not an accurate one.[61] Morant looked perhaps excessively for administrative tidiness, but by doing so enabled links to be established between the different sectors of education. Albert Mansbridge paid eloquent testimony to Morant's sympathetic attitude towards movements aimed at widening the educational opportunities of working people (1940, pp. 160-1). Morant's action in increasing grants for the university tutorial classes at Longton and Rochdale in 1906 and his appearance at the Oxford Conference on Working-Class Education in August 1907, where he gave positive encouragement to Mansbridge, bear this out. It is not generally realized that Morant was invited by Gore, the Chairman, to address the Conference. In a brief speech, Morant, after committing his department to financial aid, made an appeal:

We have made it a special point during the last few years to develop what we are beginning to call further education and adult education. What our Department is looking for is guidance from such an association or union as is represented here today, to show us the way in which this particular line of education can best be furthered. ... But I am not here to puff up a Government Department, but to endeavour to dissipate the notion that we shall in any way [word missing] and to entreat you to tell us how we can help you.[62]

On his leaving the Board, Morant told Mansbridge that:

What led up to the Oxford meeting, and the meeting itself which I had the pleasure of attending, seemed to me at the time quite one of the largest matters to which we could put our hand at this Board (Mansbridge, op.cit., pp. 160-1).

He also wrote resignedly to Mansbridge about his efforts on behalf of the educational and intellectual culture of working men, 'Misunderstandings and misrepresentations ought not really to matter to one, if one knows that they are due to misconceptions' (ibid., p. 162).

A rare insight into Morant's philosophy can be found in the minutes of an interview he had granted during Morant's time in office to Dr J. B. Paton, a leading nonconformist figure. Paton's special theory about the ideal church conceived of the education system as a means of uniting Christians in the service of man (Holland, 1915, p. 287). A tangible expression of this endeavour was his creation of the National Home Reading Union (NHRU) in 1887, in which Acland, Sadler and Percival held office. The Union was based on a pattern developed at Chautauqua in the USA, where summer holiday courses of instruction had grown up into a national system of circles of organized courses of home reading. The aim was to guide people to reading, which, as Green had pointed out, appealed to the imagination or higher feelings.[63]

Paton regarded the subsequent development of his scheme into Summer School meetings of extension classes as a deviation from his original conception. Morant actively supported the NHRU movement, and it was his Preface to the Board of Education Code for 1904 which had led Paton to seek an interview. The aims of the elementary school had been clearly set out by Morant and the Preface had ended:

> The school should enlist, as far as possible, the interest and co-operation of the parents and the home in a united effort to enable the children not merely to reach their full development as individuals, but also to become upright and useful members of the community in which they live, and worthy sons and daughters of the country to which they belong.

After the meeting at the Board on 6 February 1906 between the two men, Paton made a précis of their conversation, as an agreed unofficial record.[64] According to Paton, they were unanimous on the need to provide literature which would 'inspire our youth with a true ideal of life, and of all the finer elements that go to make good conduct and good character'. Morant promised to invite some of Her Majesty's Inspectorate to assist the Union in making an appropriate selection. Paton then described a grammar school in Manchester in which the walls were covered with pictures and mottoes which would appeal to boys' highest instincts. 'We then said – Could not the walls of every school in the country be clothed with pictures of that kind instead of growling tigers and gaping alligators, etc?'

They were of one mind as to the importance of games in day schools and the need for the younger masters and mistresses especially to associate with their pupils in the playgrounds or in games. Morant volunteered the suggestion that it might be possible to secure one hour each week where games in the playground might take place; it was agreed that Paton should get up a petition to the Board from teachers and others interested in promulgating these ideas. The last and most important part of the conversation concerned plans to set up a national committee to co-ordinate the moral training of children. Both Morant and Paton agreed that in addition to simple religious teaching, moral teaching 'of the best kind' should take place:

> Such teaching should appeal to the imagination and feelings, which are the great factors of conduct, and should deal with the actual relations of life at home, at work, in companionship, and in all civic relationships and with the discipline of personal character.

Morant's personal failings[65] have overshadowed his achievements in striving for a coherent system of national education in accordance with worked-out principles. Although he failed to carry through all his reforms during his comparatively short term as Permanent Secretary (1903-11), it is an impressive fact that five years later H. A. L. Fisher, on becoming President of the Board, remarked that Morant's enthusiastic spirit still pervaded the Office (Fisher, 1940, p. 98).

Continuation schools

A reformed system of education would not be complete without a reassessment of the provision for further education of those leaving elementary schools at an early age. Paton had, since 1885, been active in pressing for a system of evening classes which met the needs of the community and in which the idea of brotherhood and fellow service permeated educational and recreative work alike. Acland laid the foundation for progress towards this end in his Evening School Code of 1893: the Code swept away the requirement that pupils must take one or more of the 3Rs, abolished the twenty-one age limit, and encouraged the teaching of civics, recreative and practical subjects. However, the scattered provision for further education – working men's colleges, polytechnics and evening classes – was different from that conceived by Sadler and others. It was hoped that for those who had completed a day-school course there would be systematic instruction in the equivalent of a *Vorbildungsschule* or 'further progress school', the secondary school of the industrial classes.

Looking at the German pattern in 1907, Sadler mentioned two of its advantages. Technical training following on a good general education was indispensable to the industrial and commerical success of a nation: modern conditions deprived young people of the educational care which was formerly provided by apprenticeship. A more powerful reason than the economic one was the moral consideration: that the moral welfare of the nation would suffer if no measures were taken to counteract the deteriorating influences of urban life during the first years of a youth's freedom from school (Sadler, 1907a, p. 514).

Although Sadler drew attention to some of the disadvantages of a heavily centralized system such as Germany's, on balance it was advantageous in securing for the individual a measure of economic and moral freedom which was denied to many of the victims of a more individualistic society. This could be achieved by extending attendance at day schools to sixteen years, the course of training in the last year to consist largely, but not exclusively, of hand training. Sadler recognized that the time was not yet ripe for such a large-scale move and suggested in the interim a carefully devised plan of half-time attendance at day continuation schools. The national and collective good which would follow from an intelligent upbringing of children, Sadler believed, would not be maximized unless this was coupled with a sufficiently long course of liberal education which included the duties of citizenship and home-making (ibid., p. 712).[66]

The book edited by Sadler, *Continuation Schools in England and Elsewhere* (1907a), was a landmark in this field, providing a focus for the widespread agitation which existed for such provision. Mansbridge had led a deputation of WEA representatives to Morant and Anson, Parliamentary Secretary to the Board of Education, in November 1905, with the object of securing compulsory attendance at evening schools. The whole question was referred to the Consultative Committee, headed by Acland, and it was charged with reporting on the need for compulsory or otherwise attendance at continuation schools. Its findings were published in 1909 and the main recommendation was that there should be no gap between day and continuation school, as this would lead to scholars being lost to further education; various ways in which this could be achieved until such times as compulsion could be introduced were suggested. Once again, as in the case of the Bryce Commission, it was Sadler who largely drafted the final report of the Consultative Committee before it was sent to the Board (Grier, 1952, p. 153).

These recommendations were repeated in the 1918 Education Act: Section 10 envisaged the provision of part-time schooling for all between the ages of fourteen and eighteen;[67] and again in 1944, when County Colleges were to be set up. In neither instance did permanent continuation schools become a reality. Economic cutbacks in Government expenditure following the Report of the Geddes Committee on National Expenditure in 1922 and opposition from some industrialists proved too powerful a combination for the earlier system to succeed. One MP objected to the scheme, claiming that it constituted 'a very large advance towards the socialist theory that children belong to the State' (Doherty, 1966, p. 45). The Crowther Report on education from fifteen to eighteen, issued in 1959, agreed with the principle but looked to a gradual extension in stages over a number of years. The present-day problem of what constitutes the most appropriate education of the sixteen to nineteen group is one outcome of the failure to make the continuation school, in Sadler's terms, an integral part of the education system.

Educational reconstruction: Haldane and Fisher

The campaign for continuation schools was not an isolated example of the concern expressed about the state of education during the First World War. In those four years suggested ways in which reform might be attempted included a royal commission, a Board of Education inquiry and a committee appointed by the Prime Minister. Haldane had been excluded from office as Lord Chancellor in May 1915, allegedly because of his pro-German sympathies, when the Asquith coalition government was formed. He now threw his considerable energies into formulating and, he hoped, implementing a scheme of educational reform.[68]

The weapons Haldane chose were a combination of rallying public opinion and behind-the-scenes manipulation. His opportunity came with the setting up in March 1916 of the Asquith Reconstruction Committee, analogous to the Committee of Imperial Defence, which, with the assistance of sub-committees, co-ordinated the work already being done by Government departments. No action was taken at the Board of Education until Haldane, in a brilliant speech in the Lords (12 July 1916), drew attention to the deplorable waste of talent in the elementary schools and called for the establishment of continuation schools. A Reviewing Committee consisting of Cabinet and ex-Cabinet ministers to examine 'the whole field of National Education' was then announced six days later.

At its one and only meeting on 11 August, the Reviewing Committee asked Haldane 'to prepare in association with a group of English and Scottish educational experts a memorandum outlining the questions which required consideration'. All future deliberations were to be cloaked in secrecy. The course of events was carefully masterminded by Haldane. He had privately met Lloyd George in April and struck up an alliance on education and had later suggested the creation of a Reviewing Committee, a permanent organization charged with the supervision of national education. Haldane had ready to hand a comprehensive scheme of reform which he had drawn up before the war as Chairman of a Cabinet committee on education.[69]

It contained eleven propositions for consideration by a sub-committee, consisting of Board officials such as L. A. Selby-Bigge, the Permanent Secretary; H. F. Heath, Director of Special Enquiries; and, representing Scottish interests, Sir William McCormick, the educationalist, and Sir John Struthers of the Scottish Education Department.

Weekly meetings were held at Haldane's house in Queen Anne's Gate during October and November 1916. The final document for the consideration of the Reviewing Committee strongly bore his stamp (Lloyd, 1976, p. 41). Many weaknesses in the existing system were exposed. He asked for a long-term plan for education (twenty years) with provincial councils, as expounded by Arnold and Green, controlling the system and given fiscal powers. The quality and supply of elementary schoolteachers had to be improved and nursery and continuation schools established; a national system of scholarships was needed and university fees should be lowered.

Unfortunately for Haldane, in December 1916 Asquith was replaced by Lloyd George, who, as head of Government, was now determined to remove any vestiges of the Asquith regime. The Reviewing Committee was disbanded and with it much of Haldane's influence.[70] Instead, the educational problems were passed on to the new President of the Board, H. A. L. Fisher. But, as will become clear below, Haldane's work had by no means been in vain.

Fisher mentioned in his unfinished autobiography how in December 1916 Lloyd George summoned him to London from Sheffield where Fisher was Vice-Chancellor, and offered him the Presidency of the Board of Education with a seat in the Cabinet (Fisher, 1940, pp. 90-1). As normal Cabinet government was in abeyance because of the war, Fisher was able in his capacity as Minister to concentrate on securing legislative proposals which would have, in peace time, run into many obstacles. In his own words, 'I resolved to move forward at a hard gallop and along the whole front. If I did not strike my blow now, the opportunity might be lost never to return' (Ogg, 1947, p. 103).

He had entered New College, Oxford, in 1884, obtaining a first in Greats. Green's books, especially the *Prolegomena*, profoundly influenced him. After some indecision Fisher devoted himself to the study of history rather than philosophy (his best-known work being *The History of Europe*) and became a Fellow of his college in 1888.[71]

Fisher's predilection for Greek philosophy led him early in his career to lecture on Plato, whom he admired above all others for his devotion to reason and truth (ibid., p. 198). He also visited the University of Göttingen and other places, becoming absorbed in the economics of medieval Germany, reading widely and developing a lifelong love for that country. A keen Liberal in politics, he had tutored the group of active and enlightened administrators known as 'Milner's kindergarten' who were to become prominent in South Africa after the Boer War.

Fisher's view on university education emerged during the years that he was Vice-Chancellor of Sheffield. The University had grown out of an institute essentially concerned with applied science. He did not attempt to redress the balance in favour of the humanities but rather encouraged the application of science to industry, promoting research within the University. He established close links with the city, regarding the University as the central power-house of the intellectual life of the area (*DNB*, vol. 2, p. 2631). By the time he was appointed to the Board of Education, Fisher clearly knew what steps were needed: 'My sympathies were democratic. I believed in the open career for talent, and was ambitious of the honour of widening the highway from the elementary school to the university' (Fisher, op. cit., p. 98).

Fisher knew and respected Haldane; and the two men, who shared similar views, had long talks on educational affairs. 'Fisher was very sympathetic to my programme', Haldane told his sister three days before the education estimates were introduced: 'There seems to be a real prospect of getting something done. He is putting nursery schools, continuation schools, improved secondary education and physical training in his programme' (Maurice, 1939, vol. 2, pp. 45-6).

The Education Bill introduced in 1917 ran into trouble from both the Conservative and Labour parties. 'Does education give you the ablest race of men?' asked one Conservative MP (Hansard CIV, cols 429-32). Fisher was disappointed to note that the Labour Party was opposed to any form of vocational teaching; support for continuation schools was forthcoming only if they provided a good general education in the humanities. 'The idealist advisers of the Labour Party on educational questions,' Fisher wrote, 'were, I suspect, in advance not only of the older Trades Union politicians, but also of average working-class opinion and desires' (Fisher, op. cit., p. 110). He singled out Tawney as one of his most consistent supporters outside the House of Commons.

In its final form the Education Act of 1918 contained a number of interesting features. Educational progress was encouraged by giving local authorities 'percentage grants', the matching of local expenditure by a government grant; this led to an expansion of services. Salaries of both elementary and secondary schoolteachers were raised; the path to universities was made easier by the establishment of State Scholarships and the award of grants for advance courses. Fisher also adopted the recommendations of the Consultative Committee chaired by Acland in 1911, replacing the fifty-five examinations for which teachers in secondary schools could be called upon to prepare candidates, by a single general one, the School Certificate Examination. Faced with the choice of raising the school-leaving age to fifteen or providing part-time continuation schooling up to eighteen, Fisher unhesitatingly chose the latter.

Reform within the universities was also undertaken. Vice-Chancellors, especially at Oxford and Cambridge, were loth, in the name of academic liberty, to accept money from the state. Fisher was concerned with the developing requirements of applied science, and obtained grants of £30,000 per year for this purpose for the two universities. But he was aware that a larger-scale inquiry was long overdue and Asquith, now Lord Oxford and Asquith, headed a royal commission on universities which led, amongst other changes, to the setting up of a University Grants Committee composed of eminent academics, to administer state grants.

Fisher in a short space of time had achieved much: the legislation was to remain the basis for action until the 1944 Act came into force. It is fitting to sum up Fisher's conception of a unified system of education in his appreciation of the work of James Bryce, with whom he shared similar ideals:

> He [Bryce] urged that any scheme of educational reform must be comprehensive, that it must regard boys' schools and girls' schools, elementary schools and secondary schools, night schools and day schools, technical schools and universities as part of a single plan. The Education Act of 1918 embodied this, the only fruitful and legitimate conception of his work which the educational reformer should have in view (Fisher, 1927, p. 109).

R. H. Tawney

The 1918 Act when fully implemented would have satisfied many of the ideals of R. H. Tawney, whose work in connexion with the WEA movement was considered above. In many ways, Tawney was the last line of pre-war idealist thinkers who survived into the

1960s, devoting his life to educational advance. Like many of his contemporaries at Balliol at the beginning of the century, who included his friends Temple and William Beveridge, he was fired by the social idealism of the master, Edward Caird.[72] Although he was an economic historian rather than a philosopher, his 'Commonplace Books' of 1912-14 (Winter and Joslin, 1972) show clear evidence of idealist influence on him in his early years.

However, Tawney differed from T. H. Green in believing that universal citizenship would not be achieved without first attacking capitalism, which had held back the working classes from achieving self-fulfilment. The lack of harmony between the different social classes was not be resolved by Green's solution of involvement in local as well as national affairs. Tawney looked only to political activity on a national scale which would reform the system as a whole; this task could best be undertaken by Socialism. For this reason, Tawney joined the Fabian Society in 1905, the ILP in 1909, and in 1918, when individual members were accepted, the Labour Party.

A prerequisite of educational reform and true citizenship was social reform. Tawney was optimistic that education could create social solidarity, 'a means whereby men could transcend the limitations of their individual [perspectives] and become workers in a world of interests which they could share with their fellow men' (Terrill, 1974, p. 182). But capitalism denied the working classes their proper inheritance as citizens and Tawney attacked the apparatus by which the *status quo* was upheld. He wanted

> to set the realities of child-life in the centre of the stage as the criterion by which all educational arrangements are to be tested; to adapt educational organization, not to social conventions or economic convenience, but to the requirements of the children themselves; to be sensitive to the varying needs of different individuals, and merciless to the pretensions of different classes (Tawney, 1952a, pp. 154-5).

The hereditary curse on English education, Tawney stated, was its organization on social-class lines. The public schoolboy was encouraged to regard himself as one of the ruling class and acquired the aristocratic vices of arrogance and intellectual laziness. If the elementary schoolboy in 1931 was no longer taught that the world was divided by Providence into the rich and the poor, then the same lesson was taught through inferior school facilities. As early as 1912 Tawney observed:

> Class ethics is a curious thing. It is the ineradicable assumption of the upper classes that a workman should be primarily a

159

good productive tool. He is always judged from this point of view, from the assumption that all he wants or ought to want, is not to live but to work (Winter and Joslin, 1972, p. 5).

Tawney saw, then, the removal of class barriers as of prime importance in a programme of educational reform. A stream of articles, speeches and conference addresses spelt out this message. Characteristically, during the passage of the 1918 Education Bill, Tawney wrote a piece in the *Daily News* dramatically entitled 'Keep the Workers' Children in their Place', attacking a recently-issued memorandum on education by the Federation of British Industry which questioned the desirability of continuation schools (Tawney (1918) in 1964 edn, p. 49). In this, as in other writings, Tawney scorned the notion that only a minority of children were capable of benefiting from education beyond the age of fourteen. Indeed, he dismissed the whole concept of a 'ladder' into liberal education at the age of eleven, whereby individuals had to prove themselves worthy of access to a fuller life.

Amongst Tawney's papers is an official undated document signed by H. F. Heath, a civil servant and admirer of Haldane, entitled 'Suggestions for a National System of Education'. The sentiments expressed bear the stamp of Haldane, but no doubt received Tawney's approval.

Every grade of education ... needs organizing from the standpoint of what lies beyond and above it – from above downwards, not vice versa. Much thought has been given to the selection of the able boy and girl with a view to their further education. ... The really necessary needs are those of the great bulk of the people.[73]

Tawney was a practical man as well as a visionary. As a regular contributor to the *Manchester Guardian* on educational subjects, mainly in the form of leaders, from 1913 and for the next forty years, Tawney was able to influence successive generations by his writings (Williams *et al.*, 1960, p. 23). He dominated the advisory committee on education established by the Labour Party in 1918. The failure of the continuation schools led Tawney to draw up a long document which became the basis for the Labour Party's policy statement *Secondary Education For All* in 1922. It has been recently claimed that the book represents the final reconciliation of Tawney's vision of the ultimate ends of education with his view on practical schemes for educational reform. Up to 1921, his schemes for the reorganization of adolescent education had appeared to be based upon socio-economic exigencies rather than upon any theory of human personality (Brooks, 1977, p. 3). Briefly, the new plan advocated a system 'under which primary and secondary education are organized as two stages in a single and continuous process: secondary education being the education of the adolescent and primary education being preparatory thereto' (Tawney, 1922, p. 7).

This involved an improvement in primary education and the development of a public system of secondary education to which all normal children, regardless of income, class or occupation of their parents could be transferred and remain there until sixteen. Tawney agreed with Nunn in 1924 that a technical education could satisfy the requirements of a good secondary education, 'provided that inspiration is sought from the traditions of the industry or craft at their noblest' (Tawney, 1924, p. 3; quoted in Brooks, op. cit., p. 7). It was probably also about this time that he advocated, in the Consultative Committee, the need for an 'Intelligence Department' within the Board of Education. Its function would be to collect and systematize information on educational developments and problems at home and abroad. Educational research would be strengthened and 'the formation of an intelligent public opinion on educational matters by the dissemination of full and accurate information' could be achieved.[74] The scheme and the terminology employed are strongly reminiscent of Sadler.[75] Tawney was instrumental a little later in obtaining a Barnett Fellowship, tenable at his college, the London School of Economics, for Kenneth Lindsay to study the 'Free Place' and scholarship system. The results of the investigation were published in a book *Social Progress and Educational Waste*, a title which makes clear the nature of Lindsay's findings.[76] Tawney's views contained in *Secondary Education For All* and *Education: the Socialist Policy*, the latter written in 1924, remained the basis for Labour Party policy until after the Second World War (Terrill, op. cit., p. 63).

Of all the problems which had been most persistently deferred since the 1902 Education Act, that of a truly public system of secondary education was the most serious (Tawney, 1932, p. 6). Tawney's dismissal of the public schools followed from the argument that while a good school is a community with distinctive characteristics, every school had responsibilities not only to its immediate clientele but to the nation as a whole. The state had to ensure that these responsibilities were not ignored. By these criteria, the isolation of the public school was an anomaly. It was the task of those who guided the nation's schools to create the common culture which was so far lacking (Tawney, 1966 edn, p. 73).

When the first Labour Government came into office in January 1924, C. P. Trevelyan, the President of the Board of Education,

161

whose policies largely reflected Tawney's views,[77] lost no time in referring to the Consultative Committee under Sir Henry Hadow[78] the question of 'the organization, objectives and curriculum of courses of study suitable for children who will remain in full-time attendance at schools other than Secondary Schools, up to the age of fifteen'. The origins of the proposals do not concern us here, but it is remarkable that the topic was initiated by a small section of the Committee's members seeking the Minister's approval rather than through the normal procedure of receiving instructions from him. Ernest Barker, who had entered Balliol in 1893 and 'fed' himself on the writings of Green and F. H. Bradley,[79] had headed the deputation to the departing Conservative Minister in November 1923. (Tawney was not a member of this.) Barker, together with Tawney, who had served on the Consultative Committee since 1912, and Percy Nunn,[80] who had been a member of the Labour Party's educational advisory committee, formed a powerful triumvirate on a drafting sub-committee of which Barker was the chairman.

The Hadow Report influenced the reorganization of schooling into stages, with a break at eleven and a closer recognition of pupils' needs at different ages. It recommended the raising of the school-leaving age to fifteen, and the concept of a variety of types of schools which would provide for creative and practical as well as academic abilities. Tawney saw that reorganization of education which did not allow for a full four years of secondary schooling was valueless (Tawney, 1934, p. 17). He spent much time subsequently explaining and defending the report at public meetings.

It seems curious that Tawney did not see the contradiction contained in the terms of reference of the Hadow Committee: of surveying the reorganization of post-primary education without reference to the established municipal grammar schools. The exclusion of continuation schools from the Committee's deliberations also left a gap in creating a fully worked-out system. Tawney's attitude towards the nature of secondary education, as displayed in his writings, was also ambivalent. Whilst chiding the Englishman's characteristic reluctance to test the quality of an activity by reference to principles (Tawney, 1921, p. 1), he himself could be charged with possessing the same vice.

He complained, for instance, in 1934 that there was a misdirection of ability, with children entering secondary schools who were better suited to the more realistic curricula of central schools, because the former were supposed to carry an aura of social prestige; similarly, children who should go to secondary schools were attending senior schools simply because the former charged fees and the latter were free. Here Tawney looked to easier means of transfer between senior, central, junior technical and 'pure' secondary schools on the grounds that they were all different species of one genus, varying in curricula and methods but equal in quality and status (Tawney, 1934, p. 18). What he failed to appreciate was how this persistence of different types of post-primary education would undermine his campaign for secondary education for all and help to prolong the class-divided system until long after the Second World War.[81] At the time of Hadow, however, these future trends were no doubt difficult to predict.

Tawney's vision was also circumscribed by the prevailing attitudes within the Labour Party, which largely favoured traditional practice in matters concerning curricula and school organization (Barker, 1972, pp. 147-59; White, 1975, p. 18). Political and economic changes also nullified many of the better recommendations of the Hadow Committee. The school-leaving age was not raised, the necessary parity between all types of post-primary education was ignored by the Board of Education, and the possibility of a fresh start at eleven was delayed by the slow rate of school reorganization. Nevertheless, in the long term, the influence of Tawney's view can be seen in the provisions of the 1944 Education Act (Doherty, 1964, p. 126) and, within the Labour Party, in the post-war debates on secondary education.

Tawney looked both backward, to the influence of Green and Caird, and forward to the more practical ways of achieving social justice. He was sustained, as a practising Christian, by the belief that men can fulfil the purpose of God only in so far as they follow a distinctively Christian way of life. For him, all forms of economic and social organization which hindered that way of life stood condemned, and it was the obligation of Christians to replace them by others (Tawney (1935), in 1953b, p. 172). At the same time, as already noted, he saw the immense aggregations of economic power in a capitalist society as the main threat to the liberty of citizens, resulting in a social order based largely on class differences and interests. For this reason, he saw Socialism as a fellowship which should aim to end economic and political tyranny by making such power responsible to authorities acting for the nation (Tawney (1944), in 1953b, p. 91). Unlike the Fabians, Tawney did not envisage collectivism as the solution, but rather an open-ended fellowship where the entire society, not only part of it, was the arena within which individual fulfilment could be attained. Education, of course, had a major part to play in such a programme (Terrill, 1974, p. 216).

The Liberal ideology which had prevailed in the earlier period

163

collapsed after the First World War. Some of the main factors were the decline in Imperialism, the spread of totalitarianism abroad, and the absence in the Liberal Party of ideals which were relevant to the social and economic problems facing the country. Earlier idealists, notably Toynbee, Bosanquet, Caird and Jones, opposed the notion of a Socialist programme as a means of achieving their ends. To Tawney, as to his friend Haldane, on the other hand, this seemed to be the natural solution. Haldane, on joining the Labour Party in 1922, wrote to Asquith:

> Except by invoking the ideal of an enlightened democracy we cannot hope for the public insight which is the indispensable preliminary to progressive enthusiasm and so to reform in every direction. It was for this reason that three years ago I decided for the future to work with whatever party was most earnest with Education in its widest sense.[82]

Tawney too saw in Socialism the possibility of an infusion of new values in society which would lead people to recognize that 'education is the most formal and public recognition of the claims of the spirit that the modern world has permitted' (Tawney (1917), in 1953b, p. 32), a sentiment which was in the best tradition of idealism.

Religion, idealism and education

9

The link between the idealists' interest in education and their religious commitment was, as we have seen, very close. In this chapter we examine the educational work of a number of leading idealists, all of whom became prominent churchmen. To do so we need first to go back once again to the beginning of our story, that is, to the 1850s and after.

From a number of events which affected the climate of intellectual, political and social thought in the second half of the nineteenth century, two are worth singling out for special mention. The first was the political success of Dissenters in 1868 following the second Reform Act. It was hoped that their MPs would bring about the disestablishment of the Church of England, but by the time the Conservatives were returned in 1874 little had been achieved, apart from some concessions for Dissenters in Forster's 1870 Education Act. The issue was again revived with the Liberal victory of 1880, but as politicians were divided amongst themselves on this issue – Gladstone, for example, did not favour disestablishment – the question was left unresolved.

Second, and of greater importance, were the scientific discoveries which had brought into question the authority of the Bible. The Oxford Movement, led first by Newman, Froude, Keble and Pusey, had from the 1830s challenged the view that the church was dependent on the state for its authority.[1] Bishops, it was claimed, traced their succession in an unbroken line back to the Apostles. Darwin's theory of evolution, postulated in *The Origin of Species* (1859) and supported by Lyell's *Geological Evidence of the Antiquity of Man* (1863), led to the challenging of orthodox doctrines. This might be typified by the publication of *Essays and Reviews* (1860), the work of seven churchmen, Bishop Colenso's reappraisal of the *Pentateuch* (1862) and J. R. Seeley's *Ecce Homo* (1865), in which a humanized Christ was presented; this latter book was denounced by Lord Shaftesbury as 'the most pestilential book ever vomited from the jaws of Hell' (Clark, 1973, p. 94).

Green's own writings and lectures reflect an intellectual reappraisal of religion.[2] He was deeply influenced by the writings of F. C. Baur, a German Protestant theologian and biblical critic

(1792-1860) who minutely criticized the New Testament texts. Green began in 1863, but never completed, a translation of one of Baur's books, *Geschichte der Christlichen Kirche* (Grosskurth, 1964, p. 73).[3] His evangelical beliefs were expressed in two essays which were unsuccessfully entered for a theological prize in 1860. In the past, he held, a good citizen was naturally conservative, but to a modern Christian, who can 'believe in the immanence of a divine life in the church' such reverence for the past and aversion to all that is new and untried implies 'a distrust of humanity' (Green, *Works,* 3, p. xxvi). Green therefore saw the true 'church' as an institutional expression of an all-embracing spiritual life. Both civil and ecclesiastical institutions ought to be the vehicles of such a life, but it ultimately resides in the consciences of all individuals. This view sanctioned the actions of individuals who challenged the established authority of the church. As we pointed out in Part 1, Green held the Hegelian view that God reveals himself in the form of reason (see pp. 19-20); the miraculous elements in the Christian church as it existed in Green's time were quite contrary to this. For Green, the church represented 'a dead hand' in preserving traditional values. As D. G. Ritchie pointed out, Green's attitude towards religion was the only possible outcome of 'the recognition that the ethical end of self-realization is an end for all human beings, and that we must get rid of those powers of class and caste which we are in the habit of saying that Christianity has broken down' (Ritchie, 1891, p. 151).

As the son of a clergyman, Green favoured the retention of the established church, but looked beyond the union of church and state to a community embodying a rational social morality (Clark, op. cit., p. 236). He envisaged church reform mainly in terms of giving the congregation greater powers: in the appointment of clergy, in ceremonies, and in formulae used in worship. This would attract a different type of clergyman who would respond to the needs of his community. At the same time, as Green pointed out at a meeting at Merton College in 1881, disestablishment would make the clergyman of the future either a mere priest or a mere preacher 'instead of the leader in useful social work and the administration of such public business as is not directly administered by the state, as he now often is' (Green, *Works,* 3, p. cxxii).[4] He chided passionate theologians for believing that God revealed himself to man in some other form than reason: 'God is for ever reason; and his communication, his revelation, is reason ... giving life to the whole system of experience which makes the history of man' (ibid., p. 239).

Green's admiration for priests as community workers was based on their good work in parishes, especially in large towns, where they alleviated the worst effects of poverty. Green's plea for the democratization of the church was consistent with the secularizing of the social services which had attracted a number of his followers. For example, the setting up of the Charity Organisation Society in 1869 – to distribute charity on a more scientific basis, using case-work techniques – brought together the lay social worker and the clergy. Toynbee, as we have seen, canalized his religious passion into assisting the poor in the East End to understand their situation by means of education, through the teaching of economic theory and history. The Toynbee Hall notion of a settlement offering educational and other social facilities also illustrated the develop-ment of a partnership between church and secular elements.

Churchmen, from this time onwards, were faced with such challenging statements as Edward Caird's: 'No one who has breathed the atmosphere of modern science, literature or philo-sophy can any longer consent to worship as God an object or power of nature' (quoted in Jones and Muirhead, 1921, p. 341). How then to solve the problem of the relation of the human to the divine, of the spirits of men to the Absolute Being? Some who entered the church – those described by Mark Pattison as carrying off Green's honey to their hives – searched for appropriate answers.

As early as 1848 Frederick Temple had started on, and almost completed, a translation of Hegel's *Logic* with his near contem-porary, Jowett. (His other intimate friends at Balliol included Matthew Arnold and A. H. Clough.) Temple's subsequent career, as Principal of Kneller Hall Training College, a brief spell as an Inspector, Head of Rugby, one of the Taunton Commissioners, Bishop of Exeter and London, and Archbishop of Canterbury, was guided by three principles: the faith, the church and national life. Faith involved accepting new viewpoints but also safeguarding essential truth. This is apparent in Temple's correspondence with his old Balliol tutor, and Dr Arnold's successor at Rugby, Dr Tait, then Bishop of London, following his (Temple's) contribution to the notorious *Essays and Reviews* published in 1860. Writing from Rugby in 1861, Temple defended himself in the following terms:

> I for one joined in writing this Book in the hope of breaking through that mischievous reticence which go where I would I perpetually found destroying the truthfulness of religion. I wished to encourage men to speak out. I believe that many doubts and difficulties only bred because they were hunted in the dark, and would die in the light. . . . What can be a grosser superstition than the theory of literal inspiration? But

because that has a regular footing it is to be treated as a young man's mistake: while the courage to speak the truth about the first chapter of Genesis is a wanton piece of wickedness.[5]

Temple's faith was expressed in his lifelong interest in maintaining the union of religion with education. He contended that the teaching of religion should form an essential part of national education, and that the church should co-operate with the state in providing it, thus offering to each individual the power of rightly governing his own life (Sandford, 1906, vol. 2, p. 652).[6] With Arthur Acland's father, he had pioneered the system of University Local Examinations which Green eagerly supported. As one of the Taunton Commissioners, he supplied the leading ideas for the Commission's Report on the reform of secondary education in 1867. He also outlined a plan to the Bryce Commission almost thirty years later for a national system of education linking the elementary to secondary schools (ibid., pp. 649-50). However, although Temple's interest in education continued until his death in 1902, he shared with Jowett the belief that Hegel had not solved 'the problem of Truth idealized, as the Gospel of St John did' (ibid., vol. 1, p. 78).

Green's influence, both direct and indirect, on future generations of Christians is nowhere more apparent than in the persons of two very different individuals, Henry Scott Holland and Charles Gore. Holland went up to Balliol in 1866 and formed the most important friendships of his life with Green and Nettleship. Much later, Holland described Green's contribution to the formation of his religious outlook:

> He broke for us the sway of individualistic sensationalism. He released us from the fear of agnostic mechanism. He taught us the reality of the corporate life and the inspiration of the community. He gave us back the language of self-sacrifice, and taught us how we belonged to one another in the one life of organic humanity (Holland, 1920, pp. 9-10).

Especially fired by Green's teaching, he obtained a first in Greats and decided that the best chance of using his powers for the glory of God and the service of man was to take holy orders and remain within the church. Holland gained a Studentship at Christ Church in 1870, lectured on philosophy, and worked in various good causes among the undergraduates and townspeople. He feared on his ordination that Green would be disappointed with this step. Green's reply was reassuring. He recognized the competition between philosophy and dogmatic theology, each claiming to be the true rationale of religion, though he rejected the latter; at the same time orthodox Christianity, as expressed in prayer and in the ordinances of Protestant worship, were acceptable. Green saw himself, therefore, as a supplier of intellectual formulae for the religious life whether lived by an 'orthodox clergyman or a follower of Mazzini'. He assured Holland,

> I hold that all true morality must be religious, in the sense of resting upon the consciousness of God: and that if in modern life it sometimes seems to be otherwise, that is either because the consciousness of God from intellectual obstacles cannot express itself, or because the morality is not the highest – at any rate has for the time being become mechanical.[7]

Holland's lectures at Christ Church were marked by a compromise between extreme positions within the church. The spirit of universal order was demonstrated in his lectures on Plato and St John, a marriage of philosophy with religion also evidenced in some of his later sermons, such as 'The Venture of Reason'[8] and 'The Ethics of Christian Society'.[9] The church at its fullest and its best is a social organism or universal brotherhood: it should look to spiritual equality and brotherly fellowship, repudiating every arrangement which would treat men as mere instruments for the enrichment or convenience of others. In an age of industrialism the church had hitherto failed to give a lead in protesting against the conditions in which the working classes lived. The doctrine of the church and the sacraments taught that the continuous expression of the union with God was to be realized in the fellowship of men with one another (Holland, 1905, p. 66).

Holland took no direct part in educational work, but his indirect influence was important. Attracted to the East End of London, he lodged in Hoxton for a time in 1875, visiting and preaching. His biographer mentions that 'he set himself to make us active, not lookers-on, but playing our education for all it was worth against injustice and class-hatred outside Oxford' (Paget, 1921, p. 127). In a sermon preached in the Cathedral to the Co-operative Congress at Oxford in 1882, Holland condemned the old economics teaching which limited itself to man in his pursuit of wealth alone. It was impossible to isolate either individual man from his fellows or any one domain of human action from another:

> You are here today to say, to declare that in his trade man finds himself a brother among brethren – no competing foe, but one of a family, knit up by closest ties and fellowship, into an organic society of helpful co-operators.

Equally, Christ

> should break down all walls of fleshly partition, all divisions of
> blood, all severance of race or class or kind, and should raise
> the brotherhood of man into solid and actual reality (ibid.,
> pp. 105-6).

A lifelong friend of Holland, Charles Gore, had much in common with this outlook. Gore, the younger man, followed Holland
to Balliol in 1871 and was equally deeply influenced by Green's
philosophy. As with Holland, Gore's interest in programmes of
personal and social conduct and passion for the redress of social
grievances were subsidiary to the religious motive; but once certain
of the validity of the reasoning underlying his beliefs, he never
wavered in promoting them. He displayed his strong Liberal views
at the University: with Herbert Asquith, his Balliol contemporary,
he spoke at the Union in 1873 against the motion 'that trade
unions are dangerous to the welfare of the community in their
operation and tendency' (Gore, 1932, p. 69). Gore as well as
Holland actively supported the 1887 Labour demonstrations in
London.

Gore held a less optimistic view of the world than Holland,
judging it to be so bad that its redemption seemed only possible by
the immediate judgment of God (Prestige, 1935, p. 18). Together
they sought to provide a common meeting ground between churchmen who were seeking to reconcile the claims of reason and
revelation. In 1875, together with Edward Talbot, Warden of
Keble, J. R. Illingworth, the religious philosopher and former
student of Green,[10] and others, Gore adopted a plan of occupying
a small country parish – Longworth, near Oxford – each summer
for a month. The group, calling itself the Holy Party, took over the
duties from the incumbent and discussed the possibilities of forming an Anglican religious community along the lines of the Oratory
(Prestige, op. cit., pp. 25-6). Gore became the acknowledged 'Pope'
of the Party.

Out of this developed the Christian Social Union (CSU) in 1889,
with Gore as its most prominent leader. It established a worldwide
following. Its objects were threefold: to claim for Christian law the
ultimate authority to rule social practice, to study in common how
to apply moral truths and principles of Christianity to the social
and economic conditions of modern times, and to present Christ in
practical life as a Loving Master and King. Gore based his social
doctrine of the brotherhood of man on a specifically Christian
conception of the Fatherhood of God. Individuals were to be
treated as ends not as means, unequal in capacity but equal in

their right to consideration and opportunity. A lifelong hatred of *laissez-faire* led Gore naturally to the conclusion that Christians' 'ruling motive was to co-operate rather than compete' and to the statement in 1908 that 'we must identify ourselves with the ideal of socialist thought' (ibid., p. 94).

The group set down their beliefs after the Union was founded in a book, *Lux Mundi* (1889). Its publication caused an uproar in theological circles, less for views expressed on the relationship between intellectual and spiritual authority than for its questioning of the historical accuracy of portions of the Old Testament. The Holy Party became the Lux Mundi Party, and included some of the leading contributors to the book. Gore, Holland and Talbot, R. C. Moberly, Illingworth and Francis Paget (later Bishop of Oxford) met over the next twenty-five years to discuss social and religious questions.

Gore became successively Bishop of Worcester, Birmingham and Oxford, and a leader of the Liberal and philosophical wing of the High Church Party. He was one of the founders of the Synthetic Society in 1896 which invited eminent men in philosophy, science and theology to dine and read papers commensurate with the society's object 'to consider existing agnostic tendencies, and to contribute towards a working philosophy of religious belief '. Among its earliest members were Haldane, Bryce, Dicey and Holland. Gore considered the aims of the CSU too moderate and turned to more active involvement in reform: poor law, housing, trades conciliation and education. He saw the aims of education not simply in terms of academic success, but as giving individuals possession of a fuller life. Mansbridge acknowledged Gore as the spiritual progenitor of the WEA, being inspired to action by one of Gore's sermons. 'If I have constructed my secular policy upon any one man's teaching,' Mansbridge told Lansbury in 1907, 'it has been that of Bishop Gore, who knows the smallest details of all my efforts to do something for Labour.'[11]

Gore campaigned for the admission of poor boys to Oxford and Cambridge, and in the House of Lords demanded a Royal Commission on the two Universities in 1907 (see p. 126). In his opening address as Chairman of the Conference 'What Oxford can do for Workpeople' in August that year, he remarked:

> What has become apparent to all persons as a fact ... [is] that they have got to give a wide extension to the idea of the governing classes. I do not myself even like the phrase of 'the working class'. I think it is a definition unfortunate to those who are included in it and for those who are not.[12]

171

It was important for all citizens to have political and economic knowledge to improve the conditions of the country. Later, as Bishop of Oxford, he warmly supported Fisher's Education Bill, urging churchmen not to oppose it.

The influence of Gore and Holland can be seen in the careers of some of the later idealist churchmen, notably William Temple. The son of Frederick Temple, he entered Balliol in 1900 and, as with others, came under the spell of Caird. Unlike Gore, whom he called 'a veritable prophet of social righteousness' (Mansbridge, 1935, p. 88), Temple possessed a remarkable serenity that came from his unwavering faith which made it unnecessary to wrestle with his conscience (Hartley, 1963, p. 3). His powerful intellect was matched by some of his contemporaries, who included G. M. Young, Tawney, Maurice Powicke, Raymond Asquith and Beveridge. Temple's study of philosophy led him to visit Jena University with Tawney in 1905. The twin principles of liberty and justice governed his outlook. It was to education, he believed, that one had to look to in order to achieve them:

> Until education has done far more than it has yet had an opportunity of doing, you cannot have society organized on the basis of justice; for this reason, that there will always be that strain of which we have spoken between what is due to a man in view of his humanity with all his powers and capacities, and what is due to him at the moment as a member of society, with all his faculties still undeveloped, with many of his tastes warped, and with his powers largely crushed (Iremonger, 1948, p. 78).

The real root of social problems was spiritual; and if Christianity was to be applied to the economic system, an organization which rested primarily on the principle of competition should give way to one resting primarily on co-operation.

A prerequisite for action was that the church should be able to direct its own life, and to speak with the authority of its whole corporate body on the great issues confronting the world. To achieve this, Temple headed the Life and Liberty Movement, begun in 1917, which culminated in the passing of the Church of England Assembly (Powers) Act two years later;[13] this created a Church Assembly, which consisted of bishops, clergy and laity, with powers to pass measures on all matters concerning the church. In a letter to a colleague at this time, Temple's views clearly emerge:

> The Church is not concerned with the spirit of the age but

with the spirit of the ages. On the other hand the purely
traditionalist position is very liable to be dead, at least
intellectually. I feel sure that the right line is a rather difficult
balance of recognizing in the Church authority, but authority
of the moral kind. ... I am one of those who find myself
generally in sympathy with the modernists as regards their
method of approach to the problem and with the
traditionalists as regards conclusions accepted.[14]

Temple gave a lead in numerous activities which gave scope for
his beliefs. He played a leading part in COPEC, the Conference on
Christian Politics, Economics and Citizenship, in April 1924, which
replaced the Interdenominational Conference of Social Service
Unions. Later, in 1936, as Chairman of the Archbishop of York's
Committee on Unemployment, Temple was concerned both to
discover the most fruitful line of action to take and to explore the
moral and spiritual well-being of the unemployed.

More than Gore, Temple became personally involved in educational activities. The WEA movement attracted him as a vehicle
for ameliorating the position of the working classes. He became its
President. He had persuaded Gore to raise the issue of university
reform in the Lords in 1907 and was a member of the Catiline
Club, a group of dons with radical views (see p. 126, above).
Though committed to the reform of public schools, he was
appointed headmaster of Repton School in 1910. It was Haldane
who appointed him to the rectorship of St James's, Piccadilly, four
years later.

Of his writings, two books best display his attitude towards social
questions. *Christus Veritas,* published in 1924, expounded his view
that theology and philosophy mutually imply one another; what
was needed in the interests of both was a 'Christo-centric metaphysics'. For Temple, man's 'whole being is a condensation of
society. He *is* his fellow men's experience focused in a new centre.
There is no impenetrable core of self-hood which is his, and his
alone' (p. 71). Temple had joined the Labour Party in 1918, largely
as a result of Gore's influence.[15] Towards the end of his life in 1942,
when he was Archbishop of Canterbury, Temple wrote *Christianity
and Social Order,* which examined the relation of an enlightened
church to social and industrial problems. It was a fitting end to his
career that Temple should have earned the trust of fellow-
churchmen in negotiating with R. A. Butler, the President of the
Board of Education, who was then preparing the 1944 Education
Act, about the shape of the post-war system of schooling.

The influence of the churchmen discussed in this chapter on

their contemporaries, both through their thinking and their many-faceted activities, was impressive. Temple's friend at Balliol, Tawney, was attracted by Gore's religious philosophy. In a discussion in 1937 on the attitude the church should take on matters of economic and social ethics, he stated that the duty of the Christian church was not only to act on the individual conscience:

> It is also to affirm openly and ceaselessly that men can fulfil the purpose of God in so far as they follow what has been called the distinctively Christian way of life. It is to insist that all forms of economic and social organization which hinder that way of life, whatever their incidental attractions, stand *ipso facto* condemned, and that it is the obligation of Christians to replace them by others (Tawney (1937), in 1953b, p. 172).

Further, all Christians should be agreed on securing the conditions of a good life for the rising generation. Tawney took as his prime example the obstacles to individuals achieving their full potential in education. Writing in 1953, he noted that the 1944 Education Act had removed some of the barriers but that some of the anomalies remained, especially that of provision for a system of continued part-time education when full schooling had ended. Any dualism which drew a sharp line between the life of the spirit and the external order with which religion had no concern was unrealistic. The church's function, therefore, was to state its own conception of the duties and rights of men in society and to determine its attitude to the policies of all political parties by the degree to which they were in agreement with that conception. It is significant that in formulating these views, Tawney wrote that 'my debt to the thought of two great men, the late Bishop Gore and Archbishop Temple, is both obvious and beyond acknowledgement· (ibid., p. 167).

Idealists as educational theorists   10

The idealist reformers contributed more, as one might have expected, to educational practice than to educational theory. They preferred for the most part to do something directly to improve the extent and quality of education, rather than write about it from a theoretical standpoint. Not that they did not write on educational matters at all. On the contrary, many of them were prolific in this field. One only has to think of R. H. Tawney's innumerable leaders in the *Manchester Guardian* and his other educational books and articles. But then it was Tawney, too, who wrote, 'Books on education ... belong to a type of literature which, I am 'sorry to say, I cannot read' (Terrill, 1974, p. 182). Tawney's writings were not the products of reflection about education in the abstract, but weapons forged for particular campaigns in a continuing political battle for educational improvements, powerful in impact but discardable once they found their target.

At the same time, the idealists were among the most theoretically oriented of educational reformers. Their practical achievements would have been impossible without a theory of education of some sort. But the important point to note is that they did not have to *devise* such a theory: idealist philosophy, especially as it was developed in the school of T. H. Green, embodied within itself a whole philosophy of education, of its purposes, social distribution and connexions with society and the state. A theory of education adequate enough to guide the work of a social reformer lay ready to hand.

This may explain why the reformers did not need to work out an educational theory for their own purposes. But it does not show why little was done to translate idealism into specifically educational terms for the greatly enlarged teaching profession of the turn of the century, which was becoming increasingly avid for theoretical guidance. One factor, perhaps, was that the kind of educational theory which teachers and teacher-trainers felt they needed most was in an area where idealism had least to contribute. Idealism had most educational relevance when it came to the larger topics mentioned above: the aims of education and their connexions with man's nature and destiny; the enlargement of educational opportunities throughout the population; the role of social institutions other than the school in the process of education; the rights and duties of the state in the matter of educational provision. Where the teaching profession most wanted help, however, was with more immediate, smaller-scale problems: problems of how to organize their teaching, of what methods to employ to get large classes to learn efficiently and in an orderly manner. The macro-topics might be of interest to politicians, or at most, to teachers *qua* citizens; but to teachers *qua* teachers it was (as ever) the micro-topics that seemed to matter most.

But one should not conclude that idealists' influence on educational theory was entirely negligible. Indeed their *indirect* influence, on such as John Dewey, for instance, was considerable. This apart, writers who were themselves idealists contributed to educational thought in a number of ways, as we shall be indicating below. Though none of these men (T. G. Rooper, J. MacCunn, Fred Clarke and Henry Jones, for instance) are, with the possible exception of Fred Clarke, remembered today as eminent educational thinkers, their writings are important to our main thesis in this volume, since they make explicit the educational ideas implicit in general idealist philosophy, the ideas, in fact, which powered so many of the practical reforms.

A complete history of idealist educational theory remains to be written. In this chapter we do not profess to do more than outline the views of a small number of writers whose work has so far come our way. In the next chapter we shall be adding a little about another idealist educationalist, Robert R. Rusk. That there are others, perhaps subsidiary, who also belong to this category, but of whose work we are ignorant, we have little doubt. But there is one extremely well-known educational writer, about whom, although he was an idealist philosopher, we intend to say next to nothing. We refer to A. N. Whitehead, the author of *The Aims of Education*. The reason is simple. Although the book *The Aims of Education* first appeared in 1929, some ten years after Whitehead, under R. B. Haldane's influence, became an idealist in philosophy, the essay of the same name, with its famous attack on 'inert knowledge', first appeared in a book called *The Organization of Thought* published in 1917, some two years before Whitehead began to embrace idealism.[1] Though there is nothing of an idealist flavour about this essay, its successor in *The Aims of Education*, on 'The Rhythm of Education', does contain the following passage:

I think that Hegel was right when he analysed progress into three stages, which he called Thesis, Antithesis and Synthesis;

though for the purpose of the application of his idea to educational theory I do not think that the names he gave are very happily suggestive. In relation to intellectual progress I would term them, the stage of romance, the stage of precision, and the stage of generalization (pp. 27-8).

A few pages later we find: 'The final stage of generalization is Hegel's synthesis' (p. 30).

These two are the only references to Hegel, or Hegelian philosophy, in Whitehead's book. Even here there seems to be little of Hegel in Whitehead's celebrated trichotomy beyond the bare claim that progress can be trichotomized. Certainly Percy Nunn, who, as we shall see in the next chapter, was a firm anti-Hegelian, found Whitehead's trichotomy acceptable enough, since it was in his view only another way of stating Nunn's own rhythmic law 'wonder – utility – system', a formula he first published in 1905 (Nunn (1920), 1945 edn., p. 270, n.1; p. 271, n.2).

The writers whom we shall first be considering all belong, unlike Whitehead, to the mainstream of idealist thinking connected with Green and his associates. Their contributions are of different kinds.

First come translators and commentators. Plato's educational theory was especially appealing to the British idealists. Jowett's translations of the dialogues, especially of the *Republic*, have long been classics. R. L. Nettleship's essay 'The Theory of Education in the *Republic* of Plato' (1897) was followed in 1900 by Bosanquet's *The Education of the Young in 'The Republic' of Plato*. Jowett's translation, together with these commentaries, helped to make Plato's educational thought accessible to a wider circle of readers. Nettleship's essay, in particular, is especially fine, a model of clear and well-turned exposition. His *Lectures on the Republic of Plato* (1897) are still widely read by students of philosophy today.

It is possible that the work of these three Balliol philosophers on the *Republic* did more for the growth of interest in educational theory in this country than any original idealist philosophy of education. In the realm of practice, rather than theory, Platonic influences have often been alleged. Nettleship concludes his chapter on the education of Plato's Guardians with these words:

No one can doubt that, if it were possible to do something in his spirit for the training of the most influential people in the state, modern government would be considerably better than it is, for, if the function of government is the hardest and highest of all, it clearly requires the best training and the best instruments (Nettleship, 1897, p. 293).

The emphasis that the twentieth century came to place on the selection and education of an intellectual élite is well known. So, too, is the parallel often drawn between this élitism and Plato's. To what extent Plato's theory did indeed provide a model here is a topic for further research. To a large extent the impetus for modern élitism came from psychology and biology, from the eugenics movement and the rise of intelligence testing. This on its own does not, of course, rule out Platonic influence, since Plato was himself a eugenist. In addition Morant's sharpening of the line between elementary and secondary education in the years after 1900 *looks* as if it was modelled partly on Plato.[2] But fully to resolve the problem of the interconnexions between Platonic and contemporary élitism is not a task which we can undertake here.

The educational views of German, as well as Greek, idealism also became more available to British readers in this period. Millicent Mackenzie wrote an account of *Hegel's Educational Thought and Practice* (1909). She was, incidentally, Professor of Education at Cardiff, where her husband, J. S. Mackenzie, a pupil of Caird's, was Professor of Philosophy. Some years later, in 1926, G. H. Turnbull produced *The Educational Theory of Fichte*.

Fichte indirectly influenced British educational thought in the early part of our period in two other ways also. Both Herbart and Froebel had been Fichte's pupils: Herbartian and Froebelian ideas were both very influential before and just after the turn of the century. Neither thinker can be properly labelled an 'idealist'. Herbart reacted explicitly against idealism in a firmly realist direction; Froebel's thought is too unphilosophical. Yet in Herbart's case, at least, Fichte's insistence, shared by many later idealists, that while the content of education should be highly intellectual, its ultimate aim is moral improvement, was preserved. Herbart's main appeal to his less sophisticated English followers was that he appeared to provide them, in his famous doctrine of the 'four [later five] steps', with a ready-made teaching method of wide application. To the more discerning, however, his virtue lay in his having created a *comprehensive* (though not complete) educational theory, covering not only problems to do with teaching methods and the nature of mental structures, but also, in his theory of 'many-sided interest', the content of education in relation to its aim. Herbart showed them how these different topics could be interconnected in a single theory. He also stressed the importance of getting clear first about one's aims and then working out appropriate means of realizing them, in the shape of content and methods. At the level of ends, Herbart's theory dovetailed well with idealism: the aim of education was the creation of moral character,

178

as exhibited in one's interpersonal dealings, in one's life as a citizen, and, wider still, in one's 'relation with the Highest Being'. At the level of means, Herbart had little in common with the idealists, partly since the latter, as we have said, had not much to offer at the micro-level, partly since Herbart placed all the emphasis on a direct moulding of mind and character through 'instruction' and moral training, while the idealists always kept in mind the indirect educative influence of social institutions in general. Because of the macro-level connexion, however, it must have been easy for many in the teaching profession during our period to see Herbartian and idealist conceptions of education as belonging to very much the same school of thought – as indeed in many respects they did.[3]

An explicit connexion between Herbartianism and idealism is found in the writings of T. G. Rooper (1847-1903). Rooper went up to Balliol in 1866. He studied classics, became an intimate friend of Bernard Bosanquet and was deeply influenced by Jowett and, especially, by T. H. Green. After a few years as a private tutor, he became a school inspector, first in Northumberland, then in Bradford and finally, until his death in 1903, in charge of the Southampton district. He was a tireless and enthusiastic devotee of popular education. As another inspector, A. C. Legard, like him a pupil of T. H. Green, wrote of him: 'He threw himself with energy into every movement that was likely to increase the interest of teachers in their profession, and humanize their work. He saw, for example, as a student of Plato, the far-reaching benefits of children being brought up among surroundings of an elevating kind' (Tatton, 1907, p. xlvi). And again: 'Although Rooper's chief concern was for education, it must not be supposed that he did not take, as might have been expected from a pupil of T. H. Green, a keen interest in other public and social questions' (ibid., p. xlvii). Like Green, Rooper saw the aim of education as at once ethical and religious. In his essay on 'Reverence: or the ideal in education', he follows Goethe in arguing that the purpose of education is to implement in children a three-fold feeling of reverence, 'for things above, for things on earth, and for man in society'. On the last of these he writes:

> It is not the most important end of education to train a child to become a successful wage-earner, because 'making his own living' is not really the most important part of his future life. The real educational problem is not a mere industrial question. We want to know how we can make it possible for all, even the poorest, to lead a life which, however humble, shall not want its share of dignity. The boy grows to be a man, and will

179

become a workman or a professional man, but he will also be a member of a community, and an Englishman. Our problem is how to enable him to play a man's part in that community and in that country (ibid., p. 253).

In this passage we hear the authentic voice of social idealism, the same that speaks through the pages of Carlyle and Green, of Caird, Henry Jones, Lindsay and Tawney.

Most of Rooper's essays were, however, closer to teachers' practical classroom concerns. The most celebrated of them has the curious title 'The Pot of Green Feathers' (ibid., p. xlvii). It took him, he said, seven years to write. Still very readable, its theme – familiar enough to teachers today, but less so to those of eighty or ninety years ago – is the influence of a child's existing interests and understanding on his perception. The title was suggested by an actual experience of Rooper's: a little girl in an inner-city school gave the name to a pot of ferns which her teacher was using in an object lesson, never having seen this plant before. What is of especial interest for us is that Rooper sees the topic partly as an educational application of Green's philosophy of mind. As we saw in the discussion of Green's metaphysics in Part 1, he drew heavily on the Kantian point that phenomena do not exist independently of minds: how the world appears depends on the conceptual apparatus which is applied to it. What is of even further interest in Rooper's account is his awareness that this Kantian insight runs not only through British idealism but also through Herbartian psychology. Herbart, the pupil of Kant's disciple Fichte, developed Kant's idea into his well-known theory of 'apperception', which he applied in his *The Science of Education* to the pedagogical problem of trying to ensure that children are intellectually prepared to assimilate new ideas and information. In connecting Herbartianism and idealism in this way, Rooper points to a link between them, educationally speaking, not only at the macro-level in their shared insistence on moral aims, but also at the micro-level of classroom learning.[4]

John MacCunn studied at Balliol under Green a few years later than Rooper, matriculating in 1872. He later became Professor of Philosophy at Liverpool. His book *The Making of Character* was subtitled 'Some Educational Aspects of Ethics'. It was first published in 1900 in *The Cambridge Series for Schools and Training Colleges,* many times reprinted and still, according to his Balliol contemporary J. H. Muirhead, writing about the beginning of the Second World War, 'widely and justly honoured in all teacher training colleges to this day' (Muirhead, 1942, p. 50, n.1).

The book first examines various factors which help to form an individual's character. The first part concerns congenital endowment, discussing such matters as heredity, vital energy, temperament, capacities, instincts, development and habits. MacCunn draws much on the views of contemporary psychologists like Lloyd Morgan and James, and his idealist proclivities, though not absent, are less in evidence here than elsewhere, especially in his following chapters on 'Educative Influences'. These 'influences' extend much further for MacCunn than the home and the school. They even extend further than social institutions in general: one of his chapters is entitled 'Wordsworthian Education of Nature'. In this he is at pains to point out, following Wordsworth's account of his childhood and youth in *The Prelude*, that 'the influences of social and natural surroundings are not antagonistic to each other, but interfused and co-operant' (p. 70). Nature and society are not to be contrasted, as in Rousseau: they work together. Nature can influence the moral life in several ways: by deepening our emotional life, especially as 'recollected in tranquillity' or, for instance, by helping us to develop a 'healthy, care-free, outward outlook on things, which is of peculiar value in days when city-life is more and more with us' (pp. 74-5). Some of MacCunn's argument in this chapter – and elsewhere – is, as in this quotation, banal. What is of interest is the idealist framework in which it is set. Nature *must* work with society and not against it, because both nature and society are expressions of divine thought. 'Our great prophets of Nature ... have ever insisted,' writes MacCunn, 'that "half-revealed and half-concealed" there lies in visible appearances a revelation of Ideas, and of God in whom all Ideas find their source and unity' (p. 77). This is, he thinks, a doctrine which 'is not to be lightly brushed aside as misty metaphysics'. He goes on to talk of seeing 'Power in the flooded torrent, Peace in the sheen of silent and sailless days' (p. 78), and so on. Once again, intellectually this is not impressive; but the pedigree is unmistakable.

Nature does not, according to MacCunn, reveal moral values to us. 'For such things we must turn to Society' (p. 79); that is, to the various social institutions which help to shape individuals' moral character: the family, school, friendship, one's place of work, the political community and religious organizations. 'Character' (also referred to as 'moral character' or 'the character of the citizen') is, MacCunn later remarks, the 'one supreme and satisfying end for which all polities exist' (p. 125). Character, then (we may infer), is the end of education; social institutions, largely, its means.

Among these, the family is of first importance, especially in the early years. MacCunn perceptively comments that since the introduction of public education on a large scale its importance has grown considerably. It is, he says 'precisely when education is organized by public authority that there is more need than ever of a place where the individuality of the child, upon which Rousseau and Pestalozzi and Froebel laid such passionate stress, may with the discerning eyes of anxious affection be studied, cared for, tended, restrained, developed' (p. 85). But MacCunn's 'individuality of the child' is not that of individualist philosophers. 'Their social atom is an abstraction. It is the family, not the atomic individual with which ... we have to build' (p. 86). The ends which children learn to follow in the family are not of an egocentric sort. 'There are common joys and common sorrows: and, as time goes on, there come the cementing memories of a common past. There is disinterested delight in the projects and the successes of kith and kin' (pp. 85-6).

This sense of a shared well-being must extend gradually beyond the narrow family circle. If it does not, it may 'create a corporate selfishness fatal to the wider sympathies' (p. 88). The next institution MacCunn discusses – but in less than three pages – is the school. He points to its heavily qualified value in stimulating the spirit of competitiveness needed in the industrial and commercial world outside, to the influence within it of public opinion, to its 'revelation of the importance of punctuality and order' (p. 90). As to the value of any direct instruction in moral codes which it may provide, he is more doubtful, inclining to the view that 'it is the institutions that control our actions that are ... the main teachers of what our duties are' (p. 186), while recognizing at the same time the need for some kind of more reflective understanding of them. (He does not connect the latter especially with the school.)

MacCunn's chapter on 'Livelihood' is interesting for its ambivalence, typical of much of idealism, on the moral influence, for good or ill, of the industrial order. The division of labour turns men into means for the realization of non-moral ends. 'Moral ends', on the other hand, 'are deposed from that pre-eminence which they would never lose were the social organism planned, maintained and developed in the interests of the moral life of its members' (p. 97). There remains a contradiction between the narrowness of the average man's vocation and the 'breadth of moral development of which [he] is capable' (ibid.). And yet the division of labour also teaches us the importance of mutual dependence, compulsory work shows us the 'stern, but never really hostile, face of Obligation' (p. 98): however far status gives way to social mobility, men must give up any illusion that they can spin their destinies as they please. Even though the industrial order has not been devised as a school

182

of virtue, 'it may, nevertheless, in the large scheme of social evolution, be more in harmony with moral progress than might at first sight appear' (p. 99). MacCunn is more easily able to keep at bay his anxieties about the demoralizing nature of capitalism than some of his fellow-idealists. Is society not, after all, evolving according to a divine plan?

In any case, work, MacCunn tells us, is not the sole moral influence on our adult lives. There is the 'active participation in the life of citizenship which Democracy practically puts within the reach of all' (p. 101). For this 'the preparation of the citizen for his duties is a necessity. In part this is a preparation in knowledge, some knowledge at least of his country's history and laws, its political institutions and economic system. And the need for this will be intensified should these days come – as the socialists assure us they are coming – when self-government in industry and commerce will be added to self-government in politics' (p. 102). It is interesting to reflect that this passage was written eighty years ago: it is a universal political education and industrial democracy that many social reformers are still demanding today as necessary conditions of a participatory democracy, and their coming is still by no means a certainty. Knowledge alone, MacCunn goes on, is insufficient as a preparation in citizenship: it must be harnessed to a concern for the common good. This can best grow by participation in active citizenship itself. Once again, along with this radicalism, we find curious touches of Hegelian historicism: men are not always drawn into politics for moral motives, yet 'by the exceeding cunning of the national Destiny ... they may unconsciously be forming the political virtues' (pp. 104-5).

Religious organizations, finally, also have a part to play. They can help the individual to live for distant and unseen ends through participation in corporate activities dedicated to their pursuit.

But what is there to guarantee that all these several institutions, from the family through to the religious organization, will work together, to produce a unity of character in the pupil? Social institutions, MacCunn tells us, 'are not permeated by a recognized common ideal'. 'Society is out of joint and inconsistent with itself' (p. 113). The education which they provide therefore needs supplementing. Plato and Aristotle, he reminds us, thought that moral improvement at the individual level was 'impossible without the reorganization of society, the instrument of education' (p. 115). MacCunn is sympathetic to this recourse to a solution at a more global level. He thus helps to bear out our contention earlier in this chapter, that the idealists, with their interest in relating phenomena to the wider wholes which contain them, were more effective at the macro-level of educational thinking than at the micro-level. But what kind of more global solution is practicable? The chief obstacle to social reorganization, as he sees it, lies in the intractability of the economic and political system. While eschewing 'the obsolete conservatism that would ascribe to these the fixity of Nature's ordinances', their reform is likely to be a long and slow process. 'They are so wedded to their own ends, so intent upon wealth-production or wealth-distribution, or upon the reform or defence of the constitution, or upon the administration or expansion of the empire' (p. 116). Perhaps the growth of democracy will help to stem this 'scramble for wealth and struggle for power' (p. 117) by making men more unwilling to be mere means for the creation of wealth or the realization of political programmes, and insist on being treated as ends in themselves. Perhaps. But MacCunn is not confident that this will happen quickly. What, if anything, can be done in the meanwhile, short of total social reorganization?

MacCunn sees most hope in the reform of those existing social institutions which can help to shape character. At present they often work against each other. But in principle they could come increasingly to be permeated by common moral ideals.

This, then, for MacCunn, is the way ahead. Ethical philosophy can perform an indispensable service at this point. There is no shortage of moral ideals in circulation. Indeed, that fact is a partial explanation of the lack of coherence in the collective work of social institutions. What ethics can do is help men to reflect on different ideals, compare them with each other, think about their assumptions and justifications. It can also throw light on the values and disvalues of methods of imparting these ideals to others: by example, for instance; by precept; or by the institution of a moral code; and on the difficult problem of developing moral judgment in people.

All these issues are treated in some detail in the last half of the book. Presumably this discussion is meant to help not only schoolteachers, but all those whom MacCunn calls 'educators by profession', 'parents, teachers, priests and moralists' (p. 124). But, again, it is not only to these that the job of realizing ideals should ideally be left. 'They must also enlist in their service those who lead in industry and politics.' These men must look beyond their narrower ends and make their activities contribute to the moral development of their fellow-countrymen.

What is of interest in MacCunn's book as a whole is his awareness throughout of the intimate connexion between education and the general social ethos. Education is not wholly, or even primarily, a matter of instruction. Here he would have been quite at odds with the Herbartians: it proceeds, to reintroduce Hegel's term, by changes in *Sittlichkeit*. MacCunn saw, quite correctly, that the prevailing incoherence in social ideals endangered unity of moral character in the individual. His solution – in line with the aims of the Ethical Society and other idealist enterprises we have examined – was a general raising of the ethical standards of social institutions. As a contribution to educational reform, this approach has much to recommend it, being of relevance as much to our age as to his. When professional educationists discuss education, or moral or political education today, this is still too often within a school framework, or within a framework of home and school combined. The idealists, MacCunn included, help us to keep our horizons broader. This is a point to which we shall be returning in Part 3.

Let us look next at the writings of Fred Clarke. The relevant parts of them for our purposes are not extensive, consisting of the first two of his *Essays in the Politics of Education*. But they repay examination because they provide a particularly clear example of the application of idealism to educational theory, and one which has many points in common with MacCunn's.

Fred Clarke was, like most idealists, a product of Oxford, but not a conventional one. Born in that city in 1880, he won a Queen's Scholarship in 1899 to the Oxford University Day Training College as a non-collegiate scholar of St Catherine's Society. After four years of a composite course, he emerged with a first-class degree in history and a teacher's certificate (Mitchell, 1967, pp. 12-13). After teaching and lecturing in education in this country, he became Professor of Education in Cape Town, where he published his *Essays* in 1923. In 1936 he succeeded Percy Nunn as Director of the London University Institute of Education, where he remained until his death in 1952.

In his preface to the *Essays*, Clarke pays tribute to the 'wonderful philosophical work of the late Dr Bosanquet' and acknowledges his great indebtedness to him. 'I have long thought,' he goes on, 'I should like to try the rather ambitious role of attempting to point to some of the implications for education of the general idealist position as he has taught us to understand it' (Clarke, 1923, p. viii).

The first of the two essays is entitled 'The Need for a Philosophy'. It begins with the statement that 'The aim of all education is the attainment of a right understanding of the eternal and the expression of that understanding in and through the ways of common life' (p. 1). More concretely, as he says he used to put it to his student-teachers, 'the ultimate reason for teaching Long

Division to little Johnny is that he is an immortal soul' (p. 2). In T. H. Green and other idealists, the purpose of education, though evident enough from the whole body of their philosophy, had not been explicitly stated. Clarke transposes mainstream British idealism directly into educational terms. All the familiar arguments are here. 'Individualism' is a baneful influence. Society is not a construction out of atomic individuals: individuality and society are inextricably interconnected (p. 6). He shares MacCunn's attitude to social progress: 'Plato tried to teach us more than two thousand years ago that we shall get nowhere unless we begin with ... humanity writ large in the whole developed social order, instead of with seeming individuals who in themselves are unreal abstractions' (p. 7). Individualism has led to competitiveness in industry, to *laissez faire* in politics and to a conception of education as a lever for 'getting on'. In education, as elsewhere, men must be seen as social creatures, not private individuals. Pupils must learn to think in terms of 'we' not 'I'. 'So long as "others" remain simply "others", education, like society, must remain unintelligible' (p. 14). We must come to see ourselves as belonging to a 'world', a world which 'must come to speak through us and through which we are to learn to speak':

> The existing social order is a type of such a world, just as the
> course of human history is another type looked at dynamically
> as 'becoming', and both must find a place in the final
> synthesis. But if we ask what kind of a 'world' is needed to
> determine the growth and expansion of a self so as to ... give
> it the completest universality, we shall be driven on beyond
> the bounds of the 'world' of society, beyond the bounds of the
> 'world' of history to the world of Reality as a whole within
> which these must fall (ibid.).

In this explicit attachment to traditional idealist metaphysics Clarke is more uncompromising, or perhaps merely less cautious, than MacCunn. His Hegelian streak comes out again a sentence or two later, in a passage reminiscent also of Dewey:

> We are faced in education by a world of seeming
> contradictions: mind and body; individual and society;
> freedom and government; work and leisure; instinct and
> morals; religion and science; time (or history) and eternity;
> and the task of education is to *transcend* these contradictions
> without annihilating either of the terms (pp. 14-15).

If the values of idealism for education were more generally recognized, he goes on to say, a thinker like Froebel would be remembered for

> more than his invention of the kindergarten. For amid all his obscure mysticism ... he did hold fast to the conception of a concrete unity which preserved in full value and quality all the seeming contradictions of immediate experience. And he did not hesitate to call this unity God and to treat the revelation of its nature in and through the education of the individual as the real goal and significance of that education (p. 15).

This particular passage is interesting, as it shows how a theory like Froebel's, which we tend to see today as an ancestor of 'child-centred' education and so to be included under the heading of 'individualist' theories, was readily acceptable to a self-professed idealist and passionate anti-individualist like Clarke.

In one way this first chapter of Clarke's goes beyond a rather mechanical application of idealism to educational matters and begins to break new ground. 'Individualism' has been, in his view, only the first of two antipathetic influences on education. The other has been 'Science'. When we were discussing the impact of Oxford idealism in Part 1, we observed that a large part of its attraction, to a man like Dewey, for instance, was its *reconciliation* of science and religion. Clarke, on the other hand, is opposing them. But the difference between him and earlier idealists is probably more apparent than real. For when Clarke talks of 'Science', he has especially – though not wholly – in mind the new discipline of educational psychology, while his predecessors were working with a broader conception. 'Science', he points out, has been strongly individualistic. He cites Spencer, Darwin and 'our modern Eugenists' (p. 8). Individualistic science is now becoming more and more influential in education. Clarke takes as his text Percy Nunn's *Education: Its Data and First Principles*. 'Nowhere,' he complains, 'does he show a real grasp of, or even an attempt to grasp, Reality as a whole. He sets out from the conception of a human individual as "given" and exhibits education as the guided and assisted *development* of the individual as such. It is all development, the individual makes *himself*, and there is no revelation of him as a centre in which a whole universal order comes to a self-conscious realization of itself' (ibid.). Nunn has a false conception, in Clarke's view, of the aim of education. For Nunn there is no universal aim, if this is taken as implying a particular ideal of life, since each person will have his own ideal. Education aims at the most complete development of each individual, thus enabling him to 'make his original contribution to the variegated whole of human life as full and as truly characteristic as his nature permits'. Clarke has two objections to this position. First, he claims that 'there *is* a universal aim of education that holds for all alike', that is (more or less), 'to know God and enjoy Him forever'. Second, he cannot attach any sense to Nunn's 'conception of a congeries of individuals each forging "for himself" (and apparently *out of* himself) his own contribution to the variegated whole' (p. 8). Clarke does not clearly separate out these two reasons, but they are surely very different and both of them do not have to be accepted together. One could accept the second argument, for instance, on the ground that social wholes cannot be built out of atomic parts; but deny the former claim that a religious ideal of life is the only one to follow.

Clarke's objections to 'science' rest on another ground as well although this, too, is not differentiated from those already mentioned. It is the familiar idealist point that its attitude is 'analytic and abstract'. Educational psychology, no less than physical science, tends to abstract from concrete phenomena their quantifiable, measurable properties and concentrate on these. Psychological tests may set out for us 'in precise mathematical form all that there is in Johnny – except Johnny himself!' (p. 10).

In pointing out that educational psychology presupposes both that individuals are atomic entities and that understanding human nature is methodologically similar to understanding physical nature, Clarke is making important charges which will find him many sympathizers among philosophical psychologists today. But he fails to detach these criticisms from his own religious assumptions. Why does Johnny in his real individuality escape 'the cunning nets of science'? It is not merely that not all his properties are capable of being brought under laws of nature or capable of mathematical expression, but that 'when you find *him* you come across the "immortal soul" which is ... just the *wholeness* itself, while Johnny, in turn, derives from the complete wholeness' (ibid.). This barely intelligible metaphysics destroys the keen edge of Clarke's critique and makes his own position vulnerable to a scientifically inclined opponent. This will be worth recalling both when we look at the causes of idealism's decline as a force in education in the next chapter and also when we come to assess what, if anything, in it is worth reviving, in Part 3.

Clarke is not wholly opposed to educational psychology. It may help us to understand children, but it cannot help us with the most important things about them. Still less is he opposed to the application of science in general to educational matters. But, in line with his anti-atomism, he sees sociology rather than psychology as the 'controlling science' for education. The Subjective Mind studied by psychology is only a 'correlate' of Objective Mind (Hegel's term for the phenomenon of human society) and subordinate to it (p. 13). He quotes Durkheim with approval on this point.

We can extract from Clarke's statements, indeed, a hierarchical picture of the relations between the different disciplines of educational theory. 'If you wish really to *understand* education,' he says, '... you must take the synthetic and concrete position of Philosophy rather than the analytic and abstract standpoint of Science' (p. 10). Philosophy (i.e. idealist philosophy) has thus priority over science; and among the sciences, sociology has priority over psychology. This has obvious affinities with Hegel's system: one cannot understand individuals on their own without introducing society; and one cannot understand society without seeing this in its relation to reality as a whole. Clarke's hierarchical conception is of by no means purely historical interest. We shall have to examine more fully in Part 3 what abiding light – again, if any – idealist views like his can throw on the nature of educational theory.

The last part of Clarke's first essay says something more about the various 'seeming contradictions' already mentioned – between work and leisure, time and eternity, and so on – and the ways in which they may be overcome in a new 'synthesis'. Two of his central points are reminiscent of MacCunn, as well as of many other idealists. The first is his belief in the power of poetry, especially Wordsworth's, to make us sensible of an eternal reality which is not man-centred. 'I have sometimes thought,' he writes, 'I should like to try the experiment of training teachers in a two years' course where there was nothing but study of Wordsworth and contact with children. It would be interesting to compare the product of such a course with those brought up on "Method" ' (pp. 17-18). The second is his belief that the established industrial order is one of the main two obstacles in the way of the hoped-for synthesis (the other is the established ecclesiastical order). He cites Laski as support for his view that industry should be run by 'democratic co-operation'. This would help to diminish the 'waste and misdirection of spiritual energy' which it entails at present. It is no use hoping for salvation only from a reform of schooling:

What is needed is that school and industry shall alike be taken up into the same system, an *educative* system. This will mean that on the one side school will have to be brought closer to the actual needs of ... the community's economic life, as men like Dewey and Kerschensteiner have so long

189

argued. On the other side, industry must 'educationalize' itself, and that means it must 'democratize' itself (p. 19).

The general theme, that all social institutions, not at all the school alone, are potential educators, is explored further in Clarke's second essay, 'Education and Society'. 'We educate *for* society,' he points out, 'and we also educate *by* society' (p. 23). Unfortunately, we are often prone to overlook this second truth. Not only do we unduly exalt the school as the chief instrument of education; even within the school we put much more emphasis on its formal side – on 'instruction' – than on the school society itself. Our neglect of social means is evident in our acceptance of the individualistic ideas of educational reformers (like Montessori, for instance) who urge us to discourage imitativeness and encourage inventiveness, to put free activity and free expression in place of rigid discipline, to let the child shape his world for himself. These reforms may well be desirable, but not if they lead us to ignore the social nature of individuals: 'the individual consciousness must work upon social "stuff" in order to fashion itself; ... the individual is a point, as it were, around which is organized a social network of rights and duties' (pp. 25-6).

Social institutions educate us in more than one way. 'They communicate to the individual member the idea or ideal which they embody and assist the growth of that idea in him', usually otherwise than by direct instruction. They can also provide us, through our contact with many diverse minds, with manifold reflections of ourselves as seen by others, and so can guide us towards self-revelation, towards 'a good working knowledge of self' (pp. 30-1).

The first of these points once again echoes MacCunn. So does another which he goes on to make about the family: that 'the chief duty of the State is to strengthen, not to supersede it' (p. 32). The State must ensure to it that minimum of resources without which it cannot properly carry out its educative functions. Like Mac-Cunn, too, the other social institutions Clarke mentions besides the family are school, trade or profession, and church. The main job which the school does as an institution, rather than as a place of instruction, is to convey the idea of 'Abstract Justice': the pupil comes to see himself as only one unit among many, under a law made for the common good and enforced on all alike.

Clarke also has very definite views – as we have begun to see – about the proper relationship between the state and these various educative institutions. He discusses and dismisses both the theory, embodied in German education of the day, that institutions are merely to be manipulated – or ignored – by the state in its efforts to mould a certain type of citizen; and the anarchist theory found in Tolstoy, that education can occur only by the free contact of individuals, that the school is, for example, 'just a shop set up to meet the demand of those who want to buy knowledge' (pp. 36-7), and that the state, therefore, has no role whatever to play. Clarke adopts a middle position. The state *does* have a role. It cannot simply withdraw altogether and leave things in the hand of autonomous institutions or individuals. After all, 'the State itself is an institution' (p. 38), an institution arising out of the common language, beliefs and traditions of a community and thus out of something more comprehensive than any particular institution lying within it. The state is set over against these other institutions as 'a common power to keep them all in *harmony*' (p. 39). Its role is not to be a competitor among educating institutions – one educator among many – but the 'means of sustaining, stimulating, and co-ordinating the real institutions that educate' (p. 40). It will encourage the educative work of family, school, church and industry, but 'will not claim to call the tune because it pays the piper' (ibid.). Those things which it can do better – teacher-training, for instance, or the 'general organizing and standardizing of instruction' – it will do itself; otherwise it will leave other institutions considerable freedom. It is also part of its educative task to modify industry in various ways, especially as regards child labour. 'Furthermore, it will take steps to see that the life of the streets, the common amusements and places of resort of children, the periodical literature and the very shop-windows are not exercising influences hostile to the ideal of life which the State has to further and maintain' (p. 41).

The last quotation is of especial interest. It provokes the question: in what way can the state keep subordinate institutions 'in harmony'? Does this not imply a criterion of value of some sort? Is the state not, after all, going to shape and manipulate other institutions in accordance with the 'ideal of life' which it is charged to promote? If so, how does one avoid the German and Platonic excesses to which Clarke objects? Earlier Clarke has told us that the central aim of education is a religious one. The state's 'ideal of life', in virtue of which it is to control the life of the streets, is therefore a religious ideal. But, for all Clarke's arguments about the free scope left to other institutions, how can he avoid the charge that his educative society will be a closed, monistic theocracy?

He does, it is true, say things which suggest a pluralistic, rather than a monistic, outlook. For instance: 'The supreme end of the State in education will be to secure that its educational system, taken as a whole, shall be as full, as rich, as wide, as varied, as the whole complex life of the State itself. Every ideal of proved worth; every defensible view of life; every form of social observance that has value; ... all must be represented' (p. 40). But if the phrase 'every ideal of proved worth' covers ideals antipathetic to religion, Clarke seems guilty of an inconsistency; yet if it does not, the charge of arguing for a closed religious state still sticks. Is Clarke leaning over backwards, when he adopts this pluralism, to avoid this latter objection? It does not seem so. More likely, it is yet one more indication of his Hegelian inheritance. The ideal society will be a unity, but not a monistic one. It will embrace within it all kinds of diversity, resolving their contradictions in its higher harmony. The framework within which this resolution is to take place is still, it would seem, a religious one.

In his combination of religious commitment, socialism and a belief in the diversity of the educational system, he reminds one of Tawney, his almost exact contemporary and later co-member of a group of Christian activists with strong idealist connexions.[5] Many have found it odd that Tawney should have *both* advocated an end to the secondary-elementary divide in his *Secondary Education For All* (1922) *and* been a leading figure on the Hadow Enquiry which produced *The Education of the Adolescent* four years later, in which the seeds of a divided secondary education were so firmly planted. Why, one may ask, did Tawney not argue for a *common* secondary school? This may seem obviously desirable to fellow-socialists today, but it is not surprising that Tawney, with his idealist background, should not have found it at all obvious. The only commonness desirable in Tawney's society was at the level of general moral values. Within this overarching harmony, diversity was not only allowable, but positively desirable, for without it there was nothing to stop the rise of a monistic religious state.

We shall be returning to the question of the state's relationships with its subordinate educative institutions in Part 3. The tension we have found in Clarke – and also in Tawney – between a demand for social unity on the one hand and a belief in diversity on the other, is still with us today. We shall have to see, if we can, how far Clarke's solution – of state as 'harmonizer' but not as educator – is still viable today, or whether the difficulties it contains point the way forward to any more rationally acceptable alternative.

Last in our collection of idealists' writings on the theory of education is Henry Jones's essay 'The Education of the Citizen' (1917) (Jones, 1924). In genre it is more a topical reaction to current events than the works we have considered so far, all of which were pitched at a more theoretical level. But it is interesting partly because it illuminates Jones's motives in the educational enterprises of his which we have already discussed, but more especially because it is an explicit statement of the educational implications of idealism as seen by a leading exponent of that school.

Jones wrote his essay towards the end and in the light of the First World War. In it he contrasts the British and German conceptions of the purpose of education. The main difference is that the British people, unlike the German, has not seriously endeavoured to define this. For Germany the ultimate aim of education is the advancement of the state. It has helped to make Germany economically powerful, but it is 'education also which has perverted its spirit, corrupted and enslaved its soul' (p. 235). How can Britain avoid the same fate? Many will say that its strength lies in its traditional reluctance to set any national educational aim. 'It is one matter, it may be said, to control the machinery of education for industrial and commercial purposes; it is another matter for the State to presume to control the souls of its citizens by means of its educational schemes' (p. 236). Britain has proceeded empirically, 'muddling along' in a very un-German way, and not doing badly in the process. Jones sets his face against this reaction. The true solution is not to renounce national aims, but to embrace good ones. Britain should see that 'the sole end of education is the citizen himself'. States exist only for their citizens. The 'only education which should ever be given is a *moral* education' (p. 247). It is interesting that Jones also says at about the same point that the child must be taught 'for his own sake'. For an idealist, believing in the doctrine of self-realization, it was natural to identify an education directed to the pupil's own well-being with a morally-oriented education. This is a point we shall be discussing more fully in Part 3.

'How can it be reasonably said,' asks Jones, 'that the only education permissible is moral education? What of the arts and of religion, and of the whole series of crafts and industries, trades and professions?' (p. 248). He answers that the question falsely assumes that morality is a separate province of life. 'Morality *is* religion operative'; 'all man's ultimate ideals are adjectives of one another; the good is beautiful and the beautiful is good; and they are both true.' Crafts and industries he sees as 'moral opportunities, a chance of rendering a service which is free' (p. 249).

Moral education at school level is not to be a theoretical matter. We learn morality, as Aristotle pointed out, by doing good deeds: through practice, not theory. The teacher's example is important.

In a passage reminiscent of Fred Clarke, and possibly a prototype, Jones writes, 'He may be teaching the multiplication table or the paradigm of a Greek verb, . . . but his permanent care is, by any or all of these means, to liberate the possibilities of character in his pupils' (p. 251).

But a theoretical understanding of morality is also essential to citizenship. It is that which Germany has failed to provide for its own people, thus preventing them from seeing that the state is not a final end but itself has moral responsibilities at the international level. Since it is not in the school that an intellectual moral education can be provided, Britain must make some kind of national provision for post-school education in citizenship. Here the WEA points the way, especially in its system of tutorial classes. This recoils on the universities themselves, leading them 'to reform themselves in the direction of serving citizenship more directly *and much more widely*' (p. 268). Jones urges the universities to train all their own undergraduates directly in citizenship, providing courses in literature, British history, science, economics and the ethics of individual and social life. Universities should also extend their responsibilities for working-class education and, in addition, begin to do something to provide a broad education in citizenship for the employers and managers of labour, who are themselves generally not much more liberally educated than their workers. The universities, in short, are to become the spiritual-intellectual centre of the nation, not superseding the churches, who will remain the chief agencies of moral education, but working with them to create a new and more intelligent national community.

We pass now to two educationists, who, though not, like those we have just described, in the mainstream of idealist thinking, were nevertheless deeply influenced by idealism and retained important features of it in their writings. They are Edmond Holmes and John Dewey.

Rooper, MacCunn, Clarke and Jones all adhered to the two idealist doctrines: (a) that individuals are essentially social creatures, and (b) that individuals achieve their fullest self-realization as vehicles of eternal spirit. Holmes and Dewey were both influenced by idealist philosophy in their youth, but in each case the idealist strands in their thinking became so interwoven with other doctrines that neither of their resulting educational theories can properly be called 'idealist'. Putting it very roughly, each of them dropped, and each of them retained, a different one of the two idealist tenets, (a) and (b). Holmes dropped (a), the social doctrine; and retained (b), the religious. Dewey dropped (b) and kept (a).

Edmond Holmes's *What Is and What Might Be* took the educational world by storm when it appeared in 1911. In it Holmes, recently notorious through his association with Morant in the matter of the so-called Holmes' Circular (Gordon, 1978, pp. 36-40), seized the opportunity which retirement as the Board of Education's Chief Inspector afforded of being able to speak his mind publicly on educational matters, and launched on a passionate tirade against the evils of the system in which he had worked all his life. The book is divided, black against white, into two parts: I: What Is, or The Path of Mechanical Obedience; and II: What Might Be, or The Path of Self-Realization.

Holmes's strictures on traditional elementary education (its rote learning, cramming for examinations, authoritarianism, and so on) are based on close observation and important to the general historian of education in their own right. But it is not his critique, but the ideal with which he replaces it, that is of particular interest to us here. Instead of being repressed and mis-shapen by a soulless system, the pupil is to be helped towards 'self-realization'. Holmes's use of this idealist term is not coincidental. Self-realization, in both Holmes's theory and in philosophical idealism, is the highest aim, or ideal, of human life: in realizing himself, the individual is at the same time becoming united with reality as a whole. Holmes thus preserves the central religious connotation of the term.

It is not surprising that he should have done so. Born in 1850, he was an undergraduate at St John's College, Oxford, between 1869 and 1873, at a period when idealism was rapidly becoming dominant. An unpublished biography of Holmes by E. Sharwood-Smith testifies to its influence on him at that time: 'No one felt its appeal more keenly than the scholar-freshman of St John's, already possessed by a daimon – that devotion to probe into the secret depths of the mysterious Universe, and a passion for beauty and truth which never degenerated ... into emotional and sensual excess.' It was the religious doctrine of idealism which had most effect on him. T. H. Green, who 'put in the foremost place the struggle to unite in the closest sympathy with the inner strivings of the Universe' meant more to him than Jowett, with his more practical concern with fitting his pupils for statesmanship. 'Until the study of Buddhism and the Upanishads brought Holmes into closer touch with Eastern intuition, it was to Thomas Hill Green that he looked mainly for guidance and support.' The effects of Green's teachings, Sharwood-Smith points out, 'are plain to read in much of Edmond Holmes's writing.'[6]

There is little doubt that Holmes's doctrine of self-realization is an offspring of British idealism, especially that of T. H. Green. But it has other progenitors besides. One of these is the Buddhism that

Sharwood-Smith has mentioned. 'Speaking for myself,' writes Holmes, 'I will say that the vista which the idea of self-realization opens up to me goes far beyond the limits of any one earth-life or sequence of earth-lives, and far, immeasurably far, beyond the limits of the sham eternity of the conventional Heaven or Hell' (Holmes, 1911, p. 307). Elsewhere in the book he speaks of 'the ever-widening path which makes at last for Nirvanic oneness with the One Life' (pp. 176-7).

Holmes is best known today as an advocate of standing back from the child and letting his inner potentialities develop to their fullest extent. He was much influenced by a teacher in a village school in Sussex, Harriet Finlay-Johnson ('Egeria'), who ran her class in what we would now call an enlightened 'child-centred' way. He gave a theoretical backing to this practice in the shape of a theory of inborn instincts (the communicative, the dramatic, the artistic, the musical, the inquisitive and the constructive) for whose development a good teacher creates the conditions. If these instincts are allowed full rein, the child will be on the path of self-realization.

Holmes shares with Green the idea that human ends are *given,* are embedded in reality. Where he differs from him is in his conception of how these ends are attained. For Green, and for the idealists in general, it is social institutions which form our character. Our biological nature is also, of course, an influence: social forces can only get to work on what is naturally given; but our purely animal consciousness must soon give way to those higher forms of awareness which the family, school and other institutions have the task of developing. Holmes allows much more educative influence to our biological make-up, to our half-dozen major instincts.

Social influences, correspondingly, he plays down. He discusses very briefly 'the social aspect of self-realization', accepting, with the idealists, that we ought to move towards a less egoistic and competitive society, but trusting to nature to guide us towards it. 'When the growth of the soul is healthy and harmonious, the cultivation of all the expansive instincts having been fully provided for, the *communal* instinct will evolve itself in its own season; and when the communal instinct has been fully evolved, the social order will begin to reform itself' (pp. 289-90).

Holmes does not, therefore, *reject* the idealist picture of individuals as parts of social wholes, which are themselves parts of a large, metaphysical whole, but his treatment of the first of these relationships is perfunctory and naïve. How the individual could achieve Nirvana mattered to him more than how he could be fashioned into a member of a community. His shift away from Green's social idealism is evident, too, from his section on 'the moral aspect of self-realization'. For Green, of course, the social aspect and the moral aspect were inextricably connected: moral development was necessarily developed in and through and for society. For Holmes, however, being a morally good man is having managed to conquer one's sensuality and learnt to escape from self. It is the instincts, once again, which effect this escape: 'The sympathetic instincts [are] a way of escape into the boundless aether of love; the aesthetic instincts . . . into the wonder-world of beauty; the scientific instincts . . . into the world of mysteries which is lighted by the "high white star of truth" ' (p. 280). There is, therefore, nothing essentially *social* about morality: as long as all one's instincts – not only the 'sympathetic' – are allowed full scope to grow harmoniously together, the individual will necessarily escape from self.

Holmes is important in the history of educational thought because he modified the idealist concept of 'self-realization' in the way we have described. By cutting away its social connotations and building in an instinct theory, he made the first of two historic moves which were to turn the concept completely on its head, making it the pivot of a 'progressive' theory of education of an ultra-individualistic, and hence utterly anti-idealist, kind. The second move – which has occurred in the last half century – has been to cut away, too, the religious connotations, tying 'self-realization' to biology alone.

Atomic individualism and self-realization theory can now go hand in hand: the social and religious constraints which had kept them apart before have finally vanished. Again, we shall link up some of these more general observations with our wider assessment of the idealist reform movement in Part 3.

One final comment on Holmes, before passing on to Dewey. If we compare him with MacCunn and Clarke, we find none of their doubts about the tendency to over-value the school as an instrument of education; quite the contrary. Clearly, with his views, Holmes is not going to attach any educative potential to the industrial and political institutions which the others stressed; the Christian church – in whatever denomination – has little appeal to him. It is *par excellence* in emancipated schoolrooms like 'Egeria's' that education proper can take place. The schoolteacher, paradoxically perhaps, thus becomes more significant as an educator at a time when she is learning to abstain from instruction and merely guide the hand of nature. This, too, will be a point worth reflecting on again when we come to Part 3.

197

In his relation to his idealist inheritance, John Dewey is the mirror-image of Edmond Holmes. Where Holmes preserves the link between self-realization and religion but removes its link with community, Dewey does the opposite. As outlined in Part 1, Dewey was an early convert from a rather narrow nonconformism, which failed to meet the challenge of Darwinian science, to Green's idealist and rationalistic version of Christianity.

In proceeding further along a rationalist path, Dewey quickly came to lose his religious faith entirely and therewith his commitment to idealist philosophy. But he retained a number of its features in his own work. First, as with the idealists, philosophy for him remained closely tied to educational ends: it never became a hived-off end in itself. He kept, too, the basic idealist concept of self-realization, although he early changed his terminology and came to speak of it as 'growth'. Again, just as the fundamental aim of education for the idealists was the unending raising of the individual's consciousness to fit it more and more as a vehicle of divine spirit, so, too, in Dewey, education is essentially to do with promoting the growth of the individual mind without limit. Education for him has no aims outside itself: growth is an intrinsic aim. The idealists, too, might well have said the same. But for them there was a metaphysical rationale which is lacking in Dewey, or transposed into a different key. Raising men's consciousness was not, to the idealist, a means of promoting an *extrinsic* aim, namely, the furtherance of God's purposes: God only existed as reason, so the apparently extrinsic aim was, after all, intrinsic. Dewey lopped away the religious rationale, leaving only growth for its own sake. Or rather, since nature in evolution came to replace for Dewey the gradual unfolding of a divine purpose in the world, growth was important, in the final analysis, because it was in line with the open-endedness of evolutionary progress.

Dewey's shift from a religious to a biological perspective also brought with it a change in his conception of 'growth' itself. For the idealists, mental development was ratiocinative, and contemplative. For Dewey, impressed by the evolution of mind in nature, it became above all practical, taking the form of adapting new means to ends when usual means were unavailable. Intelligence was reconceptualized as problem-solving.

Like all the idealists, Dewey had an antipathy towards dualisms, and not least in education. Like them, he rejected the dichotomy between liberal and vocational education and between individualistic and social aims. On the latter issue, he accepted the idealist contention that to realize oneself is to promote the well-being of one's community. He accepted, too, the democratic and egalitarian interpretation of such a communal life which most of the British idealists adopted. For him the 'growth' which constituted both aim and process of education was to take place within a democratic form of social life, one whose worth was measured, as he writes in *Democracy and Education*, by 'the extent to which its interests are shared by all its members, and the fulness and freedom with which it interacts with other groups' (Dewey, 1916, p. 99). Individual mental growth is not, therefore, the development of practical intelligence for whatever private and idiosyncratic ends the individuals may happen to have. Since individuals are essentially members of a community, it is necessarily subservient to social ends.

11

The decline
of idealist
influence

Between the two world wars the influence of idealism on British educational thought and practice dwindled away as rapidly as the influence of the Liberal Party on British political life. (These two changes were not, indeed, unconnected, as we pointed out above.) It is true that some of the idealist reformers – Tawney and Lindsay, for instance – were still very active. The founding of Keele as late as 1949 can be seen as a very late offspring of the movement. Henry Morris's Cambridgeshire 'village colleges' may have had a tenuous connexion with idealist communitarianism: a leading influence on Morris was his old tutor, Hastings Rashdall, whose philosophy was inspired by that of T. H. Green.[1] Idealists like William Temple helped to shape the 1944 Education Act. And if we look beyond education to social policy more generally, the Beveridge Report of 1942, which laid the foundation of the post-war welfare state, is also traceable back to the Balliol idealism of the turn of the century.

We should not forget, either, that the institutions which the idealists helped to found or foster – university extension, the WEA, the new universities – continued to flourish long after the idealist heyday between 1870 and 1920. The campaign for 'secondary education for all' was continuous with the nineteenth-century demand for 'middle-class education': to a large extent it was still powered by the old idealist belief in fellowship and the brotherhood of man.

In all these ways the work of the earlier idealists was still bearing fruit. In some ways, perhaps, it still is today. But as time goes on, as one moves forward from the First World War to the present day, the strands of influence become increasingly harder to discern. As in the movement for 'secondary education for all', for instance, they become so interwoven with other lines of thought ('child-centred' educational theory, for instance, or the psychologically based doctrine of 'tripartitism') that it becomes no longer possible to talk of peculiarly *idealist* educational reforms, as one was quite happy to do for the earlier period. Above all, there was nothing after the First World War like the close-knit movement of educational reformers we found before this time. Green, Acland, Haldane, Sadler, Tawney, Jones: the work of all these men, and of many secondary figures, criss-crossed and dovetailed at innumerable points. As they shared a common philosophical background, their contacts with each other no doubt helped to reinforce their common commitments. The age, too, was behind them. Idealism was the dominant philosophy. After 1918, however, the idealist outlook – in education and in life – had formidable rivals. In the changed intellectual climate it would have been difficult to keep a cohesive idealist reform group together. Idealist ideas, as a result, became watered down, merged with theories of often quite opposite inspiration, until nothing distinctively idealist was left.

Tawney's career is a case in point. Had he been buttressed in his educational work on the Consultative Committee and within the Labour Party by men equally devoted to his views of Christian fellowship, he might have achieved more than he did. But one of his Labour Party associates and one of his colleagues on the 1926 Hadow committee, who is said to have had a large hand in drafting its Report, was Percy Nunn, who, as a realist in philosophy and an individualist in education was, as we shall see, an avowed enemy of idealism. Despite the promising early start to his career which made him the leading educational policy-maker of the Labour Party by his early forties, Tawney was unable to develop a coherent, independent educational policy after that time. In signing Hadow in 1926, the harbinger of post-war tripartitism, his views became progressively hard to disentangle both from those of the 'child-centred' theorists on the one hand and, on the other, those conservative politicians who, seeing the inevitability of 'secondary education for all', sought to deprive it of its substance by letting the old elementary-secondary divide continue under this new name.

Idealism's decline as an educational force followed hard on its removal from the dominant position it had earlier held in academic philosophy. A landmark here was an influential article by the young Cambridge philosopher, G. E. Moore, published in *Mind* in 1903. Entitled 'The Refutation of Idealism', it argues that the basic tenet of British idealism – of the metaphysics of T. H. Green and F. H. Bradley, for instance – is that reality is spiritual, and that this conclusion is based on the premise that *'esse'* is *'percipi'*. We saw in Part 1 how this premise is incorporated into Green's system. Relying on Kant's claim that the phenomenal world is one in which objects are objects *for some consciousness,* Green had argued that since objects in nature do not depend for their existence on human consciousness, they imply the existence of a non-human, i.e.

divine, consciousness. All this, however, depends on the assumption that natural objects cannot exist unless they are perceived or experienced. It was this assumption which Moore held was unjustified and against which he set the realist claim, which he saw more reason to accept, that natural objects are capable of independent existence. Being a stone, for instance, should not be conflated with being seen as a stone: the former does not entail the latter.

Realists like Moore and his fellow Cambridge philosopher, Bertrand Russell, grew rapidly to philosophical prominence about the turn of the century. The *Zeitgeist* was changing. Oxford idealism had appealed to religious young men who were perplexed by the corrosive influence of science, especially Darwinism, on their beliefs. Its metaphysical foundations, in which so many thought they had found a bulwark, were, as Moore's famous essay showed, flimsier than they looked. To an increasing number of philosophers, often reared in the sciences and without religious commitments, they were less than compelling. Institutional lag helped to keep individual philosphers in prominent university positions well beyond the First World War; but already, a decade or so before, most of the creative thinkers in British (and American) philosophy were beginning to turn their back on the old philosophy. In its place various forms of realism emerged, which denied the postulate of spirituality and created philosophical systems more congenial to empirical science. Neo-realism, logical atomism, pragmatism, logical positivism, linguistic philosophy: the new philosophical movements which rose on the ashes of idealism in the first half of this century were consistently opposed to its fundamental assumptions.

Idealist social philosophy also lost ground with the decline of idealist metaphysics. This may be only what might have been expected, since, as we saw in Part 1, Green's ethics and political philosophy depend on his metaphysics: the 'common good' at which personal and social action ought to aim was understood by him in essentially religious terms; and Hegel's political philosophy was similarly metaphysically rooted. Whether idealist social philosophy *necessarily* depends on such a metaphysics, or whether parts of it are detachable from a religious basis, is an issue we shall take up again in Part 3. Historically, however, from the First World War onwards, it *was* taken as intimately connected with its Hegelian or post-Hegelian metaphysical foundations and was often heavily criticized for that reason. The most celebrated critique was by L. T. Hobhouse in *The Metaphysical Theory of the State* (1918). This book, which is still the standard critical work on idealist political theory, was largely directed against Bosanquet's *The Philosophical Theory of the State* (1899) and also against the explicit Hegelianism in that book to which Bosanquet, more than any other of the idealists, was highly committed. Much of Hobhouse's attack focuses on the view that individuals realize themselves only as members of a state, which is seen as a supra-personal entity, or substance, and exists as an end in itself. Since actual states are manifestations of, that is, partial self-realizations of, a cosmic reason, it seems to follow that it is pointless for the individual to try to remodel society: he is rather 'to do his duty in that state of life to which it has pleased the state-god to call him' (Hobhouse, 1918, p. 87). Hobhouse excepts Green from much of his criticism, on the grounds that he was less attached than Bosanquet to Hegelian ideas; in particular, Green never argues that the state is a supra-individual substance but constantly affirms that states are nothing but communities of individuals. Despite his greater attachment to the rights of individuals, however, Green's social philosophy still runs into problems when taken together with its metaphysical foundations.

It was no accident that Hobhouse's critique appeared during the First World War. He dedicated it to his son, then serving as an officer in the RAF. In his dedication he writes, 'In the bombing of London I had just witnessed the visible and tangible outcome of a false and wicked doctrine', the 'Hegelian theory of the god-state' (op. cit., p. 6). Hegel's philosophy was thus held responsible for the Prussian state-worship which culminated in the First World War. Hobhouse saw his book as a contribution to the war effort. He considered Hegel's thought 'the most penetrating and subtle of all the intellectual influences which have sapped the rational humanitarianism of the eighteenth and nineteenth centuries.' He wrote the book to help to 'make the world a safe place for democracy'. For this, 'the weapons of the spirit are as necessary as those of the flesh' (ibid.).

Hobhouse's invective against Hegel was less than just. As we saw in Part 1, Hegel was no crude authoritarian, advocating the unquestioning worship of a god-state. His theory of the state was an attempt to satisfy the twin demands of Enlightenment rationalism and of the expressivist theory that individuals can only realize themselves by seeing themselves as bound together in larger wholes. As Avineri, Taylor and other present-day commentators on Hegel have stressed, he *continued* the 'rational humanitarianism' which Hobhouse claimed he undermined. The fact that Prussian apologists later in the nineteenth century used and contorted Hegel's theories as an intellectual prop for their doctrine that individuals should never resist established government, cannot fairly be blamed on Hegel.

Whether or not Hegel's was in fact a 'wicked doctrine', its association with Prussianism made it normal so to regard it, even for such an otherwise judicious thinker as Hobhouse. Before the First World War, critics of idealism, like Moore, would have tended to describe Hegelianism as 'misconceived'; after it, it became difficult not to think of it as morally reprehensible. Had such steps been taken after the First World War as were taken after the Second, to make Germany economically and morally strong enough to take its place in a democratic Europe, perhaps philosophers would have soon reverted to a juster appreciation of Hegel's political thought. But the rise of Hitler ensured that he remained an object of intellectual and moral contempt until long after the Second World War (as he still is for many people today). He was pilloried especially in Karl Popper's *The Open Society and its Enemies* (1945), a book in many ways the equivalent for the Second World War of Hobhouse's *The Metaphysical Theory of the State*. 'The final decision to write it,' Popper says in his Preface, 'was made in March 1938, on the day I received the news of the invasion of Austria' (Popper, 2nd edition (1959), p. viii). Hegel, along with Plato and Marx, is seen as one of the three chief enemies of an 'open' society or liberal democracy, an intellectual precursor of totalitarianism, whether of right or of left. Popper's onslaught on Hegel is no less than vitriolic. Not only is modern totalitarianism *based* on Hegel: Hegel himself is represented as having one overriding aim: 'to fight against the open society, and thus to serve his employer, Frederick William of Prussia' (op. cit., ch. 12, book 2, p. 32). Hegelianism is 'an apology for Prussianism' (p. 35). Popper states that he has 'tried to show the identity of Hegelian historicism with the philosophy of modern totalitarianism' (p. 78). 'The new generation,' he states, in a characteristically contemptuous and dismissive passage, 'should be helped to free themselves from this intellectual fraud, the greatest, perhaps, in the history of our civilization and its quarrels with its enemies. . . . The Hegelian farce has done enough harm. We must stop it. We must speak even at the price of soiling ourselves by touching this scandalous thing' (p. 79).

Which is the more scandalous – Hegel's philosophy or Popper's chapter on Hegel – may be left to the judgment of history. What is more important to us here is that, thanks to Popper, the hostility which Hobhouse expressed towards Hegelian social philosophy has been enabled to persist even into our own generation. Only very recently have Hegel's philosophy in general and his political philosophy in particular become academically 'respectable', and this only in some quarters.

The significance of this anti-Hegelianism in our account of the decline of idealism as the flywheel of an educational reform movement should be clear. It was the ethical and social doctrines of the British idealists, as much as their metaphysics, which led their disciples into the cause of education. The attack on Hegel's social philosophy could not help but diminish adherence to those political theories, like Green's or Bosanquet's, which were Hegelian-inspired. As totalitarianism continued to flourish in Europe, moral and political thinkers tended to turn their back on all 'organic' theories of society and stand firm on the rights of the individual against the threat of an almighty state. The nineteenth-century British philosophy of liberalism and individualism, against which Oxford idealism was to some extent a reaction, found a ready soil in which to re-root itself. Green's own fate is interesting in this connexion. Although, as Quinton has recently reminded us, there is no doubt at all of the Hegelian inspiration behind much of his philosophy, over the last fifty years Green's debt to Hegel has been played down and his connexion with British liberalism played up. R. G. Collingwood, for instance, stated in his *Autobiography* that the British idealists rightly repudiated the label 'Hegelian'; that their work was a continuation and criticism of indigenous philosophy; and of Green, in particular, that he 'had read Hegel in youth, but rejected him in middle age' (p. 16). That this is a massive overstatement, affected, no doubt, by the prevailing anti-totalitarianism of the time of writing (1939), should be evident from our discussion of Green's relationship to Hegel in Part 1.

An interesting example of an educational reformer influenced by Green in his youth and strongly anti-Hegelian in later life is H. A. L. Fisher. Fisher was the President of the Board of Education in Lloyd George's government, responsible for the Education Act of 1918 which raised the school-leaving age to 14 and proposed the institution of part-time continuation education up to 18. He is best known, academically, as a historian, especially, perhaps, for his *The History of Europe* (1935). His academic career began, however, as an Oxford teacher of philosophy. He records in his *Unfinished Autobiography* how although he was less attracted as an undergraduate in the mid-1880s to the prevailing Hegelian philosophy than many of his contemporaries, 'there was one book, inspired by Hegel, to which we were introduced from the first and which made a deep impression on my mind' (Fisher, 1940, p. 50). This was Green's *Prolegomena to Ethics*. Green had died in 1883, a year before Fisher went up to New College, but 'his powerful influence survived' (ibid.). By 1935, however, Fisher clearly had no time whatever for Hegel. 'The cult of an omnipotent State which prevailed among the Prussians found full and explicit warrant in the teaching of Hegel. The logic of tyranny was gilded by the ethical beauty of sacrifice. The State was God. In the name of that abstraction millions must be prepared to work, to suffer, and to perish' (Fisher, 1935, pp. 931-2).

The new insistence on the rights and autonomy of the individual as against the state, evident in general political thought and practice, was echoed, in the inter-war period, in the world of education. In educational theory, this individualism was related to the idealism it replaced in one of two ways. To some extent it developed out of it; to some extent it grew up in deliberate opposition to it. We saw above, in Chapter 10, how Edmond Holmes's advocacy of 'self-realization' as the supreme aim of education was rooted in idealism, and how he retained the Hegelian belief that individuals could only realize themselves as parts of a larger, cosmic whole. His lack of interest in that part of idealism which stressed the individual's communal ties and his relation to the state meant that there was no question, in his case, of being tarred with 'Prussianism'. Quite the contrary: his was an educational philosophy which stressed above all the salvation of the individual. To teachers and educationists sickened by the First World War and looking forward to a society where such personal sacrifice and spiritual waste would be for ever eliminated, his book, as we know, had an immediate appeal. Whether, because of its religious framework, it appealed more to believers than to non-believers, is uncertain. Its basic religious assumptions, we must remember, were not Christian, but Buddhist. This may have given it a sympathetic audience even among agnostics or atheists; and it helps a little, no doubt, to explain how the 'progressive' movement, with which the book was associated, came to lose any intrinsic connexions it had with religious beliefs which it had in Holmes. Indeed, by the end of the inter-war period, the philosophy of 'growth' or of the 'fullest development of the pupil's potential', had become assimilated to a theologically-neutral individualism: the individual pupil was to be allowed to develop for his own sake alone, as an independent entity, talk of larger cosmic wholes having receded into the background, or disappeared altogether.

The 'progressive' movement, therefore, can claim some continuity, via Holmes, with idealism, as first the social and then the religious aspects of the latter fell away to leave an educational theory of 'self-expression' or 'self-realization' of a far more individualistic sort than the idealists ever conceived.

But Holmes was not the only prophet of progressivism. At least as influential at the time we are considering – the period after the First World War – and, if anything, increasing in influence up to the Second World War and even beyond, was Percy Nunn, whose *Education: its Data and First Principles* was first published in 1920, reprinted over twenty times between the two wars, and for the last time in 1963.

Unlike Holmes, Nunn was an explicit opponent of idealism, his educational theory marking a complete break with the older tradition. For over a decade before he wrote *Education*, Nunn was already a well-known figure in philosophical circles, a prominent member of the Aristotelian Society and contributor to its proceedings. Like Moore and Russell, he was a staunch realist, being assciated with a group known as the New Realists (Passmore, 1957, pp. 259-61). Educated as a scientist and mathematician, he was thus from the start of his career closely associated with the new anti-idealist movement in philosophy. His opposition to Hegelianism is very evident in the first edition of *Education* (in a passage deleted from its later editions):

> The bitter fruit of the Hegelian ideas has ripened and been gathered under his [the reader's] own eyes. It would be absurd as well as unjust to charge upon any philosopher the whole guilt of Armageddon. . . . Nevertheless the connexion between the World War and Hegelianism is too close to be ignored. From the idealist of Jena more than from any other source, the Prussian mind derived its fanatical belief in the absolute value of the State, its deadly doctrine that the State can admit no moral authority greater than its own, and the corollary that the educational system, from the primary school to the university, should be used as an instrument to engrain these notions into the soul of a whole people
> (Nunn, 1920, p. 3).

Nunn states in a footnote to this passage that 'it should be remembered that a noble line of British thinkers – e.g. T. H. Green, the Cairds, F. H. Bradley, B. Bosanquet, Lord Haldane, Sir H. Jones – have drawn inspiration from Hegel.'[2] But he takes no pains to distinguish those parts of Hegel's philosophy which could inspire this noble thinking from those so closely associated with Prussianism. As with Hobhouse's book, the dominant impression which the average reader must have derived from *Education* was that Hegelianism was a morally repulsive philosophy which sacrificed the good of the individual to a suprapersonal entity called 'the State'.

Nunn's own educational theory rests on assumptions and arguments quite opposite from those of the idealists. Both are equally interested in the good of the individual; but whereas the idealists claim that this good can only be understood in terms of a common, social good, Nunn looks to nature, rather than society, as its source. The aim of education, for Nunn, is the fullest possible development of the pupil's individuality. Individuality is most fully developed when one's powers of self-expression are given full rein. 'Self-expression', for Nunn, is an aesthetic category. 'Human lives, like works of art,' he tells us, 'must be judged by their "expressiveness"' (op. cit., p. 249). It is artists, above all, who are most fully able to express what is within them: the artist 'shows in the clearest and most definite form what is fundamentally and ideally the way of all life' (op. cit., p. 40).

Not all self-expression is, for Nunn, of an artistic sort. He does not say in so many words that the aim of education is to turn every pupil into a painter or a poet. But it is difficult to escape the conclusion that in an ideal society he would hold that teachers could have no higher aim. Here immediately we see what a change of direction there has been since the days of the idealists. For them social realities had been omnipresent: the ignorance, poverty and despair abounding in city life made a life of social service a far surer route to the promotion of the good life than the life of the artist. As we saw above, Green encouraged those attracted to an artistic career to reflect on the magnitude of their talent, so as to see whether it was large enough to enable them better to serve the common good more in that vocation than in some other. Nunn, however, turns away from the evils and inadequacies of contemporary society. Education for him has nothing, it appears, to do with such social improvement. His book turns from actuality towards an aesthetic utopia. No doubt this, too, helps to explain its popularity among its first readers, sickened by four years of war. They may be excused for overlooking the fact that the working and living conditions of actual society did not give the mass of the people the opportunity to live the fully expressive life of which Nunn dreamed. Maybe social conditions could be so altered as to enable this, but this would take time. A socially-oriented education could have helped, no doubt, to speed up this process. If Nunn had thought on these lines, his views would not have been so very different from the idealists'. But he did not. Philosophically a 'realist', he was far more of an 'idealist', in the different and somewhat pejorative sense of a utopian, out of touch with present realities, than the philosophical idealists themselves.

But then one of the strong points of idealist writers has always been their awareness of the historical rootedness of their thinking. In reverting to the older atomist-individualist tradition of British philosophy, Nunn revives an a-historical attitude towards educational thinking.

In his 'expressivism', however, Nunn has at least one point of contact with idealism. As Charles Taylor has shown in his recent book *Hegel,* the view that man's highest end is in some sense to make his life an expression of himself, of his fundamental thoughts and feelings, became increasingly powerful in the eighteenth century as a counter-weight to the rationalism of the Enlightenment and, especially via Herder, greatly influenced Hegel and his followers, helping to shape the idealist conception of self-realization (Taylor, 1975, pp. 13 ff.). Nunn's interest in expressivism derives from the aesthetic version of the theory found in the Italian idealist, Benedetto Croce.

At the same time, Nunn's individualism served to give 'expressivism' a different connotation from that which it had had in Herder and the idealists. For them, self-expression was something essentially social. If a poem or a symphony is an expression of one's thoughts or feelings, it is an expression *to others* of these things. It is man as communicator in language who provides the model for the concept of human life as expression in a more general sense. But in Nunn, as more widely in popular aesthetic thinking in the period after the First World War, expressiveness becomes a more exclusively individualistic ideal. The emphasis comes to be put on externalizing, giving shape to, the individuality within one. The social function of expression, by contrast, its role in binding members of a community together at the level of the fundamental values they hold in common, drops out of the picture. Henceforth, creative art in schools, elevated by Nunn and others to an importance it never had before, would be justified increasingly by appeals to 'self-expression'. But as the older, social connotations dropped away, the criterion of expressiveness came more and more to be, not the power of a work to reveal to us our common nature, but its 'individuality', its lack of dependence on established traditions, its mere 'originality' (in the non-value-loaded sense of that term).

In his interest in expressiveness, and, as we shall see, in other ways, Nunn's thought is not wholly discontinuous with idealism. But his treatment of self-expression, although important as a girder in the total structure of his thought, is far from extensive in his *Education,* occupying only a few paragraphs at most. What is far more evident, almost on every page, is his picture of human beings, and of pupils in particular, as essentially biological creatures. Here his difference from idealism is at its most marked. For the idealists, man is to be understood as what he potentially is: a vehicle of eternal consciousness. His 'animal' nature is something to be transcended in the course of self-realization. Nunn, on the other hand, stresses at every point his continuity with the animal world. The highest forms of human individuality and creativeness are shown to differ only in degree from more primitive functions in sub-human mammals and creatures further down the phylogenetic scale. Nunn draws freely and widely on the work of biologists, animal psychologists and psychoanalysts in support of this thesis.

It is on the basis of such biological and psychological facts that Nunn seeks to 'justify' (Nunn, 1920, p. 26) his central contention that the aim of education is the fullest development of individuality. This is the aim of education because it is the goal of *life*, not merely of the life of particular human beings, but of life in general as a phenomenon of nature. The history of life in this sense is of 'a striving towards the individuality which is expressed most clearly and richly in man's conscious nature, and finds, therefore, in that goal the true interpretation of its earlier efforts' (p. 25).

Nunn's educational theory is a species of social Darwinism. Life has evolved from primitive states of goal-directedness towards states of greater and greater autonomy and capacity for flexible, intelligent action. In man this autonomy reaches its as yet highest form. Educators, therefore, in promoting their pupils' individuality, are handmaidens of nature, co-operators in a grand evolutionary enterprise.

A fundamental weakness in this view, which Nunn nowhere seeks to remedy or explain away, is that empirical facts – about the course of evolution in this case – cannot by themselves justify value judgments. The particular value judgment which Nunn wants us finally to accept is that we should educate for individuality. This, we have seen, rests on the more general value judgment that we ought to co-operate with the process of evolution, work in the same direction as that which it is following. But *why* ought we to do this? The fact, if it is a fact, that evolution has proceeded in a certain direction, is no justification. There is no argument here from what is to what ought to be. It might be, for all we know, our moral duty to work *against* natural, including evolutionary, tendencies.

Many, like T. H. Huxley, for instance, have argued precisely this in the face of social Darwinism. If evolution has occurred through the 'survival of the fittest', it does not follow, as some have thought, that maximum competition for wealth and other goods should be permitted so that the 'fittest' should survive. Neither does it follow, as Galton and his school believed, that social policy should be

210

directed towards the creation and maintenance of an intellectual élite, whether by eugenics or by educational selection. In line with his Darwinism, Nunn argues strongly in *Education* (p. 117) for educational élitism: it is only among the select few that individuality will reach its full flowering.

Despite, or in a curious way because of, his naturalism, Nunn's educational theory shares a fundamental assumption with idealism. This is that man's destiny is in the hands of a cosmic force. For the idealists this force is God, operating through human history and social institutions. For Nunn it is nature, operating through organic evolution. But God and nature have often, in the history of thought, been closely assimilated to each other. Even Nunn, whose book is framed throughout within the categories of natural science and hardly ever touches on religion, can write, when talking of 'expressiveness', that 'our bodies, or rather our "body-minds", are meant to be temples of the Holy Ghost, and though we are left free, each to work out his own plan, we are bound to make the building as fair as the materials and the powers at our disposal permit' (p. 249). We must, he goes on, 'use our creative energies to produce the most shapely individuality we can attain. For only in that way can we be, as we are bound to be, fellow-workers with the Divine in the universe' (ibid.).

Nunn, like Holmes, became an inspirational leader of the 'progressive' movement which grew to such prominence between the wars and is still perhaps even more widely influential today. In playing down the pupil's social ties, he strengthened that inclination to see him atomistically, as a self-contained entity, which has since been such a prominent feature of the 'child-centred' movement. As in Holmes, so in Nunn, the foundation of his theory is holistic: neither writer treats individuals as completely self-contained, since for each the individual is a member of a larger whole, whether directly of reality, as in Holmes, or indirectly of reality and immediately of a biological species, as in Nunn. One of the features of educational thinking since the time they wrote has been the falling away of such larger metaphysical backdrops, while the foreground theorizing which the metaphysics once supported has been preserved. One sees this also in intelligence testing. When this grew up under Galton, Pearson and Burt right at the beginning of this century, it was backed by the doctrine of eugenics, which itself was a form of Darwinism. Today the eugenic background has long since melted away and the intelligence test stands on its own. Piagetian theory is the same: few of today's students and teachers who describe children's learning as a development through Piagetian stages realize that Piaget's interest in children derived wholly from grand Darwinist speculation about the continuity between biological and intellectual evolution and ultimately about the relationship of mind and matter.

Nunn's 'child-centredness' is thoroughgoing. Conceptual learning is not presented as a gradual initiation into intersubjective (i.e. social) meanings, but as a process of abstraction from experience, based on a foundation of innate ideas (p. 223). As in Rousseau, the postulation of innate ideas plays an important role in Nunn's theory. It allows him to talk of a human nature 'in which there is an inborn impulse towards greater perfection or "expressiveness"' (p. 250). Hence he insists, like Rousseau, that the child be left alone as far as possible to develop by himself. While not ignoring the point of view of those who claim that school curricula will often contain subjects or activities which children left to themselves would rather not pursue, he believes that 'in our ideal school the ultimate veto lies with the pupil', though not without 'a genuine trial of the repellent subject' (p. 274).

The 'progressive' movement thus reversed the idealists' conception of the child and his education, the child becoming a self-contained, atomic entity whose links with others within a community became of subsidiary importance; and a more self-oriented ideal of education grew up to replace the older community-centred ideal. Conceptions of the school and of teachers were also fundamentally altered. For the idealist, the school is only one social institution among many which play some part in education. As we saw in MacCunn and Clarke, *all* social institutions potentially have an educative role to play, from the family, through places of work to churches and political institutions. In Nunn, however, the school becomes relatively far more important. Educating becomes a task for the expert in those biological-psychological studies which alone provide the key to an understanding of the individual pupil's nature and hence of the fundamental aims of education and its methodology. The teacher is the teacher-psychologist, no longer a mediator between the child and the social-religious world into which the child will enter, but a servant of nature, an adjutant of evolution. Both schools and teachers become increasingly detached from the community without, turning in on themselves, because in an imperfect world they almost alone can carry the torch of evolutionary progress through the generations.

It is not that schools and teachers have *no* social purposes. In saying this, we are not thinking of the several passages in Nunn's book, especially in its final chapter, where – awkwardly for his main thesis – he writes about the need to introduce children into their social heritage. We mean, rather, that social progress now becomes an aspect of natural evolution. Schools, though cut off increasingly from the society around them, are still the servants of that society, but at a more exalted level: they are helping to move that society closer to the ideal implicit in the process of evolution.

Of course, Nunn's theory, though influential, was not the only intellectual support for this conception at the time. Cyril Burt, a colleague of Nunn's at the London Day Training College and a writer frequently cited in *Education,* lent his interest in intelligence testing to the same cause. Society will best achieve its nature-given ends if it allows the unimpeded growth of an intellectual élite. It is they who will enable societies to adapt to the changed environment which the future will always bring with it. In nature species have declined or died out through their inability to adapt, their lack of flexibility; so, too, it might be with man: the quality of our human stock might otherwise diminish. Burt and Nunn and their many followers thus pressed, between the wars, for special attention to be given to the 'élite'. Burt's Galtonian doctrines that individual differences in IQ are largely of hereditary origin and that these hereditary factors, in Nunn's words, 'limit the possibilities of individuals with adamantine rigour' (op. cit., p. 117), helped to justify this élitism. If nature had made us all capable of high intelligence, our evolution might have had to follow a different path. But she has not. The less intelligent among us will still be able to develop their individuality to the full through a child-centred régime; but this individuality will not, of course, be capable of that expressiveness and creativity which we can find only among a few.

The institutional reflection of this new educational doctrine was, as is well-known, the 'tripartitism' in secondary education, foreshadowed in the Hadow Report of 1926. This story has been told often enough and we shall not repeat it here. What interests us is the general change of outlook since the days of the idealists. We have already mentioned the reversal of views on the aims of education, the nature of man, the role of the school and of the teacher. But there was also a change of attitude towards an élite. In Green and his followers one certainly finds an interest in selection, the 'ladder', different kinds of school for children of different ability, and so on. Superficially, this looks little different from the IQ-élitism of the twentieth century. There is, indeed, a difference in nomenclature: the élite education which the idealists demanded was explicitly for the middle-class above all; the call then was for 'middle-class education'. By contrast, IQ-élitism was not explicitly tied to social class, but based on the class-neutrality of science. To many – and we should remember that Nunn was an educational adviser to the Labour Party – the second kind of élitism must have seemed far less socially reactionary than the first. But this is far from the truth. The idealists did not favour a middle-class élite because they wanted to entrench the privileges of that class as against the working class below. Their fundamental objective was to raise *everyone's* consciousness so that everyone could become a vehicle of the divine purpose. The middle classes were to become co-operators in this educative enterprise: once their own cultural level was raised above the level of Arnold's philistinism, they could help, as teachers and in more indirect ways within the institutions in which they worked, to raise the cultural level of the masses. IQ-élitism, however, had no such social rationale. There would be no point in the IQ-élite's seeking to improve the intelligence of the masses, since that intelligence is genetically unimprovable. Educational priorities were reversed: the élite was no longer seen as the cultural servant of the whole community; it was rather that the community should minister to the growth of the élite, the one guarantor of evolutionary salvation.

There is yet another way in which the educational outlook changed since the days of the idealists. We saw earlier how Green, Acland, Haldane, Morant and other reformers had pressed for a cohesive, organically-related, national system of education. We saw the attempts made to demarcate more clearly different kinds of school, their objectives, the 'ladders' and paths connecting each to each: the elementary school, the secondary school, the continuation school. We saw the creation of a national network of universities and an associated network of institutions of adult education, both of which were to be interconnected in various ways not only with the lower schools beneath them, but also with the wider needs of the communities and regions which they served. After the First World War interest in systematization waned. The movement of opinion was increasingly towards institutional autonomy. In 1926 elementary schools and teacher training colleges became free to determine their own curricula and objectives, these being no longer under the control of the Board of Education and ultimately of Parliament. Secondary schools were freed in the same way in 1945. Universities began to insist more and more on 'academic freedom' and less and less on any direct role they could play in improving social welfare. WEA and university extension classes gradually lost their function as instruments in the cause of working-class education and increasingly became isolated centres of genteel culture in the middle-class suburbs.

To investigate the causes of this centrifugal tendency after 1918 would require a historical study in its own right. But the change in the *Zeitgeist* which we have already discussed must surely be a contributory factor. If metaphysics turned from an interest in organic wholes to atomic entities, social philosophy, from the state-community to individuals, and educational theory from socially-oriented aims to the promotion of individuality, it would not be surprising if this atomism were not reflected also at the level of institutions. Reaction against contemporary totalitarian moves to make all social institutions into servants of an official creed must also have encouraged institutional autonomy. Party political policy may have been a further factor. The freeing of elementary schools and training colleges from government control over their curricular objectives was the action of the Conservative President of the Board of Education at that time, Lord Eustace Percy. Whether his motive was to prevent the Labour Party from imposing their own objectives on these institutions is uncertain, though it cannot be ruled out.[3] Certainly by the Second War, R. A. Butler had defined four areas of educational activity which, in his view, were to be kept free of government control: school curricula, universities, teacher training, and the public schools. Though it was always hostile to the public schools, to a large extent the Labour Party followed the Conservatives' lead for the half-century after 1918, in leaving schools, colleges and universities considerable freedom in running themselves.

Institutional autonomy in education also found a backing in a theory like Nunn's. Schools, colleges and universities are here the servants of nature's evolutionary purposes, especially those institutions like secondary schools and universities, whose business is with the élite. Social constraints on their activities would endanger the higher, 'natural', ends to which they should be devoted. *Vis-à-vis* society educational institutions should be treated as ends in themselves. 'Child-centred' doctrine, finally, also had implications for institutional autonomy: children could not be free from the constraining influence of their teachers, if those teachers were themselves empowered by authorities outside the school to impose such and such objectives on the children.

In all these ways – in the concept of education and its aims, in attitudes towards an élite, in views on the function of the teacher, the role and autonomy of the school and other educational institutions – the vision of the idealist reformers was superseded after the First World War by a far more individualistic *Weltanschauung*. R. R. Rusk's book on *The Philosophical Bases of Education* (1928), in which 'idealism' in education is most favourably compared with 'naturalism' and 'pragmatism', failed to reverse the new flow of ideas. This is in spite of some shrewd criticism of Nunn's *Education,* his principal target in the chapter on naturalism. He points out, quite correctly, the difficulty which Nunn has in accounting for the social aspects of experience, since he sees man as predominantly a biological creature, ignoring the idealists' claim that 'man's higher or spiritual nature is essentially social' (Rusk, 1928, p. 43). Rusk likewise has no truck with the autonomous development of the individual as the central aim of education. It comes too close to justifying mere self-assertion, the paramountcy of one's own interests and rights. 'Insistence on development of individuality may result in a condition of affairs, such as Herbart described (1806, book 2, ch. iv, para. I), in which each person brags of his individuality and nobody understands his neighbour. Man must be taught to rise above his individuality, and to seek in social activities and social service the satisfaction of his spiritual needs' (Rusk, op. cit., p. 47).

What is most revealing in Rusk's book, however, is that despite his advocacy of 'idealism', it is clear from his description of it that the term has come to have a less determinate meaning than it had had at the time of Green and his followers. There is far less of a structured philosophical rationale, far more eclecticism. Religion, morality, art and knowledge are all aspects of the Absolute; as forms in which the creative activity of man manifests itself, their appreciation must form part of any comprehensive system of education. 'The idealist in Education, believing that the intangible values are the ultimate and eternal realities, will also emphasize the spiritual aspects of experience, insisting that knowledge, art, morality and religion are the aspects of life of supremest moment' (p. 109). The 'supreme task of education' for the idealist, we are later told, lies in 'the transmission and increase of [man's] cultural inheritance through its constant recreation' (p. 126). These pronouncements on the aims of education certainly have affinities with idealism. But they are too vague and general to be classified unmistakably as belonging to that school of thought: many a non-philosophical bishop might have tied education to 'intangible values' and 'eternal realities'; and, as to the second quotation, even the rejected Nunn himself can write that a school fails in its purpose 'unless it gives its pupils some understanding and appreciation of the conservative basis of their nation's life and of civilization as a whole' (Nunn, 1920, p. 36).

Rusk's 'idealism', despite occasional references to social activities and social service, has lost the vivid perception of the earlier idealists that individuals find their highest being as members of communities. In his historical review of idealism in education, Rusk traces the theory from Socrates, through Plato, Aristotle,

Rousseau, Kant, Fichte, Pestalozzi and Froebel, to Hegel. Between Hegel and the time of writing there is only one other idealist educational thinker whom he discusses. This is Gentile. Rusk's choice is significant in two ways. It shows, first, how already by 1928 the educational significance of British idealist philosophy was no longer considered worthy of note, even by an avowed supporter of idealism. It is true that he makes scattered references to Bosanquet, Caird, Green, Jones and Haldane elsewhere in the book, but these names are intermingled with such other names as R. Otto, H. H. Horne, W. Bagley, L. Bernard, without any indication to the reader that the former belong together in a cohesive and influential school of thought. The second point is that Gentile became closely associated with Mussolini's fascism, acting as intellectual spokesman for that movement. Rusk's reverence for him as the last of a great line of idealist educators can only have helped to drive the final nail in the coffin of the reform movement we have been studying.

The idealist legacy today

part 3

Education and its aims 12

What, if anything, do those concerned with education today have to learn from the idealist reformers? Has their work been only of historical interest, as having laid some of the foundations of the educational system we have today? Or do the theoretical under-pinnings of that work, their views on such things as the aims of education and its institutional embodiments, still have any relevance for us?

Let us look first at the general conception of education which one can extract from their works. The first thing to note about it is its close connexion with religion. Individual human beings are each potential vehicles of an eternal consciousness (or God, *Geist* or Absolute). This is not something which pre-exists a universe which it has created. It is embodied in the universe: it is in this that it expresses itself. Its connexion with man – as a thinking being, not simply as an animal – is more intimate than its links with nature. For in man the eternal consciousness becomes progressively aware of its own being. Its goal is self-knowledge, thought about thought. But this thought cannot take place in a divine mind detached from the universe. Since God is embodied in the world, the thought must be embodied, too. It is so in the minds of individual men. As men's minds develop beyond the lower types of awareness they share with animals towards higher forms of thought and feeling, so they become vehicles through which God can come to realize his in-trinsic purpose. As men are gradually extending their own self-knowledge, seeing themselves not as atomic entities, but as parts of larger social wholes and finally thereby as linked with the wider purposes of the universe as a whole, so God, too is expanding in self-awareness. This expansion is both in depth and in breadth. The divine purpose can be forwarded in two ways, by raising the consciousness of particular individuals to higher and higher levels, and by enlarging the number of individuals whose consciousness is so raised.

In devoting oneself to education, therefore, one is directly furthering God's purpose in the world. There is no problem of *justifying* education, for the idealist. He does not have doubts, as some of us do today, about what the proper aims of education

221

should be, or whether the continued expansion of the education system is necessarily a good thing. How could it fail to be so, provided it is working efficiently? It is an instrument fitted to a divine purpose. Looked at this way, it is not surprising that Green, Acland, Haldane, Sadler and the others whose work we have been tracing in this book should have thrown themselves so passionately into educational reform. Were it not for idealism, many of these men might have become clergymen. Some of them, like Gore and Temple, did. But neither those who did nor those who did not could have found any more certain or immediate way of serving God than through serving education.

All the idealist reformers we have been studying were religious men. Part of the reason for idealism's decline, we have suggested, has been the general secularization of life since the First World War. Many of us today would find it impossible to accept that religious justification for education which to the idealists seemed so compelling. The central difficulty resides in the claim that ultimate reality is personal, a conscious being of some sort with ends which it endeavours to realize. There are further problems which are embedded in this conception: of the relation, for instance, between this eternal being, dwelling beyond time and space, and the spatio-temporally located human beings in which he comes to be embodied. But leaving these consequential problems on one side, what reason have we to believe in the personal nature of ultimate reality, i.e. in the existence of a personal God? For some, the proposition literally makes no sense; for very many others, including ourselves, it may make sense, but there is no more reason to hold it than to hold that personal characteristics appeared in the universe only with the coming of man (or, perhaps, other creatures on other planets), and are ultimately traceable to an accident of unplanned evolution. Certainly T. H. Green's own economical demonstration of the existence of an eternal consciousness, which his disciples found so persuasive as a prop to their wavering faith, seems less than compelling once it is dispassionately examined. Green held, it will be remembered, that nature, as a system of Kantian 'phenomena', can only exist as an object of consciousness, but clearly not only as an object of human consciousness. It has an objective reality which transcends this. So the consciousness in question must be a more than human consciousness.

It is true, still following Kant, that we can have no experience of nature except as falling under conceptual schemes. But this does not imply that natural entities cannot *exist* except as conceptualized objects of consciousness. Trees, ferns and rocks can exist in the world, as they did before the appearance of animal life, even

222

though there are no creatures around to be aware of them. Green's mistake was to accept too readily Kant's distinction between 'phenomena' and 'noumena'. Kant made the existence of the phenomenal world dependent on creatures with human sensibilities, while preserving the truth that it is not man who has created nature, by introducing his unknowable world of 'noumena'. What Green did was to preserve this latter truth, not by introducing 'noumena', but by extending the concept of 'phenomena' so that these are no longer dependent on purely *human* sensibilities. He failed to see that there is another alternative solution of Kant's problem: to reject the concepts of 'phenomena' and 'noumena' altogether as unnecessary for making the distinction between nature as it is and our awareness of nature. There is only one nature picked out by these last two uses of the term: the first is not a world of 'noumena' and the second of 'phenomena'. If this is so, there is no reason at all to accept Green's theological conclusions – though this is not to say, of course, that they are not correct.

A contemporary unbeliever may well begin to look askance at the idealists' work in education, once he reflects on its religious rationale. It is not that they advocated the indoctrination of their own religious beliefs in others by closing their minds to alternatives. On the contrary: a respect for rationality and for the intellectual autonomy of the pupil was a hallmark of all their work. But the fact remains that their enthusiasm and energy spent in the service of education was born of a belief in a personal God as embodied in mankind. Suppose one drops this belief and the motivation which goes with it. What reason has one left to bother oneself with educational reform? Will it still be important to raise pupils' consciousness to higher and higher levels? Will it still be important to extend educational facilities to as many pupils as possible? If it is, then some other reason must be given than that which the idealists gave. The terrible thought occurs to one: suppose there is, in the final analysis, *no* good reason for expanding education in these ways. Was all the idealists' work, then, a pointless waste of time? Was their selfless enthusiasm perhaps completely misplaced? The thought may pass as quickly as it came: it is so obviously a good thing that we have schools and universities and adult education classes that even if the idealists promoted these things for the wrong underlying reasons, what they did was far from in vain. And yet . . . a doubt may creep back: *why* is education so obviously a good thing?

Even though the underlying reason for teaching Johnny long division may not be, as Fred Clarke thought, because he is an immortal soul, it does not follow that the idealists have nothing to

223

teach us about education and its aims. It could be that some of their central doctrines on this matter are detachable from their religious underpinnings and can stand on their own. What, for instance, of the basic belief that men should work together for a common good? This looks, on the face of it, as if it might be acceptable to many today who are community-oriented in some sense in their political and educational views, but who are at the same time not religious. Many may also be willing to adopt some of the more determinate ideas which Green and other thinkers had about the *kind* of communities whose good one should serve: the view, for instance, that a common good can and should be realized at different levels, from the family, through local communities, to state or national communities – given, as Green points out, that the service of the state or nation does not cut one off from a wider involvement in human brotherhood.

If we think on these lines, we are not left without answers to our fundamental questions about the nature of education, its aims and the value of expanding it. Education, we may say, should aim at promoting the common good, that is, at promoting the well-being of communities at different levels, and ultimately at promoting the well-being of the most all-embracing communities, that is mankind in general; or, if this is too un-concrete a community, then at least the outward-looking state or nation which can mediate between the individual and mankind.

We have an answer, too, to the question why the expansion of education – the increase in the numbers of educated men and women – is important. Or, rather, we do have an answer, provided that we give a certain interpretation to the proposition that education should aim at promoting the common good. Plato and Hegel both believed in this aim, but neither considered that anyone but a member of an intellectual élite (the Guardians, or the 'universal class') should deliberately follow it: the rest of the community could *in fact* be helping the common good without intending to do so, simply by attending to the demands of their social station or profession, perhaps because this is the conventionally accepted thing to do, or perhaps for selfish reasons. On this élitist view there is no reason for providing the non-élite with an education fitting them consciously to aim at the common good: there are limits to the need to expand an education of this sort across the population. But although there is an élitist strand in some idealist writings, the general tendency of the thinkers we have considered has been far less restrictive. It follows from their religious assumptions that *all* men should ideally become vehicles of the divine and that the more people become aware of their common destiny, the better. The early idealists' pressure for 'middle-class' education was not motivated by élitism: as the middle class became more highly educated, they would help in turn to educate the working class. Historical considerations aside, we have in this second, non-élitist, conception of education – in the view, that is, that everyone in the community should be brought up consciously to work for the common good – an educational ideal which many today may find appealing, once any religious connotations which it may once have had have been removed.

But how viable is this conception? A central problem lies in its assumption that there *is* a common good which members of a community do, or can, share. We should remember here that we are taking 'common good' in the idealist sense, minus only the religious background. A common good is, first, a unitary good. An egoistic hedonist might argue that we each have a common good, i.e. the maximization of our own pleasure. Here individual good is common only in the sense that it is *qualitatively* identical: for each of us, our good is to be described in the same way. The idealist, on the other hand, claims that the good is *numerically* the same for each of us, in the way that members of a football team have a common objective (to win the match), and not merely a set of private objectives described in the same words. Second, the idealist notion of the common good is not merely instrumental. Many liberals could accept that we share a common good, in that it is in all our interests that there be things like drains and roads and laws and armies. Many liberal educationists could accept the thesis that one aim of education should be to promote the common good in the sense of helping to ensure that such necessities of life be provided. But this instrumental notion does not imply that there must be common *ends,* as well as means: *intrinsic* goods may still vary considerably from person to person. On the idealist view this is not so: intrinsic good is unitary. A third point about this view is that the good of each individual and the common good coincide perfectly. There is no gap between them. That is why, for the idealist, the aim of education can be stated indifferently either as the realization of a common good or as self-realization.

Given these connotations, it now begins to seem far from clear that there exists, or could exist, a common good which education should seek to realize. For in what would it consist? With the religious framework added, it is not difficult to provide an answer, viz., the continued heightening of human consciousness. But without that framework, what alternative could there be? Of course, various suggestions could be put forward, but presumably we are not interested in any *arbitrary* account of the common good, but only in one which we would have reason to accept. And here one problem seems to be that any particular account is likely to be contested. Suppose someone says, for instance, that our common good consists in the maximization of intellectual and aesthetic activity pursued for its own sake. This reflects only one ideal of life. There are others. Active benevolence, a Thoreauesque return to nature, mystical contemplation, or the worship of God: there will be no end of competitors. Given this, it might reasonably be urged that it is not only arbitrary, but politically dangerous, to think of education in terms of a common good. For this may encourage the imposition of a monolithic conception of such a good which allows no room for competing ideals. Politically, it could mean a return to a closed society.

Of course, if it can be shown that our common good lies only in maximized intellectual activity (or whatever), and the argument thereto is not a rationalization of prejudice but a line of thought so clearly and irrefutably sound that competitors melt away before it, monolithism may not be such a danger after all. But, as far as I can judge, no one has yet come up with any such thing. This is partly because there has notoriously not been any rational agreement about what any *individual*'s ultimate good consists in, let alone a common good. Here again, all one finds is a mass of different life ideals. But the common good is supposed to coincide with the good of each individual in the community, so if the latter is indeterminable, so also must be the former. But even if the individual good *were* determinable, there would still be difficulties about the common good. For suppose, for the sake of argument, it were found that the highest good for any individual consisted in intellectual and aesthetic activity for its own sake, the 'activity' here would be that of the individual in question. What could then be the common good? It could not be the maximization of intellectual and aesthetic activity within the community, since it would not then coincide with the good of any individual: *his* good consists in the maximization of *his* own activity, not in any overall maximization. Yet at the same time the common good cannot be made to coincide with that of any individual A; i.e., be made to consist in the maximization of *his* intellectual and aesthetic activity, since, plainly, while this would raise no problems for A, it would be unacceptable to B, C, D and others in the community, since the common good would no longer coincide with *their* good.

How far do these various problems mean that we should dispense with the claim that education should aim at realizing the common good? It does not seem to us that the door is completely shut against it, although the difficulties in supporting it are real enough. Under what conditions could it be viable? The argument in the last paragraph shows that, given that individual good and common good are to coincide, individual good cannot consist in something limited to the individual. Individual good cannot consist in any activity or enjoyment, for instance, of the individual in question. What else could it be, then? There are still several possibilities. It could be the maximization of certain sorts of activity or enjoyment, for instance, within the community. Or it could be something more impersonal: that God's will be done, for instance, or that objects of natural and man-made beauty be preserved. These are only, of course, intended as bare logical possibilities. Arguing for these or any other version of the common good is quite a different matter; and it is here that all the trickiest problems would arise. But, at least – and this is our only point here – there is still logical space, as it were, for a conception of the common good.

Can one go further, though, and claim that the common good is not only a logical possibility but also a logical necessity? There is at least one argument which may tempt us in that direction. This argument is built on the premise, dear to all idealists, that individuals are not atomic entities out of which society is somehow constructed, but are themselves essentially social beings. This premise can nowadays be reinforced, perhaps, by arguments drawn from Wittgenstein about the necessarily interpersonal nature of conceptual schemes: given that individuals are defined as minimally capable of some kind of thinking (covering, for instance, reasoning about the means they should adopt to attain their goals, as well as theoretical reasoning, or exercising imagination); and given that this depends on the use of conceptual schemes which are necessarily shared within a community of language-users; it follows that individuals cannot but be members of a society. But if this is so, what follows about the good of individuals? If an individual A is necessarily a member of a society S, will not his good necessarily be inextricable from the good of S? It cannot, it seems, be a good which is hived off from the good of other members of the same society; but it must be shared with them.

If a common good is unavoidable, though, we come straight back to the problem which beset us just now: what can be the content of such a good? It seems that all the problems about monolithism and arbitrariness must break out all over again.

There is, in any case, a telling objection to the claim that a common good is unavoidable. It is supposed to follow from the fact that individuals are necessarily social, that individual good is necessarily a social, i.e. common, good. But does it follow? This depends on what is meant by the statement that individuals are necessarily social creatures. In so far as this rests on Wittgensteinian considerations about the inter-subjectivity of concepts, all it seems to mean is that, in order *to become* an individual, one needs to have been brought up in a society. It does not follow from this that, having become an individual, one cannot turn into the most self-centred of egoists, totally cut off from human society. Of course, such an egoist can always be mistaken about his good, believing it to reside in his self-centred concerns, whereas in fact it lies elsewhere. But the important point is that individual good *may* be located where the egoist thinks it is; we cannot conclude that the individual good which a socialized individual follows *must* be a common good, without begging the question.

But the anti-social egoist, it may be argued, must surely be an exception. It is true that individuals cannot become what they are without being brought up within a shared form of life. But the point about the social nature of man goes further than this. Humanity could not exist at all if everyone were an anti-social egoist. It must be normally the case that individuals value their links with the society which has contributed so much to making them what they are. Normally, then, they must seek to foster the well-being of society, not concentrating wholly on what they take to be a private, non-social, well-being of their own.

There are many difficulties in this line of thought, but the one most pertinent to us is that, even granted that the anti-social individual must be an exception, it has not been shown either that the normal individual's well-being must coincide with the well-being of society, or that the latter must be a *common* well-being. For his interest in the general social well-being may be nothing more than a reflection of a *moral* obligation laid upon him: as a moral agent, he has a duty to consider the good of all, not only his own good. If this is so, his pursuit of his own good may be straightforwardly at odds with his moral duty, so there is no necessary coincidence between his own and the general good. Neither is it necessary that the general good be a *common* good: if morality enjoins him to consider the good of all, this good may still fray into the separate individual goods of the different members of the society.

The upshot so far of the argument from the social nature of man seems to be that it is too weak to show that there must be a common good. This conclusion is still, at best, a mere logical possibility: it has not been shown to be well-grounded.

But perhaps there is more to the social-nature-of-man argument than this. What, one may ask, is an individual? Where does he begin and end? Where are his boundaries? A natural answer would be that these boundaries are the boundaries of his body: if there are two living human bodies in this room, then there are two individuals. But are we rationally constrained to accept this 'natural' answer? For if A is necessarily a member of society S, and if this is also true of B, then an essential part of A's nature, it seems, is likewise an essential part of B's. So boundaries cannot be drawn around A and B which exclude each from the other: each partakes necessarily in the other's being. So A's good can no longer be conceived of as the good of one person *as against* that of another: if A and B, C, D, E ... are inextricably involved in each other in this way, then the notion of the coincidence of individual goods with a common good seems hard to resist.

To be valid, this argument requires that what is necessarily shared between A and B is more than a mere description. If their common feature is that they necessarily belong to society S, then are they not formally in the same position as two triangles, both of which share the common feature of necessarily possessing three angles? If we show no inclination to say that these two triangles are not discrete entities, why should we say anything different about A and B?

In what way, though, could A and B share more than a common description? Perhaps an analogy with features of a work of art may be helpful at this point. Line one and line ten of a sonnet X may each be said to share the common description 'necessarily belonging to sonnet X'; but there is also a further connexion between them. Line one is what it is because of the part that it plays in the whole poem. But the whole poem includes line ten. Line ten thus contributes to line one's being what it is. In this case there *does* seem to be an inextricable interpenetration of parts. We confront two conflicting criteria of individuation. On the one hand we want to say that line one is a self-contained entity:

Earth hath not anything to show more fair.

Going by physical characteristics alone, the line begins with 'Earth' and ends with 'fair'; but if we look at its spiritual characteristics, its poetic meaning, we find it impossible to isolate from all the other elements of the sonnet. Perhaps the relation between individuals and society is not unlike that between the elements of a work of art and the work itself. There, too, purely physical characteristics – the clear boundedness of human beings which leads one to say unhesitatingly that there are two individuals in a room – are not, perhaps, indefeasible criteria of individuation: spiritual characteristics may play a part here, too.

All this is very tentative. It is an argument by analogy only: and it certainly falls short of proving incontrovertibly that individuals are not discrete from each other and cannot, therefore, possess non-common goods. We mean at this point only to keep the door open, to show, that is, that the claim that there must be a common good is not obviously false or misguided; further reflection may as much incline us in its direction as it may make us turn away from it, provided also that we can reach some more satisfactory conclusion than we have reached so far on what the content of this common good might be.

Our main purpose in this chapter has been to discover what, if anything, is of lasting value in the idealists' general conception of education and its aims. We began by taking the theory of the common good intact, with all its religious connotations. Stripping those away, we asked whether education could be seen as oriented towards a common good in any untheological sense. As we have seen, the answer is inconclusive, with the scales weighted, if anything, against this claim. Suppose, as may seem likely, the proposition that we share a common good is unfounded – at most a bare logical possibility, like the proposition that God exists. If it is, what becomes of our main enquiry, about the heritage of the idealists? Should we conclude that we have nothing to learn from them, since their view of education and its importance sinks or swims with the viability of the common good theory?

Such a conclusion would be premature. Just as we stripped away the theology, so we may now strip away the concept of the common good itself. A far weaker version of the idealists' theory will be left, it is true: so weak, perhaps, that it may no longer be possible to label it 'idealist', as it may be acceptable enough to those of other philosophical persuasions; but, even so, the residue may prove to be of service to contemporary educational thought. This, as we shall show, we believe to be the case. There is a strong argument for reversing or supplementing some of our current priorities in education and returning to something like the idealists' picture of it, even without their idea of the common good.

'Education,' wrote Hegel, 'is the art of making men ethical.' We saw in earlier chapters how the British idealists and their Greek and German forebears gave a central place to moral values in education. Partly this stemmed from Kant. His insistence on the supreme value of moral autonomy was taken over by his pupil Fichte and Fichte's pupil, Herbart, both of whom applied it directly to education, making its paramount aim the fashioning of moral character. More ancient influences were Plato and Aristotle. From them derived the insight that morality is inextricably political: the moral man is the citizen of a political society, his education fitting him to become one. In Hegel and his followers the two influences, the Kantian and the Platonic-Aristotelian, converged. Our references to the work and thought of the British idealist reformers show abundantly the centrality of morality as an aim, or even *the* aim, of education. It is on the one hand a socially-oriented morality: the ideal pupil is to see his moral obligations as not restricted to the face-to-face relationships of everyday life, but as extending into his wider life as a member of a local community, of a work-institution, of a national and ultimately international community. At the same time, although social ethos is allowed to play a larger part than others would admit in shaping moral character, the moral agent is not at all to become a blind conformist. He is to be guided by reason, partly directly, and partly indirectly by the rationalization of the social ethos itself. His society is to be an open, not a closed one, democratic, not authoritarian in its institutional life at all levels.

In the idealist reformers these ideas were tied to a religious rationale. But how far, once again, can they be detached from this? How far can one argue, from a non-religious point of view, that a central, or perhaps the central, aim of education should be the formation of moral character in the sense described?

Few would deny that morality has *some* place among educational ends. Children must at least be taught to be truthful, honest, tolerant, kind and fair. But it is possible to espouse these ends without going nearly as far as the idealists did in their commitment to moral purposes. For them, one's moral being is a central feature of one's life: one's dominant purposes must be governed by moral concern. A less demanding view, and one widespread today, would be that, while one's moral duties should certainly not be neglected, there is no reason why these should be allowed to become all-important. Morality as a system subserves the pursuit of individual well-being. Men must be honest and truthful and well-disposed to one another, since, if they were not, individuals would lack the ordered society necessary to their pursuing their own well-being. On this view, there is no reason why education should aim *centrally* at moral objectives: if any aim is central, it must be one to do with the pupil's own well-being.

What, if anything, can be said in favour of the idealists' more stringent conception of morality over this minimalist view? A leading thought here is that, even on the minimalist theory, the individual is urged to take an impartial, moral point of view when his interests are at odds, or might be at odds, with others'. But once the obligation to consider other people equally with oneself is conceded, there seems no non-arbitrary way of restricting it to certain points only of one's life. For it is not only when I am repaying my debts or telling the truth that I am capable of detaching myself from my own interests and thinking of others': I am able to do this at *any* point in my life. Morality cannot, in reason, be anything less than all-pervasive.

A minimalist can easily accept this latter demand, provided that he sufficiently restricts the range of moral obligations, perhaps to truthfulness, honesty and tolerance. These principles can guide him continuously even though he spends virtually all his life preoccupied with his own interests. This is because they need make no demands on his time or resources: they are, so to speak, 'negative' virtues, virtues of restraint.

But it is otherwise with benevolence. Benevolence enjoins activity, doing something to help others. Once a morality includes benevolence somewhere among its virtues – and few minimalists would deny this – then the requirement that it be all-pervasive commits one, it seems, to more than spasmodic good deeds: one must *continuously* have the well-being of others at heart. This does not necessarily imply altruism in the sense that one should live only for others and take no account of oneself. There is no *prima facie* reason why one's own well-being should be of any less moral importance than that of any other individual with whom one is morally concerned. But if one is to count only as one among many, there will, it seems, be very little difference in practice from altruism proper: in a society of any size one's own interests would appear to become negligible in comparison with all others'.

We may agree so far with the idealists, that reason urges one beyond a mere minimal morality. And not only, of course, with the idealists: moral philosophers of other persuasions have claimed as much. One thing which helps to differentiate the idealists from others is their insistence on the concretization of morality, on its localization within communities of varying extent. We stated just now that 'in a society of any size' one's own interests become negligible compared with all others'. A general problem for any moral theory is: who are the 'others' with whom one is to be morally concerned? Reason seems to indicate that one is being arbitrary in restricting this moral community in any way whatsoever: there are always others outside one's tribe, one's family, village or nation whose well-being could be taken into account. One's duty, it seems, can only be to mankind in general, and not merely that part of it alive today but also all future generations. But if one's moral vision must be as all-encompassing as this, it is seemingly impossible ever to attain it. It is a virtue of idealism that it makes the moral life concrete by locating it in communities of different kinds which mediate between the individual and mankind as a whole. One learns to apply one's moral understanding first in the family circle, widening out beyond it later to the local community, the various institutions of which one is a member, and the state-community as the final – or pehaps penultimate – mediator before one reaches mankind as a whole. We may detach from this idealist argument any historicist connotations which may once have adhered to it. We cannot justify accepting the norms of any particular community on the grounds that these have been programmed into it by God (or Spirit of Nature). But in rejecting the metaphysics behind the idealists' concretized morality, we should not reject that morality itself: there seems everything to be said in its favour, provided always that none of the nested communities ever becomes closed to the moral demands that those outside it have on its members.

A concrete morality brings us one step nearer, but not all the way back to a common good morality. It brings us at least to a common *end,* if not to a common *good.* For the end of each member of any particular community will be the same (numerically, not merely qualitatively) as that of any other member. Each will direct his efforts to promoting the good of every member of the community, himself included. This common end still falls short of a common *good,* as long as there is any question of an individual's having to sacrifice something of his own well-being in order to realize the common end: if the common end *were* a common good, there would be no question of such a sacrifice, since individual and common well-being would necessarily coincide. The recurrence of the theme of self-sacrifice and self-abnegation in the writings of the British idealists may well lead us to conclude that at the heart of their position was a common-end, rather than a common-good, morality. Or perhaps it is truer to say that they never clearly distinguished between these two moralities. Green, in particular, has often been described as much a Kantian as a Hegelian thinker. Perhaps he never succeeded in fully integrating these differing moral inheritances into a coherent scheme.

In one way – and this may help to account for the idealists' failure to separate them – the two moralities come even closer. Both when one is pursuing a common end and when one is pursuing a common good, one is pursuing, *inter alia,* one's own good. In both theories, then, there is something of a coincidence between individual good and a common end/good, sufficient, at least, to enable one to argue from the latter to the former. The crucial difference between the moralities is, of course, that only in

233

the common-good version can one argue also from the former to the latter: only in this version is it true that if I pursue my own good I am necessarily pursuing a common end/good.

We have argued that a common-end morality is more obviously defensible than a common-good one. Educationally, it provides us with what may prove to be a more acceptable alternative to the thesis that the aim of education is to promote the common good, viz., that its aim should be to promote, as a common end, the good of all members of the community.

But this alternative needs an important qualification. That educated men should above all work together for a common end may – or may not; we shall see – be a reasonable claim; but what this end should consist in is as yet by no means clear. We have taken it as read so far that the common end is the promotion of the good of each. But are we *obliged* to see it in this way? One difficulty lies in the presupposition that, in order to act morally, we must know what the good of the individuals with whom we are concerned, is. But do we know this? Is it something we can know? We may know, or think we know, what is instrumentally good for them: that they be at least fed, clothed, housed and medically treated, up to a certain minimum standard. There is no theoretical difficulty in our co-operation for a common end of a purely material kind like this. But what, if anything, do we aim at beyond these material requirements? What is intrinsically good for the individuals in question?

How is this to be determined? Some would argue that this is a subjective matter, to be left to the individual's own judgment about what, on reflection, he most wants to do. But if our common moral end is said to be to put everyone in a position, as far as possible, to realize his most cherished desires, it may well seem less than worthy. Suppose it turns out that what men most want to do is to enjoy good food, or celebrity or material comfort. There seems something less than dignified in our bending our collective moral will to producing a culture of steak bars and headline-seeking. Is it worth all that self-sacrifice?

In any case, this subjective conception of individual good is not uncontested. It is hard, indeed, to see how it could be supported: why should the good be identified with the satisfaction of one's wants? On the other hand, it is equally difficult to see what could be put in its place. Objectivist alternatives are not lacking. But none of them proposed to date has, to our knowledge, been convincingly argued for.

But if we cannot come to any firm conclusion about what individual good consists in, how can it be our moral, and hence educational, aim to promote the good of each? Don't we have to know what this is before we act?

It has certainly been a presupposition of the last few paragraphs that we *do* have to have such knowledge. But is this presupposition dispensable? It depends, perhaps, on exactly how it is interpreted. We have to know *something* about what individual good involves in order to aim at someone's good; but what we could know about it might be that it is unknowable. It is, on this view, a characteristic of human nature that we can never work out what our own good is; neither can we even discover that our good exists in some sense in the world, but unknowably. We are simply creatures for whom what one's good is must remain constantly mysterious, an eternal open question. When we think we have caught the quarry – identifying it with the satisfaction of our deepest desires, with service to the community, or whatever – there is always room for dissatisfaction, for putting forward some alternative identification. There is nothing mysterious about the fact that our good is mysterious. Nature – or God – has not built it into our make-up, not, at least, as far as we know. We have somehow achieved something of which other animals appear incapable: consciousness of self. This enables us to see the cosmic pointlessness of our lives, causing us to shift from picture to picture of the *summum bonum*. What would be a fitting response to our recognition of this pointlessness: expressing it in art or philosophy, cherishing our fellow humans all the more as equally adrift, making fun of those who think there *is* a point to it all, envying non-self-conscious animals their ability to follow their natural proclivities without reflection, etc., etc? There is no right answer. All may seem fitting at different times. Sometimes we can adopt more than one of these attitudes together; at other times one of them will dominate the field until it in turn, as it must, will cede place to another. None of this is to say that it is up to us to determine our own good, as if this were finally a matter of subjective choice. It is our situation, or rather our consciousness of it and of its pointlessness, which elicits in us one attitude or another; we are as much passive as active in this process.

If the good of the individual is necessarily unknowable in this special sense, morality, and hence a morally-oriented education, *can* get off the ground. To work for another's good is to put him in the position of seeing for himself this fact about his good. It may take a material form, of helping to free him from anxieties about food, clothing, shelter, etc.: obsessed by these, he may mistake his good, conceiving it to lie in something determinate like the possession of material goods. Or it may take an intellectual form, as it did with

235

Socrates, whose mission it was to disabuse those who thought they knew what the good was and hence to make them conscious of their ignorance. Teachers have – or should have – the Socratic attitude towards their pupils. They teach them, in their turn, also to adopt this attitude, to themselves, as well as others. They also teach them that they can work for people's good by following the material, as well as the intellectual, path.

We have extracted from idealism the thesis that education should consist in bringing children up to live a life of moral goodness within nested communities of differing extent. This may seem to some a small amount of juice to have been squeezed out of such a very large fruit; and it might also seem to be a conclusion reachable without the aid of idealism at all. Even if these objections are sound, however, it does not mean that the examination of the idealist movement which has led us to distil this conclusion has been unprofitable. Far from it: for banal though the conclusion may be to some, it presents a view of education which is radically different from many influential contemporary beliefs about it. At the very least, setting it over against the latter should force us to reflect on their soundness. It may, of course, do more than this: we might come to feel that we are in the presence of an educational ideal worth reviving.

Three conceptions of education are dominant in Britain today.

(1) First is the view that education is centrally concerned with the expansion of the understanding (or intelligence, or the mind) for its own sake. It comes in several forms: in a faculty theory version, for instance, in which the strengthening of mental powers is all-important and content secondary; in Hirst's theory of a liberal education in all the forms of knowledge; in Peters' once-held and still influential theory of education as initiation into intrinsically worthwhile activities of a predominantly theoretical sort.[1]

Two features of this point of view are worth dwelling on. First, it divorces education from social responsibility: education becomes something self-contained, driven on by its own intrinsic ends, disengaged from wider, social concerns. Secondly, attempts to justify this view of education have been notoriously unconvincing. One move has been to define 'education' in such a way that all alternative accounts are ruled out from the start. Another has been intuitionist: we simply know by intuition that being educated in this sense is a good thing.[2] Kantian, i.e. 'transcendental', arguments have also been invoked.[3] These attempts are open to in some cases obvious and in other cases not so obvious objections, which have adequately been discussed in recent work in the philosophy of education and do not need to be re-examined here.

Why should the ceaseless expansion of mind for its own sake be considered a central aim of education? It may be hard to give any reliable backing to this today, but a century ago, in the heyday of idealism, the answer would not have been far to seek: the more individuals' consciousness was raised above the level of animal existence, the more they become vehicles of eternal spirit. What has happened since that time is that the same conception of education has been retained, but without its religious rationale. John Dewey, we suggest, has played a key part in this story. Dewey, as we pointed out above, came to conceive of education as a process of continuing, unfettered growth to more and more complex levels of mental functioning. This was the idealists' doctrine of self-realization without its religious rationale. Despite the criticism which has often been levied against Dewey that his theory of growth fails to provide any criterion of value, so that it all seems as if growth in *any* direction is intrinsically desirable, his theory *was* set, as we argued earlier, within an implicit framework of values, derived partly from his idealist-inspired attachment to democracy and fraternity and partly from his social Darwinism. What happened after him, in the early (but not the later) works, for instance, of his admirer R. S. Peters, on the concept of education, was that the bonds which linked Dewey's growth theory to wider social and metaphysical concerns dropped away, leaving the thesis that education is to do with understanding for its own sake, hived off from any extra-educational attachments.

It is true, however, that none of the writers who have recently argued most forcefully for the view that education is centrally to do with mental development for its own sake – Peters, Hirst, Downie, Telfer and Loudfoot – holds that moral education is no part of the educator's task. All find a place, and some a large place, for it. But in doing so, how do they square this moral end with the end of understanding for its own sake? Obviously, moral understanding enters into moral learning; but the morally educated person is not someone who prizes this understanding for its own sake, but one who applies it to his own and others' conduct. If education is at least partly to do with the development of moral *dispositions* as well as with understanding for its own sake, the type of theory we are currently considering must be incomplete. If valid at all, it needs to be absorbed into a more all-embracing theory, in which the relation between moral and purely intellectual ends is clearly spelt out. We shall have to see later whether the idealist heritage can help us to construct this.

(2) The contemporary philosophies of education we examined in (1) share with idealism the belief that education is 'socially-

oriented' in the sense that pupils must be brought to conform to public standards of different kinds embodied in the various disciplines of thought, even if they reject or play down the contention that it must be 'socially-oriented' in the further sense that pupils must be brought up to work for the good of the community as distinct from pursuing learning for its own sake.

The second contemporary influence we wish to examine rejects, or at least minimizes, a 'social orientation' in both of these senses. This is that of the so-called 'child-centred' educators, or 'progressives'. This tradition sees the child predominantly as a natural, i.e. biological, entity, mental development as a form of biological development, and the teacher as the handmaiden of nature, helping the pupil to develop to his maximum capacity. For all its difference from the theory examined in (1) (which we shall henceforth call 'Theory (1)'), it shares with it the assumption that education is not to do with preparing people to become citizens or members of communities. Education has no aims outside itself. Indeed, many child-centred educators would reject the very idea of aims, as suggesting predetermined objectives on the part of teachers: development must be from within and accord with internal norms. The only 'aim' is that a child should develop its individuality to the full; but since each person's individuality is *sui generis*, this is tantamount to saying that there are no aims of any general sort to guide the teacher.

A difficulty with child-centred education of this kind is that there seems, *prima facie,* nothing to prevent its pupils becoming totally concerned with their own interests, to the exclusion of others'. If their teachers believe in the overriding importance of their pupils' 'individuality', is it not more than likely, in fact, that the pupils themselves will come to agree with them? Again, as with Theory (1), progressivism does not deny the need for moral or social education; but this is difficult to fit coherently into its overall naturalistic theory, except by the implausible device of making 'social development' itself a biological phenomenon, and just one facet of the individual's total development. (In this regard, progressivism has the advantage over Theory (1): the latter has no way of bringing moral and intellectual education under the same umbrella, given, that is, that the Socratic solution – that to know the good is to do the good – is out of the question.)

The central objection to progressivism is that the conceptual learning, which lies at the heart of mental growth, is necessarily a social phenomenon: acquiring a conceptual scheme is to assimilate the *public* criteria governing the sense and application of its concepts. This is not the place to take off into a more extensive critique; in any case, this job has been adequately done already.[4]

What is of more interest is that progressivism, like Theory (1), is intelligible only in the light of its relationship with idealism. Both it and the latter share the concept of self-realization. We saw above, in Chapter 10, how the connotations of that concept have changed over the last century. Its *social* implication, that to realize oneself is to work for a common good, dropped away between T. H. Green and Edmond Holmes, leaving only its *religious* implications, that self-realization is merging oneself with a divine whole. After Holmes, the religious connotations dropped away, too, leaving the claim that education should aim at self-realization obscure in its meaning and devoid of any wider rationale which might illuminate this.

A second important influence, besides Holmes, on contemporary progressivism has been Percy Nunn. We described his educational theory and the part it played in the decline of idealism in Chapter 11. Nunn is a link in the chain between idealism and present-day progressivism largely because of his explicit rejection of the former. Yet at the same time his thinking was in one respect more in tune with the idealists than it is with today's progressives. Today, the ultimate aim of education is taken, as before, to be the fullest development of individuality. But this, as we have stressed more than once, is taken as a basic postulate, without any further theory to back it up; individuality is *per se* desirable. In Nunn, however, individuality is important because this is the direction in which natural evolution tends: in promoting it, teachers are co-operators with nature in the process of evolution. This puts Nunn not so very far away, after all, from Holmes. He helped to preserve throughout another generation Holmes's thesis that to realize the self is to participate in a process of cosmic proportions. The conception of the cosmos changed, of course, from that of Holmes's misty Buddhism to that of natural science; but the underlying idea was preserved. Today for many, and probably most, progressives, the cosmic connotations of self-realization are non-existent.

Progressivism has thus descended to us from the idealists in much the same stages as Theory (1). Each we find first embraced within a wider religious world-picture. In the next stage, represented by Nunn in one case and Dewey in the other, there is still a surrounding metaphysics, but this belongs now to natural science rather than religion. In the final, contemporary stage, each theory stands alone, bereft of any supporting rationale.

Child-centred theory today, like Theory (1), is thus a direct descendant of idealism. If we are looking for residues of that philosophy – what finally remains of it once one has removed a number of its connotations – we can find them as much in these two theories as in the morally-oriented theory we discussed at length at the beginning of this chapter. Idealism contained at least the following central emphases: on self-realization; on developing reason, or understanding, to its fullest extent; on the social nature of the individual; on co-operation for a common good; and on the divine nature of the universe. In that philosophy itself, these themes were tied together into a coherent whole. What has happened over the past hundred years is that different lines of educational thought have developed from idealism, each clinging on to some themes and discarding others. Theory (1) and contemporary progressivism are two of these residues. Their inadequacies have been already mentioned. Whether the third – and less influential – descendant, the morally-oriented theory, is any more viable is the central issue of this chapter.

(3) The third of our contemporary educational influences – the utilitarian – is very far from being a descendant of idealism. In its nineteenth-century versions, in Bentham and the Mills, it antedated British idealism, whose ethics was explicitly developed in opposition to it. Utilitarianism is far from negligible as a moral force today, both in general and in education in particular.

A utilitarian view of education, as we are taking the word here, sees it as a means of maximizing individual satisfaction. The view comes in several forms, and not all our comments apply to each. Let us take two for a start. (a) Some people would lay great emphasis on the child's present happiness – i.e., while still at school – as an educational objective. This may, or may not, be committed to the biological child-centred theory that we examined in (2). (b) Others would look to the satisfaction of the child's future wants. Parents, for instance, often see education in this instrumental way, as helping one to 'get on', to land a well-paid or congenial job. Educational theorists often write about the school's function of extending the range of options, vocational or otherwise, so that the pupil will have more kinds of satisfaction open to him from among which he can choose his own preferred pattern of life.[5]

In so far as (a) or (b) is presented as the sole aim of education, it raises the difficulty, familiar from our earlier discussion of (1) and (2), that it includes no bulwark against selfishness, but indeed promotes it. In so far as its proponents find some sort of place for moral education alongside the utilitarian, they face the problem of harmonizing these two demands. If 'getting on', for instance, is the central objective, then what will happen to morality? Will it be trimmed and clipped to fit this goal, by, for instance, becoming assimilated to legality? Or if the conception of morality goes beyond this, how can self-oriented goals remain central?

(c) A third version of utilitarianism avoids this difficulty. Education, on this view, should be directed not to pupil's satisfactions alone, but to the maximization of satisfactions in general, to the greatest happiness of the greatest number. This, again, has different variants. A powerful form of it in our own society would see the education system as a means of promoting economic growth, both on the side of production, and, by exposing people to otherwise unknown sources of satisfaction, on the side of consumption also. It would not necessarily follow from this that pupils themselves should work towards this aim: a skilled worker may be motivated by selfish ends but still in fact be contributing to economic growth. For some utilitarians a vocationally oriented education, fitting pupils for positions in the division of labour, is the most desirable. One weakness in this theory is that it fails to explain why pupils should be seen largely as job-holders, since there are other aspects to human life than that. This is an essentially manipulative theory of education: pupils are treated merely as means to ends not of their own choosing, confined within specialisms which do not allow them any critical appreciation of the situation in which others wish to place them.

All these versions of utilitarianism are obviously at odds with the view with which we are contrasting them, that education should try to create morally good men. But *one* kind of utilitarian theory, so far not mentioned, would seem to meet this specification. On this view, the aim of education would be not simply that satisfactions are maximized, but also that pupils come consciously to follow this utilitarian principle as a guide to conduct.

How far, though, would this really coincide with the kind of morality – the idealist residue – that we earlier described? Two difficulties can be easily met. First, historical utilitarianism has worked with a concept of atomic, pre-social individuals. As is nowadays widely acknowledged, this concept appears to be incoherent. Second, and connected with this, since communal links between individuals are seen as contingent rather than necessary, utilitarian morality tends to be abstract rather than concrete: its stress on the *greatest* possible satisfaction urges one constantly in the direction of humanity as a whole, ignoring one's links with smaller-scale communities. But utilitarianism can be detached from its historical associations, re-equipped with a social concept of the individual and made into a concrete morality after the idealist fashion. It would still differ, however, from the idealist residue in its excessively determinate picture of a man's well-being as the satisfaction of his wants. Not only does this raise again the problem of justification (*why* this identification?) and commit us to bending our energies to help to satisfy wants simply because they are wants and regardless of any qualitative difference there may be between them (if everyone wants sixteen TV channels of light entertainment, we are doing what is morally right in sweating to provide these). It is also likely, in practice, to lead to political difficulties. 'Greater satisfaction' can be deemed to exist where there are a hundred satisfied desires than where there are ten. The 'good society' therefore comes to be seen as one in which individuals have a great number of satisfied desires. Those whose job it is to create new wants in people – and here the advertiser can be on a par with the teacher – are as much the adjutants of moral progress as those whose job it is to satisfy them.

Utilitarian governments try to satisfy continually increasing demands for more goods, more money, more services, more status, more leisure. But with limited resources they will never succeed. In a world like our own, where world-wide shortages of food and raw materials are likely to become endemic, the clash between individuals' demands and what governments can provide becomes even more marked than in our pre-crisis society. In equipping people with new wants and a knowledge of how to satisfy them, and in encouraging them to take the view that private satisfactions are of central importance in human life, the powerful utilitarian influences in our education system share the responsibility for this political disenchantment. If the latter becomes so acute as to lead to social disintegration or a new authoritarianism of the rich, anxious to maintain their customary level of want-satisfactions against the increasingly strident demands of those awakened to the vision of a life in the sun, then, too, a utilitarian education system must also share in the blame.

Utilitarianism today is not the philosophy of any one major political party. The right wing may stress the liberty of the individual to do what he wants, unfettered by government. The left wing may pay more attention to the need to remove inequalities in wealth, education, life-styles, etc. But both wings, not only the former, can be comfortably accommodated within utilitarianism. The demand for equality can easily become the demand that not only the few should have maximum freedom to lead their lives as they best see fit, but that this should be the birthright of all. Society may then be dominated by that insistence on universal 'absolute freedom' which Hegel identified as a central doctrine of the Enlightenment, and which had a direct influence on the coming of the Revolution. Not only on the Revolution: in helping to atomize society, to break the old bonds which linked man to man and to leave individuals as a mere 'heap' of isolated free agents, the ideologists of absolute freedom also unwittingly prepared the ground, in Hegel's eyes, for the Terror.

This mention of Hegel brings us back to idealism and so to the specific issue we have been tackling in this chapter: the relevance to us, if any, of the theory which we found embodied in idealism, that education should aim at moral goodness of the kind described.

The latter may seem to offer us an alternative to the utilitarian conception of society and education. A life focused on one's moral duties as a member of various democratic communities and institutions now becomes salient, not the endless pursuit of private satisfactions. Men are seen as united at every point by social bonds enabling them to co-operate fraternally for shared ends. The central purpose of education on this view is a social one, to help to create a community characterized by such co-operation. The danger of political disenchantment within such a community will be reduced, since men will take a different attitude to government. It will not be seen predominantly as a means of enlarging satisfactions on the one hand and a potential encroacher on individuals' rights and liberties on the other, but as the co-ordinating organ of a co-operative society.

Some may consider that the claim that education should aim at moral goodness is as inadequate or incomplete as the three contemporary theories have been alleged to be.

A first objection may be that this unduly constricts the scope of education, since it would exclude all those subjects, and topics within subjects, which are not necessary to bring about this moral end. Indeed, if illiterate and unschooled peasants can be virtuous, is any but the most rudimentary education strictly required at all? Virtue, it will be argued, is not something that can be taught as a school subject. 'To adopt a moral point of view, to consider other people and to develop standards of honesty, truthfulness, kindness or loyalty ... these are things which can indeed be learned, but only by practice and example.'[6]

There is much truth in this argument, but it rests on too narrow and homely a view of morality. One of the chief lessons that the idealist reformers have to teach our generation is that the morally good man is not only kind and honest and truthful in his face-to-face relationships; he is also the thoughtful citizen of a democratic community, expressing his moral commitment both in the specialized job he performs in the social division of labour and in his unspecialized role as a participant in local and central government and in the management of industry.[7]

Once one broadens out one's conception of moral goodness, it

243

becomes immediately evident that more is required to achieve this end than learning by example. A high degree of purely intellectual understanding will also be necessary. Each citizen will need to grasp, at a fairly formal level, something of the nature of the democratic form of polity, its differences from its competitors and its roots in moral and political philosophy. In order to apply this understanding to concrete situations as a participant in democratic processes, he will also have to know all kinds of other things, drawn not only from the social and economic sciences, but, since any knowledge – scientific, mathematical, historical, aesthetic – may be relevant on different occasions, from as wide a spectrum as possible.[8] But it is not only for particular judgments that the morally good man will need a broader understanding. Morality is concerned with human well-being. But, as we have seen already in this chapter, in a predominantly non-religious age what in general constitutes this well-being is not at all clear. Art, especially literature, and philosophy, especially ethics, may help us to orient ourselves in this supremely difficult area: without them, to what else could we turn?

The moral importance of a broad background of intellectual and aesthetic understanding should now be clear. It is a theme we have already met: in the 'many-sided interest' which Herbart thought necessary for the moral man; in Fichte; in Hegel; in the kind of education for citizenship which the idealists urged in their adult education work; in their conception of university studies as connected with the on-going life of the community.

But now a very different kind of difficulty will occur to some: not that a morally-oriented education demands too little in the way of intellectual understanding, but that it demands too much. It is an education intended for everyman, but does everyman possess the mental ability to encompass it? This is a complex question. Its answer may depend partly on how high the intellectual demands have to be pitched; but there is nothing to suggest that they need to be made so high that only a few can attain them. One reason why the idealist reform movement is of such potential interest to us today is that it took place before the rise of intelligence testing and its attendant pessimism about the intellectual capabilities of the great mass of the population. As is becoming increasingly clear to us with every new piece of evidence about the flimsy scientific basis of the hereditarian claims of Cyril Burt and others, there is no good reason for pessimism (Kamin, 1977, especially ch. 3). The idealists were never hampered by such thoughts: in their view all men, mental defectives presumably excepted, could, and should, become vehicles of the divine spirit; it was only such things as poverty, ignorance and intemperance which stood in the way of their being so, obstacles all removable by concerted social action. Without this belief, the idealists would have lacked the inspiration, the motivating energy, to throw themselves into their educational projects. Our own age has too long tended to look down on the 'shallow optimism' of these late Victorians and their successors writing it off as a product of religious enthusiasm or a naïve belief in the inevitability of progress. But we ourselves have been too affected by a contrary philosophy. Progress in education may not be inevitable or God-ordained; but if only we had the *will* to raise the intellectual horizons of our community far higher than we have sought to in the past, much more, we feel, could be achieved than many would now think possible.

Some will dislike a morally-oriented education if morality is to be broadened in the direction of citizenship. Will not political desiderata then be dominant over educational? Will children not then be indoctrinated into the state-worship so familiar to us – but not to the idealists – throughout a half-century of totalitarian dictatorship?

As we saw in Chapter 11, one reason for idealism's decline was its attachment to the state as a focus of moral commitments. Educationists turned away from a state-oriented picture of education to theories which made more room for individual autonomy. Child-centred education and the emphasis on understanding for its own sake are both examples.

But, once again, there are grounds for reversing this tendency. While it is true that some idealists, notably Bosanquet, appeared to make the 'state' into a suprapersonal entity endowed with its own 'real will', many others, notably Green and his followers, thought of the state in the Greek fashion, as a political *community*. When J. H. Muirhead called his book on Green's political philosophy *The Service of the State*, he was far from suggesting that it is our duty to worship some mythical entity or – and this brings in a third meaning of 'state' – to promote the interests of the Civil Service and other parts of the government machine.

Not that, as we have indicated more than once, the British idealists were exclusively interested in the state, or national, community. Communities can and should exist within the state; and the state itself is not to be parochial or selfish. The idealists' version of patriotism was the opposite of exclusive. As we saw in Part 1 (p. 43), it was for Green just one expression of a wider brotherhood of man. Individuals cannot be attached to humanity in the abstract, but only via more concrete associations at different levels. The nation-state, with its common language, literature, history and customs provides one obvious focus for a communal life. If we so think of it that it not only embraces the pluralism of values already referred to, but is also essentially internationalist and humanitarian in its external relations, there is nothing abhorrent which we can see in patriotism of this kind. Perhaps we in Britain are – understandably, to a point – too shy of this traditional virtue?

But we do not want to be dogmatic on any of these points. Perhaps for any of a number of reasons, economic reasons no less than others, a national community is impossible or undesirable and we should begin again to think of living together in smaller groups. Whatever the truth, we live at present in nation-states, which possess some, but, alas, too few, features of a full national community. We can educate our pupils to reflect on whether they can build on what exists and bring their larger society closer to a communitarian ideal or whether our large-scale structure should be dismantled.

Let us turn, finally, to what many will see as the most telling objection to a morally-oriented education: that it makes morality not only of overriding importance, but of exclusive importance: it is an education for a society of zealots, of self-sacrificing altruists with no time for private interests, aesthetic, sporting or whatever, unless these happen to serve some moral purpose, a society which subjugates Hellenism to Hebraism.

We have already rebutted the charge that T. H. Green was a Hebraist. He saw a place, at least according to Nettleship, for aesthetic and intellectual activity for its own sake: this, as much as direct moral endeavour, could 'liberate the human spirit from its own littleness' (Green, *Works,* vol. 3, p. cxlviii). But if a present-day advocate of morally-oriented education is not prepared to accept these foundations, this road away from Hebraism is not open to him. Is any other?

We believe there is. Moral goodness does not imply moral obsessiveness. First, there is no reason why the morally good person should always devote himself to 'good works'. His own judgment of his community's well-being may lead him to conclude that he could best serve it by exploiting his talents as a composer of music or as a pure mathematician: there are, as Green saw, many different routes to the same end. Second, moral goodness does not entail altruism in the sense that one always acts in others' interests and ignores one's own: as a member of the community one is just as much an object of one's moral concern as any other member. Indeed, there is even a good reason why one should often pay *more* attention to one's own needs than to other people's. We could in theory go about brushing each other's teeth and cooking each other's food, but in practice it is often so much more convenient to let people, where possible, look after themselves. Further, a society whose members always did things only for others would necessarily fail to realize the social ideal we are considering. We stated above (p. 235) that to work for another's good is to enable him to see for himself the indeterminable nature of this good and to react in his own way to this awe-inspiring fact. Now although someone else may in principle clean my teeth, no one, not even in principle, could take my place when it comes to my reflecting on my ultimate good and acting on those reflections. If the society envisaged is to keep its *raison d'être,* then as many of its citizens as possible must be encouraged to reflect and react in this way. But if we all spent all our time working only for others, no one would have any time to do this.

So there is a *prima facie* obligation on each one of us to spend at least some of his life occupied with his own ultimate ends. The obligation is only *prima facie.* Some of us may consider that social conditions are so much in need of improvement that we should devote ourselves entirely to this task (see the quotation from Green in Part 1. p. 35). Others, on the other hand, may put far greater weight on this self-oriented aim. For a few, indeed, such a 'duty to oneself' may come to seem paramount, transcending obligations towards others to which other people would give a higher priority. How far, therefore, one goes in self-attention is itself a moral problem, to which the moral agent must work out his own solution. The important thing is that one approaches this issue as a *moral* being and not as an egoist. Both types of person may be self-preoccupied to a very large extent, but the self-concern of the moralist, unlike the amoralist's, springs from prior reflection about the well-being of the whole community.

There is nothing, in short, in an 'education for morality' which excludes a concern for the pupil's self-development. On the contrary, it demands it.[9]

13 The realization of educational aims

The idealists' thoughts on the nature of education and its aims are to be extracted from their writings, including their general metaphysical and ethical philosophy. Their views on how those aims are to be realized can be discovered not only there but also, and more especially, in their practical involvement in social and educational reform. What lessons, if any, can we learn from this today?

A great virtue of the idealist reformers was their disposition to see problems in the widest possible perspective. This is evident, for instance, in the work they did in non-educational fields, such as temperance and the relief of poverty, work which helped to lay the basis of our contemporary 'welfare state'. They saw drink and indigence as evil because they hindered spiritual growth. Social reform was important because it made possible educational – i.e. spiritual – advancement: the temperance worker, no less than the schoolteacher, served the ends of education.

Contemporary beliefs about the relationship between social welfare and education are partly similar, partly different. Virtually everyone accepts today that children's educational achievements can, though need not, be adversely affected by environmental factors like poor health or housing, bad diet, poverty and so on; and that, consequently, a general advance in educational standards must be accompanied by wider social reforms. What is not so generally accepted, however, is the proposition that all social welfare has an educational rationale. The idealists saw environmental deficiencies as impediments to spirituality; we, to happiness. Poverty, ill-health, unemployment are treated as evils today because they prevent the individual from doing what he wants: we have lost, to a very large extent, the non-utilitarian outlook of the idealists. Is this a good or bad thing? Of course, the idealists were committed to social reform ultimately for religious reasons, and these weigh less with many of us than they did with them. But, as we showed in the last chapter, the utilitarian picture of human nature is not the only alternative to the religious. If what constitutes man's well-being is indeterminable and if all we can do for individuals is to equip them, not for happiness but for self-consciousness, for reflectiveness about their own being, then welfare services are important, after all, for reasons not so very different, religion apart, from the idealists'.

Organized education, on this view, is not just one social service among many, on a par with the health service or unemployment insurance as a specialized means of reducing distress or misery: it is the queen of them all, since it is essentially for educational ends that all the others exist. Today we have lost, by and large, the belief that education is not only important, but supremely important, to a society. Dominated by utilitarianism, some of us even doubt whether it is a good thing at all: if it is not at all obvious that schoolchildren are 'better off' (in a narrow sense) for all their years of compulsory schooling, we begin to urge that they be given less. Our scepticism affects other parts of the welfare state, too, and for the same reason. A better acquaintance with the idealist heritage may do something to restore our faith in it. Even in so far as education does promote personal happiness, some of us may feel that it is still not worth fighting for, or, at least, not putting up an *especial* fight for. If schools and hospitals are no more important than ice-rinks or department stores, crusading zeal seems out of place. Conversely, a conceptual shift of the kind we have been describing can bring with it a new source of motivational energy.

The reformers we have described in this book were concerned less with other necessary conditions of education than with education itself. Here, too, however, when we reflect on the specifically educational means they advocated of attaining educational ends, we are struck by their breadth of vision. Today we tend to think first of formal educational institutions: it is primarily schools, colleges, universities which do the educating. The family is also important, of course, but it is not natural to all of us to think of parents as educators, on a par with teachers. (It is again typical of our generation that we lack any clear and generally accepted understanding of what the job of the parent ought to involve.) The media, too, we may allow something of an educational role, especially in so far as they resemble schools and colleges in content or teaching methods (we think of musical concerts on radio or science documentaries on television). But we have lost, most of us, the perception which idealist educationists like MacCunn and Clarke had so keenly, that *any* social institution is a potential educator. The idea is familiar from Part 1 as Hegel's concept of '*Sittlichkeit*'. We are, or can be, educated by the laws and customs of our society, by the traditions and practices of the institutions or communities to which we belong. The qualification 'or can be' should serve as a reminder that for Hegel, as for any idealist who believes that societies are what they are at any particular time because of the guiding hand of Spirit, society and its conventions *must* be educative to some extent; while those who reject this historicism must make the weaker claim, i.e. that they *can* be educative.

This latter claim is worth reviving today. What makes it difficult to revive our predilection, as noted in the last chapter, for seeing education as hived off from social concerns, as self-contained and self-sufficient. If education is a matter of initiating pupils into academic disciplines, then of course it is schools and colleges which will be our main educators. The conclusion is no less inevitable if one shifts to the child-centred thesis, espoused by Nunn pre-eminently, that the educator is essentially an expert in child psychology, enabled thereby to perceive the way in which a child's mind is developing, as well as the constitutional limits to such development: if educating is an expertise, then, once again, it will best take place in purpose-built institutions in which the teacher-psychologists can pursue their work uncontaminated by the a-psychological prejudices of the larger world.

If, however, we revert to the morally-oriented ideal of education we set up in the last chapter in opposition to these 'purist' doctrines, then any social institution which can help to shape our moral being is potentially educative. Factories, offices, trade unions, political institutions now take on a new aspect. Work institutions, for instance, can embody different views about how one ought to behave. They can encourage obedience to authority, or critical autonomy; competitiveness and status-worship, or fraternal co-operation. If they go against the moral values of one's family or school, they can unsettle the moral character with which those institutions have helped to endow us; if they are in line with them, they may reinforce them. Their educational significance, therefore, at least on this theory of education, is undeniable.

Recent moves in the direction of industrial democracy may be a hopeful sign that this familiar idealist theme will now become increasingly prominent. Whether the hope is realized, we shall have to see: it may turn out, alternatively, that 'industrial democracy' is valued only as a means to selfish ends, and that individuals learn only to stand on their 'rights' and have no time for any kind of authority or administrative organization.[1]

Whatever the outcome in this particular field, the general point we wish to underline is that there is plenty of work available for contemporary educators and educational reformers, not only in schools and universities, but in every department of our social life. MacCunn's central recommendation in *The Making of Character* deserves our closest consideration: we can get to work *moralizing* our different social institutions, reforming and harmonizing their purposes and procedures under the aegis of a rational ethics, so that they all work together for the same moral ends. As Tawney stressed, industrial and financial companies have come increasingly, with the rise of capitalism, to insist on their autonomy *vis-à-vis* the rest of the community and its other concerns. In this they mirror, or, perhaps more accurately, are mirrored by the educational institutions of the 'liberal education' and child-centred traditions, with their similar demand for autonomy and non-interference. This drive towards institutional autonomy has hindered the progress of a shared, rational social morality. Since the idealists, and thanks partly to their insights, the tide has begun to turn to some extent, and the need to harmonize our common purposes has become plain to more and more people. But an enormous amount of this educational work – the bulk of it, in fact – is still waiting to be tackled.

In some areas this may oblige us to reconsider some of our central liberal-democratic values – the freedom of the press, for instance. Among the most powerful of potentially educative institutions are the mass media. At present educational aims, though not absent, are not uppermost, being often subordinated to commercial. There is little doubt that television, radio, newspapers and magazines could do much more, if we so willed this, to promote the community's spiritual development. But at what cost? Would not new controls be necessary? Would these not endanger freedom of expression? These are difficult questions to answer. But at least we should see that they are open ones, not closed. It is not a 'Hegelian' penchant for totalitarian solutions which leads us to raise the 'spectre' of controls. Press freedom is not valuable for its own sake, but for the sort of society, including its political arrangements, which it makes possible. The question is: what sort of a society should this be? Some might argue that freedom of expression is worthless if it merely panders to utilitarian values, to satisfying whatever individuals happen to desire. If social values are to shift in the 'spiritual' direction outlined in this chapter, it is these rather than happiness that freedom should subserve. How it should do this is, as we have said, a complex problem which we cannot tackle here.

A similar shift may occur in our conception of the family and the rights of parents. An Englishman's home, like the businessman's factory or newspaper firm, or the headmaster's school, is his castle. Parents are masters of their own private fiefs, free to bring up their children as they will, provided that they satisfy legal minima of care and attention. But should their freedom be so unrestricted? If, as should be plain on the slightest reflection, parents are potentially one of the most important educative influences on their children, should society not try to make this potentiality an actuality? Should there be a basic minimum of conceptual equipment and moral disposition expected of every child who enters the primary school? And should it not be the parents' responsibility to provide this, or, at least, if unable to do so personally, to welcome the assistance of professional educators who can do so? Should couples be discouraged from starting a family unless they are prepared to see themselves as educators? Should the state provide parental education for those willing to do this but uncertain how to go about it? Again we can do no more than raise a string of questions. In answering them, as on the issue of the freedom of the press, delicate balances will have to be struck, between the demands of spirituality or education on the one hand and the dangers of imposing monolithic structures on the other. But at the very least it should be clear that there is an issue here, and that parental autonomy is not self-evidently a good thing.

The idealists remind us that the whole ethos of a society and its institutions is an educative force. Within that broader setting, specifically educational institutions have a particular role to play. To say this is not to make a sharp contrast between education through direct instruction and the more indirect education received from the social ethos. For schools and universities, being institutions, have their own social ethos too, and this can be harnessed to educational ends. The idealists understood this well enough. Some, like Clarke, show this by an explicit theoretical discussion of the principle. Others, like Green and the dons whom he influenced, expressed their commitment to it in the changes they wrought within their own universities, trying to break down their social exclusiveness by encouraging their links with the working classes, both inside and outside their walls; their sexual exclusiveness by pressing for the higher education of women; their institutional exclusiveness by building new links between them and the towns in which they were situated.

The general point in all this, that schools and colleges teach by institutional example, as it were, as well as by direct instruction, is by no means unfamiliar to us today, although its truth is often overlooked. The ideology behind comprehensive education – that, by learning together, children from different social classes and children who will find themselves doing very different kinds of jobs will come to see themselves as belonging to the same co-operative community – is a contemporary application of this principle. It is, indeed, entirely in line with the thinking of the idealist reformers.

These stood for the comprehensive ideal in education long before comprehensive schools as such were introduced. Their own attempts at realizing this ideal – Toynbee Hall, university extension, the WEA, the campaigns for secondary education for all – may have had traces of paternalism and, in the last of these cases, exhibited too uncautious a belief that differences of ability required different types of secondary school; but these divergencies from contemporary thinking on comprehensive education, understandable as they are when see in historical context, show only that it was their methods, not the underlying ends, which were different.

There are also other ways in which the importance of the *Sittlichkeit* of schools and colleges is recognized, at least in some quarters, today. The authority-structure in a school, its system of discipline, its encouragement or discouragement of competition, its closedness or openness to the community: all these and other aspects of its organization are now widely seen as shapers of attitudes, moulders of belief. A reacquaintance with the idealists reminds us that what seem to be new or revolutionary ideas in the educational world are often rooted in more ancient traditions of thought.

In many ways the climate of educational thinking has changed over the last fifteen or twenty years, if not towards idealism – that would be too crude a judgment – then at least towards themes which the idealists held dear. Comprehensive schooling and concern for the ethos of the school are only two of several examples. Another, closely linked with these two, is the 'new' interest in strengthening the links between schools and the local community, not least by the introduction of 'community schools'. Once again, although the idealists tended, with the rest of their contemporaries, to see schools as self-contained institutions, they would no doubt applaud this communitarianism, if they came back among us today, as a further extrapolation of their own thinking. This is not mere speculation. The idealists themselves promoted the idea of the community school, we are tempted to claim, but at the university, not secondary or primary level.

In the overall organization of our national education system we have also recently begun to revert to something like the idealists' outlook. What characterized this was a vision of the educational system, from infants to adults, as a single whole, its parts harmoniously interrelated, and related in its turn, as we have just seen, with the life of the community. Links of more than one kind were proposed, in order to bind the different elements together: 'ladders' leading from one grade of school to another, as in Green or in the later introduction of the scholarship system from elementary to secondary schools; the continuation school and adult classes, bridging the gap between elementary school and higher education; the recurrent themes of educational provinces, to be created around universities, and of a National Council of Education. This was very far from system-making for its own sake. The whole structure was to be the concrete embodiment of an ideal, the ethico-religious ideal discussed at length in previous parts of this book. What cannot fail to impress one about the idealist reformers (whether or not one finally approves of it is a different matter) is the way they worked from principles of the highest generality, to do with the existence of eternal spirit and its relationship to man, downwards to the most concrete and banal details of educational organization. Hegel, for his part, may have deduced the police-force ultimately from *Geist*; but with him it was all largely on paper, enclosed within the covers of the *Philosophy of Right* or the *Logic*. What is more, the British idealists' *a priori* approach to educational policy did deliver the goods: the networks of civic universities, the WEA, scholarships, plans for continuation schools, and the rest. What, one wonders, would the English education system have looked like if Acland, Sadler, Haldane and Tawney had never existed? Not, one suspects, the neatly articulated set of structures into which they attempted to shape it. This way of proceeding was alien to our more empirical and idiosyncratic national temper, too rationalistic, perhaps too 'German', for our domestic tastes.

At all events, the decline of idealism soon after the First World War spelt the end of an era of visionary planning in education. The inner coherence of the half-finished system which the idealists bequeathed gradually faded away. Essential parts of the whole, like the plan for continuation schools, without which the working classes would all but lose any opportunity for spiritual emancipation, were quietly forgotten or filed away for future reference which never came. Universities, no longer reminded by idealist professors like Muirhead that they have a civic as well as an academic function, came increasingly to forget the former and confine their horizons to the latter. Haldane's picture of a network of universities which were to be both liberally- and technologically-oriented, and thereby well-placed to give industry a more scientific and at the same time more ethical foundation, was not realized.

Not only universities, but other institutions, too, within the system began to to look inwards and allow their links with its other parts quietly to crumble away. In 1926 elementary schools and teacher training colleges became free *de facto* to decide their own objectives and curricula; in 1945 secondary schools followed suit. The idea of a national system of education, connected by a set of shared goals, came gradually to seem more and more unreal and finally, some time after the Second World War, all but disappeared from political thinking. This is not to say that people no longer talked of a national system: the towering counter-example of the 1944 Education Act should be enough to refute that. But the kind of system they envisaged was very different from the idealists'. It is not far from the truth to say that its only guiding principle was that it should have no guiding principle. Common aims were forgotten; diversity of objectives became the new battlecry, both for schools and for individual pupils.

The pieces which the idealists tried so energetically to weld together into a unity refashioned themselves, according to the individualistic temper of the new age, as autonomous entities, often jealous of their 'rights' and defensive against intrusion by outside bodies, not least the state. Universities, teacher training colleges, schools, all conformed to the new pattern.

We must be careful not to exaggerate. After the First World War there were integrative as well as disintegrative tendencies. The organization of teacher training is one example. The disintegrative measures of 1926, whereby the Board of Education gave up its powers to determine the broad structure of training college curricula and to conduct its own examination, left the colleges theoretically free to teach what they wanted. But this centrifugal movement was balanced by new attempts to bind training colleges closer to the universities, so that these could take over the old functions of the Board to do with aims, content and assessment. This new form of integration was finally achieved with the setting up of the Area Training Organizations in 1948, following the McNair Report of 1944, whereby university institutes of education became responsible for all the training colleges in their area. In one way the ATO was the realization of an old idealist dream: Haldane's vision, inspired also by Matthew Arnold, of a nation divided into educational provinces with a university at the hub of each, responsible for the overall direction of education in its area, in training colleges and so in schools, as well as in adult education.

But the fate of the ATOs was sealed from the start. Other, disintegrative, forces had already so atomized the educational system that they had no chance. The chief obstacle was the *de facto* authority which schools now had to determine their own aims and curricula. Before 1926 there had been more of a match between the content of teacher training courses and the demands of the schools, since the overall curricular arrangements of both types of institutions were under the control of the Board. Once this control was lifted, how were training colleges to know how many teachers in each subject area they should train? The ideal number henceforth depended on what the now autonomous schools would require. And how was this to be determined? The same problem arose over aims and content. The colleges' job was to prepare teachers for schools; and since each school theoretically decided its own aims and content for itself, the aims and content of college courses would ideally have to be shaped by school demand. The role of the ATO in these circumstances was very different from Haldane's ideal of an educational province. In that ideal, the universities were intended to have a more directive role. Within the ATOs, however, the work of the training colleges tended to become disconnected from what was happening in schools; and the university institutes, charged with the general oversight of college courses, came to share the disconnectedness which afflicted the colleges themselves. This is not to say that universities and colleges ceased to have any influence on schools during this period. They often had considerable influence in specific areas. 'Progressive' theorists, in particular, became a powerful pressure group among teacher trainers, many of their students, especially those who taught in primary schools, becoming enthusiastic disciples. But what influence the universities and colleges were able to have was increasingly at the mercy of events: it was far from the rationally-planned leadership which Arnold and Haldane wanted.

Except for the ideological bonds which linked some school-teachers to their training colleges, the world of the school grew further and further apart from the world of teacher training. Schools came to see what the colleges did as 'irrelevant' to their needs. At the same time, their new autonomy over aims and content was a mixed blessing, since it left the way open to all sorts of bodies, both institutions and individuals, to put pressure on the schools in one direction or another. We have already spoken of ideological pressure from the training colleges. But it took other forms as well: the pressure of examination boards, of universities, of the inspectorate, of parents, of curriculum development agencies, of publishers.

In general, by the 1960s the education system, once visualized by the idealists as a rationally interlocking whole, had fragmented into the mass of theoretically autonomous, though in fact often far from autonomous, units with which we have been familiar until recently: primary schools disconnected in their aims and curricula from their local secondary schools; schools disconnected not only from training colleges, but also from establishments of further education; training colleges valuing their links with the university for reasons of prestige as much as for the spiritual leadership the universities could provide; an inspectorate uncertain of its role; universities without a civic conscience.

In the last few years the scene has begun to change. 'Public accountability' has come to be the new watchword. In higher education publicly-accountable polytechnics challenge the old supremacy of the universities. In teacher training, the autonomous ATOs have been disbanded and colleges of education have to a very large extent been absorbed into polytechnics or other institutions under the control of local authorities. The 'Great Debate' of 1976/7 questioned the schools' autonomy over aims and curricula. The Taylor Report of 1977 on the government of schools recommended that these matters be determined not by the school alone, but by a governing body more responsive to the local community. At the time of writing this issue is still unsettled: it is not clear what national guidelines, if any, there will be on curricular matters, and what powers will be left to governors on the one hand and school staffs on the other.

As the pendulum thus swings back from autonomy towards accountability, the work of the idealist reformers should acquire a new relevance for us. The basic issue today is: given that we require a more cohesive educational system, what role should the state play in helping to provide this cohesion? Since we have now become unaccustomed to thinking of the state as having any say in the content of education (as distinct from its distribution, or the provision of its material prerequisites), we find that we do not know how to answer this question. A first impulse, perhaps, is to identify state direction with a form of totalitarianism: if the content of education is to be decided at the centre, this will make it possible for small groups of decision-makers to shape the intellectual and spiritual life of a whole nation. If state regimentation of this sort is to be avoided, is it not better, one may ask, to leave power at the periphery?

A reacquaintance with idealist views on the role of the state may help to give us more adequate conceptual tools with which to tackle the problem. First of all, the idealists' interest in the state was the reverse of totalitarian. The idea that all initiative should come from the centre and that other institutions should simply carry out orders from above, was anathema to them. They conceived of the state not as something imposed on, and in conflict with, free institutions, but as developing out of and remaining in harmony with them. The vitality of a community lies in its free institutions. But these institutions cannot operate in blind disregard of each other. They must work with each other: what each one does must be harmonized with the work of others. To ensure this

257

harmonious co-operation there must be something standing above these separate institutions. This is the state. Its function – or rather one of its functions, since it has other functions, too, e.g., in foreign affairs – is to regulate in this non-regimenting way the work of other institutions. The educational application of this theory can best be seen in the work of Fred Clarke, to which we referred in Chapter 10.

The idealist's state is not necessarily something apart from the national community. It *can be* that community under a certain aspect, that is, as politically organized. It is not simply the government. The government acts as agent of the state: the state is the whole political community. And to say this is not to say that it is coequivalent with a mere body of voters. It is a political community activated by a common desire to promote the good of the whole society. The 'state' is thus undeniably an ideal, not necessarily actualized in political arrangements as we know them, where individual voters can and do vote according to selfish or sectional interests.

How can this ideal conception help us to determine the limits of state power over the aims and content of education? We still need, it seems, a criterion for what these limits should be. Green, and later Bosanquet, proposed as a more general criterion that the coercive power of the state should be invoked only to remove 'hindrances to hindrances'. The state cannot coerce men into goodness, since being a good man must be something which an individual has freely willed. The most the state can do is to remove obstacles in the individual's path which prevent his self-perfection. Ignorance is one such obstacle. It is for this reason that Green argued that the state has the right to compel parents to have their children educated.

The 'hindrances to hindrances' criterion lies at the root of the concept of the welfare state. In so far as disease, poverty and ignorance are hindrances to the good life, the state has the right and duty to try to prevent them. One problem with this criterion, however, is: hindrances to what? If we say 'to goodness' or 'to the good life', then what is to count as these? We discussed this question in the last section. If the idealists' notion of the good, with its religious implications, is unacceptable, then we cannot take over their conception of the state *in toto*. The state cannot, for us, have the function of removing hindrances to our leading a properly religious life.

Can anything be salvaged from the 'hindrances to hindrances' doctrine? As we interpret it today, when applied to the welfare state, we tend to yoke it to a utilitarian conception of the good: the job of state welfare provision is to remove obstacles to individuals' being able, within certain moral constraints, to do what they want. The shortcomings of utilitarianism we have already touched on. In its place we have proposed the futility of searching for any determinate picture of human good, stressing its ultimate indeterminability. On this foundation we constructed a non-utilitarian account of the end of education, as the creation of a society of moral agents whose work both for themselves and for others is inspired by this alternative picture of the good. If we accept the 'hindrances to hindrances' doctrine, the state should have the right, in the field of education, to check whatever hinders this ideal. What this might be is a further question. What necessary conditions must obtain for individuals to be able to be moral agents of this sort? Various kinds of knowledge, at least, seem to be required: all those kinds of non-moral knowledge which may be relevant to the moral judgments they may make, as well as some understanding of the nature of morality itself. Other things besides knowledge are also necessary, of course, not least moral dispositions. There seem to be good grounds to insist that the state should demand of all its citizens that they be educated up to minimum standards in these and perhaps other areas.

This is not the place to go further into detail about what should be laid down. Instead we prefer to reiterate the point already made, about the dangers of state regimentation. As Fred Clarke showed, a nice balance has to be made between the claims of the state on the one hand and institutional vitality on the other. It could so happen that, by and large, educational institutions were all working on their own initiative towards the kind of ideal suggested. If this were the case, there would be no educational hindrances for the state to hinder. At most it could formalize the actual procedures of the schools in a code of common practice which it might not have to invoke in the present but might have to if the system deteriorated in the future.

This might be thought the ideal solution. Where, however, educational institutions fall short of this, more has to be done. Assuming, perhaps unlike the idealists, that there is no inevitability about social progress, we cannot simply leave it to the institutions themselves to improve automatically over time. One thing we could do would be to follow MacCunn's suggestion, of working within these institutions and trying to infuse them with a common social purpose of the kind described. This is something which we not only could, but should, do: whoever makes the ultimate decisions about what schools and colleges should aim at and what the content of their curricula should be, nothing will be achieved unless the teachers in these institutions voluntarily accept this framework. But is it enough to improve institutions from within? In theory MacCunn's policy might be sufficient. But in practice there may well be difficulties. Teachers' attachments to traditional ways of doing things, as well as their allegiance to different educational ideologies, may mean that reform will come about, if it comes about at all, unbearably slowly. State action can help to hinder such hindrances, making it more difficult for instance, for educational diehards to hold up progress. There is no reason, in any case, why educators should be the final authorities on what schools and colleges should teach, and why. As a moral problem, this is not one on which any individual or group of individuals has a privileged voice. The ultimate authority, on this as on other such questions, must be in the hands of the political community. This is true even where what teachers would do if left to their own devices coincided perfectly with the policy of that community. Where, as is most likely, it does not coincide perfectly, there is good reason to introduce a certain measure of state control. How this is introduced, whether by mandatory legislation or recommended guidelines, is a further matter. Regimentation, we may agree with the idealists, should as far as possible be avoided, state prescriptions being ideally in line with what subordinate institutions have independently agreed to do. The balance between the two is, as we have said, a delicate one.

The theory and practice of education 14

The drive towards independence described in the last chapter has affected not only the organization of the education system but also educational theory. The autonomy given to schools and colleges in the 1920s and later shattered the vision, as yet not fully realized, of a system united in its major purposes. Traditional purposes held it together for a time, the elementary-secondary pattern persisting into the era of secondary modern and grammar schools. But in the last twenty years this older tradition has been severely eroded, and incoherences in the system have become more and more plain. One of the parts which have come adrift is educational theory. In a unified system this could have a well-defined role, helping to formulate and criticize the major aims and sub-aims of the system, the means to these ends and the obstacles to their attainment. In an autonomous system it can have no such role. Its only global function could be to provide a rationale, and a suitable pedagogy, for the autonomous system itself. Hence the persisting influence of libertarian or progressive ideologies in the last half century. But apart from this, the world of educational theory has fragmented in the same way as the larger world of educational practice. Its constituent disciplines, psychology, sociology, philosophy and the rest, have become independent principalities, each on constant guard to repel incursions from the others. But it is not as though one found a unity of purpose even in each discipline. Here and there, for a while perhaps, one may do so; but there is often as much ideological separatism within disciplines as there is between them, perhaps especially in psychology. Educational theorists are also divided in their attitudes to educational practice itself. Some wish to get in gear with it. They propose their panaceas and their utopias – Marxist, romantic, Freudian or whatever – but all except those who content themselves with rationalizing the *status quo* half believe *au fond* that their projects can never be any more than idle dreams, at least beyond a small circle of enthusiasts. Others have no hope of influencing a system which dispenses with large-scale theoretical structures, and turn towards some form of educational study for its own sake, whether it be the analytic philosopher teasing out the meaning of 'teaching' or the historian of education

261

bottoming the grammar schools of Lincolnshire in the sixteenth
century.

We do not wish to be misunderstood. We are not saying that
ideological differences or educational enquiry for its own sake
should not exist. As always, it is a question of balance, of priorities.
Our study of the idealists points to a more positive and more
rewarding role for the educational theorist. If what we have written
about the importance of unifying the education system under a
clear set of common aims is correct, then there will be work for him
a-plenty in clarifying these aims and helping to devise a suitable
pedagogy and organizational framework in which this can occur.
Philosophers, sociologists, psychologists, students of educational
administration and comparative education can work hand in hand.
That they have a moral obligation to do so should be plain enough.
Even in an autonomous system, theorists from the different disciplines ought to appreciate that if what they put across to teachers
in training fails to cohere with what other disciplines are teaching
them, the students will be left in an intellectual mess. If educational theory is to affect practice in any way at all, it has a moral
duty to make its different branches as mutually coherent as possible. In a unified system, one which has jettisoned institutional
autonomy on the scale on which we have come to know it, its
moral obligations extend beyond individual students to the
framework of the system as a whole.

The idealists' work in education has shown us how detailed
practical reforms may originate in theories of the most general
kind. It is often said not to be in the British temper to wish to
reform society from the macroscopic end. 'Grassroots' innovation
has commonly been thought of as our national forte. But a study
of our history reveals a more complex reality. Our contemporary
civilization owes much to visionary planners who saw things in the
large and set to realizing them in the small. Florence Nightingale,
for instance, is popularly remembered today as a sympathetic
Crimean nurse. In fact she was much more than this, an indefa-
tigable reformer not only of civilian and army hospitals, but also of
the living conditions of the British soldier and the indigenous
population of India. All her minute recommendations under these
and other heads were based not only on her experience at Scutari
but·also and more fundamentally on a combination of humanitarian outrage that the poor should be deprived of the basic
necessities of life, and an encyclopaedic knowledge of the best
medical practice. She is indeed a national heroine, but not for the
reason most commonly put forward. William Wilberforce, Edwin
Chadwick, Florence Nightingale, John Maynard Keynes: in these

and in other men and women we see that we are a nation of practical visionaries as well as of eccentrics and individualists. In the field of education few have possessed the vision and the practical ability of the idealist reformers. They still have much to teach us.

Biographical notes

Acland, Sir Arthur Herbert Dyke, 13th Bt (1847-1926). Educated Rugby and entered Christ Church, Oxford, 1866. Lecturer, Keble College, 1871-5. Principal, Oxford Military College, Cowley, 1875-7. Secretary of Extension Lectures Committee, 1878-85. Steward, Christ Church, 1879-83. Senior Steward, 1884. Senior Bursar, Balliol, 1883-8. Liberal M.P., Rotherham, 1885-99. Vice-President of the Committee of Council in Gladstone's and Rosebery's Ministries, 1892-5. Chairman, Consultative Committee of the Board of Education, 1900-16.

Arnold, Matthew (1822–88). Educated Laleham, Winchester and Rugby. Entered Balliol, 1841. Fellow, Oriel College, 1845. Brief spell teaching at Rugby. Private Secretary to Lord Lansdowne. President of the Committee of Council on Education, 1847-51. H.M. Inspector of Schools, 1851-86. Professor of Poetry, Oxford University, 1857-67.

Ashley, William James (1860-1927). Educated St Olave's, Southwark and entered Balliol, 1878. Fellow and History Lecturer, Lincoln College, 1885-8. Lecturer in History, Corpus Christi, Oxford, 1885-8. Professor of Political Economy and Constitutional History, Toronto University, 1888-92. Professor of Economic History, Harvard University, 1892-1901. Professor of Commerce, Birmingham University, 1901-25 and Vice-Principal, 1918-25. Knight, 1917.

Ball, Sidney (1857-1918). Educated Wellington College and entered Oriel College, Oxford, 1875. Lecturer in Philosophy and Fellow, St John's Oxford, from 1882, but mainly interested in economics.

Barker, Ernest (1874-1960). Educated Manchester Grammar School and entered Balliol, 1893. Fellow of Merton College, 1898-1905. Lecturer in Modern History, Wadham College, 1899-1909. Fellow and Lecturer, St John's College, 1909-13. Fellow and Tutor, New College, 1913-20. Principal, King's College, London, 1920-39. Chairman of the Drafting Committee of the Hadow Report on *The Education of the Adolescent,* 1926. Knight, 1944.

Barnett, Samuel Augustus (1844-1913). Educated at home, entered Wadham College, Oxford, 1862. Became curate, St Mary's, Bryanston Square, London, 1867; and rector, St Jude's, Whitechapel, 1873-94. Founder of Toynbee Hall. Canon, Bristol Cathedral, 1895.

Beveridge, William Henry, 1st Baron (1879-1963). Educated Charterhouse and entered Balliol, 1897. Stowell Civil Law Fellow, University College, Oxford, 1902-9. Sub-Warden, Toynbee Hall, 1903-5. Barrister, Inner Temple, 1904. Leader writer, *Morning Post,* 1906-8. Director of Labour Exchanges, 1906-16. Assistant General Secretary to Ministry of Munitions, 1915-16. Second Secretary, Ministry of Food, 1916-18 and Permanent Secretary, 1919. Director of the London School of Economics, 1919-37. Vice-Chancellor, London University, 1926-8. Master of University College, Oxford, 1937-45. Liberal M.P., Berwick-on-Tweed, 1944-5. Baron, 1946.

Bosanquet, Bernard (1848-1923). Educated Harrow and entered Balliol, 1867. Fellow, Lecturer and Tutor, University College, Oxford, 1871-81. On the death of his father in 1880, Bosanquet came into possession of an independent income which enabled him to follow his interests. Professor of Moral Philosophy, St Andrews University, 1903-8.

Bradley, Andrew Cecil (1851-1935). Educated Cheltenham and entered Balliol, 1869. Fellow of Balliol, 1874; Lecturer, 1876-81. Professor of Modern Literature (with Modern History also at first), University College, Liverpool, 1882-9. Professor of English Language and Literature, Glasgow University, 1889-1900. Professor of Poetry, Oxford University, 1901-6.

Bradley, Francis Herbert (1846-1924). Educated Cheltenham and Marlborough, and entered University College, Oxford, 1865. Fellow, Merton College, Oxford, 1870. Because of illness, he was unable to undertake teaching and devoted his life to his philosophical writings.

Bruce, Hon. William Napier (1858-1936), second son of 1st Baron Aberdare. Educated Harrow and entered Balliol, 1876. Barrister, Lincoln's Inn, 1883. Assistant Commissioner, Charity Commissioner under the Endowed Schools Acts, 1886-1900. Secretary, Royal Commission on Secondary Education, 1894-5. Assistant Secretary, Board of Education, 1900-3; Chairman, Departmental Committee on the organization of secondary education in Wales, 1919-20. Principal Assistant Secretary, Schools Branch, 1903; Second Secretary, 1920.

Bryce, James (1838-1922), Viscount Bryce of Dechmont. Educated Glasgow High School and Glasgow University. Entered Trinity College, Oxford, 1857. Fellow, Oriel College, 1862-89 and re-elected Professor Fellow, 1890-3. Assistant Commissioner, Schools Inquiry Commission, 1865-6. Lecturer, Owen's College, Manchester, 1868; and Professor of Law until 1874. Regius Professor of Civil Law, Oxford University, 1870-93. Liberal M.P., Tower Hamlets, 1880-5; South Aberdeen, 1885-1906. Chancellor of the Duchy of Lancaster and member of Cabinet, 1892-5. Chairman, Royal Commission on Secondary Education, 1894-5. Ambassador to Washington, 1907-13. Viscount 1914.

Caird, Edward (1835-1908). Educated Greenock Academy, Glasgow and St Andrews University. Entered Balliol, 1860. Fellow and Tutor, Merton College, 1864-6; Professor of Moral Philosophy, Glasgow University, 1866-93. Master of Balliol, 1893-1907.

Caird, John (1820-98). Brother of Edward, q.v. Educated Greenock Academy and Glasgow University. Minister, Newton-on-Ayr, Edinburgh and Glasgow. Professor of Divinity, Glasgow University, 1862-73; Principal and Vice-Chancellor, 1873-98.

Clarke, Fred (1880-1952). Educated at an Oxford elementary school, Oxford Technical College and, as a pupil teacher, won a Queen's Scholarship to Oxford. Senior Master of Method, Diocesan Training College, York. First Professor of Education, Hartley University College, Southampton, 1906-11. Professor of Education, South African College, later Cape Town University, 1911-35. Director, Institute of Education, London University, 1936-45. Knight, 1943.

Dicey, Albert Venn (1835-1922). Educated King's College School, London, and entered Balliol, 1854. Fellow of Trinity College, Oxford, 1860. Barrister, Inner Temple, 1863. Vinerian Professor of Law, Oxford University, 1882-1909. Principal of Working Men's College, London, 1899-1912.

Ellis, Thomas Edward (1859-99). Educated Bala Grammar School, Wales, Aberystwyth University College and New College, Oxford. Elected Liberal M.P., Merioneth, 1889. Became Junior Whip in Gladstone's Ministry, 1892; Chief Whip, 1894-5; and Chief Whip of the Liberal Opposition, 1895-9.

Fisher, Herbert Albert Laurens (1865-1940). Educated Winchester and entered New College, Oxford, 1884. Fellow, 1888-1912. Vice-Chancellor, Sheffield University, 1912-16. President of the Board of Education, with a seat in the Cabinet, 1916-22. National Liberal

M.P., Hallam in Sheffield, 1916-18, and English Universities, 1918-26. Warden, New College, Oxford, 1925-40.

Gore, Charles (1853-1932). Educated Harrow and entered Balliol, 1871. Fellow, Trinity College, Oxford, 1875-95, Lecturer, 1876-80. Vice-Principal, Cuddesdon Theological College, 1880-3. Librarian, Pusey House, 1884-93. Vicar of Radley, 1893-4. Canon of Westminster, 1894-1902. Bishop of Worcester, 1902-5; Birmingham, 1905-11; Oxford, 1911-19.

Green, Thomas Hill (1836-82). Educated Rugby and entered Balliol, 1855. Lecturer in Ancient and Modern History and Fellow, Balliol, 1860. Assistant Commissioner in the Midlands for the Schools Inquiry Commission 1865-6. Senior Dean, Balliol, 1866. In charge of the new Balliol Hall, 1867. Member, Oxford School Board, 1874, and of Oxford Town Council, 1876. Whyte Professor of Moral Philosophy, 1878-82.

Haldane, Richard Burdon (1856-1928), Viscount Haldane of Cloan. Educated Edinburgh Academy and Göttingen and Edinburgh Universities. Barrister, Lincoln's Inn, 1879. Q.C., 1890. M.P., East Lothian, 1885-1911. Secretary of State for War, 1905-12. Lord Chancellor, 1912-15, and from 1924-5 in the first Labour Government. Leader of the Opposition in the House of Lords, 1925-8.

Hewins, William Albert Samuel (1865-1931). Educated Wolverhampton School and entered Pembroke College, Oxford. Director of the London School of Economics, 1895-1903. Teacher of Modern Economic History, University of London, 1902-3. Tooke Professor of Economic Science and Statistics at King's College, London, 1897-1903. Unionist M.P., Hereford City, 1912-18. Under-Secretary of State for Colonies, 1917-19.

Holland, Henry Scott (1847-1918). Educated Eton and entered Balliol, 1866. Senior Student, Christ Church, 1870-86; Tutor, 1872. Canon, St Paul's Cathedral, 1884-1910. Regius Professor of Divinity, Oxford, 1910-18.

Holmes, Edmond Gore Alexander (1850-1936). Educated Merchant Taylor's and entered St John's College, Oxford, 1869. H.M. Inspector of Schools, 1875-1905. Chief Inspector, Elementary Schools, 1906-11.

Jones, Henry (1852-1922). Educated at village school, Llangernyw, leaving at the age of twelve. Bangor Normal College, 1870. Appointed headmaster of Ironworks School, 1873-5. Entered Glasgow University, 1875. Clark Fellow in Philosophy, 1878-82. Lecturer in

Philosophy, University College, Aberystwyth, 1882-4. Professor of Philosophy and Political Economy, University College. Bangor, 1884-91. Professor of Logic, Rhetoric and Metaphysics, St Andrews, 1891-4. Succeeded E. Caird, q.v., as Professor of Moral Philosophy, Glasgow University, 1894-1922. Knight, 1912.

Jowett, Benjamin (1817-93). Educated St Paul's and entered Balliol, 1836. Tutor at Balliol, 1842-70. Regius Professor of Greek, Oxford University, from 1855; Vice-Chancellor, 1882-6. Master of Balliol, 1870-93.

Lindsay, Alexander Dunlop (1879-1952). 1st Baron Lindsay of Birker. Educated Glasgow Academy and Glasgow University. Entered University College, Oxford, 1898. Clark Fellow in Philosophy, Glasgow University, 1902-4. Shaw Fellow in Philosophy, Edinburgh University, 1904-6. Fellow and Tutor, Balliol, 1906-22; Professor of Moral Philosophy, 1922-4; Master of Balliol, 1924-49. Vice-Chancellor of Oxford University, 1935-8. Principal, University College of North Staffordshire, later Keele University, 1951-2. Baron 1945.

MacCunn, John (1846-1929). Educated Greenock Academy, Glasgow, and Glasgow University. Entered Balliol, 1872. Private coach, Oxford, 1876-81. Professor of Logic, Mental and Moral Philosophy and Political Economy, University College of Liverpool, 1881-1910.

Mackenzie, John Stuart (1860-1935). Educated Glasgow High School, Glasgow University, and Trinity College, Cambridge. Subsequently Fellow, Trinity College; assistant to Professor Adamson, University of Manchester. Professor of Philosophy, University College, Cardiff, 1895-1915.

Mackinder, Halford John (1861-1947). Educated Gainsborough Grammar School and Epsom College. Entered Christ Church, Oxford, 1880. Barrister, Inner Temple, 1886. Involved with Oxford Extension Movement from 1885. Reader in Geography, Oxford University, 1887-1905. Student, Christ Church, 1892, and became Principal of the new Reading College, 1892-1903. He held the posts of Lecturer, Reader and Professor of Economic Geography and Director of the London School of Economics, 1895-1925. Unionist M.P., Camlachie Division of Glasgow, 1910-22. Knight, 1920.

Mansbridge, Albert (1876-1952). Educated Battersea Grammar School. Left school at fourteen, taking a number of clerical posts, including one in the tea department of the English and Scottish Co-operative Wholesale Societies, Whitechapel. Teacher, Co-operative Classes in Industrial History from 1897. Honorary

Secretary, 1903 and General Secretary of the Workers' Educational Association, 1905-15. Member of the Consultative Committee, Board of Education, 1906-12, 1924-39. Member of the Statutory Commission on Oxford University, 1923.

Milner, Alfred, 1st Viscount (1854-1925). Educated Tübingen Gymnasium and King's College, London. Entered Balliol, 1873. Fellow, New College, 1877. Barrister, Inner Temple, 1881. Journalist, *Pall Mall Gazette.* Chairman, Board of Inland Revenue, 1892-7. High Commissioner for South Africa, 1897-1905. War Cabinet, 1916-18. Secretary of State for War, 1918-19 and for the Colonies, 1919-21. Baron, 1901. Viscount, 1902.

Morant, Robert Laurie (1863-1920). Educated Winchester and entered New College, Oxford, 1881. Tutor, King of Siam's nephews, 1887-94, and took part in organizing the country's education system. Returned to England, 1894, resident in Toynbee Hall, 1895. Assistant Director, Officer of Special Inquiries, 1895-9. Private Secretary to Sir John Gorst, the Vice-President of the Committee of Council on Education, 1899-1902. Assistant Private Secretary to Duke of Devonshire, the Lord President, 1902. Acting Secretary, Board of Education, 1902; Permanent Secretary, 1903-11. Chairman, National Health Insurance Commission, 1911-19. Permanent Secretary, Ministry of Health, 1919-20. Knight, 1907.

Muirhead, John Henry (1855-1940). Educated Glasgow Academy and Glasgow University. Lecturer in Classics and Mental Philosophy, Holloway College, Egham, 1889-91. Lecturer in Philosophy, Bedford College, London, 1891-7. Professor of Philosophy, Mason University College, Birmingham, 1897-1900; and Birmingham University, 1900-22.

Nettleship, Richard Lewis (1846-92). Educated Uppingham and entered Balliol, 1865. Fellow of Balliol, 1869-92. Died whilst climbing Mont Blanc.

Nichol, John (1833-94). Educated Glasgow Academy and entered Balliol, 1853. Founder of the Old Mortality Society. Tutor at Oxford, 1859-62. First Professor of English Literature, Glasgow University, 1862-89.

Nunn, Thomas Percy (1870-1944). Educated at his father's private school and Bristol University College. Taught in Halifax and later London grammar schools. Science Master and Lecturer, Shoreditch Technical Institute, 1903-5. Vice-Principal, London Day Training College, 1905-22; Director, 1922, continuing when it became the Institute of Education until 1936. Professor of Education, 1913-36.

Percival, John (1834-1918). Educated Appleby Grammar School, Westmorland. Entered Queen's College, Oxford, 1855. Ordained deacon and became master under Frederick Temple at Rugby, 1860. Headmaster of Clifton, 1862-79. President of Trinity College Oxford, 1879-86. Headmaster of Rugby, 1886-95. Bishop of Hereford, 1895-1918.

Sadler, Michael Ernest (1861-1943). Educated Rugby and entered Trinity College, Oxford, 1880. Succeeded Acland as Secretary of Extension Lectures Committee (Inter Delegacy), Oxford, 1885-95. Steward, Christ Church, 1886-95. Student, Christ Church, 1890-5. Member, Royal Commission on Secondary Education, 1894-5. Director, Office of Special Inquiries, 1895-1903. Professor of History and Administration of Education (part-time) Manchester University, 1903-11. Vice-Chancellor, Leeds University, 1911-23. Master, University College, Oxford, 1923-34. Knight, 1919.

Smith, Arthur Lionel (1850-1924). Educated Christ's Hospital and entered Balliol, 1869. Fellow, Trinity College, Oxford, 1874-9. Lecturer and Tutor in Modern History, Balliol, 1879-1916; and Fellow, 1882-1916. Master of Balliol, 1916-24.

Smith, Hubert Llewellyn (1864-1945). Educated Bristol Grammar School and Corpus Christi College, Oxford. Lecturer, Oxford Extension Delegacy, 1887-8 and Toynbee Trust, living for a number of years at Toynbee Hall. First Commissioner of Labour, Board of Trade, 1893-1903; Controller-General of Commercial, Labour and Statistical Department, 1903-7, and Permanent Secretary, 1907-19. Chief economic adviser to the Government, 1919-27. Secretary of the National Association for the Promotion of Technical Education, 1889-93; and member, Royal Commission on Secondary Education, 1894-5. Knight, 1908.

Spender, John Alfred (1862-1942). Educated Bath College and entered Balliol, 1881. Editor *Eastern Morning News,* Hull, 1886-91. Assistant Editor, *Pall Mall Gazette,* 1892. Assistant Editor, *Westminster Gazette,* 1893-5; Editor, 1896-1922.

Tawney, Richard Henry (1880-1962). Educated Rugby and entered Balliol, 1899. Resident at Toynbee Hall, 1903-6. Assistant Lecturer in Economics, Glasgow University, 1906-8. Teacher, Oxford Tutorial Classes Committee, 1908-14. Fellow, Balliol, 1908-21. Reader in Economic History, London School of Economics, 1919-31; Professor, 1931-49.

Temple, Frederick (1821-1902). Educated Blundell's School, Tiverton and entered Balliol, 1839. Fellow and Tutor, Balliol,

1842-8. Ordained deacon 1846; and priest, 1847. Examiner, Committee of Council on Education, 1848-9. Principal, Kneller Hall, Twickenham, training college for workhouse teachers, 1849-55. Headmaster of Rugby, 1857-69. Member, Schools Inquiry Commission, 1864-8. Bishop of Exeter, 1869-85. Bishop of London, 1885-97. Archbishop of Canterbury, 1897-1902.

Temple, William (1881-1944). Younger son of Frederick Temple, q.v. Educated Rugby and entered Balliol, 1900. Fellow and Lecturer in Philosophy, Queen's College, Oxford, 1904-10. Headmaster of Repton, 1910-14. Rector, St James's, Piccadilly, London, 1914-17. Canon of Westminster, 1919-20. Bishop of Manchester, 1921-9. Archbishop of York, 1929-42. Archbishop of Canterbury, 1942-4.

Toynbee, Arnold Joseph (1852-83). Educated at a preparatory school, Blackheath, and entered Pembroke College, Oxford, 1873. Left because of illness and went to Balliol, 1875. Lecturer in Political Economy, Balliol, from 1875; and Tutor for Indian Civil Service probationers, 1878-83.

Urwick, Edward Johns (1867-1945). Educated Uppingham and Oxford University. Sub-Warden, Toynbee Hall, 1898-1902. Professor of Social Philosophy, University of London. Professor of Political Economy, University of Toronto.

Wallace, William (1843-97). Educated Madras Academy, Cupar, Fifeshire, and St Andrews University. Entered Balliol, 1864. Fellow of Merton, 1867. Lecturer, Oriel College, 1873-4. Succeeded Green as Whyte Professor of Moral Philosophy, 1882-97.

Warren, Thomas Herbert (1853-1930). Educated Clifton College, and entered Balliol, 1872. Fellow, 1877 and Tutor, Magdalen College, Oxford, 1878-85; and President, 1885-1928. Vice-Chancellor, Oxford University, 1906-10. Professor of Poetry, Oxford University, 1911-16. Member of Consultative Committee of Board of Education until 1906. Knight, 1914.

Zimmern, Alfred Eckhard (1879-1957). Educated Winchester, and entered New College, Oxford; Lecturer in Ancient History and subsequently Fellow and Tutor there, 1904-9. H.M. Inspector of Schools, Board of Education, 1912-15; and later joined the Political Intelligence Department, Foreign Office, 1918-19. Wilson Professor of International Politics, Aberystwyth University College, 1919-21. After this, concerned with League of Nations work, returning to Oxford as first Montague Burton Professor of International Relations, 1930-44. Knight, 1936.

Notes

Part 1   Philosophical idealism and education

1   Introduction

1 See G. Faber, *Jowett*, pp. 177-83, for further details on this paragraph.
2 It would be wrong to claim that F. H. Bradley held this view without qualification. See his criticism of it in *Ethical Studies*, pp. 202ff. For Hegel's un-Bradleian stress on social mobility, see p. 36.
3 See also E. Ashby and M. Anderson, *Portrait of Haldane at Work on Education*, pp. 5-9.

2   Nature, man and God

1 For an introduction to Fichte and to his chief metaphysical work, the *Wissenschaftslehre* (translated as *Science of Knowledge,* 1970), see F. Copleston, *History of Philosophy*, vol. 7, part 1, chs 1-4. For Fichte's educational ideas and influence, see pp. 48-51, 56-7.
2 See also C. Taylor, *Hegel,* pp. 185-8, 410-22.

3   Morality and community

1 On *Sittlichkeit*, see Hegel, *Phenomenology of Mind,* especially ch. 6; *Philosophy of Right,* parts 2, 3. See also C. Taylor, *Hegel,* pp. 376ff, 385ff.
2 See also S. Avineri, *Hegel's Theory of the Modern State,* ch. 8.
3 See A. R. Cacoullos, *Thomas Hill Green,* pp. 63ff, for a further discussion of the relationship between Green and Kant.

4   Society and the state

1 · See also p. 204.
2 See also Avineri, *Hegel's Theory of the Modern State,* pp. 171-2.
3 Hegel, *Philosophy of Right,* paras 182-208; Avineri, op. cit., pp. 98-109.
4 See Avineri, op. cit., pp. 89-96, 144-51, for a discussion of Hegel's views on poverty in the *Realphilosophie* and in *Philosophy of Right.*
5 Symonds to Mrs Green, July 1883, T. H. Green Papers.

5 Education

1 See part 2 for further details of this German influence: on Arnold, pp. 74-5; on Green, p. 81; and on Haldane, pp. 129-31.
2 Herbart's rise and fall in Britain is described in R. J. W. Selleck, *The New Education: The English Background, 1870-1914*. For the parallel American story see H. Dunkel, *Herbart and Herbartianism*. For T. G. Rooper's blending of Green and Herbart and application to educational problems, see pp. 179-80.
3 For Fichte's educational thought in general see G. H. Turnbull, *The Educational Theory of Fichte*.
4 H. Sidgwick to Mrs Green, 1 August 1882, T. H. Green Papers.
5 A. V. Dicey to Mrs Green, 17 September 1882, ibid.
6 See p. 97.
7 See pp. 220-1.

Part 2 The work of the educational reformers

6 The Oxford influence

1 For the general background to this period see L. C. B. Seaman, *Victorian England*, chs 9 and 10; G. Best, *Mid-Victorian Britain*, pp. 169-90. More specifically on educational questions are J. Lawson and H. Silver, *A Social History of Education in England*, chs 8, 9; H. C. Barnard, *A History of English Education from 1760*; and W. H. G. Armytage, *Four Hundred Years of English Education*, chs 7, 8.
2 In Scotland, four universities had been established for several centuries: St Andrews (1411), Glasgow (1451), Aberdeen (1494) and Edinburgh (1583). No new ones were created during the nineteenth century.
3 For details of the University Tests Act 1871, see L. Campbell, *On the Nationalization of the Old English Universities*, ch. 7.
4 A description of Rugby during Green's schooldays there is given in J. B. Hope Simpson, *Rugby Since Arnold*, pp. 22-36.
5 Some information on his life is contained in R. W. Macan, 'In Memory of Richard Lewis Nettleship', in *The Educational Review*, October 1892, pp. 309-15.
6 Dicey described Green in 1862 as a philosophical radical but of a rather peculiar kind:

Almost all his definite opinions might be endorsed by Bright or Cobden, but neither Bright nor Cobden could understand the process by which Green's opinions are attained, nor the arguments by which they are defended. An idealist in philosophy, he argues for the most utilitarian of political schools, on idealist principles and, attaching the greatest importance to national life, constantly expresses a contempt for so-called 'national' honour and imperial greatness which might perhaps offend the patriotism even of Mr Cobden (R. S. Rait, *Memorials of Albert Venn Dicey*, pp. 36-7).

7   It is interesting to note that Arnold's prize-winning Newdigate poem of 1843 was on Cromwell (A. L. Rowse, *Matthew Arnold: Poet and Prophet,* p. 31).

8   See also P. J. McCarthy, *Matthew Arnold and the Three Classes,* p. 117.

9   As late as 1898, five out of the eight members of the Oxford School Board were in holy orders.

10 C. A. Fyffe to Mrs Green, n.d., 1882, T. H. Green Papers.

11 Letter, Oxford School Board, 18 May 1881, Ed. 27/250, Public Record Office.

12 A. R. Vardy to R. L. Nettleship, 17 September, 1887, T. H. Green Papers.

13 Mrs Green's Account of T. H. Green's life, n.d., ibid.

14 Professor Henry Nettleship to Mrs Green, n.d., 1882, ibid.

15 See T. H. Green to T. H. Ward, 16 September, 1881, MS. Eng. Lett. e. 118, Bodleian Library.

16 *The Spectator,* 1 April 1882, pp. 417-18.

17 Further details are to be found in A. S. Bishop, 'Ralph Lingen, Secretary to the Education Department, 1849-70', in *British Journal of Educational Studies,* vol. 14, no. 2, 1968, pp. 138-63.

18 For an account of Cumin, Arnold and the 'Balliol Scholars' in the 1840s see Anon, *Patrick Cumin, Secretary of the Education Department,* pp. 6-7.

19 See 'Francis Richard Sandford', in *Blackwood's Magazine,* no. 25, March 1895, p. 470.

20 However, at least one student, L. R. Farnell, later to become Vice-Chancellor of Oxford University (1920-3), reacted against the Master's discourses when he realized that Green had in view 'no longer the Absolute, but Bethnal Green' (L. R. Farnell, *An Oxonian Looks Back,* p. 44).

21 Spender's importance in the political field is well illustrated in W. Harris, *J. A. Spender,* pp. 27, 31.

22 See V. Halperin, *Lord Milner and the Empire: The Evolution of British Imperialism,* ch. 5; and, for the Oxford influence, W. Nimocks, *Milner's Young Men,* pp. 48ff.

7   Adult education

1   A. V. Dicey became the fourth Principal of the College in 1899, holding the office until 1912. See R. S. Rait, *Memorials of Albert Venn Dicey,* pp. 175-80.

2   For an analysis of the close relationship between views of society expressed in the 1860s and those in the 1880s, see E. P. Hennock, 'Poverty and Social Theory in England: the experiences of the 1880s', in *Social History,* vol. 1, no. 1, January 1976.

3   See letter from Toynbee to his sister, 26 March 1882, and Nettleship to Toynbee's mother, 10 April 1883 (G. Toynbee, *Reminiscences and Letters of Joseph and Arnold Toynbee,* pp. 161-2, 179).

4   Milner's 'Reminiscence' in A. J. Toynbee, *Lectures on the Industrial Revolution of the Eighteenth Century in England,* p. xxi. After leaving

Oxford, Milner, who was elected a fellow of New College in 1877, returned to take part in an informal society set up by Toynbee for the discussion of political and social questions. The society continued in existence until Toynbee's death in 1883 (J. Marlowe, *Milner, the Apostle of Empire*, p. 6).

5   T. D. Acland to A. H. D. Acland, n.d., Acland Papers, 1148M, Devon Record Office.

6   Information kindly supplied by Lady Anne Acland.

7   Mandell Creighton, later Bishop of London, recalled that Acland acted as his curate at Embleton, Northumberland, for a few months from Easter 1875. Acland's request was based on health grounds and the need 'for a complete change from Oxford' (L. Creighton, *Life and Letters of Mandell Creighton*, vol. 1, p. 160).

8   In his diary, Acland described the first meeting of the Inner Ring: 'We formed a small society for studying various questions, and trying to hammer them out. We discussed House of Lords, etc. and Free Education. It was very interesting to me and will do us all good I am sure. They had supper at my house' (Acland Diary, 4 January 1884, Killerton, Devon). Further details are given in A. Hope, *Memories and Notes*, pp. 73-4.

9   T. H. Green to A. H. D. Acland, 29 March 1880. MS. Eng. Lett. d. 81, Bodleian Library.

10 Henry Scott Holland, see Chapter 9.

11 A. H. D. Acland to T. D. Acland, 4 November 1881, 51/12/1, Devon Record Office.

12 Ibid., 23 April 1883.

13 At the national level, Acland and his wife were active in promoting co-operative educational activities (T. Kelly, *A History of Adult Education in Great Britain,*, p. 210).

14 M. E. Sadler, 'Reminiscences of Arnold Toynbee and Ruskin at Oxford', n.d., typescript.

15 M. E. Sadler, 'England's Debt to German Education', an address delivered at Frankfurt am Main, 28 May 1912.

16 M. E. Sadler, address given at the opening of Bingley Training College, 21 October 1911.

17 M. E. Sadler, 'Christian Philanthropy and Rationalistic Philanthropy', n.d., typescript.

18 With uncharacteristic warmth, Acland commented on Sadler's and his wife's stay at his North Wales home, Clynnog: 'The Sadlers enjoyed their week very much. *It was really jolly*' (Acland Diary, September 1887).

19 Details of the Rotherham election, including an eye-witness account of the public reconciliation of Acland and his father, are contained in G. Gummer, *Reminiscences of Rotherham: A Retrospect of over Sixty Years*, pp. 250-3.

20 Toynbee Memorial Fund, Minute Book, 1884-98, 21 March 1884. Toynbee Hall Papers, A/TOY/1.

21 Acland has been appointed secretary to the fund in the previous year (Acland Diary, 10 June 1883).

22 Vice-Chancellor, Calcutta University, 1877-8, Reader in Indian Law, Oxford, 1878-1900. Like Toynbee, Markby was a tutor to Indian probationers at Balliol and was a Senior Bursar at the College 1893-1905. I. Elliott (ed.), *The Balliol College Register, 1833-1933,* 2nd edn., p. 145.

23 Dalhousie (1847-1887), then Lord Ramsay and a commander in the Royal Navy, wrote to a Balliol man, G. A. Spottiswoode, 'How can I understand the other half?' Spottiswoode consulted Jowett, who advised a year at Balliol (1875-6) (E. Abbott and L. Campbell, *Life and Letters of Benjamin Jowett,* vol. 1, p. 167).

24 Minute Book, op. cit., 7 May 1888.

25 Ibid., 12 March 1889.

26 Toynbee Memorial Fund. Correspondence: Sadler to Dalhousie, 13 June 1887. Toynbee Hall Papers, A/TOY/2.

27 Ibid., Acland to Markby, 23 December 1890.

28 Quoted in Anon, 'University Extension', *Rewley House Papers,* vol. 1, no. 1, 1927, pp. 8-9.

29 A. H. D. Acland's Report to the Standing Committee of the Delegacy, 27 November 1878 (Oxford University Extension Delegacy Papers). After a while, the three universities – Cambridge, Oxford and London – united to form a joint board for the appointment of lecturers and examiners. The Dean of St Paul's expressed his apprehension about the London Society to Goschen, its President, on the grounds that 'it would have a tendency to conduce and precipitate in raw and unprepared minds a good deal of loose thinking on grave subjects which goes on especially at Oxford among whom, I suppose, teachers will be mainly sought' (A. W. Church to J. G. Goschen, 8 November 1875; University of London Extension Society Papers).

30 On a visit to Oxford, Acland noted that 'There was talk about Sadler's appointment to University Extension Secretaryship' (Acland Diary, 17 July 1885). Acland himself managed to combine his work as M.P. and Extension lecturer for at least two more years. 'During these three months,' he wrote on 1 May 1887, 'I have managed to scrape through the remaining Univ. Extension Correspondence lectures' (ibid.).

31 Stuart mentioned in his autobiography that 'The Oxford scheme for University Extension never made much progress until Mr Sadler took it up with such enthusiasm and devotion, and raised the Oxford numbers above those of Cambridge' (J. Stuart, *Reminiscences,* p. 175).

32 For instance, some twenty years later A. E. Zimmern asked Beveridge to address the Club on the topic of Socialism 'from the political, moral and economic standpoint' (Zimmern to Beveridge, 12 December 1905; Beveridge Papers, IIb5).

33 Lang's biographer mentions that 'for an audience Acland brought along the members of the Inner Ring' (J. G. Lockhart, *Cosmo Gordon Lang,* p. 39).

34 An impression of the meeting is given in the essay 'Samuel Barnett and the Growth of Settlements', in H. S. Holland, *A Bundle of Memories,* pp. 92-3.

35 Among the earliest visitors were Sir Edward B. Tylor, first Professor of Anthropology at Oxford, Francis Galton and Frederic Harrison. Many were from overseas, especially the USA, with interests in social investigation, settlements and university extension (Visitors' Book, 1885-1927, Toynbee Hall Papers, A/TOY/17).

36 See Letters to Lord Milner, 1913-19, Toynbee Hall Papers, A/TOY/6.

37 Beveridge Papers: diary, 29 June 1903, Ic1 letter; Barnett to Beveridge, 28 August 1903, IIb 2; diary, 27 November 1903, Ic 1A; diary, 19 February 1904, Ic 2.

38 See interview given by Barnett in *The Christian Commonwealth*, 23 November 1893, p. 123.

39 Barnett to Francis Barnett, 30 November 1895, Barnett Papers, F/BAR/132.

40 The first course of lectures organized by the Society, held in 1876, included lectures on political economy by Herbert Asquith, who once referred to Toynbee Hall as a 'social laboratory' (J. Burrows, *University Adult Education in London*, p. 8).

41 Sadler to Marvin, 2 November 1891, Marvin Papers, e. 106.

42 An example of the high standard of teaching at the summer meetings was Muirhead's *The Service of the State*, based on four lectures on Green which Muirhead had given at the Oxford Meeting in 1907.

43 For an appreciation of Mansbridge's achievement, see R. H. Tawney's article, 'Mansbridge', in *The Highway*, vol. 44, November 1952.

44 *University Extension Journal*, May 1903. Mansbridge expressed the belief that such an alliance would 'inevitably benefit University Extension and Democracy alike, and express itself in increasing contributions to the correct thought of our time'.

45 *The Higher Education of Working Men, being the Official Report of the Joint Conference between Co-operators, Trade Unionists and University Extension Authorities at Oxford, on Saturday August 22nd 1903*, pp. 1-8. Copy in Temple House Papers.

46 See, for instance, M. D. Stocks, *The Workers' Educational Association: the First Fifty Years*.

47 Ball to Barnett, 21 March 1907, Temple House Papers. The sequel was amusing; Neild. a Co-operator, presented a paper entitled 'What Workpeople Want Oxford to Do'. Tawney in 1914 added at the end of the letter quoted above. 'Ball, not knowing the source of his and Neild's papers, commented with surprise and gratification at the similarity of their tone.'

48 Further details are given in B. Jennings, 'The Oxford Report Reconsidered' in *Studies in Adult Education*, vol. 7, no. 1, April 1975, pp. 53-65.

49 For a detailed picture of one Staffordshire class, see J. A. Mack (ed.). *The History of Tunstall II Tutorial Class, 1913-34*.

50 Gill to Mansbridge, 2 February 1908, Temple House Papers.

51 Tawney's success could be attributed in part at least to his attitude towards the work: 'Personally, as a teacher of Tutorial Classes, I never

felt tempted to engage in propaganda. A doubtless very improper conceit persuaded me that the world, when enlightened, would agree with me. I thought, therefore, that the longest way round was the shortest way home, and that my job was to promote enlightenment' (R. H. Tawney, *The WEA and Adult Education*, p. 8).

52 Immortalized by a later Oxford man, John Betjeman, in his verse autobiography, *Summoned by Bells*, p. 104:

> While Sandy Lindsay from his Lodge looks down
> Dreaming of Adult Education where
> The pottery chimneys flare
> On lost potential firsts in some less favoured town.

53 A highly sympathetic account by Dover Wilson of some of the Yorkshire WEA Classes which he attended, including one where Tawney was the tutor, is given in J. Dover Wilson, 'Adult Education in Yorkshire' in *The Journal of Adult Education*, vol. 3, no. 1, October 1928.

54 Board of Education Special Reports No. 2. *Special Report on Certain Tutorial Classes in Connection with the Workers' Educational Association*, n.d. but 1911, p. 3. Some of the students' essays are preserved among the papers at Temple House.

55 This meeting is not mentioned in Spiller. Details are given in a copy of the Minutes of the Society in the Bosanquet Papers, Trunk 1, Packet N, p. 1.

56 Except for a small book, *The Social Philosophy and Religion of Comte*, published in 1885.

57 Helen Bosanquet, *Social Work in London 1869-1902, A History of the Charity Organisation Society*, passim.

58 See *A Great Ideal and Its Champion: Papers and Addresses by Sir Charles Stewart Loch*, especially the Preface, pp. 7-13.

59 For a more detailed list, see G. Spiller, *The Ethical Movement in Great Britain*, p. 11.

60 These included independence from the Extension Authorities in planning courses and the prospect of adoption by the proposed 'new' University of London, thus offering professional opportunities for philosophers. We are grateful to Dr I. D. MacKillop of Sheffield University for these suggestions.

61 Bradley to Mrs G. Husband, 3 April 1899. The full examination paper is attached to the letter. Bosanquet Papers, Trunk I, A6.

62 Memorandum by Bosanquet dated 'London, 1899', pp. 5-6. Bosanquet Papers, Trunk I, Packet N.

63 Urwick later acknowledged his debt to J. H. Muirhead and J. S. Mackenzie in describing the relation of social philosophy to moral philosophy (*The Social Good*, p. 7).

64 Percival, though not a philosopher, was sympathetic to Green's views (W. Temple, *Life of Bishop Percival*, p. 167).

65 In the first prospectus for the College, Jones stated that its object was to supply university teaching, technical instruction adapted to the needs of the district, and popular lectures of interest to all sections of

the community (A. W. Chapman, *The Story of a Modern University: A History of the University of Sheffield*, p. 33).

66 Minutes of Evidence, 30 October 1887, Royal Commission on Oxford University (Selborne Report), Q 3306-9.

67 Oxford University Extension Delegacy Papers, 1877-97.

68 A summary of the meeting can be found in the third edition of Mackinder and Sadler's book which appeared under the title *University Extension: Past, Present and Future*, pp. 139-42.

69 Other members included the Webbs, Hewins, Haldane, H. G. Wells and Bertrand Russell. The club lasted only one year. For fuller details, see G. R. Searle, *The Quest for National Efficiency*, pp. 150-2.

70 Mackinder's Preface to the College's first Calendar (1892-3) stated:

> The object of the College is to bring education of a university type within the reach of those who cannot go to university. Its function is to stimulate the desire for intellectual life, to diffuse both 'liberal' and technical education, to train good citizens, and to erect a ladder by which the chosen intellectuals of all classes may climb to the universities themselves (W. M. Childs, *Making a University*, p. 9).

See also letter from Mackinder to Astley Clarke, the founder of University College, Leicester, 27 January 1913, in J. Simmons, *New University*, pp. 211-12.

71 Sir Richard William Livingstone (1880-1960). Educationist, friend of Temple. Interested in adult education and the study of Greek as an introduction to modern problems. President of Magdalen College, Oxford, 1938.

72 Sir John Linton Myers (1869-1954). Later Professor of Ancient History, Oxford, 1910-39.

73 Acland encouraged Spender in this campaign (Acland to Spender, 11 March 1906, Spender Papers, 46591, f. 179).

74 Zimmern to Beveridge, 12 December 1905, Beveridge Papers IIb5. The *DNB* entry for Zimmern makes no mention of his reforming activities (vol. 2, p. 2979).

75 Ibid., 4 July 1906.

76 Manuscript note by Barnett, n.d., Tawney Papers, Box 22, 21/2.

77 See, for example, Zimmern to Beveridge, 14 December 1903, Beveridge Papers IIb3.

78 Zimmern to Barnett, 17 June 1907, Tawney Papers. This followed a meeting at Toynbee Hall on 'The Old Universities and Labour'.

79 'I have just had an hour with the Chancellor – Zimmern had an hour yesterday. He means business. . . . He is very keen on "rooting Oxford in democracy" ' (Temple to Beveridge, n.d., Temple House Papers).

80 Zimmern to Tawney, 11 July 1907, Tawney Papers. See also his article 'What is the Use of University Study to Working Men?' in *The Highway*, vol. 1, no. 2, 1908, pp. 26-8.

81 Curzon opposed a Royal Commission on the grounds that 'the Government may be called upon to act on their Report. . . . There is always the risk that some element of politics or partisanship may

intrude' (Lord Curzon, *Principles and Methods of University Reform,* p. 10).

82 Haldane paid a lengthy tribute to Lotze in a lecture 'The Soul of the People', reprinted in *Universities and National Life,* pp. 24-32.

83 The Gifford Lectures were well received by those whose opinions he valued, including Caird, Bradley, Scott Holland and Pringle-Pattison (D. Sommer, *Haldane of Cloan,* p. 119).

84 Acland to Spender, 11 March 1906, Spender Papers, BL Add. MSS 46591, f.180. See also H. V. Emy, *Liberals, Radicals and Social Politics, 1892-1914,* pp. 40-1.

85 The Webb-Haldane partnership is described in E. J. T. Brennan, (ed.) *Education for National Efficiency: the Contribution of Sidney and Beatrice Webb,* pp. 44-7.

86 For the full story of this, see Ashby and Anderson, *Portrait of Haldane at Work on Education,* pp. 45-58.

87 Haldane's conception of a University of Wales with 'a living spiritual life' is enunciated in his address at the then newly-formed University College of Swansea, 'The University and the Welsh Democracy', 1922, pp. 2-5.

88 For Lindsay's earlier views on this topic, see 'The State and Society', in *The International Crisis: The Theory of the State,* pp. 92-108.

8   Towards a national system of education

1 J. A. Spender, *Sir Robert Hudson,* p. 21.

2 Smith had lectured on political economy for the Oxford University Extension, 1887-8, and was later a member of the Royal Commission on Secondary Education, 1894-5.

3 For the background to the Act, see J. R. Webster, 'The Welsh Intermediate Act 1889', in *The Welsh History Review,* vol. 4, no. 3, 1969, pp. 272-91.

4 Acland and Ellis worked hard to persuade the Welsh Liberal members that the 1889 Bill, a conservative measure, should not be opposed. E. L. Ellis, *The University College of Wales, Aberystwyth,* p. 97.

5 A. H. D. Acland and T. E. Ellis, *Free Education in Wales,* September 1890. This pamphlet was widely issued by the North Wales Liberal Federation.

6 T. E. Ellis and E. Griffith, *A Manual to the Intermediate and Technical Education (Wales) Act.* The introduction to the book was written by Acland.

7 An Oxford man, R. A. Jones, a member of the Flintshire Joint Education Committee, became secretary of the North Wales Conference and afterwards of the Conference for the whole of Wales (R. A. Jones, Diary, 24 January 1917, Clwyd Record Office).

8 A Central Welsh Board was established in 1896.

9 His plans for the democratization of Welsh universities were set out in a letter to Fisher, 16 July 1916, Fisher Papers, Box 6, 1915-16. Jones delivered an anti-Socialist speech at the annual conference of the

North Wales Quarrymen's Conference Union in 1911. He expressed his fear that the death of Liberalism would mean that emerging groups would disregard the fundamental tolerance and consensus which was the basis of democracy (C. Parry, *The Radical Tradition in Welsh Politics,* pp. 36-7).

10 Bruce, son of the first Lord Aberdare, was later a member of the University's Court Council in 1920, becoming Pro-Chancellor. From 1919-20 he also chaired a Departmental Committee which inquired into the organization of secondary education in Wales: it recommended the establishment of a National Council of Education which 'must be able to regard education as a whole' (D. Emrys Hughes, *The University of Wales: A Historical Sketch,* pp. 87, 94).

11 West read Haldane's letter to Gladstone on Monday 8 August (*Private Diaries of Sir Algernon West,* p. 45).

12 'It was with an enormous sense of relief that I was sent on by Morley to Lord Spencer . . . then had a delightful talk with him and appeared to convince him gradually. Then I went back to Morley. . . . Morley went off to the meeting at 1 Carlton Gardens at 3 where my fate was decided and I suppose the Cabinet settled' (A. H. D. Acland, Diary, 26 August 1892).

13 See, for instance, paper submitted to the Cabinet: 'Rural Local Government (Educational Authorities)', A. H. D. Acland, 6 January 1893, CAB/37/33, Public Record Office.

14 Acland to Sadler, 8 October 1892, Sadler Papers.

15 E.g., G. W. Kekewich, the Secretary of the Department to, Acland, 23 November 1892; and Acland to Kekewich, 25 November, Willesden, Ed. 16/218, Public Record Office.

16 Letter, 23 February 1893, Oxford University Extension Delegacy Papers, 1877-97.

17 Acland to Sadler, 1 September 1892, Sadler Papers.

18 Ibid., 8 October 1892.

19 Acland to Gladstone, 23 October and 13 November 1893. Gladstone Papers, BL Add. MSS 44517, ff.284, 317.

20 Acland and Bryce had worked together as the first co-chairmen of the Liberal Publications Department established in London in 1887 (B. McGill, 'Francis Schnadhorst and the Liberal Party Organization', p. 271, in P. Stansky (ed.), *The Victorian Revolution.*

21 Bryce's educational views are fully stated in *SIC,* vol. 9, pp. 770-90.

22 Mrs Green to Bryce, 24 May 1882 and 26 April 1903, Bryce Papers.

23 Diary, 30 January 1858, Bryce Papers.

24 R. E. Humphreys, 'James Bryce and the Advancement of Secondary Education', in *Gleanings for Tomorrow's Teachers,* p. 29. This statement seems to be confirmed by Bryce himself: letter to wife, 9 August 1895, UB 92, Bryce Papers.

25 Llewellyn Smith and Sadler had engineered several important changes (Grier, *Achievement in Education,* pp. 41, 43).

26 Acland to Sadler, 1 November 1896, Sadler Papers.

27 See 'Note A, The Department of Special Inquiries and Reports on Education', 17 October 1894, Sadler Papers.

28   Acland to Sadler, 17 October 1894, Sadler Papers.

29   'We are all groovy', Kekewich told Sadler, 'we want someone to help us out of our grooves' (M. E. Sadleir, *Michael Ernest Sadler,* p. 136). Kekewich was also sympathetic towards Acland's work; see *The Education Department and After,* pp. 83-91. Acland had met Kekewich when the latter became Secretary in 1890. There was close agreement between them on the changes needed in English education (A. H. D. Acland to T. D. Acland, 17 May 1890, A. H. D. Acland Papers, MS. Eng. Lett, e. 100, Bodleian Library). Others in the Department were less so. One H.M.I. told a colleague about this time, 'I lunched with Kingsford (C. L. Kingsford, Chief Examiner) yesterday. He was denouncing Acland's innovations and the Sadler appointment. I don't love M. E. Sadler but should have said he was just the man' (R. H. Land to F. S. Marvin, 3 April 1895, Marvin Papers e. 109).

30   Memorandum of the Work of the Office of Special Inquiries and Reports, M. E. Sadler, 27 February 1903, p. 2.

31   Eleven volumes had been prepared and another seven were in an advanced state of preparation when Sadler left the Office (Papers Relating to the Resignation of the Director of Special Inquiries and Reports of the 18 May 1903, Cd. 1602, p. 4).

32   For example, in a later unpublished paper Sadler proposed the setting up of a School of Education at Oxford, devoted to educational research and professional studies, drawing on the resources and personnel of the whole University. 'There is little doubt,' he wrote, 'that Oxford might easily and quickly become one of the most famous and influential centres in the world for educational research'. ('The Study of Education in Oxford: Suggestions for the Development of the School', n.d., pp. 3-5).

33   Sadler to his mother, n.d., possibly 1900, Sadler Papers.

34   Notes prepared by Sadler, 8 February 1898, Sadler Papers.

35   Morant to Bromley, 4 December 1904, Ed 23/588, Public Record Office. Sir Hugh Orange, an Accountant-General to the Board, mentioned that opposition to Sadler came from the more senior officials appointed in the 1870s, who were 'not eager for changes or for omniscience about ideas or ideals' (Notes of interview with Sir Hugh Orange by Lynda Grier, 28 October 1946, Sadler Papers).

36   Acland to Asquith, 20 January 1899, Asquith Papers, vol. 13, f. 171.

37   During one week in April 1894, for instance, Acland 'received deputations from the Dean of Canterbury and others, long conference with Pupils of Training Colleges with a view to improve Science Teaching. Dinner last night at Nat. Liberal Club to seven candidates at late bye elections – with self in chair – and the like. I have been helping John Morley every day with the Bill introduced yesterday.' This was of course in addition to Cabinet meetings and attendances at the Commons (A. H. D. Acland to T. D. Acland, 14 April 1894, Devon Record Office, 51/12/1).

38   Acland had been instrumental in persuading Grey and Haldane to accept posts in Campbell-Bannerman's Ministry. Herbert Gladstone had intimated, through J. A. Spender, that Acland would receive

political recognition for his services. This was not to be. See Spender Papers, BL Add. MSS 46391, Haldane to Acland, 28 December 1905 ff. 171-4; Campbell-Bannerman Papers, BL Add. MSS 52518, Acland to Campbell-Bannerman, 17 December 1907, f.79; Viscount Gladstone Papers, BL Add. MSS 46063, Acland to H. Gladstone, 31 December, 1905, ff. 248-9. Also R. Douglas, *History of the Liberal Party 1895-1970*, pp. 32-3.

39 Acland to W. E. Gladstone, 6 November 1892, Gladstone Papers, 44516 f. 250.

40 M. E. Sadler, 'Sir Arthur Acland', in *The Oxford Magazine*, 21 October 1926, pp. 13-14.

41 Acland to Spencer, 16 October 1899, Spencer Papers. Sadler had been asked previously by Kekewich to draw up a list of bodies who should be represented on the Committee (Kekewich to Sadler, 4 August 1899, Sadler Papers).

42 Devonshire to Salisbury, 18 June 1900, Salisbury Papers.

43 Summaries of the terms of reference of these committees are to be found in P. and G. Ford, *A Breviate of Parliamentary Papers 1900-1916*, section XIV, pp. 308ff.

44 For accounts sympathetic to Morant, see D. N. Chester, 'Robert Morant and Michael Sadler', in *Public Administration*, Summer 1950, pp. 109-116, and the same author's 'Morant and Sadler – Further Evidence', in *Public Administration*, Summer 1953, pp. 49-54.

45 Morant protested to Runciman, the President of the Board of Education, that 'steps had been taken. ... to prejudice you into thinking I was High Church' (22 May 1908, Runciman Papers, WR, 21).

46 Kitson Clark links Morant's crusading policy at the Board of Education with his Oxford days (G. Kitson Clark, *An Expanding Society*, pp. 179-80).

47 For the Siam background, see Ministry of Education, Thailand, *Education in Thailand*, p. 12. Damrong's part in educational reform is outlined in Tej Bunnag, *The Provincial Administration of Siam, 1892-1915*, pp. 82-6.

48 The full title was *Ladder of Knowledge: 50 Steps towards Speaking English* by R. L. Morant, MA, 2nd edn, 1901.

49 Morant had contemplated applying to Toynbee Hall in Summer 1884 (J. A. R. Pimlott, *Toynbee Hall*, p. 54).

50 Morant to Sadler, 19 November 1895, Sadler Papers.

51 Barnett to his brother, 23 November 1895, Barnett Papers, F/BAR/132. See also Morant to Sadler, 28 November 1895, Sadler Papers.

52 'Note A, The Department of Special Inquiries and Reports on Education', by Sadler (typed), p. 3, Sadler Papers.

53 Sadler to Dr R. F. Young, 27 November 1934, Sadler Papers.

54 For example, Sadler at first warmly welcomed the 1904 Regulations for Secondary Schools relating to the humanities. See his Special Report on Liverpool (1904), Appendix II (b) Curriculum of Public Secondary Schools for Boys and Girls in Liverpool. It was the Board's

subsequent interpretation of the Regulations which caused him concern. In later life, whilst adhering to the view that to spread Liberal education 'in widest commonalty' was the distinctive aim of education policy in a modern democratic community, Sadler regretted the overemphasis on the literary tradition in education at the expense of self-expression through the arts and crafts (M. E. Sadler, 'A Liberal Education', in *The Outlook in Secondary Education*, p. 55). The differences in practice between Morant and Sadler are described in R. Lowe, 'The Divided Curriculum', in *Journal of Curriculum Studies*, vol. 8, no. 2, 1976, pp. 139-48.

55　Sadler Papers.

56　These Regulations can be largely attributed to J. W. Mackail, Assistant Secretary, Secondary Branch. Mackail, a former student of Nettleship at Balliol, later wrote of the need 'to organically interrelate each stage of education in order to serve the final humanistic ideal' (C. Bailey, 'John William Mackail, OM' in *Proceedings of the British Academy*, vol. 31, 1945). See also E. J. Eaglesham, 'Implementing the Education Act of 1902', *British Journal of Educational Studies*, vol. 10, May 1962, pp. 155-8.

57　When in 1917 Haldane was appointed chairman of a committee to advise on the reorganization of Government departments, he chose Morant as its Secretary (M. I. Cole (ed.), *Beatrice Webb's Diaries, 1912-1924*, p. 89).

58　Morant to Haldane, 25 May 1902, Haldane Papers.

59　Ashby and Anderson, *Portrait of Haldane*, pp. 96-7. The similarity of views of the two men on educational matters is reflected in Haldane's address, *The Dedicated Life*, 1907, pp. 6-8.

60　The changeover was not much to Morant's liking. He told a correspondent, 'If you knew the *unspeakable* fights I have had with the Treasury!!! and infinitely worse since the change of Government in '05 than ever I had before' (Morant to Mrs E. M. Marvin, 10 March 1909, Marvin Papers, c.257).

61　See, for example, V. Markham, 'Robert Morant: Some Personal Reminiscences', in *Public Administration*, vol. 28, Winter 1950, p. 257.

62　MS. Report of the Oxford Joint Conference on the Education of Workpeople, 10 August 1907, Temple House Papers, ff. 28-31.

63　Acland told his father at this time of a visit to Rugby: 'I went there for a meeting about some Home Reading Assistance to supplement University Extension work and to find out about the best books, etc. Percival is a good deal interested in this' (A. H. D. Acland to T. D. Acland, 26 October 1877, A. H. D. Acland Papers, MS. Eng. Lett. e. 100, Bodleian Library).

64　The précis can be found in Ed 24/409 at the Public Record Office.

65　Morant's secretary from 1905 analysed Morant's complex personality (A. Richmond, *Another Sixty Years*, pp. 24-5).

66　The link between the continuation school movement and national efficiency is explored by D. W. Thoms, 'The Emergence and Failure of the Day Continuation School Experiment', in *History of Education*, vol. 4, no. 1, pp. 39-40.

67 J. Dover Wilson, one of the two H. M. Inspectors responsible for inspecting WEA work (see p. 113), drew up a special memorandum on day continuation schools' curriculum. It was published by the Board of Education under the title *Humanism in the Continuation School,* Board of Education Pamphlet No. 43 (1921). See F. P. Wilson and J. Dover Wilson, 'Edmund Kerchever Chambers 1866-1954', *Proceedings of the British Academy,* vol. 42, 1956, p. 257. Some descriptions of these schools in London and Manchester are given in E. A. Waterfall, *The Day Continuation School in England,* pp. 166-204.

68 For a fuller account of Haldane's work, see G. E. Sherington, 'R. B. Haldane, the Reconstruction Committee and the Board of Education 1916-18', in *Journal of Education Administration and History,* vol. 6, no. 2, July 1974.

69 See G. E. Sherington, 'The 1918 Education Act: Origins, Aims and Development', in *British Journal of Educational Studies,* February 1976, pp. 69-71.

70 Haldane's last major assignment was his chairmanship of the Machinery of Government Committee, formed in July 1917, which reported in December 1918. (See S. E. Koss, *Lord Haldane, Scapegoat for Liberalism,* p. 231.) The Committee was set up to advise on ways and means of improving the machinery of government. Haldane, who drafted the majority of the final report, noted that 'adequate provision had not been made in the past for the organized acquisition of facts and information, and for the systematic application of thought, as preliminary to the settlement of policy and its subsequent administration' (Report, p. 6). The Committee recommended a Central Intelligence Department working closely with the government departments concerned.

71 See G. Murray, 'Herbert Albert Laurens Fisher', in *Proceedings of the British Academy,* vol. 26, 1940, p. 460. For a description of Fisher at Oxford, see the same author's *An Unfinished Autobiography,* p. 92.

72 For Caird's influence on his students, see H. W. C. Davis, *A History of Balliol College,* pp. 223-4.

73 Board of Education: Suggestions for a National System of Education. Marked '1913-18', Tawney Papers, Box 23, 22/4.

74 Memorandum on the Board of Education, Tawney Papers, Box 23, 22/2.

75 In 1903, Sadler had favoured renaming the Office of Special Inquiries as the Office of Education Intelligence (J. H. Higginson, 'Michael Sadler, Pioneering Contribution to Comparative Studies in Education', *Proceedings of the Comparative Education Society,* 1976, p. 107).

76 K. Lindsay, *Social Progress and Educational Waste,* 1926. Tawney's help is acknowledged in the Preface, p. v.

77 Tawney presented a memorandum, which he had largely drafted, from the Party's advisory committee on education, to Trevelyan (R. Barker, *Education and Politics 1900-1951,* pp. 50-1). Although Trevelyan's biographer has stated that there is no direct evidence to indicate Tawney's influence on subsequent policy, Trevelyan was happy to enlist Tawney's aid in 1929, via the *Manchester Guardian,* in

his campaign to settle the denominational schools problem (A. J. A. Morris, *C. P. Trevelyan 1870-1958*, p. 177).

78 Hadow, an Oxford don, was an old friend of Fisher. During the First World War he had organized a scheme for army education in France at Fisher's request. He succeeded Fisher as Vice-Chancellor at Sheffield University. His best known publication is *Citizenship,* 1923. See *The Times,* 10 August 1937; and H. Deneke, *Grace Hadow,* pp. 34, 85.

79 E. Barker, *Age and Youth,* p. 320. His appreciation of Green, Bradley and Bosanquet appears in *Political Thought in England,* chs 2, 3. For Barker's sympathies with Green, see G. E. G. Catlin, 'Ernest Barker 1874-1960', in *Proceedings of the British Academy,* vol. 46, 1962, p. 349.

80 For an account of Nunn's educational thought see J. W. Tibble, 'Sir Percy Nunn 1870-1944', in *British Journal of Educational Studies,* vol. 10, no. 1, 1961, pp. 58-75.

81 Tawney's continuing interest in secondary schools and their curricula is well illustrated by J. Simon, 'The Shaping of the Spens Report on Secondary Education, 1933-38, An Inside View', p. 178.

82 Haldane to Asquith, 16 January 1922, Asquith Papers, vol. 18, f. 70.

9 Religion, idealism and education

1 For a full account of the Oxford Movement, see V. H. H. Green, *Religion at Oxford and Cambridge,* chs 10, 11.

2 J. A. Symonds, Green's brother-in-law, recording a conversation with Green in 1874, stated that 'he seems bent upon attacking evolution from the idealist point of view' (H. F. Brown (ed.), *Letters and Papers of John Addington Symonds,* pp. 69-70). On the other hand, one of Green's followers, Henry Jones, regarded evolution as a process of levelling upwards and not downwards and the best defence of man's spiritual needs (H. Jones, 'The Child and Heredity', in T. Stephen (ed.), *The Child and Religion,* p. 59).

3 Green's collaboration with Mrs A. H. Clough and others in translating Baur continued as late as 1869. 'I have no prospect of being able to attend to it myself for another nine months,' he told Mrs Clough, 'I will promise then, however, to assail the chapter on Gnosticism' (Letter, 12 December 1869, Bodleian Library MS. Eng. Lett. e. 76.).

4 At Oxford, Green campaigned actively for church reform (K. W. Jones, *Life of John Viriamu Jones,* p. 47).

5 Temple to Tait, 26 February 1861 (Tait Papers, vol. 80, ff. 39-40). For a description of the young Temple, see W. Tuckwell, *Reminiscences of Oxford,* pp. 214-22.

6 As early as 1854, Temple saw the need for educated teachers in all types of school. He told Lingen, then Secretary of the Committee of Council on Education, 'So far from the educated man being the less able to give the rudest and simplest instruction it is he only who can give it with effect. The fullness of his cultivation enables him to adapt

himself to the State whatever it may be of his scholar's mind' (Temple to Lingen, 22 May 1854, Jebb Papers, MS.2961, f. 103).

7 Green to Holland, 6 October 1872 (S. Paget (ed.), *Henry Scott Holland: Memoirs and Letters,* pp. 65-6).

8 Republished in *Logic and Life,* 1892.

9 Republished in *The Philosophy of Faith,* 1920.

10 A. L. Illingworth, *The Life and Work of John Richard Illingworth,* p. 84.

11 Mansbridge to Lansbury, 27 September 1907, (copy) Temple House Papers.

12 MS. Minutes of the Oxford Joint Conference on Education of Workpeople, 10 August 1907, Temple House Papers, ff. 10-15.

13 See C. B. Mortlock, 'Life and Liberty: The Man and the Movement', in *The Treasury,* September 1918, pp. 382-4.

14 Temple to Rev. J. H. Roberts, 7 February 1918, William Temple Papers.

15 Temple believed that while the church ought to be detached from politics, 'Christians should be associated with the party which on the whole they most approve' (*Personal Religion and the Life of Fellowship,* p. 52).

10   Idealists as educational theorists

1 For Whitehead's link with Haldane see J. A. Passmore, *A Hundred Years of Philosophy,* p. 340.

2 For details of Morant's division between 'education for followership' and 'education for leadership' see E. J. R. Eaglesham, *The Foundations of 20th Century Education in England,* chs 4, 5.

3 For Herbart see also pp. 49-51 and Chapter 5, note 2. The source for the comments in this paragraph about Herbart's theory in his *The Science of Education,* bks 1, 2.

4 R. G. Tatton, who edited Rooper's *Selected Writings,* and who was a contemporary of his at Balliol and later a fellow of that college, writes in his Memoir of 'The Pot of Green Feathers': 'The essay ... embodies, as he tells us, the results of his study of various writers on psychology, but he always spoke of Green's teaching as the original source to him of the ideas which are worked out in it' (Tatton, op. cit., pp. xxvii-xxviii).

5 The group was active in the 1930s. It was 'engaged in the publication of a series known as the *Christian Newsletter Books,* and also in planning a Conference on the functions and responsibilities of Church, Community and State in the modern world' (F. W. Mitchell, *Sir Fred Clarke,* pp. 92-3). Its members included, among others, Tawney, T. S. Eliot, Ernest Barker, Michael Sadler and A. E. Zimmern (ibid., n. 1).

6 All the quotations are from E. Sharwood-Smith, *Edmond Holmes,* pp. 72-4, unpublished. We are grateful to our colleague John Sharwood-Smith for lending us his father's biography and allowing us to quote passages from it.

11 The decline of idealist influence

1 The suggestion is admittedly speculative. For Rashdall's influence on Morris, see H. Rée, *Educator Extraordinary*, pp. 9, 16, 18, 80. Rashdall dedicated his main philosophical work *The Theory of Good and Evil* 'to the memory of my teachers Thomas Hill Green and Henry Sidgwick'.

2 This and the preceding quotation from Nunn's *Education* are the only passages we have taken from the first edition. All other references are to the more accessible third edition, 1945.

3 On the freeing of school and college curricula, see J. P. White, 'The End of the Compulsory Curriculum' in *The Curriculum*, 1975.

Part 3 The idealist legacy today

12 Education and its aims

1 P. H. Hirst, 'Liberal Education and the Nature of Knowledge'; R. S. Peters 'Education as Initiation'; both in R. D. Archambault, *Philosophical Analysis and Education*. See also R. S. Peters, *Ethics and Education*.

2 See R. Downie, E. Loudfoot and E. Telfer, *Education and Personal Relationships*, p. 50.

3 See R. S. Peters, op. cit., ch. 5.

4 See especially R. F. Dearden, *The Philosophy of Primary Education*.

5 See, for instance, J. P. White, *Towards a Compulsory Curriculum*.

6 M. Warnock, *Times Educational Supplement*, 8 July 1977, p. 2. For a fuller account, see her *Schools of Thought*, pp. 129-43.

7 See P. White, 'Work-place Democracy and Political Education', *Journal of Philosophy of Education*, 1979.

8 P. White, 'Education, Democracy and the Public Interest', in R. S. Peters (ed.), *The Philosophy of Education*.

9 For a fuller defence of this morally- or community-oriented education, see J. P. White, *The Aims of Education* (forthcoming).

13 The realization of educational aims

1 See C. Pateman, *Participation and Democratic Theory*, for a contemporary view on the educative value of industrial democracy.

Bibliography

A Manuscript Sources

Acland Papers – Bodleian Library, Oxford; Devon Record Office and Killerton, Devon.
Asquith Papers – Bodleian Library, Oxford.
Barnett Papers – Greater London Record Office.
Beveridge Papers – British Library of Political and Economic Science, London.
Bosanquet Papers – University of Newcastle-upon-Tyne.
Bryce Papers – Bodleian Library, Oxford.
Campbell-Bannerman Papers – British Library.
Education Papers – Public Record Office.
Fisher Papers – Bodleian Library, Oxford.
Gladstone Papers – British Library.
Herbert, Viscount Gladstone Papers – British Library.
Green Papers – Balliol College, Oxford.
Haldane Papers – National Library of Scotland.
Jebb Papers – Lambeth Palace Library, London.
Jones Papers – Clwyd Record Office, Wales.
London Extension Society Papers – University of London Extra-Mural Studies Department.
Marvin Papers – Bodleian Library, Oxford.
Oxford University Delegacy – Rewley House, Oxford.
Runciman Papers – University of Newcastle-upon-Tyne.
Sadler Papers – Bodleian Library, Oxford.
Salisbury Papers – Hatfield House, Hertfordshire.
Spencer Papers – Althorp, Northamptonshire.
Spender Papers – British Library.
Tait Papers – Lambeth Palace Library, London.
Tawney Papers – British Library of Political and Economic Science, London.
Temple Papers – Lambeth Palace Library, London.
Toynbee Hall Papers – Greater London Record Office.
Workers' Educational Association Papers – Temple House, London.

289

B Official Publications

Aberdare Report, vol. 1 (1881) *Report of the Committee appointed to inquire into the condition of Intermediate and Higher Education,* BPP, 1881, xxii.

Board of Education Special Reports No. 2 (1911) *Special Report on Certain Tutorial Classes in Connection with the Workers' Educational Association.*

Board of Education Consultative Committee on Attendance, Compulsory or Otherwise, at Continuation Schools (1909), 2 vols, Cd 4757.

Board of Education Consultative Committee on Examinations in Secondary Schools (1911), Cd. 6004.

Board of Education Report of the Consultative Committee on the Education of the Adolescent (1926).

Commission on Secondary Education (Bryce Report), vol. 1 (1895), BPP, xliii.

Royal Commission on Oxford University (Selborne Report) (1881), part 1, Minutes of Evidence, BPP, lvi.

Schools Inquiry Report (Taunton Commission) (1867-8) Reports by T. H. Green: vol. 8, *Birmingham Free School, Staffordshire and Warwickshire;* vol. 12, *Buckinghamshire and Northamptonshire.* Reports by J. Bryce: vol. 9, *Lancashire and Manchester Grammar Schools,* BPP, 1867-8, xxviii.

Special Reports on Educational Subjects, vol. 3 (1898): Morant, R. L. 'The National Organization of Education of all grades as practised in Switzerland'.

C Books, pamphlets and articles

Unless otherwise stated the place of publication is London.

ABBOTT, E. and CAMPBELL, L. (1897), *Life and Letters of Benjamin Jowett,* 2 vols, E. P. Dutton, New York.

ACLAND, A. H. D. (1883), *The Education of Citizens,* Central Co-operative Board, Manchester.

ACLAND, A. H. D. (1891), *Inaugural Address delivered at the 23rd Co-operative Congress held at Lincoln, May 18-20, 1891,* Co-operative Wholesale Society, Manchester.

ACLAND, A. H. D. (1902), *Sir Thomas Dyke Acland: A Memoir and Letters,* privately printed.

ACLAND, A. H. D. and ELLIS, T. E. (September 1890), *Free Education in Wales,* North Wales Liberal Federation, Wrexham.

ACLAND, A. H. D. and JONES, B. (1884), *Working Men Co-operators: what they have done, and what they are doing,* Cassell.

ACLAND, A. H. D. and LLEWELLYN SMITH, H. (eds) (1892), *Studies in Secondary Education*, Percival.

ACLAND, A. H. D. and RANSOME, C. (1891), *A Handbook of the Political History of England*, Rivingtons.

ADAM, GENERAL SIR R. (1956), *Problems in Adult Education*, 23rd Haldane Memorial Lecture delivered at Birkbeck College, 8 March 1956, Birkbeck College.

ALLEN, B. M. (1934), *Sir Robert Morant*, Macmillan.

ALTICK, R. D. (1973), *Victorian People and Ideas*, Dent.

ANON., 'Francis Richard Sandford', in *Blackwood's Magazine*, no. 29, March 1895.

ANON., *Patrick Cumin, Secretary of the Education Department, A Sketch*, (printed for private circulation), Hugh Rees, n.d.

ARCHAMBAULT, R. D. (1965), *Philosophical Analysis and Education*, Routledge & Kegan Paul.

ARMYTAGE, W. H. G. (1947), 'A. H. D. Acland', in *Journal of Education*, vol. 79.

ARMYTAGE, W. H. G. (1955), *Civic Universities, Aspects of a British Tradition*, Ernest Benn.

ARMYTAGE, W. H. G. (1964), *Four Hundred Years of English Education*, Cambridge University Press.

ARNOLD, M. (1861), *The Popular Education of France with Notices of that of Holland and Switzerland*, Longman, Green Longman and Roberts.

ARNOLD, M. (1864), *A French Eton, or Middle-Class Education and the State*, Macmillan.

ARNOLD, M. (1868), *Schools and Universities on the Continent*, Macmillan.

ARNOLD, M. (1869), *Culture and Anarchy*, ed. J. Dover Wilson, 1948 edition, Cambridge University Press.

ASHBY, E. (1955), *The Pathology of Adult Education*, William F. Harvey Memorial Lecture, Birmingham, 24 March 1955, Queen's University, Belfast.

ASHBY, E. and ANDERSON, M. (1974), *Portrait of Haldane at Work on Education*, Macmillan.

ASHLEY, A. (1932), *William James Ashley: A Life*, P. S. King & Son.

AVINERI, S. (1972), *Hegel's Theory of the Modern State*, Cambridge University Press.

BALL, O. H. (1923), *Sidney Ball, Memories and Impressions of 'An Ideal Don'*, Blackwell, Oxford.

BARKER, E. (1915), *Political Thought in England 1848 to 1914*, Oxford University Press.

BARKER, E. (1953), *Age and Youth, Memories of Three Universities and Father of the Man*, Oxford University Press.

BARKER, M. (1975), *Gladstone and Radicalism. The Reconstruction of the Liberal Party in Britain 1885-94,* Harvester Press, Hassocks, Sussex.

BARKER, R. (1972), *Education and Politics 1900-1951, A Study of the Labour Party,* Oxford University Press.

BARNARD, H. C. (1971 edn), *A History of English Education from 1760,* University of London Press.

BARNETT, H. (1918), *Canon Barnett: His Life, Work and Friends,* John Murray.

BELLAMY, J. M. and SAVILLE, J. (1972), *Dictionary of Labour Biography,* vol. 1, 'A. H. D. Acland' entries J. M. Bellamy and H. F. Bing, Macmillan.

BERDAHL, R. O. (1959), *British Universities and the State,* University of California Press/Cambridge University Press.

BEST, G. (1973), *Mid-Victorian Britain,* Weidenfeld & Nicolson, 1971; Panther edn, 1973.

BETJEMAN, J. (1960), *Summoned by Bells,* John Murray.

BEVERIDGE, LORD (1953), *Power and Influence,* Hodder & Stoughton.

BOSANQUET, B. (1889), *Essays and Addresses,* Swan, Sonnenschein.

BOSANQUET, B. (1892), *A History of Aesthetics,* Sonnenschein.

BOSANQUET, B. (ed.) (1895), *Aspects of the Social Problem,* Macmillan.

BOSANQUET, B. (1899), *The Philosophical Theory of the State,* Macmillan.

BOSANQUET, B. (1900), *The Education of the Young in 'The Republic' of Plato,* Cambridge University Press.

BOSANQUET, HELEN (1914), *Social Work in London 1869-1902, A History of the Charity Organisation Society,* John Murray.

BRADLEY, A. C. (1924), 'Bernard Bosanquet 1848-1923', *Proceedings of the British Academy,* vol. 11.

BRADLEY, F. H. (1876), *Ethical Studies,* H. S. King.

BRADLEY, F. H. (1893), *Appearance and Reality,* Sonnenschein.

BRENNAN, E. J. T (ed.) (1975), *Education for National Efficiency: the Contribution of Sidney and Beatrice Webb,* Athlone Press.

BROOKS, J. R. (1977), ' "Secondary Education for All" Reconsidered', *Durham Research Review,* vol. 8, Spring.

BROWN, H. F. (ed.) (1923), *Letters and Papers of John Addington Symonds,* John Murray.

BRYCE, J. (1903), *Studies in Contemporary Biography,* Macmillan.

BRYCE, J. (1909), *The Hindrances to Good Citizenship,* New Haven, Yale University Press.

BUNNAG, T. (1977), *The Provincial Administration of Siam 1892-1915. The Ministry of the Interior under Prince Damrong Rajanubhab,* Oxford University Press.

BURROWS, J. (1976), *University Adult Education in London: A Century of Achievement,* University of London, Senate House.

CACOULLOS, A. R. (1974), *Thomas Hill Green: Philosopher of Rights*, Twayne, New York.

CAIRD, E. (1877), *A Critical Account of the Philosophy of Kant*, James Maclehose, Glasgow.

CAIRD, E. (1885), *The Social Philosophy and Religion of Comte*, James Maclehose, Glasgow.

CAMPBELL, L. (1901), *On the Nationalization of the Old English Universities*, Chapman & Hall.

CARLYLE, T. (1831), *Sartor Resartus*, reprinted 1908, Dent, Everyman's Library edn.

CHAPMAN, A. W. (1955), *The Story of a Modern University: A History of the University of Sheffield*, Oxford University Press.

CHESTER, D. N. (1950), 'Robert Morant and Michael Sadler', in *Public Administration*, vol. 28, Summer.

CHESTER, D. N. (1953), 'Morant and Sadler – Further Evidence', in *Public Administration*, vol. 31, Summer.

CHILDS, W. M. (1933), *Making a University: An Account of the University Movement at Reading*, Dent.

CLARK, G. KITSON (1967), *An Expanding Society: Britain 1830-1900*, Cambridge University Press.

CLARK, G. KITSON (1973), *Churchmen and the Condition of England 1832-1885*, Methuen.

CLARKE, FRED (1923), *Essays in the Politics of Education*, Oxford University Press.

COLE, M. I. (ed.) (1952), *Beatrice Webb's Diaries 1912-1924*, Longmans, Green.

COLERIDGE, S. T. (1830), *The Constitution of Church and State*, Chance.

COLLINGWOOD, R. G. (1939), *An Autobiography*, Oxford University Press; Penguin, 1944.

CONNELL, W. F. (1950), *The Educational Thought and Influence of Matthew Arnold*, Routledge & Kegan Paul.

COPLESTON, F. (1965), *History of Philosophy*, vol. 7, part 1: *Fichte to Hegel*, Image Books, Doubleday, New York.

COUGHLAN, N. (1975), *Young John Dewey*, Chicago University Press.

CREIGHTON, L. (1904), *Life and Letters of Mandell Creighton*, vol. 1 (of 2), Longmans, Green.

CURZON OF KEDLESTON, LORD (1909), *Principles and Methods of University Reform, being a letter addressed to the University of Oxford*, Oxford University Press.

DALE, A. W. W. (1902), *Life of R. W. Dale of Birmingham*, Hodder & Stoughton.

DAVIE, G. (1964), *The Democratic Intellect: Scotland and Her Universities in the Nineteenth Century*, Edinburgh University Press.

293

DAVIS, H. W. C. (revised E. H. C. Davis and R. Hunt, 1963), *A History of Balliol College,* Blackwell, Oxford.

DAVISON, R. (1972), 'Llewellyn Smith, the Labour Department and Government Growth', in G. Sutherland (1972).

DEARDEN, R. F. (1968), *The Philosophy of Primary Education,* Routledge & Kegan Paul.

DENEKE, H. (1946), *Grace Hadow,* Oxford University Press.

Department of Elementary and Adult Education, Ministry of Education, Thailand (1970), *Education in Thailand: A Century of Experience.*

DEWEY, J. (1916), *Democracy and Education,* Macmillan, New York.

DEWEY, J. (1969), *The Early Works,* vol. 3, 1889-92. Early essays and outlines of a critical theory of ethics. Article, 'The Philosophy of Thomas Hill Green', Feffer and Simons/Southern Illinois University Press.

Dictionary of National Biography (1975), Compact Edition, Oxford University Press.

DOHERTY, B. (1964), 'The Hadow Report 1926', in *Durham Research Review,* vol. 4, no. 15, September.

DOHERTY, B. (1966), 'Compulsory Day Continuation Education: An Examination of the 1918 Experiment', in *Vocational Aspects of Further and Secondary Education,* vol. 18, no. 39, Spring.

DOUGLAS, R. (1971), *The History of the Liberal Party 1895-1970,* Sidgwick & Jackson.

DOWNIE, R., LOUDFOOT, E. and TELFER, E. (1974), *Education and Personal Relationships: A Philosophical Study,* Methuen.

DRAPER, W. H. (1923), *University Extension: A Survey of Fifty Years 1873-1923,* Cambridge University Press.

DUNKEL, H. B. (1970), *Herbart and Herbartianism,* University of Chicago Press.

EAGLESHAM, E. J. R. (1963), 'The Centenary of Sir Robert Morant', in *British Journal of Educational Studies,* vol. 12, no. 1, November.

EAGLESHAM, E. J. R. (1967), *The Foundations of 20th Century Education in England,* Routledge & Kegan Paul.

ELLIOTT, I. (ed.) (1934), *The Balliol College Register 1833-1933,* 2nd edn, Oxford University Press.

ELLIS, E. L. (1972), *The University College of Wales, Aberystwyth, 1872-1972,* University of Wales Press, Cardiff.

ELLIS, T. E. and GRIFFITH, E. (1889), *A Manual to the Intermediate Education (Wales) Act, 1889 and the Technical Instruction Act, 1889,* National Association for the Promotion of Technical and Secondary Education.

EMY, H. V. (1973), *Liberals, Radicals and Social Politics, 1892-1914,* Cambridge University Press.

EVANS, D. E. (1953), *The University of Wales: A Historical Sketch*, University of Wales Press, Cardiff.

EVANS, L. W. (1974), *Studies in Welsh Education: Welsh Educational Structure and Administration 1880-1925*, University of Wales Press, Cardiff.

FABER, G. (1957), *Jowett*, Faber & Faber.

FARNELL, L. R. (1934), *An Oxonian Looks Back*, Martin Hopkinson.

FICHTE, J. G. (1807-8), *Addresses to the German Nation*, ed. G. A. Kelly (1968), Harper Torchbooks, New York.

FICHTE, J. G. (1794-5), *Science of Knowledge* (Wissenschaftlehre), ed. and translated P. Heath and J. Lachs (1970), Appleton-Century-Crofts, New York.

FISHER, H. A. L. (1927), *James Bryce, Viscount Bryce of Dechmont, OM*, 2 vols, Macmillan.

FISHER, H. A. L. (1935), *The History of Europe*, Eyre and Spottiswoode.

FISHER, H. A. L. (1940), *An Unfinished Autobiography*, Oxford University Press.

FORD, P. and FORD, G. (1957), *A Breviate of Parliamentary Papers 1900-1916*, Blackwell, Oxford.

GALLIE, W. B. (1960), *A New University: A. D. Lindsay and the Keele Experiment*, Chatto & Windus.

GILBERT, E. W. (1977), *British Pioneers in Geography*, David & Charles, Newton Abbot, Devon.

GORDON, P. (1978), 'The Holmes-Morant Circular of 1911: A Note', in *Journal of Educational Administration and History*, vol. 10, no. 1, January

GORE, C. (ed.) (1889), *Lux Mundi: A Series of Studies in the Religion of the Incarnation*, John Murray.

GORE, J. (1932), *Charles Gore: Father and Son. A background to the early years and family life of Bishop Gore*, John Murray.

GOSDEN, P. H. J. H. (1962), 'The Board of Education Act, 1899', in *British Journal of Educational Studies*, vol. 11, no. 1, November.

GREEN, T. H. (1883), *'The Witness of God' and 'Faith': Two Lay Sermons*, ed. A. Toynbee, Longmans, Green.

GREEN, T. H. (1883), *Prolegomena to Ethics*, ed. A. C. Bradley, Clarendon Press, Oxford. Reprinted Apollo Edition, 1969.

GREEN, T. H. (1885-8), *Works*, ed. R. L. Nettleship, 3 vols, Longmans.

GREEN, T. H. (1895, reprinted 1963), *Lectures on the Principles of Political Obligation*, Longmans, Green.

GREEN, V. H. H. (1964), *Religion at Oxford and Cambridge*, S.C.M. Press.

GREEN, V. H. H. (1969), *The Universities*, Penguin.

GRIER, L. (1952), *Achievement in Education: The Work of Michael Ernest Sadler 1885-1935*, Constable.

GRIFFITH, L. W. (1959), *Thomas Edward Ellis 1859-99*, Llyfrau'r Dryw Llandybie.

GROSSKURTH, P. (1964), *John Addington Symonds: A Biography*, Longmans.

GUMMER, G. (1901), *Reminiscences of Rotherham: A Retrospect of over Sixty Years*, H. Garnett.

HADOW, W. H. (1923), *Citizenship*, Oxford University Press.

HALDANE, E. S. (1937), *From One Century to Another*, A. Maclehose.

HALDANE, R. B. (1902), 'Great Britain and Germany – A Study in Education', in *Education and Empire*, John Murray.

HALDANE, R. B. (1902-3), *The Pathway to Reality*, vol. 1: *The Gifford Lectures for 1902-3*, John Murray.

HALDANE, R. B. (1903-4), *The Pathway to Reality*, vol. 2: *The Gifford Lectures for 1903-4*, John Murray.

HALDANE, R. B. (1907), *The Dedicated Life: An Address delivered to the students of the University of Edinburgh on January 10 1907*, John Murray.

HALDANE, R. B. (1911), 'The Soul of the People', delivered at University College, Aberystwyth, 14 October 1910; reprinted in *Universities and National Life: Four addresses to Students*, John Murray.

HALDANE, R. B. (1922), 'The University and the Welsh Democracy', an address delivered at the Central Hall, University College of Swansea, 26 November 1921, Oxford University Press.

HALDANE, R. B. (1923), 'A Vision of the Future', in S. Oliver (ed.) *The Way Out: Essays on the Meaning and Purpose of Adult Education*, Oxford University Press.

HALDANE, R. B. (1929), *An Autobiography*, Hodder & Stoughton.

HALDANE, R. B. and SETH, A. (eds) (1882), *Essays in Philosophical Criticism*, Longmans.

HALPERIN, V. (1952), *Lord Milner and the Empire: The Evolution of British Imperialism*, Odhams Press. French edition, 1950.

HARRIS, W. (1946), *J. A. Spender*, Cassell.

HARRISON, J. F. C. (1961), *Learning and Living 1790-1960: A Study in the History of the English Adult Education Movement*, Routledge & Kegan Paul.

HARTLEY, H. (1963), *Balliol Men*, Blackwell, Oxford.

HARVIE, C. (1976), *The Lights of Liberalism: University Liberals and the Challenge of Democracy 1860-86*, Allen Lane.

HEATH, H. F. (1928), 'Lord Haldane: His Influence on Higher Education and on Administration', in *Viscount Haldane of Cloan, OM*, Oxford University Press. Reprinted from *Public Administration*, October.

HEGEL, G. W. F. (1807), *Phenomenology of Mind*, translated J. Baillie, Allen & Unwin, 1910. Reprinted, 1971.

HEGEL, G. W. F. (1821), *Philosophy of Right*, translated T. M. Knox, Oxford University Press. Reprinted, 1942.

HERBART, J. F. (1806), *The Science of Education*, ed. and trans. H. M. and E. Felkin, 1892, Swan, Sonnenschein.

HETHERINGTON, H. J. W. (1924), *The Life and Letters of Sir Henry Jones*, Hodder & Stoughton.

HEWINS, W. A. S. (1929), *The Apologia of an Imperialist*, vol. 1 (of 2), Constable.

HOBHOUSE, L. T. (1918), *The Metaphysical Theory of the State: a Criticism*, Allen & Unwin.

HOLLAND, H. S. (1892), *Logic and Life with other sermons*, Longmans, Green.

HOLLAND, H. S. (1905), *Personal Studies*, Wells Gardner, Darton.

HOLLAND, H. S. (1915), *A Bundle of Memories*, Wells Gardner, Darton.

HOLLAND, H. S. (1920), *The Philosophy of Faith and the Fourth Gospel*, ed. W. Richmond, John Murray.

HOLMES, E. G. A. (1911), *What Is and What Might Be*, Constable.

HOLMES, G. M. (1964), 'The Parliamentary and Ministerial Career of A. H. D. Acland 1886-97', in *Durham Research Review*, no. 15, September.

HOPE, A. (1927), *Memories and Notes*, Hutchinson.

HOPE SIMPSON, J. B. (1967), *Rugby Since Arnold: A History of Rugby School from 1842*, Macmillan.

HUGHES, D. EMRYS (1953), *The University of Wales: A Historical Sketch*, University of Wales Press, Cardiff.

HUMPHRIES, R. E. (1971), 'James Bryce and the Advancement of Secondary Education', in *Gleanings for Tomorrow's Teachers*, a symposium produced for the triennial celebration of Christ Church College, Canterbury.

ILLINGWORTH, A. L. (1917), *The Life and Work of John Richard Illingworth*, John Murray.

IREMONGER, F. A. (1948), *William Temple, Archbishop of Canterbury: His Life and Letters*, Oxford University Press.

JENKINS, R. (1964), *Asquith*, Collins. Fontana edition, 1967.

JOHNSON, R. 'Administrators in education before 1870: patronage, social position and role', in G. Sutherland (1972).

JONES, H. (1905), 'The Child and Heredity', in T. Stephen (ed.), *The Child and Religion*, Williams & Norgate.

JONES, H. (1922), *Old Memories*, Hodder & Stoughton.

JONES, H. (1924), *Essays on Literature and Education*, ed. H. J. W. Hetherington, Hodder & Stoughton.

JONES, H. and MUIRHEAD, J. H. (1921), *The Life and Philosophy of Edward Caird,* Maclehose, Jackson, Glasgow.

JONES, K. V. (1921), *Life of John Viriamu Jones,* John Murray.

KAMIN, L. J. (1977), *The Science and Politics of I.Q.,* Penguin.

KANT, I. (1785), *Groundwork of the Metaphysic of Morals,* translated H. J. Paton (1948) under the title, *The Moral Law,* Hutchinsons University Library.

KEKEWICH, G. W. (1920), *The Education Department and After,* Constable.

KELLY, G. A. (1969), *Idealism, Politics and History,* Cambridge University Press.

KELLY, T. (1970), *A History of Adult Education in Great Britain,* Liverpool University Press.

KITCHENER, F. E. (1882), 'Two Addresses to the Boys of Newcastle-under-Lyme High Schools', address delivered 28 April 1882.

KNIGHT, W. (1896), *Memoir of John Nichol,* J. Maclehose, Glasgow.

KOSS, S. E. (1969), *Lord Haldane, Scapegoat for Liberalism,* Columbia University Press, New York and London.

LAWSON, J. and SILVER, H. (1973), *A Social History of Education in England,* Methuen.

LEESE, J. (1950), *Personalities and Power in English Education,* Arnold.

LEIGHTON, SIR BALDWYN. (1872), *Letters and other writings of the late Edward Denison, M.P. for Newark,* R. Bentley & Son.

LINDSAY, A. D. (1916), 'The State and Society', in *The International Crisis: The Theory of the State.* Lectures delivered in February and March 1916 at Bedford College for Women under the scheme for Imperial Studies in the University of London, Oxford University Press.

LINDSAY, A. D. (1929), *The Essentials of Democracy* (William J. Cooper Foundation Lectures), Oxford University Press.

LINDSAY, K. (1926), *Social Progress and Educational Waste,* Routledge & Sons.

LLOYD, J. M. (1976), 'The Asquith Reconstruction Committee and Educational Reform', in *Journal of Educational Administration and History,* vol. 8, no. 2, July.

LLOYD, W. L. L. (1964), 'Owen M. Edwards (1858-1920)' in C. Gittins (ed.), *Pioneers of Welsh Education,* University of Swansea.

LOCH, C. S. (1923), *A Great Ideal and Its Champion: Papers and Addresses by Sir Charles Stewart Loch,* Allen & Unwin.

LOCKHART, J. G. (1949), *Cosmo Gordon Lang,* Hodder & Stoughton.

LOWE, R. A. (1972), 'Some Forerunners of R. H. Tawney's Tutorial Class', in *History of Education,* vol. 1, no. 1.

MCCARTHY, P. J. (1964), *Matthew Arnold and the Three Classes*, Columbia University Press.

MACCUNN, J. (1900), *The Making of Character*, Cambridge University Press.

MACCUNN, J. (1910 edn), *Six Radical Thinkers*, Edward Arnold.

MACGILL, B. (1973), 'Francis Schnadhorst and Liberal Party Organization', reprinted in P. Stansky (ed.), *The Victorian Revolution: Government and Society in Victoria's Britain*, New Viewpoints, Franklin Watts, New York.

MACK, J. A. (1935), *The History of Tunstall II Tutorial Class 1913-34*, Tunstall, Stoke-on-Trent.

MACKENZIE, M. (1909), *Hegel's Educational Thought and Practice*, Swan, Sonnenschein.

MACKENZIE, N. and MACKENZIE, J. (1977), *The First Fabians*, Weidenfeld & Nicolson.

MACKIE, J. D. (1954), *The University of Glasgow 1451-1951*, Jackson, Glasgow University.

MACKINDER, H. J. (1893), 'The Education of Citizens', in G. F. Jones (ed.), American Society for the Extension of University Teaching.

MACKINDER, H. J. (1919), *Democratic Ideals and Reality: A Study in the Politics of Reconstruction*, Constable. Reprinted, Penguin, 1944.

MACKINDER, H. J. and SADLER, M. E. (1890), *University Extension: Has It A Future?* H. Froude.

MANSBRIDGE, A. (1913), *A Study in the Development of Higher Education Among Working Men and Women*, Longmans, Green.

MANSBRIDGE, A. (1920), *An Adventure in Working-Class Education: Being the Story of the Workers' Educational Association 1908-15*, Longmans, Green.

MANSBRIDGE, A. (1935), *Edward Stuart Talbot and Charles Gore*, Longmans, Green.

MANSBRIDGE, A. (1940), *The Trodden Road: Experience, Inspiration and Belief*, Dent.

MARLOWE, J. (1976), *Milner, the Apostle of Empire*, Hamish Hamilton.

MARRIOTT, J. (1946), *Memories of Four Score Years*, Blackie, Glasgow.

MATTHEW, H. C. G. (1973), *The Liberal Imperialists: The ideas and politics of a post-Gladstonian élite*, Oxford University Press.

MAURICE, FREDERICK (1884), *The Life of Frederick Denison Maurice*, edited by his son, Macmillan.

MAURICE, F. (1939), *Haldane, vol. 2, 1915-28*, Faber & Faber.

MEARNS, A. and PRESTON, W. C. (1883), *The Bitter Cry of Outcast London*, James Clarke & Co.

MITCHELL, F. W. (1967), *Sir Fred Clarke, master teacher, 1880-1952*, Longman.

299

MONTAGUE, F. C. (1889), 'Arnold Toynbee', Johns Hopkins University Studies in Historical and Political Science, 7th Series, Baltimore.

MORANT, R. L. (1898), 'The National Organisation of Education of all grades as practised in Switzerland', in Sadler, M.E. (ed.) *Special Reports on Educational Subjects,* vol. 3.

MORANT, R. L. (1901), *50 Steps towards Speaking English,* Ladder of Knowledge Series, vol. 2, 2nd edn.

MORGAN, J. V. (ed.) (1908), *Welsh Political and Educational Leaders in the Victorian Era,* James Nisbet.

MORGAN, K. O. (1963), *Wales in British Politics 1868-1922,* University of Wales Press, Cardiff.

MORLEY, J. (1917), *Recollections,* Macmillan, 2 vols.

MORRIS, A. J. A. (1977), *C. P. Trevelyan 1870-1958: Portrait of a Radical,* Blackstaff Press.

MOUNTFORD, J. (1972), *Keele – An Historical Critique,* Routledge & Kegan Paul.

MUIRHEAD, J. H. (1908), *The Service of the State: Four Lectures on the Political Teaching of T. H. Green,* John Murray.

MUIRHEAD, J. H. (ed.) (1935), *Bernard Bosanquet and his Friends,* Allen & Unwin.

MUIRHEAD, J. H. (1936), 'John Stuart Mackenzie, 1860-1935', *Proceedings of the British Academy,* vol. 21, Oxford University Press.

MUIRHEAD, J. H. (1942), *Reflections by a Journeyman in Philosophy,* ed. J. W. Harvey, Allen & Unwin.

MURRAY, G. (1960), *An Unfinished Autobiography,* Allen & Unwin.

NETTLESHIP, R. L. (1897), *Lectures on the Republic of Plato,* first published as *Philosophical Lectures and Remains,* vol 2, Macmillan; 2nd edn, 1901. Many reprints.

NIMOCKS, W. (1968), *Milner's Young Men: The 'Kindergarten' in Edwardian Imperial Affairs,* Duke University Press, USA. Reprinted (1970) Hodder & Stoughton.

NUNN, T. P. (1920), *Education: Its Data and First Principles,* Arnold.

OGG, D. (1947), *Herbert Fisher 1865-1940,* Arnold.

OXFORD AND ASQUITH, EARL OF (1928), *Memories and Reflections 1852-1927,* 2 vols, Cassell.

Oxford and Working-Class Education: A Report of a Joint Committee of University and Working-Class Representatives on the Relation of the University to the Higher Education of Workpeople (1909), Oxford University Press.

PAGET, S. (ed.) (1921), *Henry Scott Holland: Memoirs and Letters,* John Murray.

PARRY, C. (1970), *The Radical Tradition in Welsh Politics,* Occasional Papers in Economic and Social History, vol. 2, University of Hull Press.

PASSMORE, J. A. (1957), *A Hundred Years of Philosophy*, Duckworth.

PATEMAN, C. (1970), *Participation and Democratic Theory*, Cambridge University Press.

PETERS, R. S. (1966), *Ethics and Education*, Allen & Unwin.

PIMLOTT, J. A. R. (1935), *Toynbee Hall: Fifty Years of Social Progress 1884-1934*, Dent.

PLANT, R. (1974), *Community and Ideology: An Essay in Applied Social Philosophy*, Routledge & Kegan Paul.

PLATO, *The Republic*, translated B. Jowett (1888), Clarendon Press, Oxford.

POPPER, K. (1945), *The Open Society and its Enemies*, Routledge & Kegan Paul, 4th edn. 1962.

PRESTIGE, G. L. (1935), *The Life of Charles Gore: A Great Englishman*, Heinemann.

PRICE, L. L. (1887), *Industrial Peace: its advantages, methods and difficulties: a report of an inquiry made by the Toynbee trustees*, Macmillan.

PRICE, T. W. (1924), *The Story of the WEA 1903-24*, The Labour Publishing Co. Introduction by R. H. Tawney.

PRINGLE-PATTISON, S. (1928), 'Richard Burdon Haldane', *Proceedings of the British Academy*, vol. 14.

QUINTON, A. M. (1971), 'Absolute Idealism', Dawes Hicks lecture on Philosophy, British Academy, *Proceedings of the British Academy*, vol. 57.

RAIT, R. S. (ed.) (1925), *Memories of Albert Venn Dicey: Being Chiefly Letters and Diaries*, Macmillan.

RÉE, H. (1973), *Educator Extraordinary: the life and achievement of Henry Morris 1889-1961*, Longman.

RICHMOND, A. (1965), *Another Sixty Years*, Geoffrey Bles.

RICHTER, M. (1964), *The Politics of Conscience: T. H. Green and His Age*, Weidenfeld & Nicolson.

RITCHIE, D. G. (1891), *The Principles of State Interference*, Swan, Sonnenschein.

ROACH, J. (1971), *Public Examinations in England 1850-1900*, Cambridge University Press.

ROBERTS, R. D. (1891), *Eighteen Years of University Extension*, Cambridge University Press.

ROWBOTHAM, S. (1969), 'The Call to University Extension Teaching 1873-1900', in *University of Birmingham Historical Journal*, vol. 12, 1969-70.

ROWSE, A. L. (1976), *Matthew Arnold: Poet and Prophet*, Thames & Hudson.

RUSK, R. R. (1928), *The Philosophical Bases of Education*, University of London Press.

301

SADLEIR, M. E. (1949), *Michael Ernest Sadler,* Constable.

SADLER, M. E. (n.d.), 'Christian Philanthropy and Rationalistic Philanthropy', typescript.

SADLER, M. E. (n.d.), 'Reminiscences of Arnold Toynbee and Ruskin at Oxford', typescript.

SADLER, M. E. (1904), *Report on Secondary Education in Liverpool, including the training of teachers for public elementary schools,* Eyre & Spottiswoode.

SADLER, M. E. (ed.) (1907a), *Continuation Schools in England and Elsewhere,* Manchester University Press.

SADLER, M. E. (1907b), 'Sadler, Owen, Lovett, Maurice, Toynbee', in *The University Review,* April-December.

SADLER, M. E. (1912), 'England's debt to German Educators', an address given at the meeting of the Allgemeiner Deutscher Neuphilologenverband, Frankfurt am Main, 28 May 1912.

SADLER, M. E. (1913), 'Learning from those who differ from us', an address to the Leeds Branch of the National Union of Women Workers.

SADLER, M. E. (1926a), 'In the Days of My Youth', in *T.P's and Cassell's Weekly,* 3 July.

SADLER, M. E. (1926b), 'Sir Arthur Acland', the *Oxford Magazine,* 21 October.

SADLER, M. E. (1930), 'A Liberal Education', in *The Outlook in Secondary Education,* three lectures delivered before the Faculty of Teachers' College, Columbia University.

SANDERS, C. R. (1942), *Coleridge and the Broad Church Movement,* Duke University Press, Durham, North Carolina.

SANDFORD, E. G. (ed.) (1906), *Memoirs of Archbishop Temple by Seven Friends,* Macmillan.

SCOTT, D. (1971), *A. D. Lindsay: A Biography,* Blackwell, Oxford.

SEAMAN, L. C. B. (1973), *Victorian England: Aspects of English and Imperial History 1837-1901,* Methuen.

SEARLE, G. R. (1971), *The Quest for National Efficiency: A Study in British Politics and Political Thought 1899-1914,* Oxford University Press.

SELLECK, R. J. W. (1968), *The New Education: The English Background, 1870-1914,* Pitman.

SETH, A. and HALDANE, R. B. (1883), *Essays in Philosophical Criticism,* Longmans.

SHANNON, R. (1976), *The Crisis of Imperialism 1865-1915,* Paladin.

SIMMONS, J. (1958), *New University,* Leicester University Press.

SIMON, B. (1960), *Studies in the History of Education 1780-1870,* Lawrence & Wishart.

SIMON, J. (1977), 'The Shaping of the Spens Report on Secondary Education 1933-38: An Inside View', part 2, in *British Journal of Educational Studies,* vol. 25, no. 2, June.

SMITH, M. F. (1920), *A. L. Smith, Master of Balliol (1916-1924): A Biography and some reminiscences by his wife,* John Murray.

SOMMER, D. (1960), *Haldane of Cloan,* Allen & Unwin.

SPENDER, J. A. (1930), *Sir Robert Hudson: A Memoir,* Cassell.

SPENDER, J. A. (1937), *Men and Things,* Cassell.

SPILLER, G. (1934), *The Ethical Movement in Great Britain: A Documentary History,* Farleigh Press.

STOCKS, M. D. (1953), *The Workers' Educational Association: the First Fifty Years, 1903-53,* Allen & Unwin.

STUART, J. (1911), *Reminiscences of James Stuart,* Chiswick Press.

SUTHERLAND, G. (1972), *Studies in the Growth of Nineteenth Century Government,* Oxford University Press.

SUTHERLAND, G. (1973), *Policy-Making in Elementary Education 1870-1895,* Oxford University Press.

SYLVESTER, D. W. (1974), *Robert Lowe and Education,* Cambridge University Press.

TATTON, R. G. (ed.) (1907), *Selected Writings of Thomas Godolphin Rooper,* Blackie.

TAWNEY, R. H. (1921), *The Acquisitive Society,* Bell.

TAWNEY, R. H. (ed.) (1922), *Secondary Education For All: A Policy for Labour,* Allen & Unwin.

TAWNEY, R. H. (1924), *Education: the Socialist Policy,* Independent Labour Party Publications Department.

TAWNEY, R. H. (1932), 'The New Children's Charter', *New Statesman and Nation,* 1 October 1932, and reprinted WEA, 1932.

TAWNEY, R. H. (1933), 'The School Leaving Age and Juvenile Employment' in *New Statesman and Nation,* 18 November 1933, Reprinted WEA, 1934.

TAWNEY, R. H. (1934), 'Juvenile Employment and Education', Sidney Ball Lecture, 2 May 1934. Barnett House Papers, no. 17, Oxford University Press.

TAWNEY, R. H. (1952a), *Equality,* Allen & Unwin.

TAWNEY, R. H. (1952b), 'Mansbridge', in *The Highway,* vol. 44, November.

TAWNEY, R. H. (1953a), *The WEA and Adult Education,* Athlone Press, University of London.

TAWNEY, R. H. (1953b), 'We Mean Freedom' (1944), 'Christianity and the Social Revolution' (1935) and 'A National College of All Souls' (1917), all in *The Attack,* Allen & Unwin.

TAWNEY, R. H. (1964), *The Radical Tradition,* ed. R. Hinden, Allen & Unwin. Reprinted Penguin, 1966.

TAYLOR, C. (1975), *Hegel*, Cambridge University Press.

TEMPLE, W. (1921), *Life of Bishop Percival*, Macmillan.

TEMPLE, W. (1924), *Christus Veritas, An Essay*, Macmillan.

TEMPLE, W. (1926), *Personal Religion and the Life of Fellowship*, Longmans, Green.

TEMPLE, W. (1942), *Christianity and Social Order*, Penguin.

TERRILL, R. (1974), *R. H. Tawney and His Times: Socialism as Fellowship*, Andre Deutsch.

TIBBLE, J. W. (1961), 'Sir Percy Nunn 1870-1944', in *British Journal of Educational Studies*, vol. 10, no. 1.

TOYNBEE, A. J. (1883), *'Progress and Poverty': A Criticism of Mr Henry George, Being two lectures delivered in St Andrew's Hall, Newman Street, London*, Kegan Paul.

TOYNBEE, A. J. (1884), *Lectures on the Industrial Revolution of the Eighteenth Century in England*, Rivingtons.

TOYNBEE, G. (ed.) (n.d.), *Reminiscences and Letters of Joseph and Arnold Toynbee*, Henry J. Glaisher.

TREVELYAN, G. M. (1940), *Grey of Falloden*, Longmans, Green.

TRILLING, L. (1939), *Matthew Arnold*, Norton, New York. Reissued by Columbia University Press, 1949.

TUCKWELL, W. (1907), *Reminiscences of Oxford*, Smith, Elder.

TURNBULL, G. H. (1926), *The Educational Theory of Fichte*, University of Liverpool Press, and Hodder & Stoughton.

URWICK, E. J. (1927), *The Social Good*, Methuen.

WALLACE, W. (1898), *Lectures and Essays on Natural Theology and Ethics*, Oxford University Press.

WARD, W. R. (1965), *Victorian Oxford*, Frank Cass.

WARNOCK, M. (1977), *Schools of Thought*, Faber & Faber.

WATERFALL, E. A. (1923), *The Day Continuation School in England: Its Function and Future*, Allen & Unwin.

WELCH, E. (1973), *The Peripatetic University: Cambridge Local Lectures, 1873-1973*, Cambridge University Press.

WELCH, E. (1976), 'The Prehistory of the University Class' in *History of Education Society Bulletin*, no. 17, Spring.

WEST, A. (1922), *Private Diaries of the Rt Hon Sir Algernon West*, ed. H. G. Hutchinson, John Murray.

WHITE, J. P. (1973), *Towards a Compulsory Curriculum*, Routledge & Kegan Paul.

WHITE, J. P. (1975), 'The End of the Compulsory Curriculum', in *The Curriculum: The Doris Lee Lectures, Studies in Education 2*, University of London Institute of Education.

WHITE, P. (1973), 'Education, Democracy and the Public Interest', in R. S. Peters, (ed.), *The Philosophy of Education*, Oxford University Press.

WHITEHEAD, A. N. (1929), *The Aims of Education,* Williams & Norgate.

WILLEY, B. (1949), *Nineteenth Century Studies,* Chatto & Windus.

WILLIAMS, J. R., TITMUSS, R. M. and FISHER, F. J. (1960), *R. H. Tawney: A Portrait by Several Hands,* n.p.

WINTER, J. M. and JOSLIN, D. M. (1972), 'R. H. Tawney's Commonplace Book', *Economic History Review,* Supplement 2, Cambridge University Press.

WYATT, D. K. (1969), *The Politics of Reform in Thailand: Education in the Reign of King Chulalongkorn,* Yale University Press.

ZIMMERN, A. E. (1923), 'The Evolution of the Citizen', in O. Stanley (ed.) *The Way Out: Essays on the Meaning and Purpose of Adult Education,* Oxford University Press.

Index

306

307

DATE DUE

MAR 6 '87			
MAR 2 3 '87			
APR 7 '87			
APR 2 2 '87			
GAYLORD			PRINTED IN U.S.A.